2ND EDITION

AQA AS

Economics

Ray Powell

Cardiff Libraries
www.cardiff.gov.uk/libraries

Llyfrgelloedd Caerdydd
www.caerdydd.gov.uk/llyfrgelloedd

PHILIP ALLAN FOR
HODDER
EDUCATION
AN HACHETTE UK COMPANY

Philip Allan, an imprint of Hodder Education, an Hachette UK company, Market Place, Deddington, Oxfordshire OX15 0SE

Orders
Bookpoint Ltd, 130 Milton Park, Abingdon, Oxfordshire OX14 4SB
tel: 01235 827827
fax: 01235 400401
e-mail: education@bookpoint.co.uk

Lines are open 9.00 a.m.–5.00 p.m., Monday to Saturday, with a 24-hour message answering service. You can also order through the Philip Allan website: www.philipallan.co.uk

© Ray Powell 2008, 2013
ISBN 978-1-4441-9558-3

First published 2008
Second edition 2013

Impression number   5   4   3   2   1
Year   2017 2016 2015 2014 2013

The publishers would like to thank the following for permission to reproduce photographs:

p. 6 Daniel Tackley/Fotolia; **p. 11** Apple Inc; **p. 18** Brinkstock/Alamy; **p. 23** Allstar Picture Library/Alamy; **p. 29** Advertising Archives; **p. 36** Ingram; **p. 39** Fotosenmeer/Fotolia; **p. 45** Web Pix/Alamy; **p. 46** Paul Cowan/Fotolia; **p. 53** BP plc; **p. 65** Dirk Hoffmann/Fotolia; **p. 70** Nick Gregory/Alamy; **p. 77** Ellenamani/Fotolia; **p. 86** Artstudio_pro/Fotolia; **p. 92** SeanPavonePhoto/Fotolia; **p. 98** Forber/Fotolia; **p. 108** Monkey Business/Fotolia; **p. 112** Advertising Archives; **p. 120** Topfoto; **p. 133** Ingram; **p. 142** drsg98/Fotolia; **p. 148** Roy Pedersen/Fotolia; **p. 162** Topfoto; **p. 170** Ingram; **p. 176** Ingram; **p. 181** Neil Fozzard; **p. 193** Evgeny Dubinchuk/Fotolia; **p. 202** Peter Cox/Fotolia; **p. 214** Hemera Technologies; **p. 217** Auremar/Fotolia; **p. 228** Alex Segre/Alamy; **p. 234** Rainer Plendl/Fotolia; **p. 243** Imagestate Media; **p. 253** Majeczka/Fotolia; **p. 257** Richard Levine/Alamy; **p. 269** Hunor Kristo/Fotolia; **p. 278** Stephen Bardens/Alamy; **p. 283** Nick Savage/Alamy; **p. 296** Topfoto; **p. 301** Duncan Phillips/Alamy

The front cover is reproduced by permission of Beboy/Fotolia.

Typeset by Integra Software Services Pvt., Pondicherry, India.
Printed in Italy.

Hachette UK's policy is to use papers that are natural, renewable and recyclable products and made from wood grown in sustainable forests. The logging and manufacturing processes are expected to conform to the environmental regulations of the country of origin.

P2264

Contents

Contents

Foreword

This book has three main objectives. The first and most important is to help you achieve the highest possible grades in the AQA AS economics examinations.

The second objective is to help you to become a good economist. For those of you who are not intending to study economics at university, I hope that reading the book will enable you to contribute thoughtfully and informatively when discussing economic issues with family or friends, or with prospective employers you need to impress. And for those of you who decide to study economics or an economics-related subject at university, I hope the book sets you on the right path and provides you with an enjoyable introduction to economics that prepares you for studying the subject at a higher level.

The third objective, which relates to those already stated, is to encourage you to study economics at A2, and for you to achieve a high A-level pass at the end of your 2-year course. With this in mind, I recommend that you re-read, toward the end of your AS course, the part of Chapter 1 which introduces you to 'what economists do'.

The content of the AQA AS economics specification is thoroughly covered in this book. Most chapters also include **extension material** which provides a link between AS and A2 economics. On occasion, the extension material goes further, introducing you to economic issues and events that go beyond the narrow confines of GCE economics, but which are of great interest to economists in the present day.

To meet my first objective of helping you to achieve a good grade, each chapter explains the topic in the depth required for an A-grade at AS. However, doing well in the examination also requires demonstration of appropriate and required examination skills. The required skills are summarised in the following diagram, which also indicates the importance of each of the four skills in the AS examinations.

The 'incline of difficulty', showing the skills required to do well at AS

'Higher-level' skills tested primarily by data-response questions

'Lower-level' skills tested primarily by multiple-choice questions

Evaluate economic arguments and evidence, making informed judgements	16% weighting
Analyse economic problems and issues	24% weighting
Apply knowledge and critical understanding to economic problems and issues	30% weighting
Demonstrate knowledge and understanding of the specified subject content	30% weighting

Economists sometimes distinguish between the necessary and sufficient conditions required for a particular outcome to be achieved. For example, a necessary condition for doing well at AS is to turn up and answer the questions in the examinations. However, merely attending an examination cannot guarantee success — it is a necessary but insufficient condition for doing well. The quality and relevance of what you write in the exam room is really important.

Likewise, possession of **knowledge** about the economy and economic theory is a necessary but insufficient condition for doing well. Knowledge is necessary, but on its own contributes in a limited way to examination success. To achieve a high grade, you must show understanding of knowledge, together with the ability to apply, analyse and evaluate.

If you have applied your knowledge of economic theory to help answer the question asked, if you have quoted from the data source or sources in the question, and, when relevant, if you have used your knowledge of recent developments in the economy, then you will have shown the skill of **application**. To display the skill of **analysis**, you must construct logical arguments in your answer that involve a 'chain of reasoning' and use, where relevant, clearly explained diagrams.

Evaluation is the higher-order skill which separates good answers that earn an A or B grade for the data-response question from those that at best reach grade C. Evaluation is also the skill which exam candidates find it most difficult to display. To evaluate, you must weigh up evidence, question assumptions you make in your answer, and judge the relative importance of factors relevant to the question before arriving at a reasoned conclusion. Having said that, it is always best to evaluate the strengths and weaknesses of each argument you introduce, as you progress through your answer.

Using this book

The book is organised into three sections. In the introductory section, Chapter 1 provides a general introduction to economics and to 'what economists do', while Chapter 2 introduces and explains the central economic problem of scarcity and the resulting need for choice. It is important that you familiarise yourselves with Chapter 2 because the central economic problem is what economics is all about. Consequently, it is relevant to every chapter in the textbook.

The main body of the textbook covers the content of the AS Units 1 and 2. The chapters closely follow the specification.

Special features

The text contains several special features designed to aid your understanding of the concepts and examination techniques required by AQA:

- **Learning outcomes:** a list of the intended learning outcomes is given at the beginning of each chapter. These are closely linked to the specification.
- **Key terms:** the key term boxes provide definitions of important economic terms or concepts relevant to the topics in the chapter and mentioned in the AQA AS specification. A list of the key terms is also provided at the end of each unit.

- **Exam tips:** these explain how the chapter content is relevant to the AS examinations. In some instances, these highlight the presence of useful background information in the text, designed to increase the your depth of knowledge and understanding. Full marks for a question can be earned without this background information, but it supports your knowledge.
- **Case studies:** the case studies come with follow-up questions which will help you to analyse, evaluate and improve your exam answers.
- **Summaries:** these appear at the end of each chapter and are a useful tool for revision.

Exam-style questions

At the end of every chapter (apart from Chapter 1), there are four **exam-style questions** on the two 'higher-order' skills you must display when answering data-response questions at AS. Two questions are testing the skill of 'analysis' and two are testing the skill of 'evaluation'.

 To help your revision further, additional data-response questions can be found online at www.hodderplus.co.uk. Here, each question is followed by examiner comments, and then by two example candidate answers.

In an exam answer do not try to display 'all you know', regardless of the relevance of the information to the actual question. And do not make the mistake of rewriting questions to fit a pre-prepared answer, rather than adapting what you know to the needs of the question.

The AQA economics specification requires that, for the Unit 2 exam:

> Candidates should have a good knowledge of developments in the UK economy and government policies over the past 10 years (before the date of the exam).

However, it is unwise to conclude that knowledge of earlier events is unnecessary and redundant. You cannot properly understand present-day economic events, controversies and the views of different economists, without some background knowledge of economic history covering the 'ups and downs' of the economy in earlier years. It is also worth noting that Unit 2 exam questions sometimes ask candidates to identify significant features or points of comparison in data series extending back more than 10 years. A basic knowledge of economic history and of different schools of economic thought, such as Keynesianism and monetarism, is useful to your understanding. Where helpful, this book adopts a historical approach, particularly in the way monetary policy, fiscal policy and supply-side economics have developed over the years.

Starting AS economics

If you are starting an AS course in economics, you should begin by reading Chapters 1 and 2, which introduce you to the subject. How you then use the book will depend on whether you are studying the course unit-by-unit (in which case you are probably studying Unit 1 before Unit 2, and are probably being taught by just one teacher), or whether you are studying Unit 1 and Unit 2 'side-by-side' (in which case, you are probably being taught by at least two teachers). As you read each chapter or section of a chapter, test yourself by answering the exam-style questions at the end of the chapter.

I hope that you find the book a useful adjunct to the course that your teachers deliver. I wish you every success in the AS examinations and hope that you go on to study for the full A-level qualification in economics. And while 'luck' is by no means the key ingredient in eventual examination success, may I wish you the best of luck in the course, in the examinations and in your future life!

Ray Powell

Introduction

Chapter 1

What is economics and what do economists do?

For most of you, welcome to a new subject. Unless you have studied economics at GCSE, it is probably only in the last week or so that you have given thought to the nature of the economy in which you live, and to what you must learn about the economy in the next 9 months. This chapter aims to ease you into the subject so that you quickly build up a broad idea of what you are going to study at AS in economics.

LEARNING OUTCOMES

This chapter will introduce you to:
- economics as a social science and a current affairs subject
- the difference between microeconomics and macroeconomics
- economic problems and economic policies
- what economists do

Starting from a position of ignorance

At the beginning of an economics course, you are not expected to know anything about economics. For the last 2 years all your mental energy has been directed at the GCSE subjects you have been studying, and economics might not have been one of them.

It usually takes at least a term to settle into a new subject. This is certainly the case with economics, which is different in many important respects from other subjects you may have previously studied. I hope that by February or March next year you will have settled, but if not, don't in the first instance blame yourself, blame the subject.

Economics is a current affairs related subject, so it will help if you can become interested in what is going on in the country you live in, and also in the wider world outside the UK. (However, you are not expected to possess this knowledge at the beginning of the course. Any relevant current affairs knowledge you already possess is a bonus, not a requirement.)

Nevertheless, if you are not prepared to read about current affairs in newspapers or on web pages such as BBC News (http://news.bbc.co.uk), you are unlikely to enjoy economics or to do very well in the course. So start reading newspapers (getting advice from your teachers as you go on what to read), and don't switch off the television whenever the news or the BBC2 programme *Newsnight* starts.

What is economics?

When answering this question, a good place to start is the fact that **economics** is a social science. Social science is the branch of science that studies society and the relationships of individuals within a society. Besides economics, psychology, sociology and political science are also social sciences, as are important elements of history and geography.

Psychology studies the behaviour and mental processes of an *individual*. Sociology studies the *social* relationships between people in the context of *society*. By contrast, economics, as the name suggests, studies the *economic behaviour* of both individuals and groups of people and the *economic relationships* between individuals and groups.

Let me give you two examples of what I mean.

I have taken my first example, about *individual behaviour*, from an important part of economics known as demand theory. This is covered early in the book, in Chapter 3. The theory addresses consumer behaviour, or how we behave when we go shopping. Why, for example, do people generally buy more strawberries as the price of strawberries falls?

My second example introduces an important *economic relationship*. Having explained demand, we must go a stage further and look at how consumers interact with firms or producers. Firms supply and sell the goods that consumers buy, and economists call the 'place' in which goods are bought and sold a market. Market interactions between consumers and producers are also explained early in the book (see Chapter 5).

Indeed, before you started this economics course, you may very well have heard the words 'supply' and 'demand' and thought that these are what economics is about. Well, to some extent this is true, particularly in the early chapters of this book.

Economics involves, however, a lot more than theories of individual behaviour and economic relationships between groups of individuals.

A second possible starting point for answering the question 'What is economics?' is in the word itself: 'economics'. Related to *economics* is the verb '*to economise*'. In large part, economics is the study of *economising* — the study of how people make choices about what to produce, how to produce and for whom to produce, in a world in which most resources are limited or scarce. How best can people make decisions on how scarce resources should be allocated among competing uses, so as to improve and maximise human happiness and welfare? This is the economic problem, which is explained in greater detail in Chapter 2.

Introducing microeconomics and macroeconomics

The subject of economics is usually divided into two parts, called **microeconomics** and **macroeconomics**. The AQA AS economics course is organised in this way:

- Unit 1 Markets and Market Failure is microeconomic
- Unit 2 The National Economy is macroeconomic

Microeconomics is the part of economics concerned with economic behaviour in the individual markets that make up the economy. Questions such as 'What determines the price of bread?' and 'How many workers might an employer wish to hire?' are microeconomic questions. Essentially, microeconomics investigates the 'little bits' of the economy, namely individual consumers, firms, markets and industries.

By contrast, macroeconomics is the part of economics that attempts to explain how the whole economy works. Macroeconomics addresses questions such as 'What determines the average price level?' and 'How do we explain the overall levels of employment and unemployment in the economy?' Macroeconomics examines the aggregates rather than the little bits of the economy: the aggregate levels of output, income, prices, employment and unemployment, and the trade flows that make up the balance of payments.

Economic problems and economic policies

One of the most interesting areas of economics lies in studying the economic problems facing governments and the economic policies that governments use to try to get rid of or reduce the problems. Economic problems can be microeconomic or macroeconomic, though some have both micro and macro elements.

At the micro level, covered by AQA Unit 1, the main problems lie in the field of market failure. As we shall see in Chapters 9 to 12, market failure occurs whenever markets do not perform very well — and in extreme cases fail to perform at all. Perhaps the best-known recent and current market failure stems from environmental pollution and subsequent global warming. I shall be examining a number of different government policies aimed at correcting market failures. These include taxation, subsidy and the use of regulations. Chapters 13 and 14 also explain how government failure results when government policies are ineffective or even downright damaging.

At the macro level, which is covered by AQA Unit 2, the main economic problems are unemployment, a failure to achieve and sustain a satisfactory rate of economic growth, inflation and an unsatisfactory trading and balance of payments position. Chapter 17, together with Chapters 20 to 22, investigates these macroeconomic problems. The final chapters of the book then examine the main macroeconomic policies that are used to try to solve these problems. The main policies are fiscal policy, monetary policy and supply-side policy.

Positive and normative statements in economics

A lot of economics is concerned with what people *ought* to do. This is particularly true of the government. *Ought* the government try to reduce unemployment, control inflation and achieve a 'fair' distribution of income and wealth? Most people probably think that all these objectives are desirable. However, they all fall within the remit of **normative** economics. Normative economics is about value judgements and opinions, but because people have different opinions about what is right and wrong, normative statements cannot be scientifically tested. They are just opinions.

By contrast, a **positive statement** can be scientifically tested to see if it is incorrect. If a positive statement does not pass the test, it is *falsified*. Some positive statements are obviously correct: for example, the statement that an apple is a type of fruit. But a positive statement does not have to be true. For example, the statement that the Earth is flat is a positive statement. Although once believed to be true, the statement was falsified with the growth of scientific evidence. The key point is that positive statements can in principle be tested and possibly falsified, while normative statements cannot. Words such as *ought*, *should*, *better*, *worse* and *good* and *bad* (used as adjectives) often provide clues that a statement is normative.

> **KEY TERMS**
>
> **normative:** an opinion that cannot be scientifically tested.
>
> **positive statement:** a statement of fact, or one that can be scientifically tested.

How much maths do I need to know?

At the beginning of an economics course, students often seek advice about the amount of mathematics they need to know or must learn to help them with their studies. For AS and A2 economics, the answer is not very much.

The two skills you do need to develop are:
- drawing and interpreting graphs
- interpreting statistics presented in a variety of forms: tables, line graphs, bar graphs and pie charts

You will be introduced to economics graphs and to the different ways of presenting statistics as you proceed through this book.

Nevertheless, I must issue two warnings. First, economics contains a large number of abstract ideas and concepts, similar to those employed in maths, summed up in the saying 'to an economist, real life is a special case'. A logical mind, capable of handling abstractions, will be of great help if you are to become a good economist. My second warning is that, unlike AS and A-level economics, university economics is definitely mathematical. Thinking ahead, however good your eventual A-level economics grade, you should only study economics as a single subject at university if you are good at and enjoy mathematics. If you are weak at mathematics or if you have dropped the subject, it would be far better to consider a joint honours degree: for example, economics and history, economics and French, or economics and politics.

What do economists do?

It has been said that 'economics is useful as a form of employment for economists'. This essentially means that economists give advice to other people, who pay them for the service they provide. Some economists act as private consultants, but others are employed by central and local government, and by the Bank of England.

CASE STUDY 1.1

How about working in the City of London?

In 2011, financial and insurance services contributed £125.4 billion in gross output to the UK economy, which is 9.4% of the UK's total gross output. The UK financial services industry creates employment for 1.1 million people, or 3.6% of all workforce jobs. Although they make up only a small fraction of this number, economists enjoy some of the most prestigious jobs in the City of London.

The financial firms that employ economists include banks, research companies and accountancy firms such as Deloitte. High-street banks such as Barclays own investment banking subsidiaries. Until about 40 years ago, investment banks were known by the old-fashioned name of 'merchant banks'. This name is sometimes still used today, but 'investment bank' has become a rather sexier label.

In the old days, merchant banks were relatively small companies, often family-owned and affected by nepotism in the sense that top jobs would be handed down from father to son. (Women were only employed as secretaries or cleaners.) This has now largely changed and City employees are rewarded according to their talents. Nevertheless, 'glass ceilings' sometimes prevent women from getting the top City jobs that their skills deserve. The demise of Baring Brothers provides a case study of how family-owned City firms have given way to a new breed of company in which talent is the requirement for success. These days, most investment banks are owned by international multinational financial and banking corporations such as Deutsche Bank.

Capital Economics, founded in 1999 by economist Roger Bootle, who currently writes excellent economics articles published in the *Daily Telegraph*, is an important City-based economics consultancy, supplying independent economic analysis to hundreds of business clients and institutions spread across the globe. Capital Economics, which specialises in the field of macroeconomics, employs a number of leading economists.

To find out more about what the economists employed by Capital Economics do, look up the staff listing at **www.capitaleconomics.com**.

The City of London is a prestigious place to work

Follow-up tasks

1 Find the website **www.economistjobs.com** and research the current UK job opportunities being advertised for economists.
2 Now go to **www.efinancialcareers.co.uk** to research a wider field of job opportunities in financial service industries. Click on 'Students' on the home page.

City firms such as investment banks, leading companies such as Marks & Spencer and trade unions are big employers of economists. Indeed, virtually every large UK organisation (except perhaps religious institutions) either employs its own economists or seeks the advice of economic consultancy firms. And, of course, there are also thousands of economics teachers hired by universities, schools and colleges.

The Government Economic Service (GES) is the UK's largest employer of professional economists, with over 1,000 economists based in 30 government departments and agencies such as the Treasury and the Department for Business, Innovation and Skills.

CASE STUDY 1.2

Working for the government

Central government and its agencies such as the Office for Budget Responsibility are the biggest employers of economists in the UK. Central government departments such as the **Department for Environment, Food and Rural Affairs (Defra)** take on each year 300 or so economics graduates. Defra and other government departments advertise for economists on the government website **www.civilservice.gov.uk**.

Treasury economists

Her Majesty's Treasury, by its very nature, is at the heart of government. As an assistant Treasury economist you might find yourself:

- providing analysis of tax policy
- analysing the economies of particular countries and providing advice to ministers accordingly
- advising on the economic effects of changes in competition and/or regulation policy
- advising on current and future determinants of central government current and capital expenditure
- ensuring the economic content of ministers' speeches is correct and understandable
- providing analyses of macroeconomic developments in the UK and in the global economy
- ensuring that the full range of economic costs and benefits are considered in evaluating policy options

Follow-up task

Go to the government website **www.civilservice.gov.uk** and research the jobs currently being advertised: for example, under Fast Stream Assistant Economist Appointments.

As well as providing advice to employers or clients, economists undertake research and are involved in forecasting activity. It has been said that 'An economist is a trained professional paid to guess wrong about the economy'. The question has also been asked 'What makes a good economist?' For the non-economist, the answer is 'An unshakeable grasp of the obvious!'

But, joking apart, economics pundits to look out for include Paul Mason and Stephanie Flanders, who work for the BBC, and journalists such as Jeremy Warner and David Smith (who write respectively in the *Daily Telegraph* and the *Sunday Times* newspapers). The public face of the economics profession centres on television appearances of economic experts or analysts giving advice on such issues as rising or falling share prices, exchange rates or interest rates. Whether the advice of such professional economists is useful will be for you to judge as you continue your studies over the next few months. Whether or not you have faith in economists, I hope you enjoy the course.

SUMMARY

- You don't need to know anything about economics or about the economy before you start the AS course.
- Economics is a social science and a current affairs subject.
- Economics divides into microeconomics and macroeconomics.
- Microeconomics looks at the 'little bits' of the economy.
- Macroeconomics examines the economy in aggregate.
- Government economic policies aim to reduce or eliminate economic problems.
- Microeconomic policies aim to prevent or correct market failures.
- Fiscal policy, monetary policy and supply-side policy are examples of macroeconomic policies.
- Unemployment, too low a rate of economic growth, inflation, and the state of the balance of payments give rise to the main macroeconomic problems that governments face.
- Positive statements in economics are statements that can be scientifically tested and possibly falsified, whereas normative statements are statements of opinion, involving value judgements.
- Professional economists undertake research, engage in economic forecasting and provide economic advice to clients.

The economic problem

Chapter 2

In Chapter 1, economics was defined as the study of choice and decision making in a world with limited resources. It was also mentioned that economics is the study of economising — how people make choices about what to produce, how to produce and for whom to produce, in a world in which most resources are limited or scarce. This chapter explains and explores the central economic problem in greater depth.

LEARNING OUTCOMES

This chapter will:
- relate the economic problem to scarcity and choice
- use production possibility curve diagrams to illustrate scarcity
- introduce the concept of opportunity cost
- explain the meaning of production
- explain the role of factors of production in the economy
- explain how different economic systems attempt to deal with the economic problem
- explain how UK governments have changed the UK economic system in recent decades

Economics and the economic problem

A definition of economics, similar to the one I have already given you, was put forward by Professor Lionel Robbins in *An Essay on the Nature and Significance of Economic Science* in 1932. Robbins defined economics as:

> The science which studies human behaviour as a relationship between ends and scarce means which have alternative uses.

Professor Robbins' long-established definition provides perhaps the most well-known starting point for introducing and understanding what economics is about. How best can people make decisions about the allocation of scarce resources among competing uses, so as to improve and maximise human happiness and welfare? This is the central or most fundamental **economic problem**.

KEY TERM

economic problem: only a limited amount of resources are available to produce the unlimited quantity of goods and services people desire.

The economic problem, scarcity and choice

To repeat, economics is literally the study of economising — the study of how human beings make choices about what to produce, how to produce and for whom to produce, in a world in which most resources are limited. The central economic problem exists because both goods and the resources needed to produce goods are scarce. Scarcity also means that people (even the very rich) have limited incomes.

Now, if goods are scarce and incomes are limited, choices have to be made. Consider, for example, a family with a weekly income of £1,000. The family currently spends

£300 on housing, £250 on food, £250 on other goods and services, including heating and lighting, and £120 on entertainment. The family's total weekly spending on goods and services is thus £920, meaning the family manages to save £80. Suddenly, the cost of housing rises to £400. To avoid getting into debt, and assuming that family income can't increase, one or more probably unpleasant choices will have to be made. An obvious possibility is to cut down on entertainment, such as visits to the cinema. Other possibilities could be spending less on home heating, buying cheaper food, cutting down on alcoholic drink and stopping saving. Something will have to be given up. Unless the family gets into debt or its income increases, it will have to economise even more on its spending and saving decisions.

The economic problem illustrated on a production possibility diagram

KEY TERM

production possibility diagram: a diagram that shows different possible combinations of goods that can be produced using available resources.

So far, I have explained how scarcity and choice may affect an ordinary family. In much the same way, but on an obviously much grander scale, the economy of the nation as a whole faces a similar need for choice. To explain how the economic problem affects the whole economy, I will use a diagram which you will come across again and again in your economics course, a **production possibility diagram**.

The key feature of a production possibility diagram is a production possibility frontier (or production possibility curve). This can be called the *PPF* curve. A *PPF* curve illustrates the different combinations of two goods, or two sets of goods, that can be produced with a fixed quantity of resource, providing we assume that all available resources are being utilised to the full. The *PPF* curve drawn in Figure 2.1 illustrates the different combinations of **consumer goods** and **capital goods** that the whole economy can produce when all the economy's resources are employed, with no spare capacity. To put it another way, the *PPF* curve shows what the economy can produce, assuming that all the labour, capital and land at the country's disposal are employed to the full, and assuming a given state of **technical progress**.

Figure 2.1 Using a production possibility frontier diagram to illustrate the economic problem

Given that resources and capacity are limited, a choice has to be made about the type of good to produce. Look closely at points X and Y on the diagram. Point X shows the maximum possible output of consumer goods, assuming that the economy only produces consumer goods (i.e. no capital goods are produced). Likewise, point Y shows the maximum possible output of capital goods, assuming that the economy only produces capital goods. In fact, points X and Y show the two extreme production possibilities, since all goods are either consumer goods or capital goods. Finally, the line drawn between points X and Y in Figure 2.1 shows all the different possible combinations of consumer goods and capital goods the economy can produce, given the available resources and given the state of technical knowledge. This line is the economy's production possibility frontier (*PPF*).

Capital goods are goods such as raw materials and machines that are used to produce other goods. They are also known as producer goods and intermediate goods. Capital goods are very important for economic growth. By contrast, consumer goods (which are also known as final goods) are goods bought by individuals and households to satisfy their wants and needs. Goods such as cars and television sets are **consumer durable goods** whereas shampoo and washing powder are **non-durable consumer goods**.

The purchase of capital goods (by firms) is known as **investment**. Likewise, the purchase of consumer goods (by individuals or households) is called **consumption**. As a general rule, if an economy decides to produce capital goods rather than consumer goods, economic growth will take place at a faster rate than if the people had chosen to enjoy a higher level of consumption.

Now consider point A on the *PPF* curve (Figure 2.1), which shows the economy producing K_1 capital goods and C_1 consumer goods. If people want faster economic growth, more scarce resources must be devoted to the production of capital goods and fewer to producing consumer goods. In other words, there has to be a movement from point A to a position such as point B on the *PPF*. Given this movement, capital good production rises to K_2, but at the expense of a fall in consumer good production to C_2. Society's choice has been to produce more capital goods at the expense of fewer consumer goods.

An iPhone is a consumer durable good

EXAM TIP

You must learn to draw and interpret production possibility diagrams, which are important in AS economics. In this chapter, a production possibility diagram has been used to illustrate the results of scarcity and opportunity cost. Later chapters will show you how to use these diagrams to illustrate and analyse other terms and concepts that are likely to be tested in the AS examinations.

Opportunity cost

The movement from point A to point B on the *PPF* curve in Figure 2.1 illustrates a very important aspect of the economic problem, namely the principle of **opportunity cost**. The opportunity cost of any choice, decision or course of action is measured in terms of the alternatives that have to be given up. Hence the opportunity cost of increasing the production of capital goods from K_1 to K_2 is the fall in consumer goods from C_1 to C_2.

Indeed, the concept of opportunity cost can be developed a stage further. Economists generally assume that economic agents (for example, individuals, households or firms) behave rationally. Rational behaviour means people try to make decisions in their self-interest or to maximise their private benefit. When a choice has to be made, the best alternative is always chosen, which means that the second best or next best alternative is rejected. Providing people are rational, the opportunity cost of any decision or choice is the next best alternative sacrificed or forgone.

> **KEY TERM**
>
> **opportunity cost:** the cost of the next best alternative sacrificed.

EXTENSION MATERIAL

Suppose the economy is initially producing at point Z in Figure 2.1. Because it is producing inside its *PPF*, there must be idle resources, including unemployed labour, in the economy. In this situation, the opportunity cost of increasing capital good production from K_1 to K_2 is not a fall in the production of consumer goods. Instead, it is the sacrificed opportunity for resources to remain idle.

The type of unemployment that occurs when the economy produces inside its *PPF* is called *demand-deficient unemployment*. This will be explained in some detail in Chapter 20. Chapter 17 explains how an outward movement of the economy's *PPF* curve illustrates *economic growth*.

The nature of production

As I explained in Chapter 1, and will repeat from time to time, the ultimate purpose of economic activity is to improve people's economic welfare and standard of living. For this to happen, material goods and services must be consumed, although quality of life factors, such as the pleasure derived from family and friends, also form an important part of welfare and human contentment.

But with the exception of goods that are freely available at absolutely no cost, which are known as **free goods**, almost all the goods we consume must first be produced. This requires the use of economic resources. **Finite economic resources** are used up

> **KEY TERMS**
>
> **finite resource:** a resource, such as oil, which is scarce and runs out as it is used.
>
> **free good:** a good, such as air, for which there are no costs of production and no scarcity.
>
> **production:** a process, or set of processes, that converts inputs into outputs of goods.
>
> **renewable resource:** a resource, such as timber, that with careful management can be renewed as it is used.

when they are employed to produce goods and services, and hence are not then available for further use. By contrast, as the name indicates, **renewable economic resources** can be used again and again, with careful management, and do not run out as **production** takes place.

The basic nature of production is shown in Figure 2.2. Production is a process, or set of processes, that converts inputs into outputs. The eventual outputs are the consumer goods and services that go to make up our standard of living, though inputs are of course also used to produce the capital goods that are necessary for the eventual production of consumer goods.

Figure 2.2 The nature of production

Factors of production

Economists call the inputs of the production process **factors of production**. Four factors of production are usually identified. These are **land**, **labour**, **capital** and **enterprise**, the last often being called the **entrepreneurial input**. **Entrepreneurs** are different from the other factors of production. They are the people who address the issues introduced in Chapter 1, deciding what to produce, how to produce it and for whom to produce it. An entrepreneur decides how much of the other factors of production, including labour, to employ. The costs of employing land, labour and capital become the firm's costs of production. In essence, the entrepreneur is a financial risk taker and decision maker. **Profit**, which is the entrepreneur's financial reward, results from successful decision making. Entrepreneurial profit is the profit left over after the cost of employing the other factors of production is deducted from the sales revenue gained from the sale of the goods and services the entrepreneur decides to produce.

KEY TERM

factors of production: inputs into the production process, such as land, labour, capital and enterprise.

The economic problem and economic systems

> An economic system is a set of institutional arrangements whose function is to employ most efficiently scarce resources to meet the ends of society.
>
> The United Nations Dictionary of Social Science

Although the problem of scarcity is fundamental and common to all forms of human society — from humble tribal groupings of hunter-gatherers in the Amazonian forest to rich nations such as the USA — different societies have produced different institutional frameworks and methods for allocating scarce resources among competing uses. The set of institutions within which a community decides what, how and for whom to produce is called an **economic system**.

Classification of economic systems by allocative mechanism

Perhaps the most widely used method of defining and classifying economic systems is according to the type of allocative mechanism by which scarce resources reach the people who eventually consume or use them.

There are a variety of ways in which wealth and purchasing power can be allocated among individuals, including inheritance and other types of gift, theft and chance (such as winning a fortune on the National Lottery). However, the two allocative mechanisms by which economic systems are defined are the **market mechanism** (or **price mechanism**) and the **command mechanism** (or **planning mechanism**). An economic system in which goods and services are purchased through the price mechanism in a system of markets is called a **market economy**, whereas one in which government officials or planners allocate economic resources to firms and other productive enterprises is called a **command economy** (or **planned economy**).

> **KEY TERMS**
>
> **command economy:** the planning mechanism allocates resources between competing uses.
>
> **market economy:** markets and prices allocate resources between competing uses.

Market economies

In a pure market economy, the market mechanism (the price mechanism and market forces) performs the central economic task of allocating scarce resources among competing uses. A market economy comprises a large number of markets varying in the degree to which they are separated from and interrelated with each other.

A **market** is a meeting of buyers and sellers in which goods or services are exchanged for other goods or services. Occasionally, the exchange occurs through barter or the swapping of goods. More usually, however, the buyers and sellers use money as the means of exchange. One good or service, such as labour, is exchanged for money, which is then traded a second time for other goods or services, sometimes immediately but often some time later. The exchange must be voluntary; if one party forces a transaction upon the other, it is not a market transaction.

Transport costs and lack of information may create barriers that separate or break up markets. In past centuries, such barriers often prevented markets from operating outside the relatively small geographical areas of a single country or even a small region within a country. However, while some markets exist in a particular geographical location — for example, a street market and until quite recently the London Stock Exchange — many markets do not. In recent years, modern developments have allowed goods to be transported more easily and at lower cost, and have helped in the transmission of market information via telephone, fax and increasingly the internet. This has enabled many markets, especially commodity and raw material markets and markets in financial services, to become truly global or international markets functioning on a worldwide basis.

Command economies

A complete command economy is an economy in which all decisions about what, how, how much, when, where and for whom to produce are taken by a central planning authority, issuing commands or directives to all the households and producers in the society. Such a system could only exist within a very rigid and probably totalitarian political framework because of the restrictions on individual decision making that are obviously implied.

In fact, in much the same way that a pure market economy, in which the price mechanism alone allocates resources, is a theoretical abstraction, so no economy in the real world can properly be described as a complete or pure command economy. Before the collapse of the communist political system around 1990, the countries of eastern Europe were command economies. However, they were not pure command economies. Production but not consumption was planned. Consumers often had to queue to get consumer goods, whose prices were fixed by the planners. Shortages resulted, which, together with the generally inferior quality of consumer goods, contributed to the breakdown of the command economies. Some communist countries still exist, namely the People's Republic of China, North Korea, Vietnam and Cuba. However, all these countries, with the exception until recently of North Korea, have encouraged the growth of markets to a greater or lesser extent. They have communist political systems, but they have moved away from being pure command economies.

Classification by ownership

So far I have defined economic systems in terms of the allocative mechanism (the market mechanism or the planning mechanism) used to solve the economic problem. Economic systems can also be defined in terms of who owns the means of production: **private individuals** or the **state**.

Capitalist economies

Capitalism is a system in which the means of production are privately owned by individuals (or capitalists), who employ labour to operate the capital they own, so as to produce output for sale at a profit.

Socialist economies

In contrast to capitalism, in a **socialist** economic system the means of production are owned by the state on behalf of the people.

KEY TERMS

capitalism: the means of production are privately owned.

socialism: the means of production are socially owned.

Classification by allocative mechanism and ownership

Mixed economies

Many economies, particularly those of the developed countries of western Europe such as the UK, are called **mixed economies**. A mixed economy, as the name suggests, is a mixture of different types of economic system. Figure 2.3 shows how a mixed economy can be defined both in terms

of the mechanism for allocating resources and in terms of ownership. The upper panel of the diagram shows that a mixed economy is intermediate between a market economy and a command economy. Defined in this way, a mixed economy contains a large **market sector** and a large **non-market sector**. The lower panel of the diagram shows that a mixed economy contains a large **public sector** and a large **private sector**.

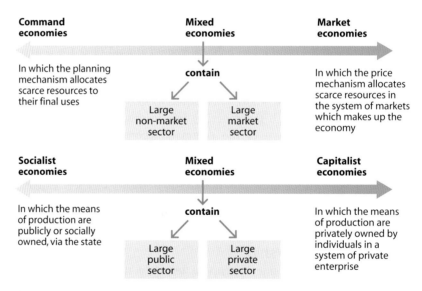

Figure 2.3
Different types of economic system

The UK as a mixed economy

The development of the mixed economy

A mixed economy developed quickly in the UK in the 1940s, when a number of important industries such as coal, rail and steel were nationalised and taken into public ownership. At the same time, the 1944 Education Act and the creation of the National Health Service extended state provision of education and healthcare.

For about 30 years after the end of the Second World War, from the 1940s to the 1970s, the majority of UK citizens (and the major political parties) agreed that the mixed economy was working well. Most people believed that certain types of economic activity, particularly the production and distribution of consumer goods and services, were best suited to private enterprise and the market economy. But people also accepted that some industries, the utility industries, which at the time were natural monopolies, ought to be nationalised, and that important services such as education, healthcare and roads should be provided by government outside the market and financed through the tax system. In short, a consensus existed around the belief that the mixed economy was right for the UK.

CASE STUDY 2.1

The UK economy and models of capitalism

To understand the UK mixed economy, it is useful to compare two models of capitalism: the **social market model**, with an emphasis on the paternalist role of the state, and the **Anglo-American model**, in which markets dominate and the role of the state is more limited.

The German social market economy has been compared to a football game:

In a good game of football it is to be noted that the game follows definite rules; these are decided in advance. The spectators of a game of football would deeply resent the players coming on with an agreement about the number of goals this or that side was to be credited with, and then not playing a fair and interesting game as expected and paid for with gate money. In a social market economy, the government lays down the order and the rules of the game, while retaining freedom of competition.

Here is an extract from the views expressed in 2008 by German Chancellor Angela Merkel on the virtues of the German social market economy:

The German way is a free market tempered by consensus-building politics and a generous welfare state. The social market economy was always against the division of society. It is a system that had and still has social cohesion and equality at its core. It tries to forge alliances. In a way, we will perhaps always insist on a higher degree of equality than in Anglo-Saxon societies.

The Anglo-American model is based on unfettered markets, self-interest, innovation and entrepreneurism, and in essence a 'winner takes all' society.

Follow-up question

Explain **two** differences between the German social market economy and the American economy.

Recent changes in the UK mixed economy

From the 1960s onwards, however, a growing minority (and perhaps eventually a majority) of economists and politicians blamed the mixed economy for the UK's deteriorating economic performance, relative to that of its main competitors in western Europe and Japan. Critics argued that the public and non-market sectors of the economy are very often inefficient and wealth consuming rather than wealth creating. The public and non-market sectors had become too big and needed cutting down to size. Critics of the mixed economy argued that a concerted effort should be made to change fundamentally the nature of the UK economy by increasing private ownership and market production.

During the 1980s and the early and mid-1990s, Conservative governments implemented policies that succeeded in changing the nature of the mix in favour of private ownership and market forces, at the expense of public ownership and state planning. The UK economy is now much closer to being a pure market and private enterprise economy than it was 40 years ago. The three main policies used to change the nature of the UK economy have been:

- **privatisation** — selling off state-owned assets such as nationalised industries to private ownership
- **marketisation** or **commercialisation** — charging a market price for goods and services that the state previously provided 'free'
- **deregulation** — removing barriers to entry and government red tape and bureaucracy from the operation of markets

Privatisation of state-owned industry in the UK occurred in the 1980s and 1990s

These policies of economic liberalisation were first introduced by Margaret Thatcher's Conservative governments in the 1980s. Thatcher believed that the mixed economy she inherited in 1979 was actually a mixed-up economy, performing inefficiently and uncompetitively. To a large extent, she established a new agenda that the Labour governments from 1997 to 2010 also accepted, continuing the process of reform (or reaction?) that they inherited. The Conservative–Liberal Democrat coalition government elected in 2010 has continued to develop these policies, though it remains to be seen what will happen if there is a change of government in 2015.

CASE STUDY 2.2

The end of history?

Few if any of you reading this book were born at the time of the collapse of the old command economies in eastern Europe at the end of the 1980s and the beginning of the 1990s. At the time, political and economic analysts, particularly those living in the USA, claimed that this was a triumph for capitalism and the market economy.

Around 1991, after the fall of the Berlin Wall and the collapse of the Soviet Union, the US political analyst Francis Fukuyama declared that the triumph of the West was so complete that it had brought about *The End of History*. American capitalism was not just the best economic system; it was the only system that could operate effectively. But by 1995, Fukuyama, had changed his views, arguing that capitalism and markets on their own are not enough for social cohesion in an economy. He was now stressing the virtues of a form of mixed economy, but with a central feature of the mix being the role of non-governmental organisations (NGOs) that lie between markets and the state. NGOs are part of the 'space between', which means all the intermediate associations, such as companies, churches and charities, critical to the functioning both of the market and of the state. Fukuyama claimed that those countries that have had the most dynamic economies are those that have had the most vigorous networks of intermediate associations: the USA, Germany and Japan. But today's problem is that the associational network is disintegrating, in the USA at least, under the stresses of headlong economic change.

Follow-up questions

1 Do you think that events since 1995 support or refute Fukuyama's views?
2 The case study briefly mentions the roles in the economy of 'non-governmental organisations (NGOs) that lie between markets and the state'. Explain the meaning of the term 'non-governmental organisation' and give two examples of important NGOs in the UK.

SUMMARY

- The economic problem is limited resources in relation to people's desires and wants.
- The economic problem results from scarcity.
- Scarcity results in the need for choice.
- Whenever a choice has to be made there is an opportunity cost.
- The opportunity cost of any decision is the next best alternative forgone.
- Economists generally assume that people are rational, choosing the best alternative available.
- Scarcity, opportunity cost and choice can be illustrated on a production possibility diagram.
- Production is a process, or set of processes, that converts input into outputs.
- The inputs into the production process are called factors of production.
- The entrepreneur is the factor of production that decides what to produce, how to produce and for whom to produce.
- Different economic systems allocate resources between different uses in different ways.
- In a market economy, the price mechanism performs the allocative task.
- The UK economy is a mixed economy, containing a mix of market and non-market sectors, and private and public sectors.
- The nature of the UK mixed economy has changed during the last 40 years.

Exam-style questions

1 With the help of an appropriate diagram, explain the central economic problem. (12 marks)

2 With the use of an example in each case, explain how decision making by both individuals and firms is affected by opportunity cost. (12 marks)

3 Evaluate the benefits and costs of solving the economic problem through the use of markets and the price mechanism. (25 marks)

4 In the 1990s, the British railway system was privatised. Different rail services between different towns and cities are now provided by different rail companies. Do you agree that British rail travellers have benefited from the changes in provision of rail services? Justify your answer. (25 marks)

Introduction key terms

capital good: a good, such as a machine, used to produce other goods, including consumer goods.

capitalism: the means of production are privately owned.

command economy: the planning mechanism allocates resources between competing uses.

consumer good: a good, such as a pineapple or an mp3 player, used by consumers to meet their needs or wants.

demand: the quantity of a good that households are willing to buy in a market.

economic problem: only a limited amount of resources are available to produce the unlimited quantity of goods and services people desire.

economics: the study of choice and decision making in a world with limited resources.

factors of production: inputs into the production process, such as land, labour, capital and enterprise.

finite resource: a resource, such as oil, which is scarce and runs out as it is used.

free good: a good, such as air, for which there are no costs of production and no scarcity.

macroeconomics: examines the economy as a whole.

market economy: markets and prices allocate resources between competing uses.

microeconomics: examines individual consumers, firms and markets in the economy.

mixed economy: contains both market and non-market sectors and a substantial public sector as well as a private sector.

normative: an opinion that cannot be scientifically tested.

opportunity cost: the cost of the next best alternative sacrificed.

positive statement: a statement of fact, or one that can be scientifically tested.

production: converts inputs or factor services into outputs of goods.

production possibility diagram: a diagram that shows different possible combinations of goods that can be produced using available resources.

renewable resource: a resource, such as timber, that with careful management can be renewed as it is used.

socialism: the means of production are socially owned.

supply: the quantity of a good that firms are prepared to sell in a market.

technical progress: improves methods of producing existing goods and enables completely new types of good to be produced.

Unit 1
Markets and market failure

Chapter 3

The demand for goods and services

Suppose you ask a person the question 'what is meant by economics?' As well as some less printable replies, one answer you may get is 'supply and demand'. Such a reply is actually very sensible because a lot of economics is about how markets work, and about how ordinary individuals such as you and I demand or supply goods and services in markets. This chapter, which focuses on demand, is followed by two chapters, the first of which considers supply, while the second brings demand and supply together to allow us to see how a market taken as a whole functions.

LEARNING OUTCOMES

This chapter will:
- explain the difference between wants, desires and effective demand
- distinguish between individual demand and market demand
- explain the 'law of demand'
- examine the slope of a market demand curve
- explain shifts of demand and the conditions of demand
- distinguish between complementary goods and substitute goods
- explain how normal goods differ from inferior goods
- distinguish between composite demand and derived demand
- explain the difference between a shift of demand and a movement along a demand curve
- consider circumstances in which consumers may respond to higher prices by increasing demand

Wants, desires and effective demand

For several years, an elderly 'bag lady' used to walk past my house. All her possessions were in the trolley she dragged behind her. From what I could gather, she had no income apart from the charity local people gave her. Her life lay outside the welfare benefit system operated by the state, which is supposed to act as a safety net for poor and downtrodden people, the cast-offs of society. Then suddenly, the poor woman vanished. A few days later, my local newspaper reported starkly that the body of an old lady had been discovered in a churchyard near my house. The lady's death was apparently due to hypothermia linked to malnutrition.

From this sad story, you can gather that my local bag lady lacked the wherewithal to meet her basic wants, namely sufficient food to provide a reasonable diet, warm clothing and shelter — the very things that most of us take for granted.

Now let's compare this poor lady's situation (when she was alive) with mine. I enjoy a comfortable middle-class life in which all my basic wants are met. However, since a very young age, I have dreamt of owning a bright-red new Ferrari. Unfortunately, the price is above £200,000. By borrowing up to the hilt, I might be able to buy the car, but no way can I pay for it out of my income. I desire the car, but to my chagrin, I cannot exercise an effective demand for a brand-new Ferrari, or at least the model I have set my sights on.

When economists refer to **demand**, they always mean **effective demand**. Effective demand is desire backed up by an ability to pay. Unlike the poor bag lady, most of us can exercise an effective demand for the goods that fulfil our basic wants, but unless we are extremely rich, with money no object, we are not in a position to buy *all* the goods we desire.

I cannot exercise an effective demand for a new Ferrari

Individual demand and market demand

Effective demand usually relates to **market demand**. This is the quantity of a good or service that all the consumers in the market wish to, and are able to, buy at different prices. By contrast, **individual demand** is the quantity that a particular individual, such as you or I, would like to buy. The relationship between market and individual demand is simple. Market demand is just the sum or addition of the demand of all the consumers in the market. Thus, if in the UK, 40 million people are prepared to buy nectarines at prices ranging between 0 and £5 a kilo, market demand is the sum of the individual demand of 40 million people.

The 'law' of demand

The 'law' of demand states that as a good's price falls, more is demanded. There is thus an inverse relationship between price and quantity demanded. Note the word 'law' is in inverted commas. This is because a law in economics is not as strong or watertight as a law in a natural science subject

KEY TERMS

demand: the quantity of a good or service that consumers are willing and able to buy at given prices in a given period of time. For economists, demand is always *effective demand*.

effective demand: the desire for a good or service backed by an ability to pay.

market demand: the quantity of a good or service that all the consumers in a market are willing and able to buy.

such as physics or astronomy. Whereas a law in physics will always hold, a social science law always has ifs and buts attached. More of a good is usually demanded as its price falls, but there are exceptions. To find out more, read the extension material later in the chapter.

The market demand curve

The market demand curve drawn in Figure 3.1 illustrates the 'law' of demand. If the price starts off high, for example at P_1, household demand is Q_1. But if the price falls to P_2, quantity Q_2 is demanded.

Demand for a good varies according to the time period being considered. For example, weekly demand is different from daily, monthly and annual demand. For this reason, the horizontal axis in Figure 3.1 is labelled 'Quantity demanded per period of time'. In later diagrams, the label 'Quantity' is used. Always remember that this is a shortcut, and stands for 'Quantity demanded per period of time'.

Figure 3.1 A market demand curve

EXAM TIP

You don't need to write 'Quantity demanded per period of time' on the horizontal axis of a demand curve diagram. When answering AQA exam questions, the label 'Quantity' is adequate.

Shifts of demand

When we draw a market demand curve to show how much of the good or service households plan to demand at various possible prices, we assume that all the other variables that may also influence demand are held unchanged or constant. This is the **ceteris paribus** assumption. *Ceteris paribus* means 'other things being equal'. Among the variables whose values are held constant or unchanged when we draw a demand curve are disposable income and tastes or fashion. Collectively, the variables (other than the good's own price) whose values determine planned demand are often called the **conditions of demand**.

KEY TERM

condition of demand: a determinant of demand, other than the good's own price, that fixes the position of the demand curve.

The conditions of demand

The main conditions of demand are:
- the prices of **substitute goods** (or **goods in competing demand**)
- the prices of **complementary goods** (or **goods in joint demand**)

- personal **income** (or more strictly **personal disposable income**, i.e. income after tax and receipt of benefits)
- tastes and preferences
- population size, which influences total market size

If any of the conditions of demand change, the position of the demand curve changes, shifting either rightward or leftward. Figure 3.2 illustrates a rightward shift of the demand curve, which is also called an **increase in demand**. Following a rightward shift of demand, more of the good is demanded at all prices. For example, at a price of P_1, the quantity demanded increases from Q_1 to Q_2. Conversely, a leftward shift of demand (known as a **decrease in demand**) causes the quantity demanded to fall at all prices.

> **KEY TERMS**
>
> **decrease in demand:** a leftward shift of the demand curve.
>
> **increase in demand:** a rightward shift of the demand curve.

Among events that might cause a rightward shift of demand are:

- an increase in the price of a substitute good or good in competing demand
- a fall in the price of a complementary good or good in joint demand
- an increase in personal disposable income (but see the following section on normal and inferior goods)
- a successful advertising campaign making people think more favourably about the good
- an increase in population

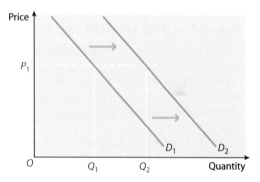

Figure 3.2 The effect of a rightward shift of demand

Normal and inferior goods

When disposable income increases, a demand curve shifts rightward, but only if the good is a normal good. A **normal good** is a good for which demand increases as income increases. However, some goods are **inferior goods**. In the case of an inferior good, demand decreases as income increases, and an increase in income shifts the demand curve leftward.

> **KEY TERMS**
>
> **inferior good:** a good for which demand decreases as income rises.
>
> **normal good:** a good for which demand increases as income rises.

To take an example, private car transport and bus travel are not just substitutes for each other; one is a normal good and the other is an inferior good. As people's incomes rise, demand for cars generally increases, while, at the same time, demand for bus travel as a form of public transport usually falls. If people respond in this way to changes in income then private transport is a normal good, but certain forms of public transport are inferior goods. For an individual, whether a good is normal or inferior depends on personal income, tastes and, possibly, age. For young children, junk food such as sweets is usually a normal good. When parents increase small children's pocket money, they generally buy more sweets. But as children get older, tastes change, and sweets may very well become an inferior good.

Complementary goods and substitute goods

An increase in the price of a complementary good (or a good in joint demand) has the opposite effect to an increase in the price of a substitute good (or a good in competing

EXAM TIP

Chapter 6 develops
the analysis of
complementary and
substitute goods
and normal and
inferior goods.

demand). For example, Sony games consoles and Sony games cartridges are complementary goods in joint demand, but Sony and Xbox consoles are in competing demand, or substitute goods. Following a significant rise in the price of Sony consoles, demand for them falls, which in turn reduces the demand for Sony games cartridges. The demand curve for the Sony cartridges shifts leftward. But the demand curve for Xbox consoles players shifts rightward, assuming that consumers consider an Xbox console to be a good substitute for a Sony console. However, all this may be changing. For decades, the cartridge games model ruled the games industry. Games players purchased the hardware and then bought packaged software titles separately. But new technology now means that games are increasingly downloaded from the internet.

CASE STUDY 3.1

Downloaded digital music replaces CDs and DVDs

Back in the year 2000, when the first mp3 players were hitting the market, it wasn't imagined that downloaded digital music sales would overtake CD and DVD sales. Even when the iTunes store opened in 2003, Apple was only vying for a small-yet-respectable market share…at least, at first.

Music technology history has just hit an important milestone. Downloaded digital music sales have finally overtaken physical music sales to the tune of a 55.9% majority. Downloaded sales have gone up 9.1% in 2012 while CD sales have decreased by 10%, though music sales in general are up 3% after a decade of pretty consistent decline.

What are we giving up by adopting the new technology? Tangible insert booklets and artwork, fold-out posters, and the joy of holding a piece of music in our hands. What are we gaining? Instant satisfaction, convenience, and mobile purchasing power. This all sounds reminiscent of the LP versus cassette or CD comparison of years past.

While we've seen record shop giants like HMV shutting up shop due to falling revenue and a general shift of music sales going to the likes of Amazon.com and Tesco, this marks the first time that we can truly imagine CDs being phased out as the years go on. It's getting harder to find physical releases of all but the highest-profile artists, and this trend is not only here to stay, but will certainly evolve further.

Music technology history has just hit an important milestone. How will our ways of consuming music evolve as time goes on?

Follow-up questions

1 Over the last 50 years, demand for recorded music has switched from vinyl records to CDs and then to downloadable digital music. Explain **two** reasons for these changes in demand.

2 How would you describe the demand relationship between CDs and downloadable digital music?

Composite demand and derived demand

Students often confuse competing demand, which occurs in the case of substitutes, with **composite demand** and derived demand. Composite demand is demand for a good which has more than one use. This means that an increase in demand for one use of the good reduces the supply of the good for an alternative use; for example, if more wheat is used for biofuel, less is available for food, unless wheat growing increases significantly. By contrast, **derived demand** for a good occurs when a good is necessary for the production of other goods. The demand for capital goods such as machinery and raw materials is derived from the demand for consumer goods or finished goods. If the demand for cars falls, so does the demand for engines, gear boxes and other car components.

Movement along a demand curve and shift of a demand curve

Another source of confusion lies in the difference between a movement along (or adjustment along) a demand curve and a shift of a demand curve. A **movement along a demand curve** takes place only when the good's price changes. As explained earlier, provided the demand curve slopes downward, a *fall* in price results in *more* of the good being demanded. This is sometimes called an **extension of demand**. Likewise, a **contraction of demand** occurs when a *rise* in price leads to *less* being demanded.

By contrast, a change in a condition of demand shifts the demand curve to a new position. As already explained, a rightward shift of demand — for example, caused by the effect of increased income on demand for a normal good — is often called an increase of demand. Conversely, a decrease of demand occurs when an event such as a rise in the price of a complementary good causes less of the good to be demanded, shifting the demand curve leftward.

EXAM TIP

In the Unit 1 exam, objective test questions and the third part of a data-response question on a market often test understanding of the difference between a movement along a demand or supply curve and a shift of the curve.

EXTENSION MATERIAL

This extension material introduces you to the way demand theory is taught in university economics — in terms of demand functions. However, you don't need to know this for AS or A2 Economics.

A demand function

A functional relationship exists between two variables whenever a change in one variable, known as the independent variable or explanatory variable, causes a change in a second variable, which is the dependent variable. The relationship between quantity demanded and price, illustrated in Figure 3.1, can be written as:

$$Q_d = f(P)$$

This tells us that the quantity demanded of a good (Q_d) is a function of the good's price (P). The symbol 'f' indicates that a change in the value of the independent variable (shown inside the brackets) causes a change in the dependent variable (on the left-hand side of the equality sign). In a demand function, changes in the good's price are assumed to cause changes in the quantity demanded.

$Q_d = f(P)$ does not indicate the precise nature of the functional relationship, but as the demand curve slopes downward to the right, the relationship is negative or inverse: an increase in price causes a fall in the quantity demanded.

$Q_d = f(P)$ is an example of a single explanatory variable demand function. But, as explained earlier, there are many other variables besides the good's own price that influence demand. Other influences, such as the level of disposable income and tastes and preferences, are the conditions of demand. The functional relationship $Q_d = f(P)$, and the demand curve in Figure 3.1, result from the *ceteris paribus* assumption (the assumption that the conditions of demand remain unchanged). Indeed, we can write:

$$Q_d = f(P), \text{ ceteris paribus}$$

Dropping the *ceteris paribus* assumption, the demand function becomes:

$$Q_d = f(P, P_s, P_c, Y_d, \text{tastes, population size...})$$

This is a multi-explanatory variable demand function. All the symbols inside the brackets except the good's own price (P) are the conditions of demand. If any of them change then the demand curve shifts to a new position. P_s, P_c, Y_d are respectively the symbols for the prices of substitute goods, the prices of complementary goods and disposable income. The dots at the end of the symbols represent any other explanatory variables that influence demand, but which have not been indicated explicitly.

Upward-sloping demand curves

Demand curves don't have to slope downward, though they usually do. In Chapter 6, it will be shown that there are circumstances in which a demand curve may be horizontal or vertical. However, as Figure 3.3 illustrates, a demand curve may also slope upward, showing that more is demanded as the good's price increases.

There are a number of possible explanations for upward-sloping demand curves. Two of these, Veblen goods and goods for which consumers perceive a high price to be an indicator of high quality, are explained in the extension material opposite.

Figure 3.3 An upward-sloping demand curve

There are two other situations in which consumers may respond to higher prices by demanding more of a good.

The first is **speculative demand**. If the price of a good such as housing, shares or a foreign currency starts to rise, people may speculate that in the near future the price will rise even further. In this situation, demand is likely to go up. In the case of rising house prices, young people who wish to become first-time buyers may scramble to buy houses, fearing that if they wait, they may never be able to afford to buy a house.

The final type of good with an upward-sloping demand curve is known as a **Giffen good**. However, there is very little evidence that Giffen goods actually exist. A Giffen good is a highly inferior good that forms a large part of the total spending of extremely poor people. Consider a situation in which a very poor family buys only two foods — potatoes and meat. Potatoes, the inferior good, are the family's main foodstuff. Meat is the luxury, which the family only eats on Sunday. In this situation, a rise in the price of potatoes means that the family's real income falls. The fall in real income increases the family's demand for potatoes, which are inferior goods (at least for this family). In effect, higher potato prices mean that the family buys even more potatoes because they can no longer afford meat.

Many students make the mistake of believing that *all* inferior goods are Giffen goods, with upward-sloping demand curves. This is wrong. Most, and possibly all, inferior goods have conventional downward-sloping demand curves. A good has to be highly inferior for it to be a Giffen good, and in any case the Giffen phenomenon can only exist for extremely poor families. While it is true that all Giffen goods (if they exist) must be inferior goods, the reverse is not true. Few, if any, inferior goods are Giffen goods.

EXAM TIP

The AQA economics specification does not require knowledge of upward-sloping demand curves. Nevertheless, exam candidates often make the mistake of referring to inferior goods as Giffen goods.

Are there any exceptions to the 'law' of demand?

According to the 'law' of demand, firms that lower their prices should sell more. Sometimes, however, you may come across a company that tries to persuade us to buy more of whatever the firm is selling precisely because its goods are more expensive than those of its competitors. The 'reassuringly expensive' advertising campaign for Stella Artois beer is a good example.

A few years ago, Interbrew, the Belgian company that owns the Stella brand, decided to sell its beer as a premium brand. Interbrew hoped that high prices would attract more customers. (Those readers enjoying a misspent youth who regularly buy beer may have noticed that, in recent years, Stella has changed tack, selling its beers on the 'stack 'em high, sell 'em fast' principle, at discounted prices.)

Perhaps more could be done to justify Stella's ridiculous price.

Aaah the exquisite Stella taste.

Aargh the excruciating Stella price. Sadly, there's very little we can do about it.

Even offering small incentives like the one on the left is beyond our means.

Making Stella properly just costs far too much money.

We could, you might suppose, adulterate our premium barley with a few bags of a more questionable grain.

Substitute ordinary hops for the rare Czech Saaz variety.

Or hoist Stella out of the vat before the customary six weeks maturation.

While these expedients might produce a price that's not ridiculous, we're afraid the same could not be said of the beer.

Stella Artois. Reassuringly expensive.

An economist might argue that the 'reassuringly expensive' campaign shows that Stella was marketing its beer as a Veblen good, named after the Norwegian economist Thornstein Veblen. A Veblen good is a good of exclusive or ostentatious consumption, or a 'snob' good. Veblen goods are sometimes called positional goods, though strictly a positional good is so scarce that only few people can ever acquire it. Some people wish to consume Veblen goods, such as the Ferrari car I mentioned earlier in the chapter, because possession of such goods indicates how well a person has done in society. Flaunting Veblen or positional goods sends signals to other (hopefully envious) people about how well off you are.

Don't confuse a Veblen good with another type of good which might attract more demand at higher prices: namely, a good for which consumers use price as a short-cut for information about quality. Consumers may lack accurate information about the quality of some of the goods they are considering buying, particularly goods such as second-hand cars, computers and, in the example below, horses. In this situation, a potential buyer may fear that a low price means low quality, and that conversely a high price means high quality.

This reflects a problem which, according to economist George Akerlof (winner of the 2001 Nobel Prize for Economics), is as old as markets themselves. It concerns how horse traders respond to the question: 'If he wants to sell that horse, do I really want to buy it?' Akerlof believes that such questioning is fundamental to the market for horses and used cars, and it is also at least minimally present in every market transaction.

SUMMARY

- Demand means effective demand, based on ability as well as willingness to pay.
- Market demand is the sum of the individual demand of all the consumers in the market.
- The 'law' of demand states that as a good's price falls, more is demanded.
- Market demand (and individual demand) can be represented on a demand curve.
- For most goods, demand curves slope downward.
- If any of the conditions of demand change, the demand curve shifts to a new position.
- The conditions of demand include the prices of substitute goods and goods in joint demand, disposable income and tastes and preferences.
- Consumer goods can be divided into normal goods and inferior goods.
- Composite demand is demand for a good which has more than one use.
- Derived demand for a good occurs when a good is necessary for the production of other goods.
- A movement along a demand curve must not be confused with a shift of a demand curve.
- A few goods may have upward-sloping demand curves. These are Veblen goods, goods for which price is an indicator of quality, goods in speculative demand and, possibly, Giffen goods.

Exam-style questions

1 Explain the relationship between the demand exercised by a particular individual for a product and market demand for the product. (12 marks)

2 Explain the significance of the *ceteris paribus* assumption in microeconomic theory. (12 marks)

3 Evaluate the view that a fall in a good's price will inevitably lead to more demand for the good. (25 marks)

4 Do you agree that whenever a person desires a particular good such as a Mercedes sports car, this will inevitably lead to more demand for the good? Justify your answer. (25 marks)

The supply of goods and services

Chapter 4

Chapter 2 introduced you to the fact that a market is a voluntary meeting of buyers and sellers, with the buyers deciding how much of a good or service they wish to buy, while firms or suppliers decide how much to sell. Chapter 3 then explained how individuals and households exercise demand in a market. This chapter looks at the other side of market transactions, investigating how firms or producers decide how much of a good they would like to supply and sell.

As you proceed through this chapter, you will note how it is similar to the previous chapter which explains the nature of demand. The similarity is no accident. For the most part, this chapter applies the same logic and line of reasoning to explain supply. Much of the explanation is similar, but do note the differences between the theory of supply and the theory of demand.

LEARNING OUTCOMES

This chapter will:

- distinguish between the supply of a single firm in a market and market supply
- explain the 'law' of supply
- examine the slope of a market supply curve
- explain shifts of supply and the conditions of supply
- explain how expenditure taxes and subsidies shift supply curves
- distinguish between joint supply and competing supply

Supply by a single firm and market supply

Normally when economists refer to **supply**, they mean market supply. **Market supply** is the quantity of a good or service that all the firms or producers in the market *plan* to sell at different prices. By contrast, as the name indicates, supply by a single firm is the quantity that a particular firm *within* the market would like to sell. As with demand, the relationship between the two is simple. Market supply is just the sum of the supply of all the firms or producers in the market. Thus, if in the UK, 20,000 farmers are prepared to sell tomatoes at various prices ranging from very low to very high, market supply sums the supply decision of all the farmers in the market.

KEY TERMS

market supply: the quantity of a good or service that all the firms in a market are willing to sell.

supply: the quantity of a good or service that firms plan to sell at given prices in a given period of time.

The 'law' of supply

The 'law' of supply states that as a good's price rises, more is supplied. There is thus a positive or direct relationship between price and quantity supplied. (There are exceptions to the 'law' of supply. To find out more, read the extension material that follows the next section on the market supply curve.)

The market supply curve

The market supply curve drawn in Figure 4.1 illustrates the 'law' of supply. If the price starts off low, for example at P_1, firms are willing to supply Q_1. But if the price rises to P_2, planned supply increases to Q_2.

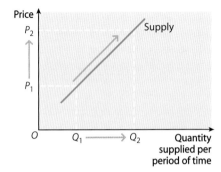

Figure 4.1 A market supply curve

The main reason for upward-sloping supply curves stems from the business objective which economists generally assume that firms have. This is the **profit-maximising objective**. It is assumed that firms always aim to make the biggest possible **profit**. From this it follows that a firm will only want to supply more of a good if it is profitable so to do.

KEY TERM

profit: the difference between total sales revenue and total costs of production.

For a firm, profit is the difference between the sales revenue the firm receives when selling the goods or services it produces and the costs of producing the goods. Now, assuming firms do not change their size or scale, the cost of producing extra units of a good generally increases as firms produce more of the good. As a result, it is unprofitable to produce and sell extra units of a good unless the price rises to compensate for the extra cost of production. The result is the upward-sloping market supply curve shown in Figure 4.1.

EXAM TIP

Figure 4.1 shows a linear supply curve: that is, a straight line. However, neither supply curves nor demand curves have to be linear. A non-linear supply or demand curve is depicted by a 'curved' curve. Both linear and non-linear curves are possible. In an exam it does not matter which you draw — providing the curve is meant to be upward sloping. Supply curves usually slope upward, although, as the extension material explains, other shapes of supply curve are possible.

As with demand, the supply of a good varies according to the time period being considered. Hence the words 'Quantity supplied per period of time' on the horizontal axis in Figure 4.1. In later diagrams, this is shortened this to 'Quantity'. But again, as with demand, remember that this is a shortcut.

EXTENSION MATERIAL

Backward-bending supply curves

Occasionally, supply curves do not slope upward. Backward-bending supply curves, illustrated here, have been observed in the markets for oil and labour. Consider a situation in which workers aim for a target weekly wage, say £750. If the hourly wage rate rises, they can achieve their target by supplying less labour, preferring more leisure time to more money. Such behaviour is quite likely in dangerous and unpleasant occupations such as coal mining.

In Figure 4.2, the supply curve of labour slopes upward in a conventional way until point X is reached. Thus, supply goes up from Q_1 to Q_2 following a wage rate rise from P_1 to P_2. However, any further wage rise, for example from P_2 to P_3, causes workers to supply less labour. Supply falls to Q_3 in this case.

Figure 4.2 A backward-bending supply curve

Shifts of supply

In Chapter 3, we saw how a market demand curve shows how much all the consumers in the market plan to buy at different prices of the good, assuming all the other factors that influence demand remain constant. These 'other factors' were called the conditions of demand and it was explained how, if any of them change, the demand curve shifts to a new position.

In exactly the same way, a market supply curve shows the quantities of the good that all the firms in the market plan to supply at different possible prices, assuming the **conditions of supply** remain unchanged. Again, if the *ceteris paribus* assumption no longer holds, one or more of the conditions of supply change, and the supply curve shifts to a new position.

> **KEY TERM**
>
> **condition of supply:** a determinant of supply, other than the good's own price, that fixes the position of the supply curve.

The conditions of supply

The main conditions of supply are:
- costs of production, including
  - wage costs
  - raw material costs
  - energy costs
  - costs of borrowing
- technical progress
- taxes imposed on firms, such as VAT, excise duties and the business rate
- subsidies granted by the government to firms

As I have noted, if any of the conditions of supply change, the supply curve shifts to a new position. A rightward shift of supply is also known as an **increase in supply**, whereas a leftward shift is known

> **KEY TERM**
>
> **increase in supply:** a rightward shift of the supply curve.

as a **decrease in supply**. An increase in wage costs, which for many firms are the most important cost of production, shifts the supply curve leftward (or upward). Firms reduce the quantity of the good they are prepared to supply because production costs have risen. For example, when the price is P_1 in Figure 4.3, a leftward shift of supply from S_1 to S_2 causes the quantity firms are prepared to supply to fall from Q_1 to Q_2.

Figure 4.3 A leftward shift of the supply curve

EXAM TIP

Chapter 5 explains how, following an increase and a decrease in supply, there is a resulting adjustment or movement along the demand curve. Likewise an increase or decrease of demand results in an adjustment or movement along the supply curve. Examination questions often test your understanding of the difference between a shift of a curve and an adjustment in response to a price change along the other curve which has not shifted.

Supply curves also shift when technical progress occurs, or when firms enter or leave the market. Technical progress generally reduces production costs and shifts supply curves rightward. The entry of new firms into the market has a similar effect. Conversely, the supply curve shifts leftward when firms leave the market.

CASE STUDY 4.1

Fluctuations in commodity prices

The Unit 1 exam sometimes contains data about changing conditions of demand or supply for a product, and the reasons for, or consequences of, a shift of a demand curve or a supply curve in the market. Very often the market is a commodity market, for an industrial raw material such as copper or a source of energy such as oil.

Volatile oil prices

Some commodity price fluctuations are inevitable in a market-based economy. But high price volatility creates uncertainty and risk. Much recent volatility in oil prices can be related to unrest in the Middle East, in itself caused by the Arab Spring. The political and in some cases military upheavals in Libya, Egypt, Syria and other countries, the boycott of Iranian crude oil in response to its nuclear weapons programme, and the risk of terrorist attacks all have conspired to make oil markets more volatile.

Other factors contributing to price volatility are the time lags in oil production and speculation. However, greater oil production from the United States, Canada and other politically stable countries provides a critical hedge against price volatility.

Now watch a very good Money Week '*Introduction to Commodities*' video clip on YouTube (**www.youtube.com**).

Follow-up questions

1 Explain how 'time lags in oil production and speculation' can lead to price volatility.
2 Explain how greater production in politically stable countries can act as a hedge against price volatility.

How expenditure taxes and subsidies shift supply curves

A supply curve also shifts leftward (or upward) when the government imposes an **expenditure tax** such as customs and excise duties or value added tax (VAT) on firms. From a firm's point of view, the tax is similar to a rise in production costs, so the supply curve shifts leftward. Firms try to pass the tax on to consumers by increasing the price of the good. For this reason, expenditure taxes provide examples of **indirect taxes**. The higher price charged means consumers indirectly pay the tax, even though the firms and not the consumers pay the tax to the government (see Figure 6.9 in Chapter 6 for an example).

How the supply curve shifts depends on whether the tax firms are forced to pay is an ***ad valorem* tax** or a **specific tax**. In the case of an *ad valorem* tax such as VAT, which is levied at the same percentage rate (e.g. 20%) on whatever the price would be without the tax, the new supply curve is steeper than the old supply curve. This is shown in the left-hand panel of Figure 4.4. But in the case of a specific tax or unit tax, such as the excise duty levied on tobacco, alcohol or petrol, the tax levied on each unit of the good is not affected by the good's price before the tax was imposed. Because of this, the new and old supply curves are parallel to each other, as the right-hand panel of Figure 4.4 illustrates.

> **KEY TERMS**
>
> ***ad valorem* tax:** a percentage expenditure tax such as VAT.
>
> **expenditure tax:** a tax levied by the government on spending by consumers. The firms selling the good pay the tax to the government, but consumers indirectly pay via the resulting price rise.
>
> **unit tax** or **specific tax:** a tax levied on a unit of a good, irrespective of the good's price.

Figure 4.4
An expenditure tax shifting a supply curve

How subsidies shift supply curves

A **subsidy** given by the government to producers has the opposite effect to an expenditure tax. In the case of a specific subsidy, which is illustrated in Figure 4.5, the sum of money paid to firms for each unit of the good produced is the same whatever the price of the good. By contrast, the size of the subsidy would vary if the subsidy were dependent on the price of the good before the subsidy was paid.

> **KEY TERM**
>
> **subsidy:** a payment made by government, usually to producers, for each unit of the subsidised good that they produce.

Figure 4.5 A specific or unit subsidy shifting a supply curve

Joint supply and competing supply

Chapter 3 explained the difference between complementary goods (or goods in joint demand) and substitutes (or goods in competing demand). It then went on to explain how, if the price of a complementary good increases, the demand curve for the other good in joint demand shifts leftward. In the case of substitute goods, the opposite relationship holds: a rise in the price of the substitute leads the demand curve for the good in competing demand to shift rightward.

With supply curves, there are rather similar relationships when goods are in **joint supply** and when they are in **competing supply**. These relationships are, however, a little bit different from the demand relationships. Joint supply occurs when production of one good also leads to the supply of a by-product. For example, the slaughter of a cow to provide meat leads to production of one extra cow hide, which increases the supply of leather. In this example, meat is the main product and leather is the by-product, though the relationship could be reversed.

Suppose now the price of beef increases and farmers believe the high price will continue in future years. More cattle will be bred for slaughter, and the supply of leather will also increase. Thus a rise in the price of the first good (beef) shifts the supply curve of the other good in joint supply.

Now consider what happens if two goods are in competing supply rather than in joint supply. The relationship between food and biofuel provides a highly topical example. As Case Study 4.2 explains, increased demand for biofuels such as ethanol has diverted crop production away from food supply to the supply of fuel for motor

More cattle will be bred if beef prices rise

vehicles. Because farmers producing crops such as wheat, maize and sugar can earn a higher price by selling their produce to energy companies, the supply curve of such products for food is shifting leftward.

Think how you could use a production possibility curve diagram to illustrate how competing supply involves switching productive resources between different forms of production.

CASE STUDY 4.2

Competing supply: biofuel and food

Record-breaking food prices in 2011 led experts to warn of the danger of another global food crisis. There are many causes of recent increases in food prices, but the growth in production of biofuels is one of the most important. About 40% of US corn or maize production goes into biofuels. In 2011, 18% of biofuels used in the UK were made from wheat and corn that are staple foods in the developing world. Yet just a year earlier, the UK hardly used either of these.

Increased demand for biofuels inevitably drives food prices higher. And biofuel use is only set to grow.

Less food is planted as biofuel production increases.

Follow-up questions

1 Explain how diverting crop production to meet the demand for biofuel is affecting world poverty.
2 Explain **two** causes, other than increased biofuel production, of recent increases in food prices.

SUMMARY

- A market supply curve shows how much of a good all the firms in the market plan or intend to supply at different prices.
- A market supply curve is derived by adding together the individual supply curves of all the firms or producers in the market.
- If one or more of the conditions of supply change, the supply curve shifts to a new position.
- If costs of production, such as wage costs, increase, the supply curve shifts leftward or upward.
- Technical progress usually reduces production costs and shifts the supply curve rightward or downward.
- An expenditure tax shifts the supply curve leftward or upward.
- A subsidy granted to producers shifts the supply curve rightward or downward.

Exam-style questions

1 Explain **three** reasons why a supply curve may shift rightward or downward. (12 marks)

2 With the help of an appropriate diagram, explain the effect of a government subsidy granted to producers of the good on the good's price. (12 marks)

3 Evaluate **two** policies the government could use to increase the supply of housing. (25 marks)

4 Do you agree that governments should intervene in agricultural markets to force farmers to grow crops only for food and not for other purposes? Justify your answer. (25 marks)

Bringing demand and supply together in a competitive market

The comedian Sacha Baron Cohen, in his guise as Ali G, once interviewed the eminent, now sadly deceased, economist J. K. Galbraith, then in his late eighties. Ali G asked: 'What is supply and demand? Is it like with me Julie? I supply it and she demand it.'

Poor old JKG replied, 'Supply and demand is an old economic expression…', but was unable to complete his sentence. I am sure that, had he been able to do so, Professor Galbraith would have summarised some of the rest of this chapter, though of course what he said would have been much more eloquently expressed. I am not going to repeat the rest of the 'interview', interesting as it was; the language hardly befits an economics textbook. If you are interested, you can of course find the whole interview on the internet.

LEARNING OUTCOMES

This chapter will:
- distinguish between goods markets and factor markets in the economy
- explain the difference between a competitive market and an uncompetitive market
- bring demand and supply curves together in a supply and demand diagram
- distinguish between market equilibrium and disequilibrium
- explain how a shift of supply or demand disturbs market equilibrium
- distinguish between a shift of a supply or demand curve and an adjustment along a curve
- examine the adjustment process that restores equilibrium in a market
- survey the functions that prices perform in a market or mixed economy

Goods markets and factor markets

Market economies and mixed economies contain a large number of markets. Many of these markets can be grouped under the heading of either **goods markets** (or **product markets**) or **factor markets**. These markets are respectively markets for *outputs* or *final* goods and services (consumer goods and services), and markets for the factors of production or *inputs* necessary for final goods eventually to be produced. Households and firms operate simultaneously in both sets of markets. In goods markets, households exercise demand for consumer goods and services produced and supplied by firms. For household demand in the goods market to be an *effective* demand — that is, demand backed up by an ability to pay — households must sell their labour, or possibly the services of any capital or land they own, in factor markets. In these factor markets it is the firms which exercise the demand for the factor services sold by the households as inputs into the production process.

EXAM TIP

One of the data-response questions in the Unit 1 exam is likely to be on a goods market: for example, the housing market or the toy market.

Competitive markets and uncompetitive markets

The extent to which markets are **competitive** or **uncompetitive** is of great importance. At one extreme a market is highly competitive when the very large number of firms in the market produce uniform products, incur similar costs of production and have no ability to influence the ruling market price (or equilibrium price) set by supply and demand in the market as a whole. Highly competitive markets lack **entry barriers**, which means that new firms can enter. Likewise, firms already in the market can leave if they wish to. Because there is also a high degree of transparency in the market, firms can find out what their competitors are doing.

KEY TERM

competitive market: a market in which the large number of buyers and sellers possess good market information and easily enter or leave the market.

At the other extreme is a market in which there is no competition at all, simply because there is only one firm in the market, protected by entry barriers. Such a market is called a **monopoly**. As Chapter 12 explains, monopolies can often exploit consumers: for example, by hiking up the price, restricting the output they make available and also restricting consumer choice.

Real-world markets usually lie somewhere between the extremes of a high degree of competition and monopoly. In many markets, such as the market for mobile phones, real-world firms use factors such as style and fashion to make one firm's product differ from the competitors' products. As a result, prices usually vary for the branded products sold by each of the firms in the market. However, the ability to influence consumers in this way is not nearly so prevalent in the market for an agricultural good such as tomatoes, where large numbers of farmers produce a similar uniform product. The next sections of this chapter explain how such a market functions.

Tomato farmers produce a similar, uniform product

CASE STUDY 5.1

To do with the price of fish

For a market to be competitive, buyers and sellers need accurate information about supply and demand. Before the use of mobile phones, fishermen in southern India lacked information about prices being charged for newly caught fish in other fishing villages along the coast. This lack of adequate information about conditions of supply and prices being charged led to small, separated and relatively uncompetitive fish markets.

If a fisherman made a good catch, other fishermen operating out of his home port and fishing in the same area would also catch a lot of fish. But when all the fishing vessels sailed back home, fish prices in the local village fish market would slump because of excess supply.

Another possibility was to sail down the coast after the catch was made, in the hope that in other villages fish catches were less bountiful and prices were therefore better. But, because of high fuel prices and uncertainty about what might be happening elsewhere, fishermen generally chose to return to their own village. This was wasteful because oversupply led to fish being thrown away, even though they might have been sold in slightly more distant fish markets.

Another result was wide variations in fish prices in different fishing villages.

However, after mobile phones had been introduced in southern India, while they were still at sea fishermen began to call markets all along the coast to find out where prices were highest. Having obtained this information, fishermen were now prepared to market their fish further afield, despite the fuel costs involved. The number of unsold fish that previously had been thrown back into the sea fell dramatically. Fish prices also fell. The 'law of one price' was operating — there now being a single price along the coast for more or less identical fish. By improving the exchange of information between fishermen, mobile phone technology has therefore contributed to the growth of a larger and much more competitive market.

Follow-up questions

1 Explain how the case study illustrates how better information on the part of buyers or sellers improves the way a market functions.

2 Name **two** UK markets that have been made more competitive as a result of the growing use of mobile phones.

Bringing demand and supply curves together in a competitive market

I will now bring together the market demand and market supply curves (explained in Chapters 3 and 4) to see how the equilibrium price is achieved within a single competitive goods market in the economy. The market we shall look at is the tomato market. The essential features of the market are shown in Figure 5.1.

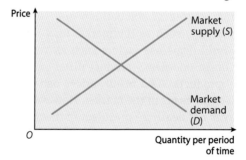

Figure 5.1 A supply and demand graph for the tomato market

Note that later diagrams in this chapter label the curves D and S, and the horizontal axis is labelled 'Quantity'. D, S and 'Quantity' are shorthand for 'Market demand', 'Market supply' and 'Quantity per period of time'.

The market demand curve drawn in Figure 5.1 shows how many tomatoes all the consumers in the market plan to purchase at different prices in a particular period of time. In a similar way, the market supply curve shows how many tomatoes all the farmers and firms in the market wish to supply at different prices in the same time period.

The equilibrium price

The concepts of **equilibrium** and its opposite, **disequilibrium**, are of great importance in economic theory and analysis. You should think of equilibrium as a *state of rest* or a *state of balance between opposing forces*. In a market, the

> **KEY TERM**
>
> **equilibrium:** a state of rest or balance between opposing forces.

opposing forces are supply and demand. **Market equilibrium**, which is shown in Figure 5.2, occurs where the demand curve and the supply curve cross each other. At price P^*, households *plan* to demand exactly the same quantity of tomatoes that firms *plan* to supply. P^* therefore is the equilibrium price, with Q^* being the equilibrium quantity.

> **KEY TERM**
>
> **market equilibrium:** when planned demand equals planned supply in the market.

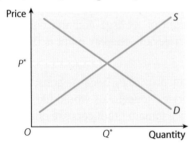

Figure 5.2 Market equilibrium in the tomato market

> **EXAM TIP**
>
> It is important to understand the concepts of equilibrium and disequilibrium in economics. You will come across many other examples besides market equilibrium and disequilibrium explained in this chapter. In your later studies, look out for macroeconomic equilibrium and balance of payments equilibrium.

Disequilibrium in the market

It is impossible at *most* prices for both households and firms simultaneously to fulfil their market plans. In Figure 5.3, P_1 is a **disequilibrium** price for tomatoes because the tomato growers and sellers cannot fulfil their plans at this price. When price is P_1 in Figure 5.3, firms would like to supply Q_2, but households are only willing to purchase Q_1.

> **KEY TERM**
>
> **market disequilibrium:** when the market fails to clear. The market plans of consumers and firms are inconsistent with each other.

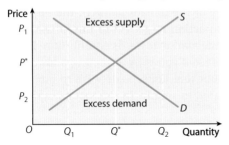

Figure 5.3 Disequilibrium and equilibrium in the tomato market

To explain this further, it is useful to divide the market into two 'sides' — the *short side* and the *long side*. When the price is P_1, households, or the people wishing to buy tomatoes, are on the short side of the market, while tomato producers are on the long side. The economic agents on the short side can always fulfil their market plans, but those on the long side cannot! Thus, when the price is P_1, households can purchase exactly the quantity of tomatoes they wish to, namely Q_1. Farmers and other tomato producers, however, are in a different situation. They would like to sell Q_2, but can only sell Q_1, as long as the price remains at P_1. The difference between Q_2 and Q_1 is **excess supply** or unsold stock.

> **KEY TERM**
>
> **excess supply:** when firms wish to sell more than consumers wish to buy, with the price above the equilibrium price.

Many students never really get to grips with microeconomic analysis because they fail to understand the difference between market plans and market action. Your market plans are what you want to do when you go shopping; your market action is what you *end up* doing.

At P_1, as at any other price, *actual* or *realised* demand equals *actual* or *realised* supply. However, this is largely irrelevant; the key point is that at price P_1, *planned* supply exceeds *planned* demand.

The market is also in disequilibrium at price P_2, because households are unable to buy as much as they wish to at this price. Households would like to buy Q_2 of tomatoes, but they can't, because at this price tomato producers are only willing to supply Q_1. The situation is now reversed compared to P_1. Tomato buyers are on the long side of the market and farmers and tomato sellers are now on the short side. In this case, the difference between Q_2 and Q_1 is **excess demand** or unfulfilled demand. Households end up buying Q_1 of tomatoes because this is the maximum quantity tomato producers are prepared to sell at this price. Once again, *actual* demand *equals* actual supply (namely Q_1), but *planned* supply is now less than *planned* demand.

KEY TERM

excess demand: when consumers wish to buy more than firms wish to sell, with the price below the equilibrium price.

I will now introduce a most important assumption about economic behaviour which recurs throughout economic theory and analysis. I will assume that whenever an economic agent, such as a household or firm, fails to fulfil its market plans, it has an incentive to change its market behaviour. When excess supply exists in the market (as at P_1 in the tomato market), the market mechanism or price mechanism swings into action to get rid of unsold stocks. By doing this, the price mechanism moves the market towards equilibrium. Economists assume that firms react to stocks of unsold goods by accepting a lower price. Eventually the price falls until the amount that households wish to buy equals exactly the quantity that firms are prepared to supply. In the tomato market, equilibrium is reached at price P^*.

In the case of excess demand, it is useful to divide households into two groups of customers. In the tomato market, the first group, depicted by the distance from O to Q_1, are *lucky* customers who buy the good at price P_1 before the available quantity runs out. By contrast, *unlucky* households, shown by the distance from Q_1 to Q_2, cannot buy the good at P_1, possibly because they turned up too late. However, in order to be able to purchase the good, unlucky consumers bid up the price until, once again, equilibrium is reached at P^*.

The equilibrium price, P^*, is the *only* price which satisfies both households and firms. Consequently, once this price is reached, neither group has reason to change their market plans. At P^*, planned demand equals planned supply and the market clears.

Here is a summary of the main conclusions of this very important part of the chapter.
- A market is in disequilibrium when:
  - planned demand < planned supply, in which case the price falls, or when
  - planned demand > planned supply, in which case the price rises.
- A market is in equilibrium when:
  - planned demand = planned supply, in which case the price does not change.

How a shift of supply disturbs market equilibrium

Once supply equals demand in a market, for example at point X in Figure 5.4, the market remains in equilibrium until an external event hits the market and causes either the market supply curve or the market demand curve to shift to a new position. Figure 5.4 illustrates what happens in the tomato market when an event such as a bumper harvest causes the supply curve of tomatoes to shift rightward, from S_1 to S_2. Before the shift of the supply curve, P_1 was the equilibrium price of tomatoes. However, once the supply curve shifts, P_1 becomes a disequilibrium price. Too many tomatoes are offered for sale at this price, which means there is excess supply in the market. The excess supply is shown by the distance Q_2 minus Q_1, or from X to V. To get rid of this unsold stock, tomato producers reduce the price they are prepared to accept. The market price falls from P_1 to P_2, which eliminates the excess supply. In the new equilibrium, planned supply once again equals planned demand, but at the lower equilibrium price of P_2.

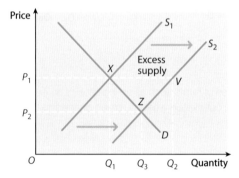

Figure 5.4 The effect of a rightward shift of the market supply curve of tomatoes

EXAM TIP

Make sure you can distinguish between a *shift* of a supply or demand curve, and the adjustment to a new equilibrium along the curve that does not shift.

Shifts of supply or demand curves and adjustments along a curve

As noted in Chapter 3, students often confuse a *shift* of a supply or demand curve with an *adjustment* or *movement* along a curve. Figure 5.4 can be used to explain the distinction again.

In Figure 5.4, the market supply curve of tomatoes *shifts* from S_1 to S_2, creating excess supply equal to the distance between X and V. The adjustment process then kicks in, reducing the price from P_1 to P_2. The adjustment involves a movement *along* the demand curve from X to Z (and also along the supply curve from V to Z). The shift of the supply curve is often called an increase in supply, whereas the resulting adjustment along the demand curve is known as an extension of demand.

The next diagram, Figure 5.5, shows an increase in demand, followed by an extension of supply. You can draw your own diagrams to illustrate (a) a decrease in supply and a contraction of demand and (b) a decrease in demand and a contraction of supply. You should also at this point go back to Chapters 3 and 4 to refresh your knowledge of the different conditions of demand and conditions of supply that determine the position of demand and supply curves. A bumper harvest shifts the supply curve of tomatoes rightward, and a change in consumers' incomes, described in the next section, shifts the market demand curve.

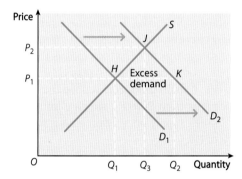

Figure 5.5 The effect of a rightward shift of the market demand curve for tomatoes

EXAM TIP

AQA does not require use of terms such as an increase or an extension of demand. By all means use these terms, but explain what you mean on the first occasion you use the terms in your answer.

How a shift of demand disturbs market equilibrium

Figure 5.5 shows what happens in the market for tomatoes following an increase in consumers' incomes.

People who enjoy eating tomatoes usually consider tomatoes to be a normal good: that is, a good for which demand increases as income increases. Before the increase in consumers' incomes, the equilibrium price of tomatoes was P_1, determined at the intersection of curves D_1 and S. At this price, planned demand equals planned supply. However, increased incomes shift the market demand curve rightward from D_1 to D_2. Immediately, disequilibrium replaces equilibrium in the market. The rightward shift of demand creates excess demand in the market, as long as the price remains at P_1. Excess demand is shown by Q_2 minus Q_1, or the distance between H and K.

The market adjustment mechanism now swings into action to get rid of the excess demand. The price increases to P_2 to eliminate the excess demand, and the quantity of tomatoes bought and sold rises to Q_3. In response to the increase in demand from H to K, there is an adjustment along the supply curve between H and J (an extension of supply) to establish the new equilibrium.

EXTENSION MATERIAL

Auctions and establishing an equilibrium price

These days almost all students are aware of eBay, the internet-based auction on which all new and second-hand goods that you can think of are traded. Economists believe that auctions provide a quick, and indeed an almost instantaneous, way of eliminating excess demand and establishing market equilibrium. Consider, for example, the situation shown in Figure 5.5 immediately following the increase in demand. If tomatoes were to be auctioned, the price would rise to that offered by the highest bidder at P_2. The market would clear instantly. But would it? It is highly unlikely that a single consumer would wish to buy all the tomatoes sold in the market. The auction would have to be more complicated, perhaps enabling different consumers to buy at different prices between P_1 and P_2. Auctions are in fact quite rare. To find out more about auctions, read Case Study 5.2.

CASE STUDY 5.2

Auctions

In theory, an auction provides a quick and efficient method of establishing equilibrium in a market. An auction is a kind of economic activity that has been brought into many people's everyday lives by the internet, through sites such as eBay. But auctions also have a long history that spans many different domains. For example, the US government uses auctions to sell Treasury bills and timber and oil leases; Christie's and Sotheby's use them to sell art; and Morrell & Co. and the Chicago Wine Company use them to sell wine.

Each bidder has an intrinsic value for the item being auctioned; he or she is willing to purchase the item for a price up to this value, but not for any higher price.

Three types of auction when a single item is being sold are:

1 **Ascending-bid auctions, also called English auctions.** The seller gradually raises the price, bidders drop out until finally only one bidder remains, and that bidder wins the object at this final price.

2 **Descending-bid auctions,** also called **Dutch auctions.** The seller gradually lowers the price from

some high initial value until the first moment when some bidder accepts and pays the current price. These auctions are called Dutch auctions because flowers have long been sold in the Netherlands using this procedure.

3 **First-price sealed-bid auctions.** In this kind of auction, bidders submit simultaneous 'sealed bids' to the seller. The terminology comes from the original format for such auctions, in which bids were written down and provided in sealed envelopes to the seller, who would then open them all together. The highest bidder wins the object and pays the value of her bid.

Follow-up questions

1 eBay is the best-known and the largest internet-based auction. Give your views on the advantages and disadvantages of trading goods on eBay.

2 Explain how the use of the internet has affected the costs consumers incur when searching for goods they want to buy.

The functions prices perform in the economy

Chapters 2, 3 and 4, and indeed this chapter, have provided you with lots of information about the role of prices in a market economy or a mixed economy. So far, however, the *precise* functions that prices perform in an economy have not been explained. I shall conclude this chapter by explaining these functions. They are:

- the **signalling function**
- the **incentive function**
- the **rationing** or **allocative function**

The signalling function

Prices provide information that allows all the traders in the market to plan and co-ordinate their economic activities. Let me provide one example. Most Friday afternoons, I visit my local street market to buy fruit and vegetables, including tomatoes and lettuce. The prices, which are shown on white plastic tabs stuck into each tray of produce, help me to decide what to buy. Of course, information about prices alone is not enough. I also need information about the quality of the goods on sale, which I try to get by looking carefully at the size of the produce and for blemishes such as bruising on apples or pears.

The incentive function

The information signalled by relative prices, such as the price of tomatoes relative to the price of lettuce, creates incentives for people to alter their economic behaviour.

Suppose, for example, I go to my local market intending to buy, along with other vegetables, a kilo of tomatoes and one lettuce. As it is Friday afternoon, by the time I arrive at the market, the street traders have cut the price of tomatoes by 50% to try to prevent unsold stock accumulating, whose quality might deteriorate overnight. A fall in the price of tomatoes, relative to the price of other goods that I could buy, creates an incentive for me to buy more tomatoes, provided of course that I believe the quality hasn't deteriorated.

The rationing or allocative function

Suppose I respond to a fall in the relative price of tomatoes by buying more, say 2 kilos rather than the single kilo I had intended to buy as I made my way to market. Because my income is limited, spending more on

Prices perform three functions in a market or mixed economy

one good usually means I spend less on other goods. Prices, together with income, ration the way people spend their money. Suppose tomato prices fall, not only in my local street market on a Friday afternoon, but throughout the economy for a sustained period of time. Tomatoes are now cheaper relative to other goods in the economy. On the one hand, the lower relative price causes households to increase their demand for tomatoes, substituting tomatoes in place of other vegetables. But, on the other hand, a lower relative price may indicate that growing tomatoes is not a very profitable activity. In response, farmers grow fewer tomatoes. If these events happen, the information signalled by changing relative prices creates incentives for economic agents to alter their market behaviour, and changes the way scarce resources are rationed and allocated between competing uses.

EXAM TIP

It is important to recognise that when markets perform well, prices convey accurate information and create suitable incentives for economic agents to respond to. But when one or more of the three functions of prices performs unsatisfactorily, or in extreme cases breaks down completely, market failure occurs.

SUMMARY

- A competitive market contains a large number of firms producing similar goods or services.
- New firms can easily enter a competitive market, and incumbent firms can easily leave.
- The price mechanism allocates scarce resources between competing uses in a competitive market.
- In a competitive market, a good's price is determined by supply and demand.
- When planned demand equals planned supply, a market is in equilibrium.
- Market disequilibrium means that excess demand or excess supply exists in the market.
- Firms respond to excess supply by reducing the quantity of the good they are prepared to supply.
- Consumers respond to excess demand by bidding up the price of the good.
- A shift of a supply or demand curve disturbs equilibrium and leads to excess supply or demand.
- A rightward shift of demand, known as an increase in demand, leads to an extension of supply.
- A rightward shift of supply, known as an increase in supply, leads to an extension of demand.
- Prices perform three functions in a market or mixed economy: signalling, creating incentives, and rationing and allocating resources between competing uses.

Exam-style questions

1 Explain the difference between goods markets and factor markets in an economy. (12 marks)

2 Explain why the market for tomatoes is competitive whereas the market for tap water is uncompetitive. (12 marks)

3 Assess the importance of markets in a mixed economy such as the UK economy. (25 marks)

4 Do you agree that governments should never intervene in markets? Justify your answer. (25 marks)

Chapter 6

Elasticity

Whenever a change in one variable (such as a good's price) causes a change to occur in a second variable (such as the quantity of the good that firms are prepared to supply), an elasticity can be calculated. The elasticity measures the proportionate responsiveness of the second variable to the change in the first variable. For example, if a 5% increase in price were to cause firms to increase supply more than proportionately (say by 10%), supply would be elastic. In this example, a change in price induces a more than proportionate response by the producers. But if the response were less than proportionate (for example, an increase in supply of only 3%), supply would be inelastic. And if the change in price were to induce an exactly proportionate change in supply, supply would be neither elastic nor inelastic — this is called unit elasticity of supply. Elasticity is a useful descriptive statistic of the relationship between two variables because it is independent of the units, such as price and quantity units, in which the variables are measured.

LEARNING OUTCOMES

This chapter will:
- explain the elasticities you need to know
- investigate price elasticity of demand
- distinguish between the slope of a curve and its elasticity
- outline the factors determining price elasticity of demand and price elasticity of supply
- relate price elasticities to the shapes of demand and supply curves
- explain how price elasticity of supply and the shape of supply curves is different in the short run and the long run
- relate income elasticity of demand to normal goods and inferior goods
- relate cross-elasticity of demand to goods in joint demand and to substitute goods
- analyse how price elasticity of demand affects who bears the burden of an expenditure tax

The elasticities you need to know

Although, in principle, economists could calculate a great many **elasticities**, indeed one for each of the economic relationships in which they are interested, the four main elasticities you must know are:
- price elasticity of demand
- price elasticity of supply
- income elasticity of demand
- cross-elasticity of demand

KEY TERM

elasticity: the proportionate responsiveness of a second variable to an initial proportionate change in the first variable.

EXAM TIP

Make sure you don't confuse the four main elasticities. It is very easy to confuse price elasticity of demand, price elasticity of supply and income elasticity of demand. You must also avoid writing the formulas 'upside down'.

The following formulas are used for calculating these elasticities:

$$\text{price elasticity of demand} = \frac{\text{proportionate change in quantity demanded}}{\text{proportionate change in price}}$$

$$\text{price elasticity of supply} = \frac{\text{proportionate change in quantity supplied}}{\text{proportionate change in price}}$$

$$\text{income elasticity of demand} = \frac{\text{proportionate change in quantity demanded}}{\text{proportionate change in income}}$$

$$\begin{array}{l}\text{cross-elasticity of}\\ \text{demand for good}\\ A \text{ with respect to}\\ \text{the price of } B\end{array} = \frac{\text{proportionate change in quantity of } A \text{ demanded}}{\text{proportionate change in price of } B}$$

Price elasticity of demand

Price elasticity of demand measures consumers' responsiveness to a change in a good's price. (Price elasticity of demand is sometimes called an 'own price' elasticity of demand to distinguish it from cross-elasticity of demand. Cross-elasticity of demand measures the responsiveness of demand for a particular good to a change in the price of a completely different good.)

KEY TERM

price elasticity of demand: the proportionate change in demand for a good following an initial proportionate change in the good's own price.

A simple rule for detecting whether demand is price elastic or inelastic

As an alternative to using the formula stated above to calculate price elasticity of demand between two points on a demand curve, a simple rule can be used to determine the general nature of the elasticity between any two points on the demand curve:

- if total consumer expenditure increases in response to a price fall, demand is elastic
- if total consumer expenditure decreases in response to a price fall, demand is inelastic
- if total consumer expenditure remains constant in response to a price fall, demand is neither elastic nor inelastic: i.e. elasticity = unity (1)

Price elasticity of demand and slope

It is important not to confuse the absolute response indicated by the slope of a curve with the proportionate response measured by elasticity. Take a careful look at the two demand curves in Figure 6.1. In Figure 6.1(a), a straight line (or linear) demand curve has been drawn. Obviously, a straight line has a constant slope. But although the slope is the same at all points on the curve, the elasticity is not.

Moving down a negatively sloping linear demand curve, the price elasticity of demand falls from point to point along the curve. Demand is elastic (or greater than unity) at all points along the top half of the curve. Elasticity equals unity exactly half way along the curve, falling below unity and towards zero along the bottom half of the curve.

Figure 6.1 Price elasticity of demand

If elasticity falls from point to point moving down a linear demand curve, it follows that a non-linear curve (i.e. a curved line) is needed to show the same elasticity at all points on the curve. Figure 6.1(b) shows a demand curve with a constant elasticity of 1 at all points on the curve: that is, elasticity equals unity at all points on the curve. Mathematicians call this a rectangular hyperbola. Whenever the price falls, the proportionate change in quantity demanded exactly equals the proportionate change in price. In this case, consumer expenditure remains unchanged following a rise or fall in price.

EXAM TIP

It is easy to confuse elasticity with the slope of a curve. Remember to include the word 'proportionate' (or a % sign) above and below the dividing line when calculating elasticities.

Infinite price elasticity of demand and zero price elasticity of demand

Horizontal and vertical demand curves have constant elasticities at all points on the curve. A horizontal demand curve, such as the demand curve in Figure 6.2(a), is infinitely elastic or perfectly elastic. At the other extreme, the vertical demand curve in Figure 6.2(b) is completely inelastic, displaying a zero price elasticity of demand at all points on the curve. When the price falls, for example from P_1 to P_2, the quantity demanded is unchanged.

(a) Infinitely elastic demand

(b) Zero elasticity of demand

Figure 6.2 Horizontal and vertical demand curves

EXTENSION MATERIAL

Mathematicians draw demand and supply diagrams with quantity on the vertical axis and price on the horizontal axis. When demand and supply diagrams are drawn in this way, vertical curves are infinitely elastic, while horizontal curves have a zero elasticity. This is the opposite to the way economists draw demand and supply diagrams.

Negative elasticities

Usually demand curves are neither horizontal nor vertical, but have a negative slope, showing that as the good's price falls, the quantity demanded rises. In this situation, elasticity as well as slope is also negative. However, economists usually ignore the minus sign of the elasticity. Ignoring the minus sign, all elasticities larger than 1 are elastic and all less than 1 are inelastic.

CASE STUDY 6.1

Elasticity and tobacco taxation

Various studies have calculated the price elasticity of demand for cigarettes of different groups in society such as the young and the old, and men and women.

A World Bank review concluded that price rises of about 10% would on average reduce tobacco consumption by about 4% in richer countries. Smokers in poorer nations tend to be more sensitive to price changes.

Reviewing 86 studies, Gallet and List found a mean price elasticity of −0.48, meaning that, on average, a 10% increase in price will be followed by a decrease in consumption of 4.8%. They also found greater responsiveness among younger people, with an average price elasticity of −1.43 for teenagers, −0.76 for young adults, and −0.32 for adults. They found an average price sensitivity of −0.50 for men and −0.34 for women. Studies have also tended to show greater price sensitivity among low-income groups.

Follow-up questions
1 Most of the elasticity statistics quoted above lie between zero and −1. Discuss the significance of this for governments.
2 Suggest **two** reasons why adult smokers may be less responsive to a rise in the price of cigarettes than teenage smokers.

Summary: different demand curves and their price elasticities

Figure 6.3
The five demand
curves you need
to know

The factors determining price elasticity of demand

Substitutability

Substitutability is the most important determinant of price elasticity of demand. When a substitute exists for a product, consumers respond to a price rise by switching expenditure away from the good, buying instead a substitute whose price has not risen. When very close substitutes are available, demand for the product is highly elastic. Conversely, demand is likely to be inelastic when no substitutes are available.

Percentage of income

The demand curves for goods or services upon which households spend a large proportion of their income tend to be more elastic than those of small items that account for only a small fraction of income.

Necessities or luxuries

It is sometimes said that the demand for necessities is price inelastic, whereas demand for luxuries is elastic. However, this statement should be treated with caution. When no obvious substitute exists, demand for a luxury good may be inelastic, while at the other extreme, demand for particular types of basic foodstuff is likely to be elastic if other staple foods are available as substitutes. The existence of substitutes really determines price elasticity of demand, not the issue of whether the good is a luxury or necessity.

The 'width' of the market definition

The wider the definition of the market under consideration, the lower the price elasticity of demand. Thus the demand for the bread produced by a particular bakery is likely to be more elastic than the demand for bread produced by all bakeries. Quite obviously, the bread baked in other bakeries provides a number of close substitutes for the bread produced in just one bakery. And widening the possible market we are considering still further, the elasticity of demand for bread produced by all the bakeries will be greater than that for food as a whole.

Time

The time period in question will also affect the price elasticity of demand. For many goods and services, demand is more elastic in the long run than in the short run because it takes time to respond to a price change. For example, if the price of petrol rises relative to the price of diesel fuel, it will take time for motorists to respond because they will be 'locked in' to their existing investment in petrol-engine automobiles. However, in certain circumstances, the response might be greater in the short run than in the long run. A sudden rise in the price of petrol might cause motorists to economise in its use for a few weeks before getting used to the price and drifting back to their old motoring habits.

Motorists may 'overreact' to petrol price rises in the short term

Price elasticity of supply

Whereas demand curves are generally downward sloping, supply curves usually slope upward. A rise in price causes firms to respond by supplying more of the good. The mathematical properties of upward-sloping (or positive) supply curves are different from those of downward-sloping (or negative) demand curves. As with demand curves, the 'flatness' or 'steepness' of a supply curve is a misleading indicator of elasticity. The key point is not the slope of the curve, but whether the supply curve intersects the price axis or the quantity axis.

Upward-sloping straight-line (linear) supply curves display the following price elasticities:

- if the supply curve intersects the price axis, the curve is elastic at all points, though elasticity falls towards unity moving from point to point up the curve
- if the supply curve intersects the quantity axis, the curve is inelastic at all points, though elasticity rises towards unity moving from point to point up the curve
- if the supply curve passes through the origin, elasticity equals unity (+1) at all points on the curve

> **KEY TERM**
>
> **price elasticity of supply:** the proportionate change in supply of a good following an initial proportionate change in the good's own price.

(a) Elastic supply

(b) Inelastic supply

(c) Unit elasticity of supply

Figure 6.4 Price elasticity of supply and linear supply curves

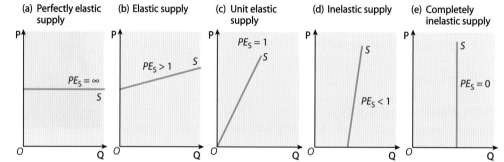

Figure 6.5
The five linear supply curves you need to know

Non-linear supply curves

Figure 6.6 shows how elasticity can be observed at any point on an upward-sloping, non-linear supply curve. This is done by drawing a tangent to the point and noting the axis which the tangent intersects. Because the line drawn tangential to point *A* intersects the price axis, supply is elastic at point *A*. The tangent to point *B* intersects at the origin, so supply at point *B* is unit elastic. Finally, the tangent to point *C* intersects the quantity axis, so supply is inelastic at point *C*. With this supply curve,

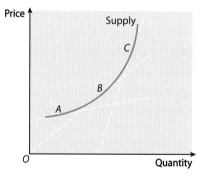

Figure 6.6 Price elasticity of supply and a non-linear supply curve

elasticity falls moving from point to point up the curve. Supply is elastic in the lower section and inelastic in the upper section of the curve.

A closer look at perfectly elastic demand and supply

Figure 6.7 shows a perfectly elastic demand curve and a perfectly elastic supply curve. (These can also be labelled infinitely elastic demand and infinitely elastic supply.) Although the two parts of Figure 6.7 appear to be identical (apart from the labels), this is very misleading. The apparent similarity disguises a significant difference between perfectly elastic demand and perfectly elastic supply. In Figure 6.7(a), demand is infinitely elastic at all prices on or *below* the demand curve, though if the price *rises* above the demand curve (for example from P_1 to P_2), the amount demanded immediately falls to zero. This is because perfect substitutes are available when demand is perfectly price elastic. Customers cease to buy the good as soon as the price *rises* above the demand curve, switching spending to the perfect substitutes whose prices have not changed.

By contrast, in Figure 6.7(b), supply is infinitely elastic at *all* prices on or *above* the supply curve, though if the price *falls* below the supply curve (for example from P_1 to P_2), the amount supplied immediately drops to zero. P_1 is the minimum price acceptable to firms. If they are paid this price (or any higher price), firms stay in the market, but the incentive to stay in the market disappears at any lower price. Firms leave the market, unable to make sufficient profit.

Figure 6.7 Perfectly price elastic demand and supply curves

CASE STUDY 6.2

Housing market elasticities in the UK

UK households have an income elasticity of demand for housing that exceeds +1. However, demand for housing is price inelastic. These demand elasticities, combined with a low price elasticity of supply for housing, push the UK's housing market towards long-term rising prices.

New housing would need to have a price elasticity of supply of +10 for supply to equal demand in the long term. But if the price elasticity of supply for new housing remains low, as the table shows, house prices will never be stable in the UK when the demand for housing is increasing.

Table 6.1 The price elasticity of supply of new housing in selected countries

Country	Price elasticity of supply
Canada	+1.2
UK	+0.4
USA	+2.0
France	+0.3
USA	+1.4
Ireland	+0.6

Follow-up questions

1 Suggest why the price elasticity of supply of new houses is lower in the UK than in the USA.

2 'New housing would need to have a price elasticity of supply of +10 for supply to equal demand in the long term.' Explain this statement.

The factors determining price elasticity of supply

The length of the production period

If firms can convert raw materials into finished goods very quickly (e.g. in just a few hours or days), supply will tend be more elastic than when several months are involved, as with many agricultural goods.

The availability of spare capacity

When a firm possesses spare capacity, and if labour and raw materials are readily available, production can generally be increased quite quickly in the short run.

The ease of accumulating stocks

When stocks of unsold finished goods are stored at low cost, firms can respond quickly to a sudden increase in demand. Alternatively, firms can respond to a price fall by diverting current production away from sales and into stock accumulation. Likewise, the ease with which stocks of raw materials or components can be bought from outside suppliers and then stored has a similar effect.

The ease of switching between alternative methods of production

When firms can quickly alter the way they produce goods — for example, by switching between the use of capital and labour — supply tends to be more elastic than when there is little or no choice. In a similar way, if firms produce a range of products and can switch raw materials, labour or machines from one type of production to another, the supply of any one product tends to be elastic.

The number of firms in the market and the ease of entering the market

Generally, the more firms there are in the market, and the greater the ease with which a firm can enter or leave, the greater the elasticity of supply.

Time

I have already noted that *demand* is more elastic in the long run than in the short run because it takes time to respond to a price change. The same is true for supply. Figure 6.8 shows three supply curves of increasing elasticity, S_1, S_2 and S_3, which illustrate respectively market period supply, short-run supply and long-run supply.

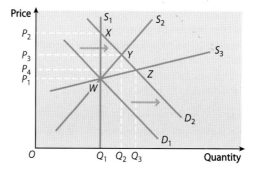

Figure 6.8 The effect of the time period upon price elasticity of supply

- **Market period supply** — the market period supply curve S_1 is shown by a vertical line. S_1 depicts the situation facing firms following a sudden and unexpected rightward shift of demand from D_1 to D_2. When surprised by a sudden increase in demand, firms cannot immediately increase output. In the market period, supply is completely inelastic, and the price rises from P_1 to P_2 to eliminate the excess demand brought about by the rightward shift of the demand curve.
- **Short-run supply** — the higher price means that higher profits can be made, creating the incentive for firms to increase output. In the short run, firms

increase output by hiring more variable factors of production such as labour. The short-run increase in output is shown by the movement up the short-run supply curve, S_2. The short-run supply curve is more elastic than the market period supply curve, S_1. In the short run, supply increases to Q_2, and the price falls from P_2 to P_3.

- **Long-run supply** — if firms believe the increase in demand will be long lasting, and not just a temporary phenomenon, they may increase the scale of production by employing more capital and other factors of production that are fixed in the short run, but variable in the long run. When this happens, firms move along the long-run supply curve S_3. Output rises to Q_3, and the price falls once again, in this case to P_4.

EXAM TIP

You should remember that, for most goods, both the demand curve and the supply curve are more price elastic in the long run than in the short run.

In a competitive industry with low or non-existent barriers to entry, elasticity of supply is greater in the long run than in the short run, because in the long run (but not the short run) firms can enter or leave the market. Short-run supply is less elastic because supply is restricted to the firms already in the industry.

Income elasticity of demand

The nature of **income elasticity of demand** — which measures how demand responds to a change in income — depends on whether the good is a normal good or an inferior good. Income elasticity of demand is always negative for an inferior good and positive for a normal good. This is because the quantity demanded of an inferior good falls as income rises, whereas the quantity demanded of a normal good rises with income. Normal goods can be further divided into superior goods or luxuries, for which the income elasticity of demand is greater than +1, and basic goods, with an income elasticity lying between 0 and +1. Although the quantity demanded of a normal good always rises with income, it rises more than proportionately for a superior good (such as a luxury car). Conversely, demand for a basic good such as shoe polish rises at a slower rate than income.

KEY TERMS

income elasticity of demand: the proportionate change in demand for a good following an initial proportionate change in consumers' income.

cross-elasticity of demand: the proportionate change in demand for a good following an initial proportionate change in price of another good.

Cross-elasticity of demand

Cross-elasticity of demand measures how the demand for one good responds to changes in the price of another good. The cross-elasticity of demand between two goods or services indicates the nature of the demand relationship between the goods. There are three possibilities:

- joint demand (or complementary goods)
- competing demand (or substitutes)
- an absence of any discernible demand relationship

Joint demand or complementary goods

Complementary goods, such as computer games consoles and computer games, have negative cross-elasticities of demand. If the manufacturer increases the price of the games consoles (the hardware), demand for the consoles falls. This causes the demand for games (the software) to use in the consoles also to fall. A rise in the price of one good leads to a fall in demand for the other good.

Competing demand or substitutes

The cross-elasticity of demand between two goods which are substitutes for each other is positive. A rise in the price of one good causes demand to switch to the substitute good whose price has not risen. Demand for the substitute good increases.

No discernible demand relationship

If we select two goods at random — for example, pencils and bicycles — the cross-elasticity of demand between the two goods will be zero. A rise in the price of one good will have no measurable effect upon the demand for the other good.

EXAM TIP

The size and sign (positive or negative) of income and cross-elasticities of demand affect how a good's demand curve shifts following a change in income or a change in the price of a substitute or good in joint demand.

How the effect of an expenditure tax depends on elasticity of demand

If you refer back to Figure 4.4 in Chapter 4, you will see that an expenditure tax imposed by the government on firms shifts the good's supply curve leftward. From the point of view of the firms that produce and sell the good, the tax has the same effect as a rise in costs of production: for example, a rise in wage costs or raw material costs. As is the case with cost increases, by raising the price of the good to cover the tax, firms try to increase the price charged to customers by the full amount of the tax. However, their ability to do this depends on price elasticity of demand (or on the elasticity of the curve that hasn't shifted). Figure 6.9 shows that when demand is relatively elastic, consumer resistance means that some, but not all, of a tax (in this case a specific tax) is passed on to consumers as a price rise. The tax per unit (labelled T in Figure 6.9) is measured by the vertical distance between S_1 (the supply curve before the tax was imposed) and S_2 (the supply curve after the tax was imposed). Immediately after the imposition of the tax, firms may try to raise the price to $P_1 + T$, passing all the tax on to consumers. However, there is excess supply at this price. Via the market mechanism, the price falls to P_2, thereby eliminating the excess supply. In the new equilibrium, part, but not all, of the tax has been passed on to consumers as a price rise. When demand is relatively elastic, as in Figure 6.9, this amounts to less than 50% of the tax.

Figure 6.9 Shifting the incidence of a tax when demand is price elastic

The part of the tax passed on to consumers as a price rise is called the **shifted incidence** of the tax. The rest of the tax (the **unshifted incidence**) is borne by firms or producers. In Figure 6.9, the total tax revenue paid by firms to the government is shown by the rectangle bounded by heavy black lines. The part of the tax rectangle above what was the equilibrium price (P_1) before the tax was imposed, shows the shifted incidence of the tax. The part of the tax rectangle below P_1 shows the unshifted incidence.

You should now draw diagrams similar to Figure 6.9, but with perfectly elastic, unit elastic, relatively inelastic and completely inelastic demand curves. The diagrams will show that firms' ability to pass the incidence of a tax on to consumers as a price rise is greatest when demand is completely inelastic, and non-existent when demand is perfectly elastic.

Students often confuse the effect of an increase in an indirect tax imposed on firms with the effect of a direct tax such as income tax imposed on individuals. Whereas a tax imposed on firms shifts the supply curve of a good, by reducing consumers' incomes, income tax shifts the demand curve for a good. An increase in income tax shifts the demand curve for normal goods leftward, but if the good is an inferior good, the demand curve shifts rightward.

Finally, note that subsidies granted to firms have the opposite effect to taxes imposed on firms. Subsidies shift the supply curve rightward or downward, showing that firms are prepared to supply more of the good at all prices.

Shifts of demand and supply curves, and adjustments along demand and supply curves

The extent to which price or output changes following a shift of demand or supply depends upon the slope and elasticity of the curve that has not shifted. Figure 6.10 shows a demand curve shifting rightward — along a gently sloping supply curve in Figure 6.10(a) and along a much more steeply sloping supply curve in Figure 6.10(b). Prior to the shift of demand, equilibrium occurs at point X in both panels of the diagram. In each case, the rightward shift of demand induces an adjustment along the supply curve to a new equilibrium depicted at point Z. With the elastic supply curve shown in Figure 6.10(a), the quantity adjustment is greater than the price adjustment. The reverse is true in Figure 6.10(b), where the supply curve is inelastic.

(a)

(b)

Figure 6.10 The adjustment to a new equilibrium following a shift of demand

You should apply elasticity analysis when answering exam questions on the effects of a shift of a demand or supply curve. The extent to which the good's price or equilibrium level of output changes depends on the price elasticity of the curve that has not shifted. For example, when the supply curve shifts leftward, the price elasticity of the demand curve determines the extent to which the good's price and quantity changes.

SUMMARY

- Elasticity measures the proportionate responsiveness of a second variable to an initial change in a first variable.
- You need to know about price elasticities of demand and supply, and income and cross-elasticity of demand.
- Make sure you know the formulas for all four elasticities.
- Don't confuse elasticity with the slope of a curve.
- It is important to understand the determinants of all the elasticities of demand and supply.
- The availability of substitute products is the main determinant of price elasticity of demand.
- Income elasticity of demand is positive for normal goods and negative for inferior goods.
- Cross-elasticity of demand is positive for substitute goods and negative for complementary goods or goods in joint demand.
- Knowledge of elasticities, particularly price and income elasticity of demand, provides useful information that aids decision making by businesses and the government.

Exam-style questions

1 Explain how price elasticity of demand affects total consumer spending when a good's price changes. (12 marks)

2 Explain how the price elasticity of supply of new housing has affected UK house prices in recent decades. (12 marks)

3 Evaluate the view that the ability of firms to exploit their customers depends on the price elasticity of demand for their products. (25 marks)

4 'When demand is elastic, taxing a good can succeed in switching consumer expenditure away from the good; it is less successful at raising revenue for the government.' Evaluate this statement. (25 marks)

Markets at work

Chapter 7

Chapters 3 to 6 explained the theory of how a market for a good or service operates. In this chapter, I will apply supply and demand theory to a number of real world markets and sets of markets, concentrating on markets which could provide the scenario for a Unit 1 data-response question on how a market functions. The markets we shall look at are agricultural markets, markets for other primary products (such as oil and metals), housing markets and sports markets.

LEARNING OUTCOMES

This chapter will:
- explain why markets for farm products and other primary products are prone to unstable prices
- explain how speculation affects markets for primary products such as the markets for metals
- describe how OPEC affects the market for crude oil
- investigate the factors determining demand and supply in UK housing markets
- examine some of the characteristics of sports markets

Why prices are often unstable in agricultural markets

Throughout recent history, agricultural markets for foodstuffs and **primary products** such as rubber have experienced two closely related problems. First, until recently, there was a long-run trend for agricultural prices to fall relative to those of manufactured goods and, second, prices have fluctuated considerably from year to year. Agricultural markets are prone to disequilibrium and random shifts of the supply curve from year to year, caused by climatic factors. This leads to unacceptable fluctuations in agricultural prices that, as Chapter 14 explains, require government intervention to stabilise the price.

The long-run fall in agricultural prices

The long-run downward trend can be explained by shifts of the demand and supply curves for agricultural products over extended periods of time. This is shown in Figure 7.1, where the equilibrium price for an agricultural product in an early historical period is P_1. Over time, both the demand and supply curves have shifted rightward, caused for example by rising incomes and population growth shifting the demand curve, while improved methods of farming have increased supply. But for many farm products, the shift of supply, brought about by improved crop yields and increased agricultural productivity, has greatly exceeded the shift of demand, resulting in a fall to the lower equilibrium price P_2.

However, since 2007/08 we might be seeing the beginning of a long-run trend for food prices to rise. Can you think of reasons why this might be happening?

Figure 7.1 The long-run fall in the price of agricultural products

Short-run fluctuations in agricultural prices

Figure 7.2 provides an explanation of fluctuating farm prices. In the diagram, price volatility is caused by random shifts of the short-run supply curve in response to fluctuations in the harvest. The diagram shows two short-run supply curves: a 'good harvest' supply curve, S_1, and a 'bad harvest' supply curve, S_2. Weather conditions and other factors outside farmers' control shift the position of the supply curve from year to year between the limits set by S_1 and S_2. As a result, market prices fluctuate from year to year within the range of P_1 to P_2.

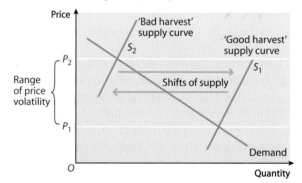

Figure 7.2
Fluctuating agricultural prices caused by shifts of supply

If you turn forward to Chapter 14, you will see that the government or a government agency, or indeed a co-operative of the farmers themselves, can try to stabilise the price of an agricultural good with a support-buying policy, which involves the accumulation of a **buffer stock**. Buffer stock intervention has sometimes also been used to stabilise the prices of other primary products, particularly metals.

EXAM TIP

Support buying and buffer stocks are explained in Chapter 14. Exam questions are often set on methods of government intervention in primary product markets.

CASE STUDY 7.1

Rising food prices

Food prices rose by 2–3% each year between 1990 and 2012, and in some years by more. There are four main reasons for this. First, the US government subsidises maize production that is used for biofuels. This takes maize out of the food supply, raising prices. Second, the World Trade Organization (WTO) limits the amount of corn and wheat that the USA and European Union (EU) can subsidise and store in stockpiles. This reduces the cushion available to add to the food supply when there are shortages, thus adding to food price volatility. Third, as more people around the world grow richer, they eat more

meat. Grains are diverted into feeding the animals that provide meat, further reducing the supply for foods such as bread. Fourth, higher crude oil prices lead to higher food prices. Food is transported long distances, especially when imported. Higher fuel prices increase shipping costs, which then leads to higher food prices.

Food riots occurred in 2008 and in 2011, caused by sudden increases in food prices. It is likely that as prices continue to rise, food riots could take place every year somewhere in the world.

Follow-up questions

1 Why do the prices of commodities such as wheat and copper fluctuate more from year to year than the prices of consumer goods such as cars?

2 Using a demand and supply graph, explain the effects of commodity speculation on the price of a foodstuff such as sugar.

EXTENSION MATERIAL

The cobweb theory

Agricultural production often has a relatively long production period, compared for example with many types of manufacturing. Arable farmers make decisions to grow crops several months before the harvest, while, in a similar way, livestock farmers must breed animals for meat production many months before slaughter. As a result, farmers may form market plans on how much to supply on the basis of last year's price rather than on the prices current this year. The length of the production period means there is a supply lag between the decision to produce and the actual supply coming on to the market. A possible effect of a supply lag can be explained by the cobweb theory illustrated in Figure 7.3.

Figure 7.3 shows a stable cobweb in the pig market, in which the market price eventually converges to equilibrium at price P_1, located where the long-run demand and supply curves intersect. Suppose an outbreak of swine disease reduces pig supply from Q_1 to Q_2 in Year 1 (but does not affect the position of the demand curve or the supply of healthy pigs in future years). In the current year (Year 1), the maximum number of pigs that can be sold on the market is shown by a vertical line drawn through Q_2. The vertical line is the completely inelastic supply curve for Year 1. This means that the price rises to P_2, determined at point A on the vertical line. The now higher price of P_2 encourages farmers to breed Q_3 pigs for slaughter in Year 2.

Figure 7.3 A stable cobweb

When Year 2 arrives, the vertical line drawn through Q_3 depicts maximum possible supply. But the slaughter of Q_3 pigs causes the market price to fall to P_3, which means that farmers breed fewer pigs (Q_4) for slaughter in Year 3. In subsequent years, price and output continue to oscillate in a series of decreasing fluctuations until eventually — in the absence of any further shock hitting the market — the market converges again to a long-run equilibrium.

In the diagram, the cobweb eventually converges to a long-run equilibrium because the long-run demand curve has a gentler slope than the long-run supply curve. This is a stable cobweb. However, an unstable cobweb is also possible. Instability occurs if the long-run demand curve is steeper than the long-run supply curve. In this case, the market diverges in a series of yearly oscillations further and further away from the long-run equilibrium.

The effect of speculative activity in commodity markets

The importance of speculative demand

Farm products are not the only goods whose prices fluctuate wildly from year to year. The same is true for many primary products, especially metals such as copper and nickel. Part of the reason for this stems from the fact that it takes years to open new mines, with the result that sudden increases in demand cannot easily be met from supply.

Another reason is **speculation**. Many of the people and organisations that buy and sell commodities such as copper never intend to use the metal, or indeed ever to actually see or take delivery of the product. Instead, when they think that the price of copper is going to rise, probably in conditions of increasing global demand while supply is limited, speculators step into the market and buy copper, believing that the price

> **KEY TERM**
>
> **speculation:** occurs when people buy or sell a good or service because they believe the price is going to rise or fall in the future. Successful speculation means people benefit from capital gains or avoid capital losses.

will then rise still further in the future. If speculative demand is large enough, the speculators themselves force the price up. In these circumstances, higher future prices become self-fulfilling. In a similar way, when speculators start to sell in the belief that copper prices are going to fall, the act of speculative selling forces down the price of copper.

The price of crude oil

Speculation has also affected the price of crude oil, but for this product, as Case Study 7.3 explains, rising world demand and the activities of the Organization of Petroleum Exporting Countries (OPEC, a producers' organisation and cartel) have been the main factors determining the price of oil. Cartels are price rings which sometimes restrict output in order to raise the price of a good.

Exam questions have often been set on the market for crude oil, or on the markets for petrol and diesel fuel. Cartels will not appear explicitly in AS questions, but questions have been set on the way OPEC has restricted supply.

CASE STUDY 7.2

Should governments intervene to prevent speculation?

In 2011, the House of Commons Select Committee on Science and Technology became concerned by reports of financial institutions entering commodity markets and buying up significant quantities of strategic metals. The committee recommended that the UK government investigate whether there are increasing levels of speculation in the metals markets and, if there are, their contribution to price volatility, and whether markets that allow high levels of speculation, with associated price volatility, are an acceptable way to deliver strategic commodities to end users.

Speculative demand can affect the price of copper

Follow-up questions

1 What is meant by speculation?
2 Draw a supply and demand diagram to illustrate the effect of speculative demands on the price of a commodity such as copper.
3 Do you think speculation should be banned? Justify your answer.

CASE STUDY 7.3

OPEC and the price of crude oil

Most people are familiar with the price of crude oil, which is often mentioned when motorists are complaining about the high price of petrol or diesel fuel. In fact, in the UK, the high prices of these fuels are largely a result of the high expenditure tax that the British government levies. But, as Figure 7.4 shows, the world price of crude oil has generally been rising rapidly in recent years, though in real terms it is not (as yet) as high as it was around 1980. Part of the reason for high oil prices lies in the activities of OPEC, the Organization of Petroleum Exporting Countries.

OPEC was created in 1960 to protect the interests of oil-producing countries. OPEC allows oil-producing

countries to guarantee their income by co-ordinating policies and prices among them. The creation of OPEC was a response to the efforts of Western oil companies to drive oil prices down.

Before recent discoveries of new oil sources, two-thirds of world oil reserves were believed to be located in OPEC countries and OPEC members were responsible for half of the world's oil exports.

OPEC's aim has been to keep crude oil prices within a particular range. To do that, OPEC countries attempt to control the amount of crude oil they export and avoid flooding or squeezing the international marketplace. But the oil market is notoriously difficult to balance, as demonstrated by sharp price swings in the years since OPEC was set up. OPEC members do not necessarily have identical interests, and often find it difficult to agree on their price and output strategies.

In the early 2000s, the price range was between about $25 and $30 a barrel, later upped to between about $55 and $65 a barrel. The fact that by late 2007, crude oil's price had risen to over $90, with occasional spikes to over $100, shows that OPEC has not been completely successful in controlling the price of oil.

OPEC attempts to control the price of crude oil, not through a buffer stock scheme, but by altering the rate at which its members release or supply oil on to the market. This is an example of a **retention scheme**, which operates through shifting the supply curve of a

product rather than through purchasing a stockpile of the good.

Some OPEC economies, such as Saudi Arabia, are completely reliant on oil. Their long-term interest is to prevent oil prices rising too high, as this would speed up research in industrialised countries for alternatives to oil. Oil producers such as Dubai realise that they must diversify their economies before oil runs out. They are using oil revenues to finance the growth of other industries, particularly financial services and tourism. But other OPEC members, such as Nigeria, are swayed by their short-term interest to keep oil prices as high as possible to finance the champagne lifestyle of ruling elites and the consequent need to pay for luxury imports.

Figure 7.4 World price of crude oil, 1973–2011, since the first OPEC price 'spike' in 1973

Follow-up questions

1 Using supply and demand diagrams, explain the difference between a retention scheme and a buffer stock scheme. (See Chapter 14 for information about buffer stock schemes.)

2 Why can't OPEC completely control the world price of oil?

Housing markets in the UK

Housing markets can be separated according to the type of property (flats, semi-detached and detached houses, etc.), but most importantly by the type of tenure enjoyed by the household living in the

EXAM TIP

Exam questions may be set on aspects of the UK housing market.

property. (A household is not the same as a family. For example, a family placing an elderly grandparent in sheltered accommodation creates a new one-person household. Likewise a teenager leaving the family home to live in a flat becomes a new household.)

There are two main types of tenure in the UK housing market. These are **owner-occupation**, which means that at least one member of the household living in the property owns the accommodation, and **privately rented housing**. In the latter case, a private landlord owns the property, which is rented to a tenant. There are also various forms of **socially owned housing** such as **council houses** and flats (owned by local authorities) and **housing associations**. The UK housing market can be divided into sub-markets containing different types of property.

Regional housing markets

Newspapers often refer to the North–South divide, which certainly exists in the UK housing market. House prices and private rents are much higher in London and the southeast region than they are in other UK regions, though there are pockets of high-priced housing outside the southeast in locations such as the Manchester and Leeds commuter belts and Edinburgh. By 2013, the average price of houses in Greater London had risen above £461,000 and the number of 'millionaire' properties was proliferating, while at the other extreme, run-down houses in declining and increasingly derelict northern manufacturing regions were selling for less than £5,000 — if a buyer could be found.

The factors explaining differences in regional house prices include the immobility of housing and the poor quality of housing in some locations (though much badly built housing in London now commands high prices), but are primarily supply and demand factors.

Factors affecting the supply of housing in different regions include the availability of building land and the operation of planning controls. Demand factors, which relate strongly to the relative success of regional economies, include population density and growth (both of which are in turn affected by migration between regions), and marked regional differences in personal income and wealth, together with the lending policies of financial intermediaries such as banks and building societies.

The markets for new and second-hand housing

New houses are mostly bought from specialist house-building companies. A few, large, house-building companies account for most of the new houses built in the UK. Second-hand houses are generally bought from their existing occupiers who wish to sell. With these transactions, the act of selling a house simultaneously creates a demand, in the sense that the seller needs another house to live in.

The long-run rise in the price of housing

There has been a long-run trend for house prices to rise in the UK, ignoring short-run booms and busts. Both the demand for and the supply of housing have increased (or shifted rightward) in the long run, but unlike in the case of agricultural goods described earlier, demand has increased faster.

Supply has increased because the quantity of new houses added to the housing stock each year exceeds the number demolished or converted to other uses. The supply of housing for owner-occupancy increases fastest when landlords withdraw from the rental market and sell their properties. Sometimes however, as in recent years, housing market conditions are more favourable for private letting and the reverse happens. The main causes of the long-run rightward shift of demand have been: population growth; the growth in the number of households; real income growth (housing being a normal good with a positive income elasticity of demand); and people switching to owner-occupancy, which they treat as a superior good (income elasticity of demand $> +1$) and away from the perceived inferior substitute, rented accommodation.

The level of economic activity in the national economy also affects the construction industry. Since the 1970s, the house-building industry has become increasingly dominated by a small number of 'volume' builders. The building companies buy land and hold the land in a 'land bank'. Houses are then built in the expectation of being sold during or shortly after construction. The process tends to be speculative — very few houses are built to meet customers' specific requirements. The construction process itself is sometimes contracted out to smaller builders, who depend on hired plant and equipment and who mainly employ casual labour. In recessions or economic slow-downs, there is often a high level of bankruptcy among smaller building firms and subcontractors, and unemployment among building workers soars.

Short-run fluctuations in the price of housing

Short-run price fluctuations are explained primarily by the short-run demand curve shifting rightward or leftward along the near-vertical short-run supply curve. Figure 7.5 shows the demand curve increasing, shifting rightward from D_1 to D_2, causing house prices to rise from P_1 to P_2, with a smaller resulting expansion of supply.

EXAM TIP

Practise drawing this diagram. It is the most important diagram on the housing market.

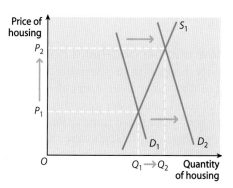

Figure 7.5 Short-term changes in the price of housing

The short-run supply of housing

In the short run, as Figure 7.5 shows, the supply of housing is highly price inelastic or unresponsive to price changes. The factors that explain this include: the general shortage of land; the effect of planning controls, which make it difficult to convert land from other uses; and the length of time taken to build a new house.

CASE STUDY 7.4

Britain's housing crisis

According to the housing pressure group Shelter, Britain is suffering a massive housing crisis. There simply aren't enough decent, affordable homes. More than 2 million people find their rent or mortgage a constant struggle or are falling behind with payments.

Against a background of mounting debt across the country, huge numbers of homeowners are having their homes repossessed because they are no longer able to keep up with their mortgage repayments. Second home ownership is pricing local people out of many rural areas. Over 1.7 million households are currently waiting for social housing.

Some homeless households — many with dependent children — wait for years in temporary accommodation. Families renting privately on low incomes have to put up with poor living conditions and little security.

The number of new households is increasing faster than the number of house builds. And at the sharpest end, many hundreds of people sleep rough on the streets every night, cold and fearing for their safety. Shelter believes this situation is unacceptable.

Around 7.4 million homes in England fail to meet the government's Decent Homes Standard. The UK is now more polarised by housing wealth than at any time since the Victorian era.

Housing is an issue that affects every one of us. We all know how important having a decent home is. From our health and emotional well-being, to our achievement in education and our ability to get work, where we live has an enormous impact on our lives.

A home is a place that provides security, privacy, decent living conditions, and links to a community. A home must be suitable to the needs of its residents — providing adequate space, affordable costs and linked support where necessary.

Shelter campaigns for better housing policies and laws to end homelessness. The only solution to the current housing crisis is to build more homes. According to Shelter, the government's proposal to build 150,000 affordable homes over 4 years is less than a third of what is needed. This will leave millions of families stuck in limbo on housing waiting lists, and push house prices further out of the reach of those on ordinary incomes.

Bad housing is closely linked to many wider social problems that blight neighbourhoods, such as crime and antisocial behaviour. And Shelter believes these problems can be best addressed once the underlying housing issues have been resolved.

Follow-up questions

1 Describe **three** causes of homelessness in the UK.
2 Evaluate **three** policies the government could use to reduce or eliminate the problem of homelessness in the UK.

The demand for housing

As with all consumer goods, people demand housing for the utility or welfare derived from the consumer services that houses provide. All houses provide basic shelter, but each and every house also has a particular combination of other consumer attributes, such as location, a view, a garden, car parking and rooms suitable for work, leisure and hospitality. However, the demand for housing is also affected by a number of special factors. Housing is a consumer durable good, delivering a stream of consumer services over a very long period, often a century or more. Unlike most durable goods, such as cars and television sets, which **depreciate** and lose value during their lives, most houses — or certainly the land on which they are built — **appreciate** and gain value. This means that the demand for housing is determined not only by people's need for shelter, but by the fact that people treat housing as a form of investment. Housing is an attractive wealth asset — indeed, the main wealth asset owned by many UK residents.

In a rising house market, first-time buyers may try to buy before houses become unaffordable

As a result, far from reducing demand, a rise in house prices can trigger a speculative bubble in the housing market in which rising prices drive up demand, causing a further rise in prices, with the process continuing until the bubble bursts. Rising house prices mean that owner-occupiers already on the 'housing ladder' have a vested interest in further price rises. Existing owner-occupiers become wealthier because the value of their property rises but the value of their **mortgages** generally stays the same. They benefit from **capital gains** — the difference between the price paid for the house and its current higher market value. In this situation, there is an increase in the number of 'first-time buyers', as young people, desperate to get on the 'housing ladder', try to buy houses before they become unaffordable. Moreover, wishing to become even more wealthy, existing owner-occupiers put their houses on the market and 'trade up' to buy larger properties or houses in more desirable locations. Both these events shift the demand curve for housing rightward and fuel a further rise in house prices. During housing market booms, activity soars with increases in both the number of people trying to sell and the number trying to buy property. However, demand rises faster than supply.

House prices can be determined by speculative demand, and also by the fact that people treat housing as an investment good.

Sports markets

It is not possible in this chapter to examine all the special features of sports markets that make such markets interesting. I will start by introducing a feature of markets not previously explained: the possibility of a **secondary market** or **black market** emerging. I will then examine shifts of demand in sports markets for sports in competing demand (or substitutes) and also for sporting activities which are in joint demand (complementary goods). The chapter will be completed by looking at pricing at different sporting events, while Case Study 7.5 explains a peculiar feature of competition in the market for competitive sports such as football or rugby.

Secondary markets in tickets for sports events

Secondary markets that occur when governments impose maximum price laws or price ceilings are of course illegal, though criminalised trading still takes place in such markets. However, some secondary markets are perfectly legal: for example, markets in tickets for popular sports events such as the FA Cup Final. In these cases, the secondary market emerges because the agency promoting the event under-prices tickets.

This is illustrated in Figure 7.6(a). The supply curve for tickets is vertical, reflecting the capacity of the stadium in which the event takes place. The number of seats in the stadium is around 90,000. Given the position of the demand curve, if tickets were priced at £150, the primary market would work efficiently. There would be no excess demand, and hence no need for a secondary market. But if the Football Association prices tickets at £50, 150,000 fans want to see the match. Excess demand is 60,000. In this situation, a secondary market enables 'unlucky' supporters, who are prepared to pay more than £50 to watch the match, to buy tickets sold by 'lucky' fans, who are prepared to sell at a price above £50.

Black markets or secondary markets occur when demand exceeds supply in sports markets. Such black markets are not necessarily illegal.

Figure 7.6(b) shows a situation more common in lower league football and in other less popular sports. Because of the position of the demand curve, only 5,000 tickets are sold at the price set by the club hosting a lower league football match, even though stadium capacity is 20,000. There is an excess supply of 15,000 seats at the price set by the football club. Indeed, in this example, some seats would remain empty even if tickets were given away free. To fill the stadium, the club would have to pay people to watch the match.

Figure 7.6 Excess demand and excess supply at football matches

Shifts of demand in leisure markets

When two leisure activities are substitutes or complementary goods, a change in the price of one leisure activity causes the demand curve for the other to shift.

Suppose, for example, there is a fall in the price of tickets to see soccer matches. This might lead to a leftward shift of the demand curve for tickets for rugby football matches. This is shown in Figure 7.7(a). The size of the leftward shift will depend on the extent to which, from a spectator's point of view, the two types of football are substitutes for each other. However, a fall in the price of tickets for soccer matches will trigger a rightward shift in the demand curve for complementary goods, such as the replica shirts worn by many spectators. This is shown in Figure 7.7(b).

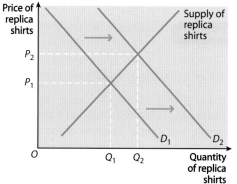

Figure 7.7 Shifts of demand for substitute and complementary goods, following a fall in admission prices to soccer matches

Charging different prices at a sports event

One way in which the providers of sport and leisure facilities can increase revenue is by charging different prices, both for different events available at the facility and for different customers. Football clubs charge higher prices for big games: for example, against a top club or a local rival. Likewise, some theatres charge different prices for different plays or shows. Also, sports fans are charged different prices for seats in different parts of the stadium. Some seats provide a better view than others, so the quality of the product varies according to where the seat is located. Customers are prepared to pay more for a high-quality view and comfort than for lower quality. Lower prices for children and old-age pensioners are a common feature of pricing for sports and leisure events and facility use. A further variant is lower prices for frequent users: for example, in the form of season ticket pricing.

CASE STUDY 7.5

The strange nature of competition in competitive sports

Some professional sports markets, such as the football market, provide an interesting mix of competition and monopoly. (Monopoly is one firm only in a market.) In football, clubs or teams compete in a league. The purpose of competition is to win the league and to be generally successful from year to year.

In most conventional markets, becoming a monopoly by driving rivals out of business represents ultimate success for a firm. But if a soccer club bankrupts all its rivals, there is no one to play against!

If Manchester United were always to win the Premiership, the league would become boring and fans would lose interest. Scottish football, where Celtic and until recently Rangers have dominated, has already suffered this problem, though the two leading teams are still well supported.

The top teams in the UK, and in other European countries such as Spain and Italy, might seek to solve the problem by abandoning national leagues, and forming a new 'super league' where competition promises to be stiffer and the market more interesting for fans.

In the 1990s, with the aim of allowing firms in all markets to compete on a level playing field undistorted by artificial barriers, the European Union created a single market. An ultimate logic of the single market is the growth of EU-wide leagues in professional sports such as football and rugby, and the decline of national sporting leagues.

Follow-up questions

1 Name **two** examples of monopoly other than in sports markets.
2 The owners of American football clubs playing in the NFL have ensured that their clubs can't be relegated. Why does the possibility of relegation make competition interesting in the UK soccer premiership?

SUMMARY

- Prices in markets for primary products, including agricultural goods, are often unstable.
- For many agricultural goods, there has been a long-run fall in prices caused by supply curves shifting rightward by more than the rightward shift of demand.
- Short-run fluctuations in agricultural prices are often caused by good and bad harvests, resulting from changing weather conditions.
- Speculation affects prices in commodity markets and also in the housing market.

- Prices of crude oil and of petrol and diesel fuel have been affected by OPEC — a producers' organisation and price ring.
- In the short run, the main determinant of house prices has been the demand curve for housing shifting up and down the inelastic supply curve for housing.
- Black markets or secondary markets are common in the markets for tickets for sports events.
- Substitute and complementary good relationships are common in sports markets.

Exam-style questions

1 Explain why agricultural prices are often unstable.   (12 marks)

2 Explain the main reasons for changes in average house prices in the UK.   (12 marks)

3 Evaluate **three** ways in which the government could intervene in UK housing markets to make
housing more affordable.   (25 marks)

4 Black markets or secondary markets often exist in markets for tickets to attend sporting events such as
Wimbledon tennis finals. Assess the extent to which black markets perform a useful economic function.   (25 marks)

Production, specialisation and exchange

Chapter 8

The meaning of production was first explained in Chapter 2 — in the context of the role of production in trying to solve the fundamental economic problem of scarcity. This chapter begins by reminding you of the meaning of production, before introducing and explaining a number of production-related concepts: namely, productivity, productive efficiency, the division of labour and specialisation. For specialisation and the division of labour to be worthwhile, the exchange of goods and services must be possible. Exchange can take place through barter, but in modern economies, money is almost always used as the medium which allows exchange to take place. I complete the chapter by explaining the main features of a firm's average cost curve and then use average cost curves to illustrate economies and diseconomies of scale.

LEARNING OUTCOMES

This chapter will:
- remind you of the meaning of production
- distinguish between production and productivity
- explain the various forms of productivity, including labour productivity
- introduce the concepts of specialisation and the division of labour
- explain how successful specialisation and division of labour require exchange to take place
- introduce average cost curves
- explain the meaning of productive efficiency
- with the use of cost curves, explain economies and diseconomies of scale

Production

Earlier in the book, in Chapter 2, I introduced the meaning of **production**, and also the roles of factors of production such as labour and capital in the production process. Before proceeding any further with this chapter, refer back to Chapter 2 and read again the section on production. The key point to remember is that production converts inputs, or the services of factors of production such as capital and labour, into final outputs of goods and services.

KEY TERM

production: converts inputs or factor services into outputs of goods.

Also remember that production is a *means to an end*, and not the end itself. I cannot stress too often that the purpose of economic activity is to increase human happiness or economic welfare in a sustainable way, without destroying the ability of future generations to enjoy the resources the planet provides. Most, but not all, economic welfare is obtained from consumer goods and services, which have ultimately been produced by extracting and then using the earth's natural resources. Production is a necessary precondition for eventual consumption; without production, human life as we know it would not be possible.

Productivity

Students often confuse productivity with production. While closely related, they do not have the same meaning. At AS, **productivity** usually means **labour productivity**, which is output per worker. However, **capital productivity** and **land productivity** can also be measured, as can **entrepreneurial productivity**. In reality, of course, all the employed factors of production contribute to both a firm's current level of output and any increase in the level of output. To reflect the fact that *all* the factors of production contribute to production, **total factor productivity (TFP)** can be measured. A change in total factor productivity measures the change in a firm's total output when more than one factor of production is changed.

> **KEY TERM**
>
> **productivity:** output per unit of input (e.g. labour productivity is output per worker).

> **EXAM TIP**
>
> Productivity is a key concept in both AS Unit 1 and Unit 2. Questions usually centre on labour productivity, although candidates should be aware of other meanings of the term. Questions could also mention the UK's productivity gap, which is the difference in productivity levels between the UK and competitor countries.

Labour productivity or output per worker is extremely significant in manufacturing industries, such as the car industry. In the 1990s and early 2000s, the Rover Car Group (which has since been bankrupted) struggled to survive in the UK car industry. Rover was unable to compete with Japanese car makers such as Nissan and Toyota. Nissan had invested in a state-of-the-art factory near Sunderland. Labour productivity in the ramshackle Rover factories amounted to only 33 cars per worker per year. By contrast, Nissan produced 98 cars per worker in its brand new factory. Given these figures, it is not surprising that the Rover Group was forced to stop production.

Specialisation and the division of labour

Over 200 years ago, the great classical economist, Adam Smith, first explained how, within a single production unit or firm (he took the example of a pin factory), output could be increased if workers specialise at different tasks in the manufacturing process.

Smith had established one of the most fundamental of all economic principles: the benefits of **specialisation** or the **division of labour**. According to Adam Smith, there are three main reasons why a factory's total

> **KEY TERMS**
>
> **division of labour:** this concept goes hand in hand with specialisation. Different workers perform different tasks in the course of producing a good or service. Different workers may also produce different goods or services.
>
> **specialisation:** a worker only performing one task or a narrow range of tasks.

output can be increased if workers perform specialist tasks rather than if each worker attempts all the tasks himself or herself. These are as follows:

- A worker will not need to switch between tasks, so time will be saved.
- More and better machinery or capital can be employed. (Employing 'more of the same' capital is called **capital widening**, while investing in 'state of the art' new technology is called **capital deepening**).
- The 'practice makes perfect' argument that workers become more efficient or productive at the task they are doing, the greater the time spent on the specialist task, although this latter advantage can easily become a disadvantage if it involves 'de-skilling' and the creation of boredom and alienation among workers.

Trade and exchange

For specialisation to be economically worthwhile for those taking part in the division of labour, a system of **trade** and **exchange** is necessary. This is because workers who completely specialise can't enjoy a reasonable standard of living if forced to consume only what they produce. The obvious solution is to produce more than what the worker actually needs, and then for him or her to trade the surplus for that produced by others.

KEY TERM

exchange: specialisation and the division of labour mean that goods and services must be exchanged for each other. Money and the use of barter are mediums of exchange.

Blacksmiths might exchange services with farmers

Until quite recently, people living in rural communities within the UK could specialise and then trade whatever they produced through **barter**. Thus a farmer might harvest wheat, part of which was then exchanged for services provided by local grain millers and village blacksmiths.

But successful barter requires a **double coincidence of wants**. Not only must the farmer require the services of the blacksmith; the blacksmith must want the wheat produced by the farmer, and a rate of exchange must be agreed for the two products. As this example suggests, it is reasonably easy to achieve the double coincidence of wants in a small community where people live close to each other and where only a few goods and services are produced and exchanged. However, in modern economies in which a vast number of goods are produced, reliance on barter holds back the growth of the economy. In such economies, barter is an extremely inefficient method of exchange.

These days, when we buy or sell a good or service, we almost always use **money**. We finance the transaction, either with cash, or with a debit card or cheque drawn on a bank or building society deposit. Using money is much more efficient than bartering, as there is no need for a double coincidence of wants when money is used as a medium of exchange. Suppose I want to buy a television from you and you have a second-hand car you wish to sell. If we barter the goods, you must want my television set and I must want your car. We must also agree that the two goods have the same value. But if we use money rather than barter, you pay for my car with money, which I can then use to buy whatever I want from somebody else. I could also save the money rather than spend it. Used in this way, money enables the economy to achieve much greater specialisation and division of labour than is possible if we were to rely on barter.

CASE STUDY 8.1

Pin factories and car manufacturing

Specialisation and the division of labour have been essential for the development of modern economies. They enable firms to increase labour productivity and produce goods on a global scale.

The advantages of specialisation and the division of labour were first recognised in the eighteenth century by Adam Smith in his classic book *The Wealth of Nations*. Smith used the example of a pin factory, describing how dividing the pin-making process into individual tasks, and training workers individually to perform each task, increased labour productivity within the factory.

Labour specialisation involves splitting a job into separate parts, with each task performed by different workers. For example, no worker in a modern car factory makes an entire car from start to finish. Instead, some workers specialise, with the help of robots, in assembling car bodies, others in painting the bodies, while others add wheels and install windows and seats. Scores of specific tasks are involved in manufacturing an automobile, and each task involves different workers.

Follow-up questions

1 The case study describes the division of labour within pin and car factories. How is division of labour relevant to different countries specialising in producing different goods and services?
2 Explain the meaning of labour productivity and how increased labour productivity affects costs and competitiveness.

Average cost curves

When studying microeconomics, we generally assume that a firm's main business objective is to make the largest possible profit. This is called the profit-maximising objective. Profit depends on both the demand conditions and the supply conditions facing a firm, with the latter depending on whether average costs of production fall or rise as the firm's output increases.

Average cost or unit cost is calculated by dividing the firm's total cost of production by the size of output produced. Average costs for each level of output can be shown on an average cost curve, such as the curve drawn in Figure 8.1.

KEY TERM

average cost: the cost per unit of output; also called unit cost.

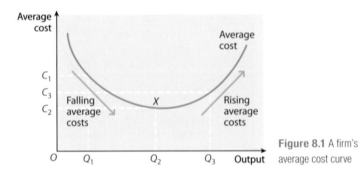

Figure 8.1 A firm's average cost curve

In Figure 8.1, the firm's average costs of production initially fall as the size of output increases. For example, when the firm produces output Q_1, average cost per unit of output is quite high at C_1. But when the firm increases output to Q_2, average cost per unit falls to C_2. However, for higher levels of output, average costs rise, for example to C_3 when output increases to Q_3.

The average cost curve in Figure 8.1 is U-shaped, showing average costs falling and then rising as the level of output increases. Point X, which is in the diagram above level of output Q_2, locates the **cost-minimising level of output**.

Productive efficiency

Economic efficiency is one of the most important economic concepts you need to know. There are a number of different types of efficiency, but the only one you need to know at AS is **productive efficiency**. There are two contexts in which we define productive efficiency — at the level of a single firm within the economy and at the level of the whole economy.

KEY TERM

productive efficiency: occurs when a firm minimises average costs and produces at the lowest point on its average cost curve.

EXAM TIP

If an exam question asks for a definition of productive efficiency, you can use either (or both) of the definitions given in this chapter.

If you have to apply the concept, *choose* the definition that is most appropriate to the question — the first definition if you are explaining a firm's costs, and the second definition if you are discussing resource allocation in the economy.

For a single firm to achieve productive efficiency, the firm must use the techniques and factors of production which are available to produce the cost-minimising or optimum level of output described in the previous section. In Figure 8.2, the productively efficient level of output is Q_1, where the average costs are minimised. Q_1 is located at the lowest point on the U-shaped average cost curve. All other levels of output, including Q_2, are productively inefficient because higher average costs are incurred.

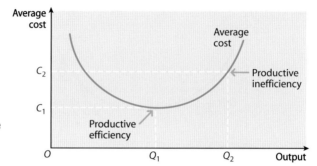

Figure 8.2 Productive efficiency for a firm in the economy

The **whole economy is productively efficient** when production takes place on the economy's production possibility frontier. To illustrate this in Figure 8.3, I have redrawn Figure 2.1 (which in Chapter 2 illustrates scarcity as the economic problem) to show productively efficient and inefficient levels of output for the whole economy.

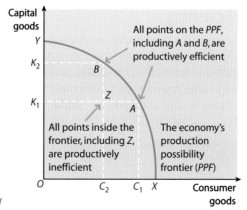

Figure 8.3 Productive efficiency for the whole economy

All points on the economy's production possibility frontier, such as A and B, show output being maximised from the available inputs or factors of production, given the technology available for the economy to use. Note that, at point *A* for example, it is impossible to increase output of capital goods without reducing production of consumer goods, and vice versa. By contrast, all points inside the frontiers, such as *Z*, are productively inefficient. At *Z*, it is possible to produce more capital goods without reducing output of consumer goods.

Economies of scale

As a firm grows in size by investing in new plant or buildings, it can benefit from **economies of scale**. However, beyond a certain size, the firm may eventually suffer from **diseconomies of scale**. Economies of scale are defined as falling average costs of production that result from an *increase* in the size or scale of the firm.

Figure 8.4 illustrates the nature of economies of scale. In the diagram, I assume initially that the size or scale of the business is shown by firm size 1. If there is spare capacity, the firm can increase output to meet an increase in demand by taking on more workers and employing more variable capital. Increasing production in this way is shown by the movement along horizontal arrow A, drawn to the right of firm size 1. Eventually, however, the firm runs into a capacity constraint, which means that it can't produce any more output solely by employing more workers and machines. In order to produce more output, the firm must expand by increasing its total productive capacity. In Figure 8.4, this is depicted by the movement along vertical arrow *X* to firm size 2.

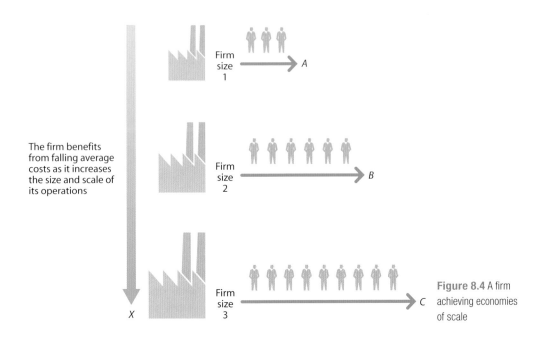

The firm benefits from falling average costs as it increases the size and scale of its operations

Figure 8.4 A firm achieving economies of scale

Once it has reached firm size 2, the firm meets any further increase in demand, in the first instance, by moving along horizontal arrow B. Then, when full capacity has again been reached, the firm meets further increases in demand by investing in new capacity, which takes the business to firm size 3.

EXAM TIP

At AS, you don't need to know the difference between variable and fixed capital. Nevertheless, knowledge of the difference is useful. As the name implies, fixed capital, such as a firm's buildings, cannot quickly be changed. By contrast, variable capital, such as raw materials, can be quickly changed.

Types of economy of scale

There are various types or causes of economy of scale, the main ones being technical economies of scale, managerial economies of scale, marketing economies of scale, financial economies of scale and risk-bearing economies of scale and economies of scope.

EXAM TIP

You may be required to explain two or three types of economy of scale and two or three causes of diseconomies of scale.

Technical economies of scale

The main types of technical economy of scale are listed below.

- **Indivisibilities.** Many types of plant or machinery are indivisible in the sense that there is a certain minimum size below which they cannot efficiently operate. A firm requiring only a small level of output must, therefore, choose between installing plant or machinery which it will be unable to use continuously, buying from an outside supplier, or using a different but less efficient method to produce the smaller required level of output.

EXAM TIP

You may be required to link economies of scale to the growth of monopolies. In the case of a 'natural' monopoly (explained in Chapter 12), there is only room in the market for one firm (i.e. a monopoly) benefiting from full economies of scale.

- **The spreading of research and development costs.** Research and development (R&D) costs associated with new products also tend to be indivisible and independent of the size of output to be produced. With large plants, R&D costs can be spread over a much longer production run, reducing unit costs in the long run.
- **Volume economies.** These are also known as **economies of increased dimensions**. With many types of capital equipment (e.g. metal smelters, transport containers, storage tanks and warehouses), costs increase less rapidly than capacity. When a storage tank or boiler is doubled in dimension, its storage capacity actually

increases eight-fold. And since heat loss depends on the area of the container's walls (which will only have increased four-fold) and not upon volume, a large smelter or boiler is technically more efficient than a small one. Volume economies are thus very important in industries such as transport, storage and warehousing, as well as in metal and chemical industries where an increase in the scale of plant provides scope for the conservation of heat and energy.

- **Economies of massed resources.** The operation of a number of identical machines in a large plant means that proportionately fewer spare parts need be kept than when fewer machines are involved. This is an application of the 'law of large numbers', since we can assume that not all the machines will develop a fault at the same time. (The massing of resources also allows for firm-level economies of scale. A multi-product multi-plant firm may also benefit from the cross-fertilisation of experience and ideas between its various subsidiaries.)
- **Economies of vertically linked processes.** Much manufacturing activity involves a large number of vertically related tasks and processes, from the initial purchase of raw materials, components and energy through to the completion and sale of the finished product. Within a single firm, these processes may be integrated through the linkages between the various plants owned by the firm — with the output of one plant providing an input or source of component supply for another plant further along the route to the finished product. Alternatively, the tasks or processes may be integrated within the workshops of a single large plant, enabling the plant to benefit from substantial economies of scale. The linking of processes in a single plant can lead to a saving in time, transport costs and energy, and the close physical proximity of specialist workshops within the plant may allow a subsequent stage in the production process to be sure of obtaining exactly the supplies it needs in the right quantity and technical specification at the right time.

Managerial economies of scale

The larger the scale of a firm, the greater the ability to benefit from specialisation and the division of labour within management as well as within the ordinary labour force. A large firm can benefit from a functional division of labour, namely the employment of specialist managers: for example, in the fields of production, personnel and sales. Detail can be delegated to junior managers and supervisors.

Marketing economies of scale

Marketing economies of scale are of two types: **bulk-buying** and **bulk-marketing economies**. Large firms may be able to use their market power both to buy supplies at lower prices and also to market their products on better terms negotiated with wholesalers and retailers.

Financial or capital-raising economies of scale

Financial or capital-raising economies of scale are similar to the bulk-buying economies just described, except that they relate to the 'bulk-buying' or the bulk-borrowing of funds required to finance the business's expansion. Large firms can often borrow from banks and other financial institutions at a lower rate of interest and on better terms than those available to small firms.

Risk-bearing economies of scale

Large firms are usually less exposed to risk than small firms, because risks can be grouped and spread. Large firms can spread risks by diversifying their output, their markets, their sources of supply and finance and the processes by which they manufacture their output. Such economies of diversification or risk bearing can make the firm less vulnerable to sudden changes in demand or conditions of supply that might severely harm a smaller less-diversified business.

Economies of scope

Economies of scope are factors that make it cheaper to produce a range of products together than to produce each one of them on its own. An example is businesses sharing centralised functions, such as finance or marketing.

Diseconomies of scale

In contrast to economies of scale, **diseconomies of scale** occur when average costs (or unit costs) rise as the scale or size of the firm grows. Managerial diseconomies of scale are particularly important. They can be caused by communication failure, which occurs when a

> **KEY TERM**
>
> **diseconomy of scale:** rising average or unit cost as a firm increases its size or scale.

firm becomes too large and there are many layers of management between the top managers and ordinary production workers. In this situation, decision making and the ability to respond to customers' needs or to problems arising in the course of production both suffer. As a result, the resources the business uses are not allocated as effectively as they could be. Top management loses touch with junior managers and employees and with the problems facing the business.

Economies and diseconomies of scale and the firm's average cost curve

Figure 8.5 shows how a firm's U-shaped average cost curve can illustrate economies and diseconomies of scale. The curve has been drawn under the assumption that average costs change as the firm changes the scale of its operations: that is, changes its overall size. Economies of scale are shown by the downward-sloping section of the curve, while the upward-sloping section (at a higher level of output) illustrates diseconomies of scale. This particular average cost curve also contains a flat middle section, lying between the downward-sloping and upward-sloping sections of the curve. The flat section depicts a range of output in which there are no economies or diseconomies of scale. Graphs which show economies and diseconomies of scale often do not have a flat middle section.

> **EXAM TIP**
>
> You may be required to illustrate economies and/or diseconomies of scale on a firm's average cost curve.

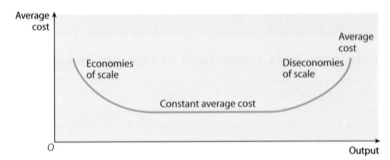

Figure 8.5
Economies and
diseconomies
of scale

You will come across average cost curves again when studying Unit 3 at A2. At A2, it is necessary to know and understand the difference between short-run cost curves and long-run cost curves. Strictly, because economies and diseconomies of scale occur when the scale or size of a firm changes, the cost curve in Figure 8.5 is a *long-run* cost curve. The long run is defined as the time period in which all the factors of production can be changed. By contrast, a short-run cost curve depicts a situation in which at least one factor of production — usually assumed to be capital — is held fixed.

However, because knowledge of short-run and long-run cost curves is not required at AS, you will not be tested at AS on the difference between the two types of cost curve.

Internal and external economies and diseconomies of scale

All the economies and diseconomies of scale so far described are examples of **internal economies and diseconomies of scale**. These occur when a firm grows and changes its scale and size.

By contrast, **external economies of scale** occur when a firm's average or unit costs of production fall, not because of the growth of the firm itself, but because of the growth of the industry or market of which the firm is a part. Very often, external economies of scale are produced by cluster effects, which occur when a lot of firms in the same industry are located close to each other, providing markets, sources of supply and a pool of trained labour for each other.

External diseconomies of scale occur in a similar way, with the growth of the whole market raising the average costs of all the firms in the industry. As with external economies of scale, external diseconomies can arise from cluster effects. When a large number of similar firms locate close to each other, not only do they create benefits which aid all the firms in the cluster; they may also get in each other's way. Competition for labour amongst the firms may raise local wages, which while being good for workers, increases the unit wage costs of their employers. There may also be an increase in local and regional traffic congestion, which lengthens delivery times and raises delivery costs both for firms and for their customers.

EXAM TIP

The Unit 1 specification only asks for knowledge of economies and diseconomies of scale. Because the specification does not mention external economies or diseconomies of scale, exam questions will only require knowledge of *internal* economies and diseconomies. Nevertheless, it is useful to know about external economies and diseconomies of scale.

CASE STUDY 8.2

Are economies of scale now less important in the car industry?

In the twentieth century, car manufacturing grew to become perhaps the most important industry in modern industrialised economies. Though car manufacture began in Germany and France, the main growth of car manufacturing in its early years took place in the USA. Henry Ford's adaptation of the <u>moving assembly line</u>, which allowed car factories to benefit from <u>economies of scale</u>, marked the beginning of <u>mass production</u>.

Garel Rhys, director of the Centre for Automotive Industry Research at Cardiff University, has calculated that economies of scale reach their peak at 250,000 cars a year in an assembly plant, although for the body panels the figure could be as high as 2 million.

However, economies of scale in car production are now not as important as they used to be. Reasons for this include: <u>market fragmentation</u>, leading to <u>lower production runs</u>; building cars to order rather than in large-scale batches of identical cars; and new ways of assembling finished cars in which manufacturers such as Toyota are <u>outsourcing</u> more and more of the car to outside suppliers. With car buyers demanding a wider choice of vehicles, production runs have to get smaller.

As car companies produce an ever-wider range of vehicles, so the way cars are made is changing. There is less need for huge, capital-intensive factories and barriers to entry into the car industry are falling.

A modern car assembly line

Follow-up questions
1 Explain the meaning of each of the concepts underlined in the passage.
2 Describe some of the economies of scale that have contributed to lower average costs in the UK car industry.

How internal economies and diseconomies of scale affect particular industries

Case Studies 8.3 and 8.4 focus on two industries or markets that are affected by economies and diseconomies of scale. Study the two case studies, and then consider the following questions.

■ Using the concepts of economies and diseconomies of scale, discuss the advantages and disadvantages of bendy buses, first for Transport for London, the organisation that provided the buses, and second for members of the general public.

■ How could the oil tanker industry be organised to get round the problem mentioned in Box 8.4 about the disadvantages of large super-tankers?

CASE STUDY 8.3

The rise and fall of London's bendy buses

The end of London's bendy experiment has brought shouts of joy from some people. Motorists didn't like the long, low monsters getting stick round narrow crossroads. Cyclists hated the crushing menace they seemed to present. Transport for London found too many fare-dodgers hopping on and off.

'Bendy buses' were used on 12 routes over the decade from 2002 to 2011 but Mayor Boris Johnson called them 'cumbersome machines' which were too big for narrow streets and encouraged fare-dodgers. Johnson has introduced nearly 500 new double-decker buses to replace the 'bendies'. But the 'bendies' could fit 120 on board, while their replacements take only 85. Even if there are plenty of seats available, well over half of them are usually upstairs. Many old people and young mothers with infants don't use stairs and can't reach the upper deck. They have to be downstairs. The 'bendies' were all single decker, so with their replacement, there's been a massive loss of accessible seats. 'The most accessible bus in London' is now being missed by the old, wheelchair users and mothers with young children.

CASE STUDY 8.4

Super-tankers and volume economies of scale

The large super-tankers that are used to transport crude oil across seas and oceans from oil fields to industrial markets benefit significantly from volume economies of scale. However, super-tankers can also suffer from a diseconomy of scale. This is because large super-tankers cannot enter shallow ports. A wider tanker with a shallow draught does not yield as many economies of scale as a conventional super-tanker, but is more flexible and can enter more ports.

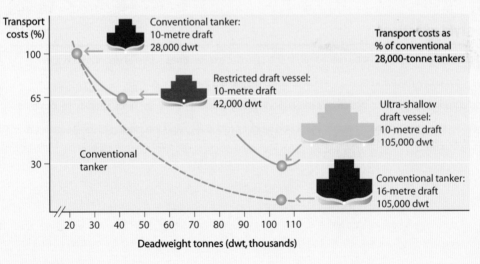

Follow-up question

Give **two** other examples of volume economies of scale.

SUMMARY

- Production is a process, or set of processes, that converts inputs into outputs.
- Productivity is measured by output per unit of input.
- Labour productivity, or output per worker, is the most commonly used measure of productivity.
- The division of labour means that different workers do different jobs.
- The division of labour and specialisation occur together.
- Specialisation and the division of labour require trade and exchange.
- Money is the main medium of exchange in modern economies, though barter still sometimes takes place.
- Average cost is cost per unit of output.
- A firm's average cost curve is typically U-shaped, showing average costs first falling and then rising as output increases.
- A firm is productively efficient when producing the cost-minimising level of output.
- For the whole economy, all points on the economy's production possibility frontier are productively efficient.
- Economies of scale mean that a firm's average costs fall as the scale or size of the firm increases.
- There are a number of different types of economy of scale, such as technical economies.
- Diseconomies of scale mean that a firm's average costs rise as the scale or size of the firm increases.
- Economies and diseconomies of scale can be shown on a U-shaped average cost curve, drawn to show average costs changing as the size of the firm increases.
- External economies and diseconomies of scale result from the growth of the industry rather than from the growth of a firm within the industry.

Exam-style questions

1 Using examples other than those mentioned in the chapter, explain **three** types of economy of scale. (12 marks)

2 Explain how economies and diseconomies of scale may affect the size of a firm. (12 marks)

3 Do you agree that large firms are always more productively efficient than small firms? Justify your answer. (25 marks)

4 'International competitiveness requires increased labour productivity and the closing of the economy's productivity gap.' Evaluate this statement. (25 marks)

Introducing market failures

Chapter 9

Earlier chapters have explained how markets work. This is the first of four chapters that explain how markets fail. In this short introductory chapter on market failure, I introduce the general idea of market failure. Specific market failures, such as public goods and monopoly, are then explored in detail in Chapters 10, 11 and 12.

EXAM TIP

Because the title of Unit 1 is Markets and Market Failure, you should expect one of the two data-response questions in the Unit 1 exam to be mostly on market failure.

LEARNING OUTCOMES

This chapter will:
- explain the meaning of market failure, distinguishing between complete and partial market failure
- relate market failure to the important economic concepts of efficiency and equity
- discuss market failure in terms of the breakdown of the three functions of prices
- examine three introductory case studies of market failure

The meaning of market failure

Market failure occurs whenever the market mechanism or price mechanism performs badly or unsatisfactorily, or fails to perform at all. There are two main ways in which markets fail.
- Markets can function inequitably.
- Markets can function inefficiently.

KEY TERM

market failure: a market completely failing to provide a good or service, or providing the wrong quantity (i.e. a quantity that leads to a misallocation of resources in the economy).

It is also useful to distinguish between **complete market failure**, when the market simply does not exist, and **partial market failure**, when the market functions, but produces the wrong quantity of a good or service. In the former case, there is a **missing market**. In the latter case, the good or service may be provided too cheaply, in which case it is over-produced and over-consumed. Alternatively, as in monopoly, the good may be too expensive, in which case under-production and under-consumption results.

Markets functioning inequitably

Equity means fairness or justness (though in other contexts, such as the housing market, equity has a very different meaning, namely wealth). As soon as equitable considerations are introduced into economic analysis, normative or value judgements are being made, 'socially fair' distributions of income and wealth are discussed, and questions are raised about the goods and services people *ought* to produce and consume.

KEY TERM

equity: fairness or justness.

As the experience of many poor countries shows, unregulated market forces tend to produce highly unequal distributions of income and wealth. Some economists, usually of a free-market persuasion, dispute whether this is a market failure. Some argue that the people who end up being rich deserve to be rich and that the people who end up being poor deserve to be poor. According to this view, the market has not failed — it merely creates incentives which, if followed, cause people to generate more income and wealth.

However, most economists reject as too extreme the view that the market contains its own morality with regard to the distributions of income and wealth. They argue that markets are 'value-neutral' with regard to the social and ethical desirability or undesirability of the distributions of income and wealth resulting from the way the market functions. Few economists now believe that markets should be replaced by the command mechanism. There is, however, much more agreement that, instead of *replacing* the market, governments should *modify* the market so that it operates in a more equitable way than would be the case without government intervention. Taxing the better-off and redistributing tax revenues as transfers to the less well-off is the obvious way of correcting the market failure to ensure an equitable distribution of income and wealth. (However, as Chapter 14 explains, redistributive policies can promote new types of inefficiency and distortion within the economy.)

Markets functioning inefficiently

Monopoly and other situations in which there is little competition provide examples of market failure resulting from markets performing inefficiently. The *wrong* quantity is usually produced in monopoly and the *wrong* price is charged. *Too little* is produced and is sold at *too high* a price. Scarce resources are not utilised in the most efficient way, and resource misallocation results.

The next three chapters

In the next three chapters, six causes of market failure that result from inefficient functioning of markets are examined. These occur in the context of:
- **public goods** and **externalities** in Chapter 10
- **merit goods** and **demerit goods** in Chapter 11
- **monopoly** and the **immobility of labour** in Chapter 12

(Chapter 11 also explores further the market failure mentioned earlier in this chapter: namely, **income and wealth inequalities**, resulting from the inequitable functioning of markets.)

Market failure and the three functions of prices

In Chapter 5, when explaining how the price mechanism distributes scarce resources between alternative uses in a market or mixed economy, you were introduced to the three functions that prices perform in such economies. These are:

- signalling information
- creating incentives to influence people's behaviour
- allocating and rationing resources in response to the information signalled and the incentives created by changing prices

As a generalisation, we can say that when all three of these functions perform well, markets also work well and market failure is either non-existent or trivial. However, when one or more of the three functions of prices significantly breaks down, market failure occurs. In Chapter 10, you will see how in the case of pure public goods and externalities, the price mechanism breaks down completely. If an alternative method of provision does not exist, complete market breakdown means that markets fail completely and none of the public good is produced. A useful service is not provided — hence the market failure. In the case of an externality such as pollution, firms (and indeed consumers) that generate pollution simply dump it on other people (whom we call **third parties**). There is no market in which the unwilling consumers of pollution can charge producers for the discomfort they suffer. The lack of a market means there is no incentive for the polluter to pollute less. Hence, again, the market failure.

EXAM TIP

Market failure can also be defined as a situation in which one or more of the three functions of prices breaks down, either partially or completely.

Three case studies to introduce you to possible market failures

This chapter concludes by introducing you to three case studies that illustrate market failures which are explained in greater depth in the next chapters.

Case Study 9.1 focuses on the first of the alleged market failures looked at in Chapter 10: namely, public goods. National defence and the police are often regarded as **pure public goods**, which markets cannot provide. However, as you read through this case study, which describes how worried neighbours have set up their own private police force in the state of Georgia in the USA, you should question whether in fact markets are unable to provide police services. The employment of private security guards at UK shopping malls could provide a similar example.

CASE STUDY 9.1

Paying for protection

With the disappearance of the 'neighbourhood bobby' patrolling the streets, many people feel they are not properly protected by the local police force. One disaffected resident became so fed up about the increasing number of break-ins and car thefts in her street, she gathered together a group of neighbours to protect themselves. 'We don't get many police patrolling in our neighbourhood, so we had to organise our own patrol group, hiring off-duty policemen,' she said.

Crime has dropped in the neighbourhood. The 260 paying members think the £300 a year they each pay is a price well worth paying, even though over 1,000 other local households benefit from the extra protection they are getting.

Atlanta residents have formed a private police force

Follow-up questions

1 To what extent are police services a public good? Justify your answer.
2 The case study illustrates the 'free-rider' problem. With the use of the example in the passage, explain what this means.

The second case study centres on the other example of market failure discussed in Chapter 10. Some of you will be familiar with the debate that has taken place in recent years about 4 × 4 vehicles such as sports utility vehicles (SUVs) and their alleged contribution to global warming pollution and traffic accidents (both of which are negative externalities or external costs).

In the March 2006 budget, Gordon Brown, then the UK chancellor of the exchequer and the country's most important economics minister, introduced higher road taxes for 4 × 4 vehicles such as Land Rovers and other allegedly higher polluting vehicles, popularly known as 'Chelsea tractors'.

CASE STUDY 9.2

The following passage is an extract from a letter written by an aggrieved 4 × 4 driver to a popular newspaper.

Should 4 × 4 drivers pay higher road taxes?

It is my opinion that 4 × 4s have all been branded, rather unfairly, with this 'Chelsea tractor' gas-guzzler image. But the 4 × 4s are no more polluting than any other correctly maintained vehicle, and owners are already paying huge amounts of tax when buying these vehicles. Why increase taxes related to running them when these drivers are currently being penalised in this way?

It is said the size of the vehicle warrants the tax. However, most 4 × 4s take up no more room than a big family saloon car, such as a Ford Mondeo. There are already benefits in reduced taxation for people who drive smaller cars by choice, and there is already a tax penalty for larger vehicles. So why put more taxes on top of that and say they need to be penalised even more?

Follow-up questions

1 Explain the economic factors that may be responsible for the increase in sales of 4 × 4 vehicles.
2 Given the large increase in sales of 4 × 4 vehicles, with the use of a demand and supply diagram assess whether taxation can reverse the trend back to sales of small cars.

The final case study switches attention to demerit goods, which are explained in Chapter 11. A demerit good, such as an alcoholic drink (e.g. whisky), is both bad for the wider community and possibly also for the person consuming it.

The case study article is not on alcohol, but on a rather similar demerit good, tobacco. But, as the article indicates, there may be a case for encouraging people to consume demerit goods — so that they die early and thus save the taxpayer the cost of paying pensions and keeping them alive into extreme old age.

CASE STUDY 9.3

Preventing smoking can save lives, but it does not save money

It costs more to care for healthy people who live years longer, according to a Dutch study which counters the common perception that preventing people smoking would save the government millions of pounds.

'It was a small surprise,' said the Dutch economist who led the study. 'But it also makes sense. If you live longer,

then you cost the health system more.' The research found that the health costs of thin and healthy adults are more expensive than those of smokers. Low-income people, who smoke most, are probably subsidising the healthcare of the better-off, who have largely given up smoking.

Follow-up questions

1 Taking account of the information in the passage, should cigarettes be classified as a demerit good or as a merit good?
2 Discuss the effects of tobacco taxes on the real incomes of different groups in society.

These three market failure case studies were chosen to try to get you to approach the various market failures you need to know about in a sceptical frame of mind. Not all economists agree that the market failures included in the AQA AS specification are indeed failures of the market. But, whatever views you form, don't rest on blind assertion. An important skill to learn at both AS and A2 is that of justifying your arguments.

SUMMARY

- Market failure occurs whenever the market mechanism or price mechanism performs badly or unsatisfactorily, or fails to perform at all.
- Complete market failure (and missing markets) should be distinguished from partial market failure.
- Markets can fail because they are inefficient or inequitable.
- Public goods, externalities, merit and demerit goods, monopoly, and the immobility of factors of production are the main examples of microeconomic market failure resulting from the inefficient functioning of markets.
- The unequal distribution of income and wealth is the main market failure resulting from the inequitable functioning of markets.

Exam-style questions

1 Explain how markets can function inefficiently. (12 marks)

2 What is the difference between complete market failure and partial market failure? (12 marks)

3 Do you agree that government policies which aim to correct market failure are always successful? Justify your answer. (25 marks)

4 Assess the view that people should pay a price every time they call for an ambulance or a fire engine. (25 marks)

Private goods, public goods and externalities

Chapter 10

Chapter 9 explained how market failure occurs whenever a market does not function very well or, in extreme cases, does not function at all. This chapter explains two of the market failures briefly mentioned in Chapter 9: public goods and externalities. By way of establishing a clear understanding of the nature of public goods, the chapter starts by explaining their opposite: namely, private goods. The chapter also explains how public goods and externalities provide examples of complete market failure or missing markets.

LEARNING OUTCOMES

This chapter will:
- explain the difference between a private good and a public good
- distinguish between public 'goods' and public 'bads'
- show how an externality is a form of public 'good' or public 'bad'
- distinguish between negative and positive externalities
- introduce the concept of the margin and use marginal analysis to explain why market failure occurs when negative and positive externalities are generated

Private goods

I am using my laptop computer to write this paragraph. A few minutes ago, a window cleaner came into my study. Suppose he had said to me: 'That's a nice computer; I'm going to steal it.' Not surprisingly, I would try to stop the theft. The computer is mine and not his. It is my **private good**.

> **KEY TERM**
>
> **private good:** a good, such as an orange, that is excludable and rival.

Most goods, such as my laptop computer, are private goods which possess two defining characteristics. The owners can exercise **private property rights**, preventing other people from using the good or consuming its benefits. This property is called **excludability**. The second property is called **rivalry**, though this is better illustrated by a good such as a sweet rather than by my computer. If I eat the sweet, you, or anyone else, cannot. In this sense, we are rivals. (Rivalry is sometimes called **diminishability**. When one person consumes a private good such as a sweet or a banana, the quantity available diminishes.)

Public goods

A **public good** exhibits the opposite characteristics of **non-excludability** and **non-rivalry** or **non-diminishability**. It is these characteristics that lead to market failure.

A lighthouse, or rather the beam of light provided by a lighthouse, is an example of a public good. Suppose an entrepreneur builds

> **KEY TERM**
>
> **public good:** a good, such as a radio programme, that is non-excludable and non-rival.

the lighthouse shown in Figure 10.1, and then tries to charge each ship that passes in the night and benefits from the beam of light. Providing ships pay up, the service can be provided commercially through the market.

Figure 10.1
A lighthouse as
a public good

However, the market is likely to fail because the *incentive* function of prices breaks down. Because it is impossible to exclude **free-riders** (in this case, ships that benefit without paying), it may be impossible to collect enough revenue to cover costs. If too many ships decide to 'free-ride', profits cannot be made and the incentive to provide the service through the market disappears. The market thus fails to provide a service for which there is an obvious need. There is then a need for alternative provision by the government in its public spending programme, or possibly by a charity (such as Trinity House in the UK).

KEY TERM

free-rider: somebody who benefits from a good or service without paying for it.

EXAM TIP

Make sure you understand the difference between a private good and a public good, and can give examples of both.

Other examples of public goods

Other examples of public goods include national defence, police, street lighting, roads, and television and radio programmes. Consider a situation in which the state does not provide national defence. Instead, the government lets individual citizens purchase in the market the defence or protection they want. But markets only provide defence when entrepreneurs can successfully charge prices for the services they supply. Suppose an aspiring citizen, who believes a fortune can be made in the defence industry, sets up a company, Nuclear Defence Services Ltd, with the aim of persuading the country's residents to purchase the services of nuclear missiles strategically located around the country. After estimating the money value of the defence received by each individual, Nuclear Defence Services bills each household accordingly and waits for the payments to flow in…

But the payments may never arrive. As long as the service is provided, every household can benefit without paying. Nuclear Defence Services Ltd cannot provide nuclear defence only to the country's inhabitants who are prepared to pay, while excluding the benefit from those who are not prepared to pay. Withdrawing the benefit from one means withdrawing it from all. But all individuals face the temptation to consume without paying, or to free-ride. If enough people choose to free-ride, Nuclear Defence Services Ltd makes a loss. The incentive to provide the service through the market thus disappears. Assuming, of course, that the majority of the country's inhabitants believe nuclear defence to be necessary (i.e. a good rather than a 'bad'), the market fails because it fails to provide a service for which there is a need. The result is a **missing market**.

Goods and 'bads'

A **good** such as a loaf of bread provides benefits to the person or persons who consume it. Consumer goods yield usefulness or utility, and sometimes pleasure and satisfaction. (Using economic jargon, we say that consumer goods increase economic welfare.)

> **KEY TERM**
>
> **good:** a good yields utility, unlike a 'bad', which yields disutility.

In everyday language, we generally use the word 'bad' as an adjective: for example, a bad film or a bad football match. However, economists also use the word as a *noun*. In this usage, an economic 'bad' is the opposite of a good, yielding disutility, dissatisfaction or displeasure. For most people, consumption of a bad such as rotten meat *reduces* rather than *increases* economic welfare.

Public bads

The free-rider problem, which was explained in the context of public goods, also affects a group of bads which are known as public bads. An example of a public bad is rubbish or garbage. However, the free-rider problem is a little different in the case of public bads. People are generally prepared to pay for the *removal* of an economic bad, to avoid the unpleasantness otherwise experienced. But in the case of rubbish or garbage, payment can be avoided by dumping the bad in a public place or on someone else's property.

In the UK, local authorities generally empty dustbins without charging for each bin emptied. Suppose this service is not provided, and private contractors remove rubbish and charge households £1 for each dustbin emptied. To avoid paying £1, some households may decide to dump their waste in the road or in neighbours' dustbins. (Builders' skips provide a good example of this practice. A household hiring a skip is well advised to fill the skip as quickly as possible, before the rest of the street takes advantage of the facility.) If too many households free-ride, it is impossible for the private contractor to make a profit, and a service for which there is a need is no longer provided. Hence the case for free local authority provision, financed through taxation.

Free-riding can be a problem with public bads such as rubbish dumped in the street

EXTENSION MATERIAL

Public goods can be divided into **pure public goods** and non-pure public goods. National defence and police are examples of pure public goods — defined as public goods for which it is impossible to exclude free-riders. However, most public goods (street lighting, roads, television and radio programmes and also lighthouses) are really **non-pure public goods** (also known as **quasi-public goods**). Methods can be devised for converting the goods into private goods by excluding free-riders (e.g. electronic pricing of road use). Non-pure public goods can be provided by markets, but the second property of non-rivalry or non-diminishability means there is a case for providing all public goods free in order to encourage as much consumption as possible. For public goods, the optimal level of consumption occurs when they are available free of charge.

Public goods and government goods

Public goods are goods for which there is a need. But because of the missing market problem, markets may fail to provide public goods. This means (as will be explained in greater detail in Chapter 13) there is a case for the state providing public goods at zero price to the consumer.

EXAM TIP

Don't confuse a public good with a government good, or with a merit good.

Students often wrongly define a public good as a good that is provided by the government: that is, as a government good. This is confusing *cause* with *effect*. The word *public* in public good refers to the fact that members of the general public cannot be excluded from enjoying the good's benefits. It is this that *causes* market failure. To try to correct the market failure, governments provide public goods. This is the *effect*. Government goods include public goods such as defence, police and roads, but they also include *merit goods* such as education and healthcare, which are explained in the next chapter.

CASE STUDY 10.1

The Tragedy of the Commons

In Britain before the eighteenth century, much farm land was open common land on which farmers could graze as many animals as they wished, for free.

As long as poaching and disease keep the numbers of animals below the carrying capacity of the land, common land grazing works well. However, it is in a herdsman's self-interest to graze more and more animals, since his gain, the money earned from selling slaughtered additional animals, exceeds any loss he incurs from the gradual deterioration of the common. He receives all the proceeds from the sale of an additional animal, but the effects of over-grazing are shared by all the herdsmen.

A rational herdsman concludes that the only sensible course for him to pursue is to add another animal to his herd. And another. And then another... But this is the conclusion reached by each and every rational herdsman sharing a commons. Therein is the tragedy. Freedom of the commons brings ruin to all. Each herdsman is locked into a system that compels him to increase his herd without limit — in a world that is limited.

Source: Harding, G., 'The Tragedy of the Commons', *Science*, 1969.

Follow-up question

Do you agree that over-fishing of North Sea cod and global warming are the result of the Tragedy of the Commons? Justify your answer.

Externalities

An **externality** is a special type of public good or public 'bad' which is 'dumped' by those who produce it on other people (known as **third parties**) who receive or consume it, whether or not they choose to. The key feature of an externality is that there is no market in which it can be bought or sold — externalities are produced and received *outside* the market, providing another example of a missing market.

KEY TERM

externality: a public good, in the case of an external benefit, or a public bad, in the case of an external cost, that is 'dumped' on third parties outside the market.

As with the public goods and public bads, externalities provide examples of the free-rider problem. The provider of an external benefit (or positive externality), such as a beautiful view, cannot charge a market price to any willing free-riders who enjoy it, while conversely, the unwilling free-riders who receive or consume external costs (or negative externalities), such as pollution and noise, cannot charge a price to the polluter for the bad they reluctantly consume.

EXAM TIP

Candidates often fail to understand that externalities are generated and received outside the market. Remember that both public goods and externalities provide examples of missing markets.

Negative production externalities or external costs

Consider the power station illustrated in Figure 10.2, which discharges pollution into the atmosphere in the course of producing electricity. We can view a negative production externality (or external cost) such as pollution as being that part of the *true* or *real* costs of production which the power station evades by dumping the bad on others: for example, the people living in the houses and the businesses in the commercial forestry industry. The price that the consumer pays for the good (electricity) reflects only the *money* costs of production, and not all the *real* costs, which include the external costs (including the eyesore or visual pollution also shown in the diagram). In a market situation, the power station's output of electricity is thus under-priced. The incentive function of prices has once again broken down — under-pricing encourages too much consumption of electricity, and therefore over-production of both electricity and the spin-off, pollution.

Figure 10.2 The discharge of negative externalities by a power station

Positive production externalities or external benefits

Figure 10.3 shows the power station illustrated in Figure 10.2 again, but in this case the production of electricity yields positive externalities (or external benefits) rather than negative externalities. I have assumed that the power station discharges warm (but clean) water into the lake adjacent to the power station. Warmer temperatures increase fish stocks and commercial fishing boats and private anglers then benefit. Unless it owns the lake, the power station company cannot charge the fishermen for the benefits they are receiving. (You might, of course, query my assumption that the water discharge creates positive rather than negative externalities. In all likelihood, disruption of a local ecosystem might cause negative externalities, such as algae pollution.)

Figure 10.3 The production of positive externalities by a power station

Different types of externalities

As I have explained, externalities divide into external costs and external benefits (which are also known as negative externalities and positive externalities). However, it is possible to go a stage further and identify pure production externalities, pure consumption externalities and externalities involving a mix of production and consumption. Table 10.1 illustrates both these methods of classifying externalities. The two columns to the right of the table depict external costs and external benefits, while the rows in the table show the various forms of production and consumption externalities.

EXAM TIP

Make sure you can give examples of external costs and external benefits and are aware of the difference between production and consumption externalities.

Table 10.1 Examples of the different types of externality

Types of externality	External costs	External benefits
Pure production externalities (generated and received in production)	Acid rain pollution discharged by a power station which harms a nearby commercially run forest	A farmer benefiting from drainage undertaken by a neighbouring farmer
Mixed production externalities (generated in production but received in consumption)	Dust pollution discharged by a brickworks breathed by asthmatic children living nearby	Commercially owned bees pollinating fruit trees in neighbouring gardens
Pure consumption externalities (generated and received in consumption)	Noisy music at a party disturbing neighbouring households	Households benefiting from the beauty of neighbouring gardens
Mixed consumption externalities (generated in consumption but received in production)	Congestion caused by private motorists increasing firms' transport and delivery costs	Commercial beekeepers benefiting from the private gardens of nearby houses

Using marginal analysis to analyse externalities

The last part of this chapter introduces a method of economic analysis which becomes very important in the microeconomics studied at A2. This is called **marginal analysis**. However, at AS, you are only required to know about, and to apply, marginal analysis in two contexts. These are externalities (the second of the two topics in this chapter), and merit and demerit goods, which are explained and analysed in the next chapter.

The meaning of the 'margin'

As I said earlier in the chapter, I am writing this book by typing on my laptop computer, alone in my study. Being the only human being in the room, I am the marginal person: namely, the last person to have entered the room. But I can hear footsteps — it's my window cleaner returning. As soon as he enters the room, my window cleaner becomes the marginal person. He wants to be paid, but I have no money with me. (Maybe he'll think again about stealing my computer.) Fortunately, my son Tom has heard what's going on and runs into the room with my wallet. Tom is now the marginal person, though I wish he'd brought his own money rather than mine. However, that indeed is wishful thinking.

I hope this story gives you a grasp of what is meant by the '**margin**'. Whichever economic activity we are investigating, the marginal unit is always the *last* unit of the activity undertaken. If one more unit of the activity is now added, the previous unit, which up to that point had been the marginal unit, can no longer be classified in this way.

> **KEY TERM**
>
> **margin:** refers to the last unit undertaken of an activity.

Marginal costs and marginal benefits

Let me turn again to the coal-burning power station illustrated in Figures 10.2 and 10.3. If we focus to start with on negative externalities (and ignore for the time being the possibility of positive externalities), then as already explained the power station incurs the private costs of electricity production, but also discharges external costs which are suffered by other people. I shall now introduce another cost concept: **social cost**. Social cost is defined as **private cost** plus **external cost**:

social cost = private cost + external cost

> **KEY TERMS**
>
> **marginal benefit:** the benefit resulting from the last unit of a good.
>
> **marginal cost:** the cost of the last unit of a good.
>
> **social cost:** the total cost of an activity, including the external cost as well as the private cost.

At the next stage, the concept of the margin is brought into the analysis. **Marginal private cost** is the extra cost incurred by the power station when producing the last unit of electricity. Likewise, **marginal external cost** is the extra cost dumped on the wider community when the power station produces the last unit of electricity. And finally, **marginal social cost** is the extra cost (private plus external) borne by everybody, as a result of producing the last unit of electricity. Bringing these together, we get the following relationship:

marginal social cost = marginal private cost + marginal external cost

or:

$MSC = MPC + MEC$

Turning now to positive externalities, and using similar reasoning, we arrive at:

social benefit = private benefit + external benefit

> **KEY TERM**
>
> **social benefit:** the total benefit of an activity, including the external benefit as well as the private benefit.

and

marginal social benefit = marginal private benefit + marginal external benefit

or:

$MSB = MPB + MEB$

Bringing together marginal costs and marginal benefits

At the heart of microeconomic theory lies the assumption that, in a market situation, an economic agent considers only the private costs and benefits resulting from its market actions, ignoring any costs and benefits imposed on others. For the agent, **private benefit maximisation** occurs when:

marginal private cost = marginal private benefit

or

$MPC = MPB$

However, **social benefit maximisation**, which maximises the public interest or the welfare of the whole community, occurs when:

marginal social cost = marginal social benefit

or

$MSC = MSB$

The important point to understand is that households and firms seek to maximise private benefit or private self-interest, and not the wider social interest of the whole community. They ignore the effects of their actions on other people. However, when externalities are generated, costs and benefits are inevitably imposed on others, so private benefit maximisation no longer coincides with social benefit maximisation.

Using marginal analysis to show how negative production externalities cause market failure

It was assumed earlier in the chapter that when a coal-burning power station generates electricity, only negative externalities are discharged and there are no positive externalities. Given this simplification, the marginal private benefit accruing to the power station from the production of electricity, and the marginal social benefit received by the whole community, are the same and shown by the downward-sloping curve in Figure 10.4. But, because pollution is discharged in the course of production, the marginal social cost of electricity production exceeds the marginal private cost incurred by the power station. In the diagram, the MSC curve is positioned above the MPC curve. The vertical distance between two curves shows the marginal external cost (MEC) at each level of electricity production.

> **KEY TERMS**
>
> **private benefit maximisation:** occurs when $MPC = MPB$.
>
> **social benefit maximisation:** occurs when $MSC = MSB$.

> **EXAM TIP**
>
> At AS, Unit 1 examination questions require use of marginal analysis, but only for externalities and for merit and demerit goods, which are explained in the next chapter.

Figure 10.4 A coal-burning power station discharging pollution

The power station maximises private benefit by producing output Q_1, where $MPC = MPB$. Q_1 is immediately below point A in Figure 10.4. However, the socially optimal level of output is Q_2, where $MSC = MSB$. Q_2 is immediately below point B in Figure 10.4. The privately optimal level of output is thus greater than the socially optimal level of production. To put it another way, market forces over-produce electricity by the amount Q_1 minus Q_2. The market fails because the power station produces the *wrong* quantity of the good: namely, too much electricity. Over-production has occurred.

Using marginal analysis to show how positive production externalities cause market failure

Whereas *negative* production externalities (which are illustrated in Figure 10.4) lead to the marginal social costs of production exceeding marginal private costs of production, when *positive* production externalities are generated, the marginal social costs of production lie *below* the marginal private costs incurred by the producers of the good or service. This is illustrated in Figure 10.5, which shows the costs incurred when a commercial forestry company plants trees.

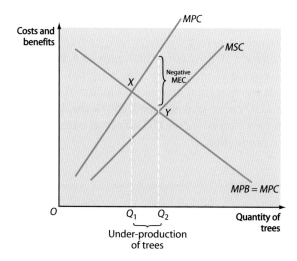

Figure 10.5
A commercial forestry company generating positive production externalities

The positive production externalities generated by tree planting include improved water retention in the soil and a carbon sink effect, whereby trees absorb greenhouse or global-warming gases from the atmosphere. As stated, positive production externalities such as these mean that the *MSC* curve is positioned *below* the *MPC* curve. The vertical distance between the two curves shows a *negative* marginal external cost (*MEC*) at each level of tree planting. (A *negative* marginal external cost is really the same as a *positive* marginal external benefit enjoyed by society as a whole.)

In order to maximise its private benefit, the commercial forestry plants Q_1 trees. Q_1 is immediately below point X, where *MPC* = *MPB*. However, Q_1 is less than the socially optimal level of output Q_2, located below point Y, where *MSC* = *MSB*. Figure 10.5 illustrates the fact that, when positive production externalities are generated, the market fails because too little of the good is produced and consumed. Under-production and under-consumption are depicted by the distance Q_2 minus Q_1.

EXAM TIP

The negative and positive externalities described in this and the previous section are generated in the course of production. In the next chapter on merit and demerit goods, the diagrams show consumption externalities and not production externalities. Make sure you understand the difference between consumption and production externalities.

Government policy and externalities

There are two main ways in which governments can intervene to try to correct the market failure caused by externalities. To eliminate or reduce production of negative externalities such as pollution and traffic congestion, governments can use **quantity controls** (or **regulation**), including in the extreme, prohibition of the externality. Governments can also **tax** the polluter. Regulation directly influences the quantity of the externality that a firm or household can generate. By contrast, taxation adjusts the market price at which a good is sold and creates an incentive for less of the negative externality to be generated.

And just as governments *discourage* the production of negative externalities, in much the same way they try to *encourage* the production of positive externalities. As with negative externalities, the government can choose to regulate and/or to try to change the prices of goods and activities that yield external benefits. In the latter case, subsidies rather than taxes are used to encourage production and consumption. These government policies are fully explained in Chapter 13.

EXTENSION MATERIAL

At A2, but not at AS, in the context of market failure, students are required to know about **property rights**. A property right is the exclusive right to determine how a resource such as land is used. Extreme free-market economists argue that, if property rights can be traded freely in markets, there is no need for government intervention in markets through the use of taxes, subsidies and public provision; and likewise there is no case for regulating markets.

In 1960 Professor Ronald Coase used the example of sparks discharged by the wood-burning locomotives passing through farmers' fields in nineteenth-century America to make this argument. A passing train lets off sparks which burn farmers' crops. To prevent this happening, the law could require the trains to buy and install spark catchers to prevent these fires. However, if that is expensive (i.e. more than the value of the burned crops), the railway companies may decide to pay the farmers for the damage done to the crops. By contrast, if instead the railway companies have the legal right to emit sparks, the farmers may decide to put up with burned crops or (if that is too expensive) they could pay the train companies to put on spark catchers. The problem of harmful externalities is dealt with through decisions to trade or not trade the property right entitlements of farmers and railway companies. As long as legal property rights exist and can be traded in markets, there is no need for government intervention other than to maintain the law.

SUMMARY

- A private good, such as a car, is excludable and rival.
- A public good, such as national defence, is non-excludable and non-rival.
- In the case of a public good, people free-ride by benefiting without paying for the good.
- In the case of a public 'bad', such as garbage, people free-ride by dumping it on others (e.g. by fly-tipping).
- A negative externality (external cost), such as pollution, is a public 'bad' dumped on others.
- A positive externality (external benefit), such as a beautiful view, is a public good that benefits others.
- The margin refers to the last unit undertaken of an activity.
- Private benefit maximisation occurs when $MPC = MPB$.
- Social benefit maximisation occurs when $MSC = MSB$.
- When an activity generates only negative externalities, $MSC > MPC$ and the socially optimal level of the activity is less than the privately optimal level.
- When an activity generates only positive externalities, $MSB > MPB$ and the socially optimal level of the activity is greater than the privately optimal level.
- Governments use regulations, including prohibition, and taxation to prevent or reduce production of negative externalities.
- Governments use regulations, including compulsory consumption, and subsidies to enforce or encourage production of positive externalities.

Exam-style questions

1 With examples, explain the difference between a pure and a non-pure public good. (12 marks)

2 With examples, explain the difference between positive and negative externalities. (12 marks)

3 Do you agree that governments should in all circumstances provide public goods? Justify your answer. (25 marks)

4 Evaluate different forms of government intervention to deal with the problems caused by negative externalities. (25 marks)

Merit goods and demerit goods

Chapter 11

Chapter 10 explained how market failure occurs when externalities are produced by firms, households and, indeed, the government. A negative externality causes too much of an activity to be undertaken, while conversely a positive externality leads to the opposite outcome: namely, too little of the activity. This chapter develops the analysis of externalities, showing how consumption of a demerit good such as tobacco harms both the smoker and other people who breathe the tobacco fumes, while consumption of a merit good such as healthcare benefits both the patient and the wider community.

LEARNING OUTCOMES

This chapter will:
- explain the difference between a merit good and a public good
- distinguish between a merit good and a demerit good
- explain how externalities lead to market failure in the case of merit and demerit goods
- use marginal analysis to illustrate how externalities lead to market failure
- introduce information problems to explain under-consumption of merit goods and over-consumption of demerit goods
- explain the importance of value judgement when deciding whether a good is a merit or demerit good

The difference between a merit good and a public good

Students often confuse merit goods with public goods, largely because both types of good are often provided by the state, with the provision funded through the tax system. Indeed, both merit goods and public goods provide examples of government goods, which were defined in the previous chapter.

EXAM TIP

Make sure you don't confuse merit goods with public goods.

However, merit goods are not the same as public goods. As we saw in the last chapter, public goods are defined by two characteristics: they are non-excludable and non-diminishable. Because of these characteristics, a market may fail to provide a pure public good such as national defence. By contrast, markets can and do provide merit goods such as healthcare and education, but arguably, they under-provide. While public goods can result in a missing market or **complete market failure**, merit goods (and also their opposite, demerit goods) lead to **partial market failure**. As goods such as private healthcare and private education clearly show, markets provide merit goods, but they provide the 'wrong' quantity. Likewise, markets provide demerit goods such as tobacco, alcoholic drink and hard drugs such as cocaine, but, by over-providing, they again provide the 'wrong' quantity.

Merit goods, demerit goods and externalities

A **merit good**, such as education or healthcare, is a good or service for which the social benefits of consumption enjoyed by the whole community exceed the private benefits received by the consumer. Consumption by an individual produces positive externalities that benefit the wider community.

As their name suggests, **demerit goods** are the opposite of merit goods. The social costs to the whole community which result from the consumption of a demerit good, such as tobacco or alcohol, exceed the private costs incurred by the consumer. This is because consumption by an individual produces negative externalities that harm the wider community. The private cost can be measured by the money cost of purchasing the good, together with any health damage suffered by the person consuming the good. But the social costs of consumption also include the cost of the negative externalities.

EXAM TIP

Many exam candidates assert that any good that is 'good for you' is a merit good. This assertion is wrong.

Healthcare is a merit good

Examples of merit goods

Education and healthcare are the best-known examples of merit goods. However, many goods can be classified as merit goods, though you must avoid the temptation that many students succumb to, to define any good that is 'good for you' as a merit good. Most consumer goods are good for you, but economists don't classify them as merit goods. Besides education and healthcare, other examples of merit goods are car seat belts, crash helmets, public parks and museums.

CASE STUDY 11.1

Museums as merit goods

Museums perform the important cultural function of conserving, interpreting, researching and displaying heritage. Museums have a mix of ownership patterns. For example, over 40% of UK museums are governed by public authorities, with the rest privately owned, mostly on a non-profit basis. Museums cover a very wide range of institutions of varying size and reputation, ranging from internationally renowned institutions such as the British Museum to a very large number of relatively small, often locally focused museums.

The funding of museums remains a source of considerable debate. Government subsidy or provision may be justified on the basis that museums generate external benefits: for example, knowledge acquired by a visitor may be passed on to others. Museums may also be regarded as merit goods, generating a better-educated and informed public and collective pride.

Government subsidy of museums may also be justified on the ground that a welfare-optimising price, based on marginal cost, would be near to zero, but this would not ensure financial viability. The case *against* government subsidy is that it may encourage inefficiency, lead to government failure and favour the well-off.

Follow-up questions

1 Do you agree that a museum is a merit good? Justify your answer.
2 Some argue that if entry to museums is free, people will not value what museums have to offer. Explain why you agree or disagree.

How positive consumption externalities lead to under-consumption of a merit good

As just noted, consumption of merit goods such as education or healthcare produces positive externalities which benefit the whole community. As a result, the social benefit of consumption exceeds the private benefit enjoyed by the consumer. The community benefits from an educated (and civilised) population, and a healthy population means there are fewer people to catch diseases from.

As Figure 11.1 shows, when education is available only through the market, at prices unadjusted by subsidy, too little of the merit good ends up being consumed. Many people (especially the poor) end up uneducated, or at least relatively uneducated. The privately optimal level of consumption is Q_1, where $MPC = MPB$. But this is below the socially optimal level of consumption, Q_2, located where $MSC = MSB$. Free-market provision of merit goods therefore leads to under-consumption, and hence to under-production. In a free market, too few scarce resources are used to produce merit goods.

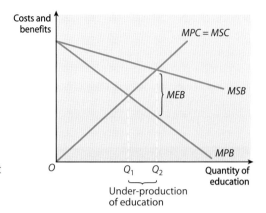

Figure 11.1 A market under-producing a merit good

How negative externalities lead to over-consumption of a demerit good

Consumption of a demerit good such as tobacco leads to a situation in which the marginal social benefit (*MSB*) of the whole community is less than the marginal private benefit (*MPB*) of the person consuming the demerit good. Private cost can be measured by the money cost of purchasing the good, together with any health damage suffered by the person consuming the good. However, the social costs of consumption include the costs of damage and injury inflicted on other people, resulting, for example, from passive smoking and road accidents caused by drunken drivers. Also included are the costs imposed on other people through taxation to pay for the care of victims of tobacco- and alcohol-related diseases.

EXAM TIP

Make sure you don't confuse a demerit good with an economic 'bad', which was explained in the previous chapter. When consumed, a 'bad' yields disutility, whereas a demerit good provides utility to the consumer, at least in the short run.

In the same way as the consumption of merit goods generates positive externalities which benefit the wider community, the consumption of demerit goods leads to the dumping of negative externalities on others. Figure 11.2 shows that too much of a demerit good is consumed when bought at market prices. At least in the short term, the privately optimal level of consumption is Q_1, where $MPC = MPB$. This is greater than the socially optimal level of consumption, Q_2, located where $MSC = MSB$. Free-market provision of demerit goods therefore leads to over-consumption, and hence over-production. In a free market, too many scarce resources are used to produce demerit goods. It is important to remember that smokers generate negative *consumption* externalities, such as the smoke breathed in by passive smokers who don't enjoy the fumes they inhale. In Figure 11.2, the marginal social benefit (*MSB*) curve of the whole community lies below the marginal private benefit (*MPB*) curve of the smokers themselves, with the distance between the two curves showing the negative externality.

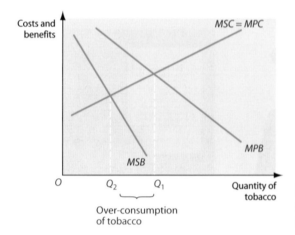

Figure 11.2 How over-consumption of tobacco occurs in a free market

Figure 11.2 indicates that some smoking is socially optimal. There may, of course, be more extreme situations in which the social costs resulting from the consumption of demerit goods are so severe that the good should be banned. But, because of the addictive or habit-forming nature of the consumption of demerit goods such as heroin and cocaine, attempts to ban their use are often counterproductive. Consumption is not abolished; the market is simply driven underground. Indeed, the social costs of consumption in an illegal and completely unregulated market may well exceed the social costs occurring when consumption is legal but closely regulated. Because of this, as will be explained in Chapter 13, governments often prefer to discourage or limit consumption of demerit goods by taxation and regulations, which stop short of an outright ban. Examples include spatial limits on where the demerit good can legally be consumed: for example, no-smoking areas and licensed premises for the sale of alcohol, restrictions on young people consuming the good, and limits on times of day when alcohol can be consumed in a public place.

Examples of demerit goods

CASE STUDY 11.2

Smoking yourself 'fit'

Strange as it seems, early cigarette ads, such as the Kensitas ad from 1929, often boasted the 'health benefits' of smoking, claiming 'relief' for asthma, wheezing, hay fever and obesity. In 1946 the American tobacco company Camel ran a series of adverts claiming that Camel were the 'doctor's choice'.

By the 1950s, research began to link smoking to cancer. Worldwide, tobacco use causes more than 5 million deaths per year, and current trends show that tobacco use will cause more than 8 million deaths annually by 2030, largely through the growth of smoking in developing countries.

1929 Kensitas magazine advert (left) and 1946 Camels magazine advert (right)

Follow-up questions

1 Most economists agree that tobacco is a demerit good. Why is this so?
2 Why do governments in countries such as the UK and USA now ban advertisements like these?

Cigarettes, and other tobacco products, and alcoholic drink are the two best-known examples of demerit goods. These days, governments in countries such as the UK either ban tobacco and drinks advertising, or severely regulate what the adverts can show. This has not always been the case, as the examples of advertisements for Kensitas and Camel cigarettes demonstrate.

Tobacco and drinks companies want to make their products appealing to young people, possibly in the hope that if teenagers develop the habit, they will be hooked on cigarettes and alcohol for the rest of their lives. To combat claims that the industry has been acting in an irresponsible way, the UK firms that produce alcoholic drinks have set up a public relations organisation, the Portman Group, to monitor adverts that might bring the drinks industry into disrepute. Here is an example of a recent drinks advert that was banned, not directly by the Portman Group, but by a local Trading Standards office.

CASE STUDY 11.3

Scratch-off label 'too sexy' for UK

Bottles of a Belgian lager whose labels showed a young lady wearing a swimsuit that could be scratched off have been banned in the UK. The 'Rubbel Sexy Lager' product breached the Portman Group's Code of Practice on the Naming, Packaging and Promotion of Alcoholic Drinks.

The Chief Executive of the Portman Group said: 'Some people might think this is harmless fun but there is a serious issue involved. Drinking excessively can affect people's judgement and behaviour, leading to them engaging in activity which they later regret. Our Code disallows drinks marketing being linked to sexual success.'

Follow-up question

Is self-regulation, by organisations such as the Portman Group, the best way of limiting consumption of a demerit good? Justify your answer.

Merit and demerit goods and the information problem

Some economists argue that under-consumption of merit goods and over-consumption of demerit goods stems not so much from the externalities that consumption generates, but from an **information problem**. Many people become addicted to demerit goods in their teenage years. Because of peer-group pressure and related factors, teenagers are heavily influenced by factors relating to lifestyle and personal circumstances, while at the same time ignoring, downplaying or being *myopic* about how their addictions may affect them many years ahead.

> **KEY TERM**
>
> **information problem:** this occurs when people make wrong decisions because they don't possess or they ignore relevant information. Very often they are *myopic* (short-sighted) about the future.

For a merit good, the *long-term private benefit* of consumption exceeds the *short-term* private benefit. But when deciding how much to consume, individuals take account of short-term costs and benefits, but ignore or undervalue the long-term private cost and benefit. Preventative dentistry provides a good example. Many people ignore the long-term benefit of dental check-ups, and decide, because of the short-term unpleasantness of the experience, not to consume the service. Unfortunately, these people can end up later in life with rotten teeth or gum disease, saying: 'If only I had visited the dentist more often when I was younger.'

In the case of demerit goods, it is the *long-run private costs* rather than the long-run private benefits that are significant. For a demerit good, the long-term private cost of consumption exceeds the short-term private cost of consumption. A person who started smoking at a young age may regret the decision later in life when affected by a smoking-related illness. But when a person starts to smoke and gradually becomes addicted to tobacco, private costs that will only appear many years into the future are often ignored. Even if we ignore externalities, the information problem means that a demerit good is likely to be over-consumed.

Merit goods, demerit goods and value judgements

The left-hand and right-hand columns of Table 11.1 list a number of goods that are accepted by most people as clear-cut examples of merit goods or demerit goods. However, for the goods listed in the middle panel — for example, contraception — the position is less clear. Because people have different values and ethics (often related to their religions), contraception is viewed by some people as a merit good, but by others as a demerit good. Whether a good is classified as a merit good or a demerit good, or indeed as neither, thus depends crucially on the value judgements of the person making the classification. This provides an important example of the distinction between **positive statements** and **normative statements**, a distinction first explained in Chapter 1. A positive statement is a statement of fact or a statement that can be tested to see if it is right or wrong. For example, statements that the earth is round and that the earth is flat are both positive statements, though scientific evidence shows that the second statement is wrong. By contrast, a normative statement is a statement of opinion, involving a value judgement. Thus, a statement that the earth *ought* to be flat is normative.

> **KEY TERMS**
>
> **normative statement:** a statement of opinion based on a value judgement.
>
> **positive statement:** a statement of fact, or one that can be scientifically tested.

Table 11.1 Merit and demerit goods, and less clear-cut cases

Merit goods	Merit or demerit goods?	Demerit goods
Education	Contraception	Tobacco
Healthcare (e.g. vaccination, preventative dental care, AIDS testing)	Abortion	Alcohol
Crash helmets	Sterilisation	Narcotic drugs, such as heroin and crack cocaine
Car seat belts		Pornography
Museums and public parks		Prostitution

Government policy towards merit and demerit goods

As in other situations in which positive externalities occur, governments can use **regulation** (including making consumption compulsory), **subsidy** or both to enforce or encourage consumption of merit goods. Likewise, governments can use regulation (including making consumption illegal), **taxation** or both to prevent or discourage consumption of demerit goods. These government policies are fully explained in Chapter 13.

Vaccination as a merit good

Vaccination, which is a form of healthcare, is listed as a merit good in Table 11.1. But as well as being a merit good in the conventional sense, vaccination also illustrates the free-rider problem, which I explained in the previous chapter in the context of public goods. Suppose for a serious infectious disease, vaccination is 100% effective in preventing people catching the disease. The vaccination has no adverse side-effects, but the market price of vaccination is £50. The disease is contagious and spreads rapidly through the country if a significant number of people in the population choose to remain unvaccinated. Given this information, we might conclude that everybody chooses to purchase vaccination for themselves and for their children, believing it is well worth spending £50 for complete protection from a contagious disease.

However, some people may choose to remain unvaccinated. This is because for each individual, the best possible solution is to remain unvaccinated — provided everyone else chooses vaccination. In this way, the person saves £50 and free-rides on the rest of the community. If everyone else is vaccinated, there is nobody from whom to catch the disease. However, other people will make their choices in exactly the same way, and if too many people choose to free-ride, the 'best solution' for the individual breaks down. Vaccination becomes under-consumed and an epidemic occurs. Therefore, it makes sense to subsidise the provision of vaccination, and possibly to make it compulsory, to ensure that everyone benefits from the merit good.

Think about how you could apply the analysis of vaccination as a merit good to help explain why a measles outbreak occurred in 2013, particularly in south Wales. Did some parents decide not to vaccinate their children because they chose to 'free-ride', or were they scared that the vaccination was unsafe?

Merit goods and uncertainty, moral hazard and adverse selection

Uncertainty about future long-term benefits and costs contributes to under-consumption of merit goods. For example, a person usually does not know in advance when, if ever, the services of a specialist surgeon might be needed. Sudden illness may lead to a situation in which a person cannot afford to pay for costly surgery, if provided solely through a conventional market. One market-orientated solution is for private medical insurance to pay for the cost of treatment at the time when it is needed. However, private medical insurance often fails to pay for treatment for the chronically ill or for the poor. Private insurance may also fail to provide medical care for **risk-takers** in society who decide not to buy insurance, as distinct from **risk-averters**, who are always the most ready customers for insurance.

EXAM TIP

You don't need to know about moral hazard and adverse selection at AS. However, understanding these concepts can add depth to an AS answer on merit goods.

Like all private insurance schemes, healthcare insurance suffers from two further problems, both of which lead to market failure. These are the problems of moral hazard and adverse selection. **Moral hazard** is demonstrated by the tendency of people covered by health insurance to be less careful about their health because they know that the insurance company will pick up the bill in the event of accident or illness. **Adverse selection** relates to the fact that people whose health risks are greatest are also the people most likely to try to buy insurance policies. Insurance companies react by refusing to sell health policies to those who most need private health insurance. For those to whom they do sell policies, premium levels are set sufficiently high to enable the companies to remain profitable when settling the claims of customers facing moral hazard or who have been adversely selected.

Public collective provision, perhaps organised by private sector companies but guaranteed by the state and funded by compulsory insurance, may be a better solution. Both private and public collective provision schemes are a response to the fact that the demand or need for medical care is much more predictable for a large group of people than for an individual.

SUMMARY

- Along with public goods, merit goods such as education are often provided by governments.
- Although both are often government goods, a merit good should not be confused with a public good.
- A merit good is a good that yields positive externalities that benefit the wider community.
- The privately optimal level of consumption of a merit good where $MPC = MPB$ is less than the socially optimal level where $MSC = MSB$.
- A demerit good is a good that yields negative externalities that harm the wider community.
- The privately optimal level of consumption of a demerit good where $MPC = MPB$ is greater than the socially optimal level where $MSC = MSB$.
- Information problems also contribute to under-consumption of merit goods and over-consumption of demerit goods.
- Governments encourage consumption of merit goods through state provision and subsidy.
- Governments discourage consumption of demerit goods through regulation and taxation.
- Private provision of a merit good such as healthcare may be affected by moral hazard and adverse selection.

Exam-style questions

1 With examples, explain the difference between a merit good and a public good. (12 marks)

2 Explain **two** policies a government can use to promote the optimal level of consumption of a demerit good. (12 marks)

3 Do you agree that people should be left to their own devices to choose how much of a merit good to consume? Justify your answer. (25 marks)

4 Evaluate the view that if merit goods are provided free by the state, the socially optimal level of consumption is always achieved. (25 marks)

Monopoly and other market failures

Chapter 12

Much of the earlier part of this book focused on how scarce resources are allocated between different uses by the forces of supply and demand in the competitive markets that were assumed to make up the economy. This chapter switches the focus away from competitive markets to monopoly, examining the extent to which monopoly is a market failure, together with circumstances in which monopoly may improve resource allocation. The chapter also surveys two other possible causes of market failure: the immobility of factors of production and inequalities in the distribution of income and wealth.

LEARNING OUTCOMES

This chapter will:
- define monopoly and provide examples of monopoly
- survey the causes of monopoly and market concentration
- explain how monopoly may lead to market failure and resource misallocation
- explain the potential benefits of monopoly, including economies of scale
- examine causes of immobility of factors of production
- consider whether income and wealth inequalities lead to market failure

The meaning of monopoly

Economists use the word **monopoly** in two rather different ways, in terms of a *strict* definition and in terms of a rather *looser* definition. The strict definition refers to **pure monopoly**, which occurs when a single firm produces the whole of the output of a market or a pure monopolist faces no competition at all, since there are no other firms to compete against. The looser definition refers to a market in which there is a dominant firm, but there are also some other firms in the market. According to this second meaning, monopoly is a *relative* rather than an *absolute* concept.

KEY TERMS

monopoly: a market dominated by one firm.

pure monopoly: one firm only in a market.

An effective monopoly must be able to exclude rivals from the market through **barriers to entry**. However, even when a firm is a monopoly producer of a particular good or service, the monopoly position is weak if close substitutes exist, produced by other firms in other industries. The closer the substitutes available, the weaker the monopoly position. A monopoly is therefore strongest when it produces an essential good for which there are no substitutes — or when demand is relatively inelastic.

Examples of monopoly

The US company Microsoft provides a very good example of a monopoly in the second, looser, meaning of the word. Microsoft is the dominant producer in both the US and the world markets of personal computer operating systems. Microsoft is also the largest producer of computer software applications. Its products, Word and Excel, dominate the word processor and spreadsheet markets. However, although Microsoft controls over 90% of the PC operating system market, it faces some competition: for example, from Linux and Apple.

Pure monopolies, by contrast, are extremely rare. Usually pure monopoly exists only when a government outlaws competition. Until about 20 years ago, **nationalised industries** (industries owned by the state) were more or less pure monopolies. However, this is no longer the case, as all the previously nationalised industries, such as British Gas and BT, have been privatised and exposed to competition. The Dutch company TNT now competes with Royal Mail in delivering first class mail and the Royal Mail itself was privatised in 2013. However, the water industry, which was privatised more than 15 years ago, continues to provide a good example of a pure monopoly. For many people, bottled water provides the only substitute to the tap water sold to you by a monopoly water company.

CASE STUDY 12.1

Nothing lasts forever

There was a time in the 1990s and early 2000s when Microsoft was at least as dominant as Apple now is in ICT markets. These days, Microsoft is still around, but actually it's an ailing giant – profitable but no longer innovative, trying (and so far failing) to get a foothold in the post-PC, mobile, cloud-based world. The same could be said for Kodak. The company's monopoly position in the camera and photographic film industry had disappeared under the onslaught of digital technology.

Apple's current strength is that it makes iPods, iPhones and iPads that people are desperate to buy and on which the company makes huge profits. But the logic of the ICT hardware business is that those profits will decline as the competition increases, so Apple will become less profitable over the longer term. What will determine Apple's future is whether it can come up with new, market-creating products. If the company fails to do this, Apple may become a footnote in history. Just like Microsoft, in fact.

Follow-up questions

1 Explain how the passage illustrates how developments in technology erode monopoly power.
2 Identify **two** similar examples of companies whose monopoly power has been eroded in this way.

Natural monopoly

In the past, **utility industries** such as water, gas, electricity and the telephone industries were regarded as **natural monopolies**. Because of the nature of their product, utility industries experience a particular marketing problem. The industries produce a service that is delivered through a distribution network or grid of pipes or cables into millions of separate businesses and homes. Competition in the provision of distribution grids is extremely wasteful, since it requires the duplication of fixed capacity, therefore causing each supplier to incur unnecessarily high fixed costs or overheads. Until quite recently, utility industries were generally monopolies.

KEY TERMS

natural monopoly: a market in which there is only room for one firm benefiting to the full from economies of scale.

utility industry: an industry, such as the post, which delivers its service to millions of separate customers.

However, governments had to choose whether utilities should be publicly owned monopolies (e.g. nationalised industries), or privately owned monopolies, possibly subject to public regulation. For historical reasons, until the 1980s, most UK utility industries were nationalised industries. In the 1980s and early 1990s, utilities such as the British Gas Corporation and BT were privatised, becoming privately owned utilities. Immediately following privatisation, they remained monopolies, protected from competition, though subject to a certain amount of state regulation: for example, Ofcom regulating British Telecom (BT).

CASE STUDY 12.2

Privatising Royal Mail and opening the business up to competition

In 2013 the government intends to sell off the Royal Mail, prompting fears that people in rural and remote areas could end up having to pay more for deliveries. The Royal Mail's universal service obligation currently prevents this.

A cross-party group of MPs has called on the UK government to guarantee that any moves to privatise Royal Mail and introduce more competition will not mean the end of standard postal charges throughout the country. Opponents of privatisation believe that new competitors will 'cherry pick' customers, leaving the Royal Mail with the job of providing a universal service to unprofitable customers.

To introduce more competition, privately owned TNT is currently trialling 'end-to-end' mail delivery in west London. Previously only Royal Mail 'posties' delivered letters over the 'final mile' to their eventual destinations. If successful, 'end-to-end' competition will eventually be introduced throughout the UK.

Competition in delivery – the 'final mile' – has been slow to develop, due mainly to the difficulty of competing with Royal Mail's economies of scale. Because of its universal service obligation, the Royal Mail also enjoys VAT exemptions which mean it can charge 20% less than rivals.

Follow-up questions

1 Explain the meaning of the underlined terms: 'universal service', 'privatisation', 'cherry pick' and 'economies of scale'.
2 Why is it difficult to expose the Royal Mail to competition in delivering letters over the 'final mile': that is, to people's front doors?

Other causes of monopoly

Geographical causes of monopoly

A pure natural monopoly would be rather different from the natural monopolies described in the previous section, occurring when for climatic or geological reasons a particular country or location is the only source of supply of a raw material or foodstuff. Monopolies of this type are quite rare, but geographical or spatial factors quite commonly give rise to another type of monopoly. Consider the case of a single grocery store in an isolated village, or of a petrol company that owns all the land around a busy road junction on which it has built a filling station. In the former case, entry to the market by a second store is restricted by the fact that the local market is too small, while in the second example the oil company uses private property rights to exclude immediate competition. In both these examples, no monopoly exists in an absolute sense, since the villagers can travel to the nearest town to buy their groceries, or motorists can drive on to the next convenient filling station. Nevertheless, the grocery store and the petrol station still exercise considerable market power, stemming from the fact that for many villagers and motorists it is both costly and inconvenient to shop elsewhere. Prices charged are likely to be higher than they would be if competition existed in the immediate neighbourhood.

Village shops exercise considerable market power

Economies of scale

Many manufacturing industries — for example, the aircraft building industry — benefit from economies of large-scale production. However, the size of the national market, and in extreme cases the world market, limits the number of firms that can coexist in an industry and continue to benefit from full economies of scale. **Economies of scale** thus help to explain the existence of a natural monopoly, which occurs when there is room in the market for only one firm benefiting from full economies of scale.

KEY TERM

economy of scale: falling average or unit costs as a firm increases its size or scale (see Chapter 8).

Government-created monopolies

Governments sometimes create monopoly in industries other than utility industries or natural monopolies. In the UK, industries such as coal, rail and steel were nationalised in the 1940s by a Labour government and turned into state-owned monopolies. At the time, the Labour government believed on the one hand that these industries were the commanding heights of the economy, and were essential for the well-being and planning of the whole economy. At the same time, the government believed that, on the other hand, state ownership was required for the industries to operate in the public interest, rather than in the narrower interest of their previous private owners.

In other instances, government may deliberately create a private monopoly. Examples include the granting of a broadcasting franchise to a commercial television company or a gambling franchise to a casino. Both these are examples of the state using monopoly to regulate the consumption of a good or service. State monopolies can ensure standards of supply of merit goods such as public service broadcasting, or prevent the worst excesses of consumption of a demerit good such as gambling.

Patent law provides another example of government-created monopoly. Patents and other forms of **intellectual copyright** give businesses, writers and musicians exclusive right to innovations or creative work (such as a novel or a piece of music) for several years, though the right may be difficult or impossible to enforce.

Control of market outlets and raw materials

Firms may try to obtain exclusive control over market outlets in order to deny access to their competitors. UK examples have included oil companies buying up garages and petrol stations, and breweries acquiring public houses. In a similar way, firms may obtain exclusive control over sources of raw materials or components for their products, starving their competitors of a source of supply or charging artificially high prices.

Advertising as a barrier to entry

Monopolies and other large firms can prevent small firms entering the market with devices such as saturation advertising. The small firms are unable to enter the industry because they cannot afford the minimum level of advertising and other forms of promotion for their goods which are necessary to persuade retailers to stock their products. The mass-advertising, brand-imaging and other marketing strategies of large established firms effectively crowd-out the newcomers from the market place.

How monopoly may lead to market failure and resource misallocation

Figure 12.1 illustrates how a monopoly may lead to market failure. If the market is competitive, all the firms in the market produce output Q_1, which they sell at price P_1. Suppose a monopoly now replaces the competitive firms. The monopoly uses its market power to restrict output to Q_2 and to hike the price up to P_2. Market failure and resource misallocation occur because, compared to the competitive market, output falls and the price rises, leading to under-consumption of the good the monopoly produces.

EXAM TIP

At AS, exam questions may require analysis and evaluation of the case against monopoly and the case justifying monopoly. The two diagrams you need to know are Figures 12.1 and 12.2 overleaf.

Figure 12.1 A monopoly restricting output and raising the price

The absence of competitive pressure in monopoly, which in competitive markets serves to reduce the profit that firms make, means that a monopoly may be able to enjoy an easy life, incurring unnecessary production costs and thus making satisfactory rather than the highest possible profit. This can occur because the monopoly is protected by entry barriers. As a result, the absence or weakness of competitive forces means there is no mechanism to force a monopoly to eliminate unnecessarily high costs of production. This is a further reason for resource misallocation.

How entry barriers protect monopolies

EXAM TIP

Make sure you understand the meaning of entry barriers and are able to give at least two examples.

Monopolies and firms in concentrated markets use entry barriers to protect the firm's position in the market. There are two main types of entry barrier: natural barriers and artificial or man-made barriers.

Natural barriers, which are also known as *innocent* barriers, are barriers such as economies of scale and indivisibilities, which have not been created by firms already in the market (i.e. by incumbent firms) to deter new firms from entering the market. Economies of scale mean that established large firms produce at a lower average cost, and are more productively efficient, than smaller new entrants, which suffer from higher average costs of production. Indivisibilities prevent certain goods and services being produced in plant below a certain size. Indivisibilities occur in metal smelting and oil refining industries.

Artificial or **man-made entry barriers**, which are also known as *strategic* barriers, are the result of deliberate action by incumbent firms to prevent new firms from entering the market. Strategic entry barriers include:

- **Patents** — incumbent firms acquire patents for all the variants of a product that they develop.
- **Setting prices deliberately low** to deter entry by new firms or to kill off small firms which have already entered the market.

- **Deliberately building excess capacity** — firms considering entering a market may be put off by excess capacity owned by firms already in the market. Excess capacity allows incumbent firms to step up production in order to drive down the price to a level at which new entrants cannot compete.

The potential benefits of monopoly

The conclusion that a competitive market produces a better resource allocation than monopoly depends on an assumption that no or few economies of scale are possible in the market in which the firms produce. When substantial economies of scale are possible in an industry, monopoly may lead to a better outcome than competition. Figure 12.2 illustrates a natural monopoly where, because of limited market size, there is insufficient room in the market for more than one firm benefiting from full economies of scale.

EXAM TIP

Chapter 8 provides more detail about a firm's average cost curve.

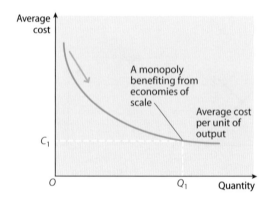

Figure 12.2 How economies of scale may justify a monopoly

In Figure 12.2, economies of scale are shown by the downward-sloping average cost curve. By assumption, a monopoly is able to produce output Q_1 at an average cost (or unit cost) of C_1, whereas competitive firms are unable to produce this output without destroying the competitive market.

A monopoly may also benefit from a second advantage possibly denied to firms in a competitive market. For example, protected by a patent that prevents competitors from free-riding on its success, a monopoly may be able to use high monopoly profit to finance product innovation. Monopoly profit can fund research and development (R&D), which leads to better ways of making existing products and to the development of completely new products.

Factor immobility as a cause of market failure

As explained in earlier chapters, the price mechanism allocates scarce resources between competing uses in both market and mixed economies (though in the latter the planning mechanism also has an important role). In both market and mixed economies, the price mechanism operates in two different types of market: the economy's **goods markets** (or **product markets**) and the economy's **factor markets**, including **labour markets**.

As Figure 12.3 shows, households and firms function simultaneously in both sets of markets, but their roles are reversed. Whereas firms are the source of supply in goods markets, in the factor markets firms exercise demand for factor services supplied by households. It is the incomes received by households from the sale and supply of factor services that contribute in large measure to the households' ability to demand the output supplied by the firms in the goods market. Indeed, the relationship between households and firms in the two sets of markets is essentially circular. In goods markets, output or finished goods flow from firms to households in return for money revenues. In factor markets, the money revenues received enable the firms to purchase factor services supplied by the households. The circle is complete when households spend this income on the goods produced by the firms.

Figure 12.3
The relationship between goods markets and labour markets

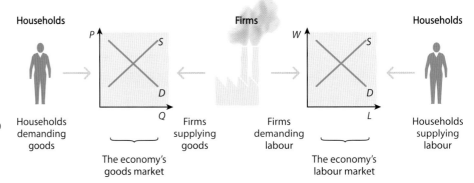

Usually when economists talk of market failure, they refer to failures occurring in goods markets, such as over-production of demerit goods, a failure to produce public goods and under-production of merit goods. However, market failure can also occur in factor markets and especially in labour markets. Whereas in a fully developed market economy or mixed economy, markets are usually pretty good at arranging the efficient exchange of goods for money, **labour immobility** means this is often not the case for workers. Occupational and geographical immobility of labour mean that economic resources are not fully utilised in areas of high unemployment, while at the same time economic growth is held back by labour shortages in areas, regions and countries benefiting from full employment.

KEY TERM

immobility of labour: the inability of labour to move from one job to another, either for occupational reasons (e.g. the need for training) or for geographical reasons (e.g. the cost of moving to another part of the country).

CASE STUDY 12.3

Labour immobility has an international dimension as well as a regional dimension within a nation state such as the UK. As the extract below mentions, one of the reasons for US economic success has been labour mobility across a continent.

Polish plumbers

Since 1 May 2004, workers in countries such as Poland and Hungary have had an opportunity to migrate to the richer countries of western Europe. Arguably, the resulting 'Polish plumber' phenomenon eased labour shortages in the boom years from 2004 to 2008 and helped to create more flexible labour markets in countries such as the UK, while mopping up unemployment in the poorer countries of the east. However, as the passage states, Europe still has a very long way to go to match the labour mobility of North America.

Has immigration been good for Britain?

Tony Blair, the former prime minister, has suggested that the debate over immigration should be 'handled with care'. Otherwise, it could descend into racism and nationalism. Blair went on to say that 'the Polish community contributes a lot to this country'.

'Of course it has to be controlled, and illegal immigration has to be tackled head on. It's important that we do that,' he said. 'But overall I would like to say that I think immigration has been good for Britain. So don't make them a scapegoat for our problems.'

In the USA it is far more common for workers to cross state lines in search of jobs. In fact, such labour mobility is a vital part of the US economy's success.

Just 2% of Europeans live and work in a foreign EU country. Amazingly, that percentage has hardly changed over the last 35 years. It compares with a figure of 8% of Americans who live and work outside their home state.

Whatever the headlines say — Europe needs more mobility, not less.

Follow-up questions

1 Do you agree that labour immobility is an example of a market failure? Justify your answer.
2 Evaluate how UK markets have been affected by the migration of labour from EU countries in central and eastern Europe.

Occupational immobility of labour occurs when workers are prevented by either natural or artificial barriers from moving between different types of job. Workers are obviously not homogeneous or uniform, so differences in natural ability may prevent or restrict movement between jobs. Some types of work require an innate ability, such as physical strength or perfect eyesight, which prevent a worker immediately switching between labour markets. Examples of artificial barriers include membership qualifications imposed by professional bodies such as accountancy associations, and trade union restrictive practices which restrict employment to those already belonging to the union. Various forms of racial, religious and gender discrimination are also artificial causes of occupational immobility of labour.

Geographical immobility of labour occurs when factors such as ignorance of job opportunities, family and cultural ties, and the financial costs of moving or travel, prevent a worker from filling a job vacancy located at a distance from his or her present place of residence or work. Perhaps the most significant cause of geographical immobility within the UK in recent years has been the state of the housing market, which itself reflects imperfections in other factor markets. Particularly during house price booms, low-paid and unemployed workers in the northern half of Britain find it difficult or impossible to move south to fill job vacancies in the more prosperous southeast of England. The prices of owner-occupied housing soars out of reach and there is very little housing available at affordable rents in either the private or the public sectors. At the same time, workers living in their own houses in the southeast may be reluctant to apply for jobs elsewhere in the country, for fear that they will never again be able to afford to move back to southern England.

The distribution of income and wealth

In Chapter 9, when the concept of market failure was introduced, it was explained that there are two main ways in which markets fail. Markets can function *inefficiently* or they can function *inequitably*. So far, in Chapters 10 and 11, and also earlier in this chapter, I have been focusing on the first of these two types of market failure, with the partial exception of merit and demerit goods. However, the final type of market failure you need to consider results from the inequitable functioning of markets.

Equity means fairness or justness (though in other contexts, such as the housing market, equity has a very different meaning: namely, wealth). As soon as equitable considerations are introduced into economic analysis, normative or value judgements are being made about a 'socially fair' distribution of income and wealth, and about the goods and services people *ought* to produce and consume.

Income is a *flow*, received per week, per month or per year, whereas **wealth** is a *stock*, which for rich people tends to accumulate over time. Examples of income are wages, salaries, rents and the dividend income received by shareholders. Shares themselves, together with other financial assets such as money deposited in banks, are a form of wealth. People also keep their wealth in physical assets, notably property or housing.

In the UK, as in most other countries, the distributions of income and wealth are both unequal, but the distribution of wealth is significantly more unequal than the distribution of income. The link between wealth and income partly explains this. For the better-off, wealth generates investment income, part of which, being saved, then adds to wealth and generates even more income. The poor, by contrast, who possess little or no wealth, have incomes (from low-paid jobs and/or **welfare benefits**) that are too low to allow saving and the

> ### KEY TERMS
>
> **income:** a flow of money received (e.g. as a wage) from supplying labour.
>
> **wealth:** a stock of assets that a person or firm owns.
>
> **welfare benefits:** transfers of money by the government to people in low income groups or with special needs (e.g. disabled people).

CASE STUDY 12.4

Growing income and wealth inequalities in the UK

The Organisation for Economic Co-operation and Development (OECD) has reported that income inequality among working-age people has been rising faster in Britain than in any other rich nation. The gap has been caused by the rise of a financial services elite who, through education and marriage, have concentrated wealth into the hands of a tiny minority.

OECD reports that in 2008 the annual average income in the UK of the top 10% was just under £55,000, about 12 times higher than that of the bottom 10%, whose average income was £4,700. The average income gap in developed nations is nine to one.

The rise of the top 1% in rich societies and the falling share of income going to poorer people are especially pronounced in Britain.

Just prior to the global recession, the OECD says, the very top of British society – the 0.1% of highest earners — accounted for a remarkable 5% of total pre-tax income and a level of wealth hoarding not seen since 1945.

At the same time as accumulating great wealth, the rich have seen tax rates fall. The top marginal income tax rate dropped from 60% in the 1980s to 40% in the 2000s, and is now 45%.

Although spending on public services in Britain had gone up in the past decade, at the same time benefits to the poor were worth less and taxes were less redistributive.

The effect has been a dramatic weakening in the state's ability to spread wealth throughout society. From the mid-1970s to the mid-1980s, the tax/benefit system offset more than 50% of the rise in income inequality. It now manages just 20%. The OECD warned of sweeping consequences for rich societies — and pointed to the rash of occupations and protests, especially by young people, around the world.

Although the OECD figures end just before the recession, economists believe the trend continued into the downturn.

Follow-up questions

1 Explain the difference between income and wealth.
2 The distribution of wealth in the UK is more unequal than the distribution of income. Why is this so?

accumulation of wealth. The tax system also hits income harder than wealth. In the UK income is usually taxed, but wealth is largely untaxed (except through inheritance tax and capital gains tax which, for the wealthy, are quite easy to avoid).

Unregulated market forces tend to produce a highly unequal distribution of income and wealth. I mentioned on page 90 that some economists, usually of a free-market persuasion, dispute whether an unequal distribution of income is a type of market failure. They argue that people who end up being rich deserve to be rich, and that people who end up being poor deserve to be poor. The market has not failed — it merely creates incentives which, if followed, cause people to generate more income and wealth, which, via a trickle-down effect, will also benefit the poor.

A version of this argument has recently been used to justify low or non-existent UK taxation for those of the world's super-rich who choose to live in London. If the super-rich, or 'non-doms', are taxed as if they are ordinary UK citizens, then, so the argument goes, they will move to tax havens outside the UK.

However, most economists reject as too extreme the view that the market contains its own morality with regard to the distributions of income and wealth. They argue that markets are 'value-neutral' with respect to the social and ethical desirability or undesirability of the income and wealth distributions resulting from the way the market functions.

Few economists believe that markets should be replaced by the command mechanism. There is, however, much more agreement that, instead of *replacing* the market, governments should *modify* the market so that it operates in a more equitable way than would be the case without government intervention. Taxing the better-off and redistributing tax revenues as transfers to the less well-off is the obvious way of correcting the market failure to ensure an equitable distribution of income and wealth.

However, as Chapter 14 explains, redistributive policies can promote new types of inefficiency and distortion within the economy.

EXAM TIP

Make sure you don't confuse *equality* and *equity*. 'Equality' is a positive term that can be measured. 'Equity' is a normative term based on what is considered to be fair or just.

SUMMARY

- Pure monopoly means only one firm in a market.
- A concentrated market dominated by one firm can also be regarded as a monopoly.
- In the past, utility industries were natural monopolies.
- Economies of scale can also lead to monopoly.
- Monopoly leads to market failure if it restricts output and raises prices, compared to the situation in a competitive market.
- Entry barriers protect monopolies and enable a monopoly to exploit consumers.
- Monopoly can be justified if economies of scale allow a monopoly to cut prices.
- Monopoly can be justified if it uses its profit to finance R&D and innovation.
- Immobility of labour leads to the inefficient use of productive resources.
- An unequal distribution of income and wealth can be regarded as a market failure because it is inequitable.

Exam-style questions

1 Explain how monopoly may lead to market failure. (12 marks)

2 Explain how the immobility of labour may lead to market failure. (12 marks)

3 Evaluate the case for and against monopoly. (25 marks)

4 Do you agree that a highly unequal distribution of income is a market failure? Justify your answer. (25 marks)

Government intervention in the economy

Chapter 13

When people think of government intervention in the economy, they often focus on the government's budget, in which decisions are made about overall levels of taxation and government spending in the whole of the economy, and on interest rate changes made by the Bank of England. However, these provide examples of government intervention in the macroeconomy, which is part of the subject matter of Unit 2 and Chapters 23–25 in particular. The content of this and the next chapter is rather different, examining government intervention at the microeconomic level, in the individual markets that make up the total economy.

LEARNING OUTCOMES

This chapter will:
- survey the reasons against and for government intervention in markets
- link government intervention in the economy to the correction of market failure
- explain why governments often intervene to provide public goods
- describe how regulation and taxation are used to improve resource allocation in the cases of negative externalities and demerit goods
- describe how regulation and subsidy are used to improve resource allocation in the cases of positive externalities and merit goods
- explain permits to pollute
- describe how government intervention may deal with the problems posed by monopoly
- examine government policies to reduce income and wealth inequalities

The reasons against and for government intervention in markets

To understand why governments intervene in markets in mixed economies such as the UK, it is useful to divide economists (and politicians) into two different groups: those who believe that unregulated markets generally work well, and those who argue that markets are prone to market failure. The former group are non-interventionists who want to leave as much as possible to market forces, while the latter group believe that government intervention can make markets work better.

Pro-free market economists see a market economy as a calm and orderly place in which the market mechanism, working through incentives transmitted by price signals in competitive markets, achieves a better or more optimal outcome than can be attained through government intervention. In essence, risk-taking business men and women who will gain or lose through the correctness of their decisions in the market place know better what to produce than civil servants and planners cocooned by risk-free salaries and secured pensions. And providing that markets are sufficiently competitive, what is produced is ultimately decided by the wishes of consumers, who know better than governments what is good for them. According to this philosophy, the correct economic function of government is to act as 'night-watchman' by maintaining law and order, providing public goods and possibly merit goods when the market fails, and generally ensuring a suitable environment in which 'wealth-creating' firms can function in competitive markets, subject to minimum interference and regulation.

EXAM TIP

Consumer sovereignty means the 'consumer is king'. Households and individuals ultimately decide what is produced. *Producer sovereignty* means the 'producer is king'. Firms use monopoly power to exploit consumers.

By contrast, **interventionist economists** believe that all too often markets are uncompetitive, characterised by monopoly power and producer sovereignty, and prone to other forms of market failure. Additionally, uncertainty about the future and lack of correct market information are destabilising forces. By intervening in the economy, especially to correct market failures, the government 'knows better' than unregulated market forces. It can anticipate and counter the destabilising forces existent in markets, achieving a better outcome than is likely in an economy subject to market forces alone.

Correcting market failures

There are various methods open to a government for correcting, or at least reducing, market failures. At one extreme, the government can **abolish the market**, using instead the command or planning mechanism, financed from general taxation, for providing goods and services. At the other extreme, the government can try to influence market behaviour by providing information, and by exhorting and **'nudging'** firms and consumers to behave in certain ways (e.g. not to use plastic bags). Between these extremes, governments can **impose regulations** to limit people's freedom of action in the market place, and use **taxes** and **subsidies** to alter prices in the market in order to change incentives and economic behaviour.

Government provision of public goods

EXAM TIP

Refer back to Chapters 5 and 9 to make sure that you understand the functions of prices and the meaning of market failure. When the signalling, incentive and allocative functions of prices work well, markets do too, and there is little need for government intervention. But, if one or more of the functions of prices breaks down, market failure occurs. This leads to resource misallocation in the economy, which means that the economy fails to make best use of resources.

Because of the free-rider problem (explained in Chapter 9), markets may fail to provide pure public goods such as national defence and police services. When free-riding occurs, the incentive function of prices breaks down. If goods are provided by a market, people can free-ride rather than pay a price, so the firms that are trying to sell the goods can't make a profit. Given that there is a need for public goods, governments often step into the gap and provide the goods, financing the provision out of general taxation.

However, with many so-called public goods (non-pure public goods or quasi-public goods) such as roads, free-riders can be excluded — in this case, by toll gates or electronic pricing — and prices can be charged successfully. There may still be a case for free provision by the government outside the market. Provided the road is uncongested, the socially optimal level of road use occurs when motorists can drive their cars without having to pay to use the road. But once congestion occurs, there is a case for road pricing.

CASE STUDY 13.1

Police services: public good or private good?

Policing is normally considered to be a form of public good which the market can, in principle, provide, but which it would under-provide. However, certain aspects of policing are a private good rather than a public good. The specific task of guarding a particular property, such as a shopping mall, can be done by private security firms such as Group 4 Securicor (G4S). Since the private benefits in such cases are large, there is a strong case for charging the person or business receiving the private benefits.

As an alternative to private security firms, the police could provide specific guard duties and charge for the service. They already charge for providing security inside football grounds. If private security firms were not allowed to operate, the police would have a monopoly and might charge very high prices. Also the quality of the service might be poorer than that provided by private security companies, which are competing against each other for business. But on the other hand, the police are likely to have greater experience, and there are economies of scale to be gained from the police providing security services.

Follow-up question

Give your own views on whether policing is a public good, a private good or some form of 'mixed good'.

Government intervention, negative externalities and demerit goods

There are two main ways in which governments can intervene to try to correct the market failures caused by negative externalities and demerit goods. The government can use quantity controls (or **regulation**) or it can use **taxation**. Regulation directly influences the quantity of the externality that a firm or household can generate, and the level of consumption of a demerit good such as tobacco. By contrast, taxation adjusts the market price at which a good that generates the externality is sold, or the price of the demerit good. For example, taxing pollution discharged by power stations and taxing tobacco create incentives for less pollution to be generated and less tobacco to be consumed.

Regulation or quantity controls

In its most extreme form, regulation can be used to ban completely, or criminalise, the generation of negative externalities such as pollution or the sale and consumption of a demerit good such as heroin. However,

KEY TERMS

regulation: involves the imposition of rules, controls and constraints, which restrict freedom of economic action in the market place.

taxation: a tax is a compulsory levy imposed by the government or some other authority to pay for its activities. Taxes can be used to achieve other objectives, such as reduced consumption of demerit goods.

it may be impossible to produce a good or service such as electricity in a coal-burning power station without generating at least some of a negative externality. In this situation, banning the externality has the perverse effect of preventing production of a good (e.g. electricity) as well as the bad (pollution). Because of this, quantity controls that fall short of a complete ban may be more appropriate. These include maximum emission limits and restrictions on the time of day or year during which the negative externality can legally be emitted. In the case of 'milder' demerit goods, smoking can be banned in public places, while shops would break the law by selling alcohol to younger teenagers.

Taxation

Completely banning negative externalities and demerit goods is a form of market replacement rather than market adjustment. By contrast, because taxes placed on goods affect incentives which consumers and firms face, they provide a market-orientated solution to the problems posed by negative externalities and demerit goods. Taxation compensates for the fact that there is a missing market in the externality. In the case of pollution, the government calculates the money value of the negative externality, and imposes this on the firm as a pollution tax. This is known as the **polluter must pay** principle. The pollution tax creates an incentive, which was previously lacking, for less of the bad to be dumped on others. By so doing, the tax **internalises the externality**. The polluting firm must now cover all the costs of production, including the cost of negative externalities, and include these in the price charged to customers. By setting the tax so that the price the consumer pays equals the marginal social cost of production ($P = MSC$), resource allocation in the economy is improved. However, a pollution tax, like any tax, itself introduces new inefficiencies and distortions into the market, associated with the costs of collecting the tax and with creating incentives to evade the tax illegally: for example, by dumping pollution at night to escape detection. This is an example of **government failure**. Government failures are explained in Chapter 14.

Until recently, governments have been much more likely to use regulation rather than taxation to reduce negative externalities such as pollution and congestion. Indeed in the past, it was difficult to find examples of pollution taxes outside the pages of economics textbooks, possibly because politicians feared that pollution taxes would be too unpopular. But in recent years, governments have become much more prepared to use congestion and pollution taxes. This reflects growing concern, among governments and the public alike, of environmental issues such as global warming and the problems posed by fossil fuel emissions and other pollutants. It may also reflect both the growing influence of green or environment pressure groups such as Friends of the Earth, and a growing preference to tackle environmental problems with market solutions rather than through regulation. For example, read Case Study 13.2 — which includes some of the advice given to the UK government by Lord Nicholas Stern about the need for carbon pricing in the *Stern Review on The Economics of Climate Change*, published by the UK Treasury in October 2006.

To analyse how the imposition of a tax on a demerit good such as tobacco affects consumption of the good, refer back to Figure 6.9 in Chapter 6. The diagram shows that imposing an expenditure tax on a good in fairly elastic demand is effective in reducing demand for the product. However, because of their addictive properties, the demand for demerit goods such as alcohol, tobacco and hard drugs can be inelastic. Taxing demerit goods can raise lots of revenue for the government, but does not do much to reduce consumption. And if the tax is set at a very high rate, it may lead to smuggling and to black market activity.

Climate change may be caused by industrial emissions

EXTENSION MATERIAL

Climate change and market failure

Many people living in advanced developed economies such as the UK agree with Lord Nicholas Stern, who is quoted in Case Study 13.2 as stating that climate change provides the greatest market failure facing humankind. Governments have not as yet taken sufficient action to reduce the rate at which climate change is taking place, let alone to reduce the total adverse effect of climate change.

An explanation for this, which is provided in the passage below, is that individual governments take too little action because they are victims of what economists call a *prisoner's dilemma game*. You should come across the prisoner's dilemma game, and possibly other examples of *game theory*, in your A2 course next year. However, it is possible, at least in theory, to escape the prisoner's dilemma if governments cooperate to introduce policies to tackle climate change.

Playing games with the planet

Suppose you believe that flying long-haul for a holiday in Australia contributes to global warming. You also believe that global warming will be reduced if everybody chooses to take local holidays rather than to enjoy vacations on the other side of the planet. However, you also know that if you alone stop flying, it will have only a minute effect on global warming. By contrast, if everybody else stops taking long-haul holidays, global warming will be reduced even if you book your flight to Australia.

Deciding to carry on flying, irrespective of what other holiday makers do, is in fact your best strategy. Unfortunately it is the best strategy for everyone else! Result: everybody continues to take long-haul holidays and there is no reduction in global warming!

Using similar reasoning, we can see that all countries and all governments benefit from a stable climate, but any single country or government may be reluctant to reduce CO_2 emissions. The immediate benefit for an individual country of continuing to pollute is perceived to be greater than the uncertain future benefit to all countries if they all take action to reduce CO_2 emissions. This helps to explain why intergovernmental agreements to reduce pollution (e.g. the Kyoto Protocol signed in 1997 and the 2012 Doha talks) have not been very effective in reducing the pace of global warming.

CASE STUDY 13.2

Lord Stern on the economics of climate change

Climate change presents a unique challenge for economics: it is the greatest and widest-ranging market failure ever seen. The economic analysis must therefore be global, deal with long time horizons and have the economics of risk and uncertainty at centre stage.

Policy to reduce emissions should be based on three essential elements: carbon pricing, technology policy and removal of barriers to behavioural change. Leaving out any one of these elements will significantly increase the costs of action.

The first element of policy is carbon pricing. Greenhouse gases are, in economic terms, an externality: those who produce greenhouse gas emissions are bringing about climate change, thereby imposing costs on the world and on future generations, but they do not face the full consequences of their actions themselves.

Putting an appropriate price on carbon — explicitly through tax or trading, or implicitly through regulation — means that people are faced with the full social cost of their actions. This will lead individuals and businesses to switch away from high-carbon goods and services, and to invest in low-carbon alternatives. Trading schemes can be an effective way to equalise carbon prices across countries and sectors, and the EU Emissions Trading Scheme is now the centrepiece of European efforts to cut emissions.

The second element of climate-change policy is technology policy. The development and deployment of a wide range of low-carbon technologies is essential in achieving the deep cuts in emissions that are needed. Public spending on research and development has fallen significantly in the last two decades and is now too low.

The third element is the removal of barriers to behavioural change. Information policies, including labelling and the sharing of best practice, can encourage behavioural change. They can help consumers and businesses make sound decisions, and stimulate competitive markets for low-carbon and high-efficiency goods and services.

Governments have a role in providing a policy framework to guide effective adaptation by individuals and firms in the medium and longer term. There are four key areas:

- High-quality climate information and tools for risk management will help to drive efficient markets.
- Land-use planning and performance standards should encourage both private and public investment in buildings and other long-lived infrastructure to take account of climate change.
- Governments can contribute through long-term policies for climate-sensitive public goods, including natural resources protection, coastal protection and emergency preparedness.
- A financial safety net may be required for the poorest in society, who are likely to be the most vulnerable to the impacts and least able to afford protection (including insurance).

Follow-up questions

1 What action, if any, has been taken by national governments and by international organisations to implement Lord Stern's recommendations since the publication of his report in 2006?
2 Find out what Lord Stern now thinks about the rate at which global warming is taking place (see the article 'Nicholas Stern: 'I got it wrong on climate change – it's far, far worse, 26 January 2013, www.guardian.co.uk)

Pollution permits

Until quite recently, the main choice of policy for dealing with the problem of pollution was between regulation and taxation. As I have explained, the former is an *interventionist solution* whereas taxation, based on the principle that the polluter must pay, has been seen as a more *market-orientated solution*, but nevertheless one which required the government to levy and collect the pollution tax. In the 1990s, another market-orientated solution started in the USA, based on a trading market in **permits** or **licences to pollute**. And as the Stern Review notes (see Case Study 13.2), the 'EU **Emissions Trading** Scheme is now the centrepiece of European efforts to cut emissions'.

A permits to pollute scheme (for electricity) still involves regulation: for example, the imposition of maximum limits on the amount of pollution that coal-burning power stations are allowed to emit, followed by a steady reduction in these ceilings in each subsequent year (say, by 5%). But once this regulatory framework has been established, a market in traded pollution permits takes over, creating market-orientated incentives for the power station companies to reduce pollution because they can make money out of it.

> **KEY TERM**
>
> **emissions trading:** emissions trading systems allow policy-makers to set a pollution target, and then issue tradable permits corresponding to that amount. Companies that wish to pollute must hold permits equal to their emissions.

A tradable market in permits to pollute works in the following way. Energy companies able to reduce pollution by more than the law requires sell their spare permits to other power stations that, for technical or other reasons, decide not to, or cannot, reduce pollution below the maximum limit. The latter still comply with the law, even when exceeding the maximum emission limit, because they buy the spare permits sold by the first group of power stations. But in the long run, even power stations that find it difficult to comply with the law have an incentive to reduce pollution, so as to avoid the extra cost of production created by the need to buy pollution permits.

EXAM TIP

The introduction of a pollution permit system is an attempt to work with the market and provide a market-orientated way of reducing market failure caused by negative externalities.

Government intervention, positive externalities and merit goods

EXAM TIP

At this stage you should refer back to Chapter 4 to refresh your knowledge of the effect of a subsidy on the supply curve of a good.

Just as governments discourage the production and consumption of negative externalities and demerit goods, in much the same way they try to encourage the production and consumption of positive externalities and merit goods. Again, the government can choose to regulate, or to try to change the prices of merit goods and other goods and activities which yield external benefits. In the latter case, **subsidies** rather than taxes are used to encourage production and consumption.

Regulation can force firms and consumers to generate positive externalities. For example, local authority bylaws can require households to maintain the appearance of properties, and the state may order landowners to plant trees. In this situation, it is illegal not to provide external benefits for others. In the case of merit goods, the government may require people to be vaccinated against disease and to wear seat belts in cars and crash helmets on motor bikes.

In the UK, education is both compulsory and completely subsidised, at least for children between the ages of 5 and 16. Low-income families would be in an impossible situation if required to pay for education as well as to send their children to school. Subsidies can, of course, be paid to private providers of education and healthcare: namely, to private schools and private hospitals. However, in the UK, education and healthcare are also provided by the state, forming an important part of public spending. Nevertheless, private sector provision is growing. One reason for growing private sector provision of merit goods lies in the fact that state provision does not necessarily mean *good-quality* provision.

> **KEY TERM**
>
> **subsidy:** a payment made by government, usually to producers, for each unit of the subsidised good that they produce. Consumers can also be subsidised: for example, bus passes given to children to enable them to travel on buses free or at a reduced price.

CASE STUDY 13.3

Regulating BAA's monopoly over UK airports

The UK government's monopoly policy is implemented by a number of government agencies, which are responsible to a government department, the Department for Business, Innovation and Skills. The principal agency, the **Competition and Markets Authority**, starts operating in April 2014 following the merger of two former regulatory agencies, the Office of Fair Trading (OFT) and the Competition Commission. There are also a number of industry-specific regulatory agencies such as the **Office of Communications (Ofcom)**, which have the power to regulate the prices charged by the privatised industries they oversee.

The extract below outlines what has happened to BAA, an airport monopoly which, amid calls for BAA to be broken up, was investigated by the Competition Commission in 2009. The commission's job was to investigate whether BAA's monopoly power over airports resulted in anti-competitive business practices.

Rebranding London main airport

In 1986 BAA was formed when a Conservative government privatised the airports it had previously owned. In 2006 BAA became the UK subsidiary of a foreign-owned company, having been taken over by a Spanish consortium. In 2009 BAA's monopoly position in the airport industry was referred to the Competition Commission. After its investigation, the commission ordered BAA to sell off Gatwick and Stansted airports, along with a Scottish airport.

In 2012 BAA decided to change its business name to 'Heathrow' to reflect the fact that Heathrow is the only London airport that the company now owns. Heathrow's chief executive said: 'We are a different company today from when BAA was formed. Heathrow now accounts for more than 95% of our business.' He added: 'We are now starting the process of rebranding each of the airports we still own.'

Follow-up questions

1 Before privatisation in 1986, Heathrow airport was part of a nationalised industry. Explain the meaning of privatisation and nationalisation.

2 Outline **two** benefits Heathrow's passengers may now enjoy since the break-up of the monopoly BAA.

The government and monopolies

EXAM TIP

Knowledge of the different policies that governments can use to deal with a monopoly will also be useful in your A2 studies.

In the previous chapter, it was explained how monopoly can be both good and bad. Arguably, by restricting output and choice, and by raising the price, monopoly is bad more often than it is good. However, monopoly can be justified in certain circumstances, especially in the case of natural monopoly where economies of scale can reduce the firm's costs.

For this reason, a government may adopt a 'cost–benefit' approach to monopoly, investigating each case on its merits to see if the advantages of monopoly outweigh the disadvantages. Other approaches to monopoly are possible, however.

- The **compulsory breaking up** of all monopolies, or 'monopoly busting'. Many free-market economists believe that the advantages of a free-market economy, namely economic efficiency and consumer sovereignty, can only be achieved when the economy is fully competitive. Monopoly, as such, is bad, and impossible to justify. On this line of reasoning, the government should follow an automatic policy rule to break up monopolies wherever they are found to exist. UK policy-makers have rarely adopted such a monopoly-busting approach, though powers do exist that allow the government to order the break-up of an established monopoly.

- The use of **price controls** to restrict monopoly abuse. These have been used by the regulatory agencies established by UK governments, to regulate industries that were privatised in the 1980 and 1990s. For example, Ofgem regulates energy industries such as gas and electricity, although price controls have mostly been dropped.

- **Taxing monopoly profits.** As well as controlling prices directly, the government can tax monopoly profit to create an incentive for monopolies to reduce prices and profits. Monopoly taxes have not generally been used in the UK, except on a few occasions when a tax has been imposed on the windfall gain that landlords receive when the land they own is made available for property development, and when windfall profits received by banks from high interest rates have been subject to a special tax.

- **Rate of return regulation.** In the USA, the regulators have imposed maximum rates of return on the capital that the energy companies employ. This is meant to act as a price cap, as the utilities are fined if they set prices too high and earn excessive rates of return. However, in practice, instead of increasing productive efficiency, rate of return regulation often has the opposite effect, having the unintended consequence of encouraging energy companies to raise costs (knowing they are protected by entry barriers), rather than to cut prices to comply with the rate of return regulation.

- **Changing monopoly ownership.** This can work in one of two ways. Either the government can **nationalise** and take into public ownership large firms or whole industries in the private sector of the economy, changing them into state-owned monopolies; or the government can sell back to the private sector, or **privatise**, previously state-owned monopolies. The choice will be explained further in Chapter 14, in the context of government failure.

- **Deregulation and the removal of barriers to entry.** Nevertheless, most economists believe that privatisation alone cannot eliminate the problem of monopoly abuse, since it merely changes the nature of the problem back to private monopoly and the commercial exploitation of a monopoly position. The fact that the privatisation of the telecommunication and gas monopolies was accompanied by the setting up of regulatory bodies (now known as Ofcom and Ofgem) is a recognition of this problem. One method of exposing monopolies — including the privatised utility industries — to increased competition is to use deregulatory policies to remove artificial barriers to entry and also to expose them to international competition.

> **KEY TERMS**
>
> **nationalisation:** the state taking over firms or industries previously in the private sector.
>
> **privatisation:** the state selling nationalised firms or industries to the private sector.

Government policy and the distribution of income and wealth

The UK government has sometimes tried to make the distribution of income and wealth less unequal and arguably more equitable, but not always with success. The main policy that governments use to achieve this end is **fiscal policy**. Fiscal policy is explained in detail in Chapter 24. However, for discussing how economic policy can be used to make the distribution of income and wealth more equal, at this stage just two elements of fiscal policy will be introduced: **progressive taxation** and **government transfers**.

In a progressive tax system, the proportion of a person's income paid in tax increases as income rises, while in a regressive tax system, the proportion paid in tax falls. A tax is proportionate (or a flat tax) if exactly the

> **KEY TERMS**
>
> **fiscal policy:** government policy that uses the fiscal instruments of taxation, government spending and the government's budgetary position to achieve particular policy objectives.
>
> **government transfers:** a payment of money from a government to an individual for which no good or service is given in return.
>
> **progressive taxation:** a progressive tax is where the tax rate increases as income rises. As a result, the rich pay a larger proportion of their income in tax than the poor.

same proportion of income is paid in tax at all levels of income. The word 'progressive' is value-neutral, implying nothing about how the revenue raised by the government is spent. Nevertheless, progressive taxation is used by governments to achieve the social aim of a 'fairer' distribution of income. But progressive taxation cannot by itself redistribute income or wealth. Progressive taxation used on its own merely reduces post-tax income differentials compared to pre-tax income differentials.

For redistribution to take place, transfers in the government's public expenditure programme are required. The government *transfers* income when paying tax revenue collected from certain groups in society to other groups, without the latter producing any goods or services in return. Although transfers are not always directed to the poor and are not always used to reduce income inequalities, usually they are, at least in countries such as the UK. When used in this way, transfers are also called welfare benefits: for example, income support and housing benefit paid to poor families and households in the UK.

SUMMARY

- Governments intervene in the economy to try to correct or reduce market failures.
- Governments often provide public goods directly, arguably because markets fail to supply them.
- Regulation and taxation are used to discourage the production of negative externalities such as pollution, and to discourage production and consumption of demerit goods.
- Governments are now using emissions trading or markets in permits to pollute as an extra approach to the problem of pollution.
- Along with subsidy, regulation is also used to encourage the production of positive externalities such as a beautiful view, and to encourage production and consumption of merit goods.
- UK governments generally use a cost–benefit approach to reduce the problems caused by monopoly, although other methods of intervention can also be used.
- Progressive taxation and transfers are used to make the distribution of income and wealth more equal.

Exam-style questions

1 Explain how subsidies and taxes may be used to promote the consumption of merit goods or deter the consumption of demerit goods. (12 marks)

2 Using the concept of elasticity, explain why taxing demerit goods may be relatively ineffective in reducing their consumption. (12 marks)

3 Evaluate **three** different policies a government might use to deal with the problem of monopoly abuse. (25 marks)

4 Do you agree that governments should use progressive taxation and transfers to the poor to reduce inequalities in the distribution of income and wealth? Justify your answer. (25 marks)

Government price controls and the problem of government failure

This final chapter on markets and market failure continues and completes the coverage of government intervention in markets. The chapter starts by looking at government intervention to influence or indeed to control prices in competitive or relatively competitive markets. The last part of the chapter completes the coverage of Unit 1 specification content by examining the nature of government failures in the economy.

LEARNING OUTCOMES

This chapter will:
- compare price ceilings or maximum price laws with price floors or minimum price laws
- explain how buffer stock intervention attempts to stabilise the prices of agricultural products
- discuss the problems that buffer stock intervention leads to
- relate buffer stock intervention to the European Union's Common Agricultural Policy
- explain the meaning of government failure
- compare government failure with market failure
- introduce the 'law of unintended consequences'
- provide examples of possible government failures

Price ceilings or maximum price laws

Perhaps the simplest ways in which a government can impose a price control is through the use of a price ceiling or a price floor. Suppose, for example, that in a particular market — say, the market for bread — the government imposes a **price ceiling** or **maximum legal price**, shown as P_1 in Figure 14.1. Because the price ceiling has been imposed *below* the free-market equilibrium price of P^*, it creates excess demand, shown by the distance between Q_1 and Q_2. In a free market, market forces would raise the price and eliminate the excess demand. But, because the price ceiling prevents this happening, there is no mechanism in the market for getting rid of excess demand. Rather than **rationing by price**, households are **rationed by quantity**. Queues and waiting lists occur, and possibly bribery and corruption through which favoured customers buy the good, but others do not.

KEY TERM

price ceiling: a price *above* which it is illegal to trade. Price ceilings, or maximum legal prices, can distort markets by creating excess demand.

EXAM TIP

Exam questions often ask for a description and an explanation of ways in which government intervention can affect the price of a good or service.

The emergence of a **secondary market** (sometimes called a black market) is also likely. Secondary markets emerge when primary markets (or free markets) are prevented from working properly. A secondary market is a meeting place for lucky and unlucky customers. In the secondary market, some lucky customers, who bought the good at price P_1, resell at a higher price to unlucky customers unable to purchase the good in the primary market. (Note: later in the chapter, the issue of whether a black market provides an example of government failure will be discussed.)

KEY TERMS

secondary market: a market that comes into existence when the primary market is not allowed to function properly.

price floor: a price *below* which it is illegal to trade. Price floors, or minimum legal prices, can distort markets by creating excess supply.

Price

Supply

Free market price

P^*

Price ceiling
or maximum
legal price

P_1

Excess demand

Demand

O Q_1 Q^* Q_2 Quantity
of good

Lucky   Unlucky
customers   customers

Figure 14.1 The effect of a maximum price law or price ceiling

Price floors or minimum legal prices

Sometimes governments impose **minimum price laws** or **price floors**. For a minimum price law to affect a market, the price floor *must* be set *below* the free-market price. Figure 14.2 illustrates the possible effect of the national minimum wage imposed in UK labour markets. A **national minimum wage rate** set at W_1 (which is *above* the free-market wage rate of W^*) creates an excess supply of labour, thereby causing unemployment equal to the distance between L_1 and L_2. It may also cause rogue employers to break the law: for example, paying 'poverty wages' to vulnerable workers such as illegal immigrants. Note also that whereas a price ceiling imposed *above* the free-market price in Figure 14.1 would have no effect on the price at which bread is traded in the market, a national minimum wage set *below* the free-market wage rate in Figure 14.2 would have no effect on unemployment. This is the situation in many UK labour markets.

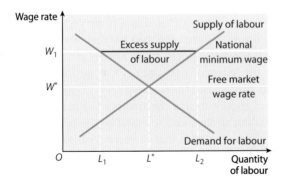

Wage rate

Supply of labour

Excess supply   National
of labour   minimum wage

W_1

Free market
wage rate

W^*

Demand for labour

O L_1 L^* L_2 Quantity
of labour

Figure 14.2 The possible effect of the UK national minimum wage

141

Buffer stock intervention to stabilise agricultural prices

KEY TERM

buffer stock: a store of an agricultural good or primary product which is added to in the event of a surplus and released onto the market in the event of a shortage.

At this point, you should refer back to the reasons given in Chapter 7 to explain why the prices of agricultural goods are often unstable and fluctuate wildly from year to year. To remind you, agricultural prices fluctuate because supply curves shift leftward or rightward in response to factors outside farmers' control: namely, climate, weather and the resulting state of the harvest. This cause of price instability is illustrated in Figure 7.2 in Chapter 7.

EXAM TIP

Unit 1 exam questions often require knowledge and analysis of buffer stock intervention.

Because a completely unregulated free market can lead to price volatility, governments, or their agencies, often intervene in agricultural markets to try to stabilise prices. They believe intervention is in the interest of farmers, or consumers, or possibly both groups.

Agricultural prices are unstable

Buffer stock intervention is one method of stabilising farm prices. Two forms of buffer stock intervention are illustrated in Figures 14.3 and 14.4. The first diagram is similar to Figure 7.2, except that a third supply curve, the 'normal harvest' supply curve, is located mid-way between the 'bad harvest' and the 'good harvest' supply curves. Suppose that the government, or an agency of farmers, decides to stabilise the good's price at the 'normal' year price, P^*. If no intervention takes place, the quantity of the good available on the free market is Q_1 when there is a good harvest. However, the glut of supply means the free-market price has fallen to P_1. But to prevent the price falling so low, and to stabilise the price at P^*, the government buys quantity Q_3 minus Q^*. (Note that farmers wish to supply Q_3 at price P^*, so the difference between Q_3 and Q^* has to be bought by the government and stored as a buffer stock.)

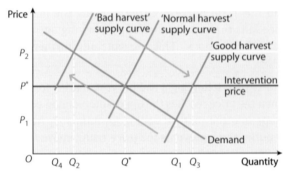

Figure 14.3 Buffer stock intervention to stabilise completely the price of an agricultural commodity

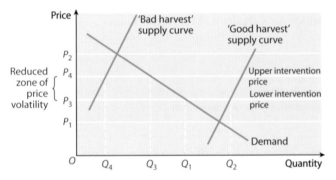

Figure 14.4 A buffer stock policy based on upper and lower intervention prices

Suppose that next year, following a bad harvest, the free-market quantity (assuming there is no intervention) falls to Q_2, with the price rising to P_2. To prevent the price rising above P^*, the government supplements supply by releasing from its buffer stock quantity Q^* minus Q_4. The sale of Q^* minus Q_4 prevents the price rising to P_2, and stabilises the price at P^*. (Note, in this case, Q_4 is the maximum quantity farmers are willing to supply at the intervention price P^*, so quantity equal to Q^* minus Q_4 has to be sold by the government to keep the price at P^*.)

Summarising, the government, or an association of producers, accumulates a buffer stock when the harvest is good and releases this onto the market in the event of a crop failure.

Lower and upper intervention prices

Figure 14.4 illustrates a slightly different form of buffer stock intervention. In this case, rather than completely stabilising the price, support buying and selling *reduces* rather than *eliminates* the fluctuations resulting from free-market forces. Two **intervention prices** are set — a **lower intervention price** at P_3 and an **upper intervention price** at P_4. Following a bumper crop, the supply

KEY TERM

intervention price: a price at which a buffer stock agency starts to buy or sell a good, thereby adding to or depleting the buffer stock.

curve shifts to the 'good harvest' curve, causing the market price to fall toward P_1. As the price falls through P_3, the support-buying agency steps into the market and purchases a buffer stock. This prevents any further fall in the price, which stabilises at P_3.

Suppose that next year, following a bad harvest, market forces cause the price to rise toward P_2. When the price reaches the upper intervention price of P_4, the government once again steps into the market, selling Q_3 minus Q_4 from the buffer stock. The release of the buffer stock prevents the price rising above P_4.

By purchasing a buffer stock when the price falls to the lower intervention price of P_3, and selling from the buffer stock when the price rises to the upper intervention price of P_4, support buying is meant to be self-financing. In theory, costs of management and administration are financed from the margin between the lower and upper intervention prices. In practice, however, buffer stock intervention leads to a number of problems, which are explained in the next section.

EXAM TIP

Exam candidates sometimes confuse the decision to hold back the supply of a good (i.e. a *retention* policy) with *buffer stock* intervention.

Problems resulting from buffer stock policies

Buffer stock policies can cause a number of problems, which harm and can ultimately undermine both the policy and the agricultural economy. The problems include:

- Good and bad harvests may not alternate. A succession of bad harvests could lead to a situation in which the government's buffer stock was exhausted and it could no longer prevent the price from rising.
- However, the opposite problem of over-production is more likely. A succession of good harvests could result in continuous over-production, with the government or support agency accumulating an ever-growing buffer stock.
- As a result, the fund used to finance the purchase of the buffer stock may run out. A few years ago, the tin-producers support-buying scheme collapsed, basically because it ran out of money.
- Suppose farmers stop producing crops which lack government support, and start producing crops which are supported. The supply curve of these crops will shift permanently to the right as more farmers enter the market, leading to permanent over-production.

EXAM TIP

Buffer stock intervention can lead to government failure. It is important to understand the problems that buffer stock intervention causes.

CASE STUDY 14.1

The EU's Common Agricultural Policy (CAP)

Currently the CAP is split into two 'pillars'. Pillar 1, making up about 75% of the UK CAP budget, includes payments made to farmers to support their income — the Single Farm Payment — and payments and policies made to enable farmers to compete in global markets and deal with the unpredictability that comes with free trade in agriculture (e.g. export subsidies that enable EU farmers to export their products at prices below the cost of production). Pillar 2, which makes up about a quarter of the CAP budget across Europe, covers most of the environment and rural development measures.

The EU has recently reformed its support systems so that farm export subsidies are now less likely to distort world markets. At the Doha round of international trade talks, the EU proposed eliminating export subsidies altogether in 2013, as well as significantly reducing import duties on farm produce. The reform is a major rethink of the whole of the CAP.

To find out more about the CAP, read the EU factsheet on the Civitas website (www.civitas.org.uk) and 'Q&A: Reform of EU farm policy' on the BBC News website (www.bbc.co.uk).

Follow-up questions

1 Find out more details of the 2013 CAP reforms and evaluate their success.
2 Find out whether support buying and buffer stock intervention have ever been part of the CAP.

Farm support policies in the UK and the European Union

When the UK joined the EEC (now the European Union (EU)) in 1973, a fundamental change took place in British agricultural policy. UK farmers are relatively high-cost producers when compared to farmers in such countries as the USA, Canada and Australia, but they are efficient within the constraints imposed by the British climate and average farm size. Compared with many European farmers employed on even smaller and less mechanised farms, British farmers are relatively low-cost producers.

Prior to 1973, imports of food were allowed into the UK at the world price and subsidies were paid to British farmers to keep them in business. Thus Britain had a 'cheap food' policy.

By contrast, the EU's **Common Agricultural Policy (CAP)** results in relatively expensive food for consumers. The CAP imposes an **external tariff** or **levy**, which brings some of the prices of imported food up to the level of European costs of production. The levy has increased EU food production, but at the expense of cheap food imports.

An aim of the CAP was to eliminate the food shortages that had occurred in western Europe in the 1940s and 1950s. But the EEC's import controls and payments to Community farmers more than succeeded in this aim. Chronic over-production — the accumulation of wine 'lakes' and butter and wheat 'mountains' — was the result. Over-production still continues, at great expense to EU taxpayers who finance the CAP. Poor developing countries outside the EU also suffer. Many have been denied free access to the rich EU export market, and have suffered from the EU **dumping** (selling at below cost) the surplus production in their markets. Dumping destroys indigenous agriculture in poor countries.

Government failure

When studying market failure, it was assumed that market failure can be reduced or completely eliminated, once identified, through appropriate government intervention: for example, by imposing taxes, controls and regulation. But there is another possibility. When the government intervenes to try to deal with a problem, far from curing or ameliorating it, intervention actually makes matters worse. When this happens, the problem of **government failure** replaces the problem of market failure.

> **KEY TERM**
>
> **government failure:** occurs when government intervention in the economy is ineffective, or wasteful or damaging.

Government failure versus market failure

Students often confuse government failure with market failure, usually by wrongly arguing that a failed or ineffective government policy is an example of market failure. As Chapter 9 explains, market failure occurs when markets perform unsatisfactorily or badly. As noted in the last paragraph, having identified a case of market failure, the government may then intervene to try to reduce or indeed eliminate the market failure.

> **EXAM TIP**
>
> Government failure often results from the failure of interventionist government policies to correct market failure, or when the costs of intervention exceed any benefits.

EXTENSION MATERIAL

Public interest theory versus public choice theory

The rather benign view of the role of government in the economy — centring on the use of public policy to correct market failure wherever it is found to exist — is part of the **public interest theory** of government behaviour. Public interest theory argues that governments intervene in a benevolent fashion in the economy in order to eliminate waste and achieve an efficient and socially desirable resource allocation.

Public interest theory was extremely influential in the UK from the end of the Second World War (in 1945) until around 1979. Interventionist government policies then gave way to a revival in the belief in free-market forces. At that time, the influence of public interest theory gave way to a growing influence of public choice theory. According to **public choice theory**, not only can *market failure* arise in the situations described in Chapter 9; there is also the possibility — perhaps even the likelihood — of government failure occurring whenever the state attempts to improve on the working of the market. As was explained in Chapter 13, pro-free market economists regard a market economy as a calm and orderly place in which the price mechanism, working through the incentives signalled by price changes in competitive markets, achieves a more optimal and efficient outcome than could result from a policy of government intervention.

The 'law of unintended consequences'

This 'law', which has become very fashionable in recent years, predicts that, whenever the government intervenes in the market economy, effects will be unleashed which the policy-makers had not foreseen or intended. Sometimes of course, the unintended effects may be advantageous to the economy, while in other instances, they may be harmful but relatively innocuous. In either of these circumstances, government intervention can be justified on the grounds that the social benefits of intervention exceed the social costs and therefore contribute to a net gain in economic welfare. But if government activity — however well intentioned — triggers harmful consequences which are greater than the benefits that the government intervention is supposed to promote, then government failure results.

Some examples of possible government failure

Black markets

Earlier in the chapter, it was explained how a price ceiling or maximum price law can create excess demand in a market, which is then relieved through trading in a secondary market or **black market**. Price ceilings are normally put in place to protect consumers from high prices. However, the rising price of a product may simply reflect market forces and the changing nature of supply or demand in the market. A higher price might be needed to create incentives for consumers to economise and for firms to divert more scarce resources into producing the good. The price ceiling may prevent this happening. The controlled price can send out the wrong signals and create the wrong incentives, thus contributing to resource misallocation. And since it may be a criminal activity to break the price law, black markets are sometimes characterised by corruption and the threat of the use of illegal force.

EXAM TIP

There are various forms of black markets or secondary markets. One type results from government-imposed price ceilings, a second from under-pricing of tickets for sport and entertainment events, a third from a government-imposed price floor, and a fourth from banning consumption of a demerit good such as a hard drug.

However, economists of a free-market persuasion often justify black markets on the ground that they do the job that the primary market should do: that is, equate demand with supply. A price ceiling prevents the primary or 'over-ground' market from working properly. Arguably, the touts, spivs and dealers who act as middle men in the black market or underground economy contribute to better resource allocation, although their contribution would not be needed if there were no price controls. A black market or secondary market only comes into existence because price controls distort the primary market.

Merit and demerit goods

Various examples of government failure may occur when the state provides merit goods such as education at zero price for the consumer, or taxes or bans production and consumption of demerit goods. When education is provided free by the state, shortages emerge for places in so-called 'good' schools. Parents who are unable to get their children into these schools sometimes lie about where they live, in the hope of winning places in the 'post code lottery' through which the local education authority offers places to the children living nearest to the school.

In the case of demerit goods, the imposition of high taxes on goods such as alcohol and tobacco has encouraged 'booze cruise' trips to France to buy beer, wine, spirits and cigarettes at lower French prices. Not only does this erode the UK government's tax base, it also unnecessarily diverts productive resources into car and van journeys that would not otherwise take place, which in turn leads to unnecessary carbon pollution. And, however worthy it is, banning the production and consumption of demerit goods such as cocaine and heroin creates black markets characterised by crime and racketeering.

CASE STUDY 14.2

The landfill tax and government failure

Government policies that aim to reduce the discharge of negative externalities can also lead to government failure. Almost every economic activity produces waste: for example, household rubbish and the waste created by building and construction. A large fraction of UK waste is either incinerated (which discharges pollutants into the atmosphere) or collected by local government and placed in landfill sites. Landfill also causes pollution, and a further problem arises as all the available landfill sites fill up.

In 1996, the UK government imposed a landfill tax which it hoped would create jobs and reduce waste. But to evade the tax, rogue building contractors and some households began to fly-tip and to dump rubbish in public places and on other people's land. This was an unintended and adverse consequence of a tax that was intended to improve the environment.

The scale of fly-tipping uncovered

Many blame the controversial landfill tax for the rise in organised unauthorised dumping. The tax increased the costs of taking waste to licensed sites by up to a third. The cost of getting rid of one truck-load of rubble could be as high as £400. Finding alternative dumping grounds, where off-loading a lorry costs little or nothing, allows the unscrupulous to make a fortune. But the cost to the environment is immense.

The unintended consequence of the landfill tax

Research published in 2011 by the Countryside Alliance uncovered the enormous scale of illegal fly-tipping in England and Wales. Figures obtained under the Freedom of Information Act reveal that illegal fly-tipping cost taxpayers over £40 million in 2010. At least 656,000 incidents of unlawful rubbish dumping were recorded in England and Wales between April 2010 and March 2011, which works out at 75 incidents of fly-tipping every hour — more than one per minute!

The cost of clearing the waste alone was just under £25 million, yet only one in 50 cases led to a prosecution.

In cash-strapped rural local authorities, the rate of prosecutions dropped to just 3 in every 1000. If waste is dumped on private land, the owners, irrespective of having no part in the fly-tip, have a duty of care and are bound by law to clear it up in their own time and at their expense.

The Chief Executive of the Countryside Alliance said, 'With the Coalition Government raising the landfill tax and with more cuts coming to council budgets, this problem is only going to get worse.'

Follow-up questions

1 Relate fly-tipping to the concept of negative externalities.
2 Do you agree that landfill illustrates both market failure and government failure? Justify your answer.

CASE STUDY 14.3

Progressive taxation – an example of government failure?

Over the last 40 or so years, the distribution of income has become more unequal. Some people believe that this is an example of market failure, but others argue that by causing poverty, government policies to make the distribution more equal lead to government failure. Some people argue that the UK tax system should be made more progressive. However, a counter-argument can be made that, if the rich are taxed more heavily, the incentives to take financial risks and to be entrepreneurial will be weakened. Economic growth then slows down. As a result, the poor end up less unequal (compared to the rich) but also poorer than they would be if greater inequality was allowed to persist.

Does progressive taxation help the poor?

■ **Yes:** progressive taxation helps combat extreme poverty. This is because the lowest zero tax band will apply to earnings beneath an initial threshold. Therefore, the less one earns, the higher the percentage of one's pay that is not taxable. The cost of basic survival needs is by definition a larger proportion of a lower earner's income and therefore a certain 'block' at the bottom of each income may be tax free altogether to allow for these needs. This protection for the poorest is important, because most countries also operate customs tariffs and sales taxes, which tend to hit the poor more than the rich in terms of the proportion of their income going in indirect taxation; progressive direct taxation redresses the balance.

■ **No:** the European experience demonstrates that progressive taxation stifles economic growth. Of course, no one gets hurt more by reduced economic growth than the poor. For the better off, progressive taxation reduces the incentive to work hard. Entrepreneurial flair is discouraged. Why put more effort into work if much of the income received disappears into the government's coffers? And if the tax revenues are used to finance transfers paid to the poor, why bother to work when you can live off the state? Progressive taxation and increased welfare benefits are part of the creeping growth of the state and the spread of a dependency culture and climate of entitlement amongst those who do not work.

Follow-up questions

1 How can progressive taxation help to make the distribution of income more equal?
2 Do you agree that the high salaries paid to company directors and top managers should be reduced? Justify your answer.

Government failure and monopoly

In Chapter 13, it was mentioned that a government could attempt to deal with the problems posed by private monopolies (namely, restricting output and choice and hiking up prices) by nationalising the firm or taking it into public ownership. Some 50 and more years ago, British Labour governments nationalised industries such as coal mining in the belief that monopoly problems only arise when the monopoly is privately owned.

However, opponents of nationalisation argued that state ownership produces particular forms of abuse that would not be experienced if the industries were privately owned. These include a general inefficiency and resistance to change which stem from the belief by workers and management in the state-run monopolies that they will always be baled out by government in the event of a loss.

According to this view, monopoly abuse occurs in nationalised industries, not from the pursuit of private profit, but because the industries are run in the interest of a feather-bedded workforce which is protected from any form of market discipline.

In the 1980s and 1990s, the Conservative governments that were opposed to nationalisation decided to denationalise or privatise previously state-owned industries such as coal, gas and electricity. But because the governments realised that, once back in the private sector, a privatised monopoly might use its market power to raise prices at the expense of consumers, government agencies such as Ofgem were set up to regulate and police the privatised industries.

However, some critics argue that the regulatory agencies have been weak and ineffective, and that they have lacked sufficient knowledge of technical conditions in the industries they regulate to do their job properly.

SUMMARY

- Governments impose price ceilings or maximum legal prices to prevent prices rising above desired levels.
- A price ceiling imposed below the free-market price distorts the market and creates excess demand.
- In this situation, a secondary market or black market is likely to emerge.
- Black markets can perform the useful economic function of dealing with shortages and equating demand with supply.
- Governments impose price floors or minimum legal prices, such as the national minimum wage, to prevent prices falling below desired levels.
- Buffer stock intervention is used to try to stabilise the prices of agricultural goods and primary products.
- Support buying of buffer stocks has been an important part of the EU's Common Agricultural Policy.
- Buffer stock intervention can lead to government failure, generally through the accumulation of unwanted stocks of surplus goods (e.g. butter mountains and wine lakes).
- Government failure occurs when government intervention in markets leads to unsatisfactory or bad results.
- There are many different forms of government failure.

Exam-style questions

1 With the help of an appropriate diagram, explain how a maximum legal price may distort a market. (12 marks)

2 Explain why buffer stock intervention often fails. (12 marks)

3 Do you agree that government intervention in a market to correct a market failure inevitably leads to government failure? Justify your answer. (25 marks)

4 Assess the view that by eroding personal incentives, progressive taxation and transfers to the poor always lead to government failure. (25 marks)

Unit 1 key terms

ad valorem **tax:** a percentage expenditure tax such as VAT.

average cost: the cost per unit of output; also called **unit cost**.

buffer stock: a store of an agricultural good or primary product which is added to in the event of a surplus and released onto the market in the event of a shortage.

competitive market: a market in which the large number of buyers and sellers possess good market information and easily enter or leave the market.

condition of demand: a determinant of demand, other than the good's own price, that fixes the position of the demand curve.

condition of supply: a determinant of supply, other than the good's own price, that fixes the position of the supply curve.

cross-elasticity of demand: the proportionate change in demand for a good following an initial proportionate change in price of another good.

decrease in demand: a leftward shift of the demand curve.

decrease in supply: a leftward shift of the supply curve.

demand: the quantity of a good or service that consumers are willing and able to buy at given prices in a given period of time. For economists, demand is always **effective demand**.

demerit good: a good, such as tobacco, for which the social costs of consumption exceed the private costs.

diseconomy of scale: rising average or unit cost as a firm increases its size or scale.

division of labour: this concept goes hand in hand with specialisation. Different workers perform different tasks in the course of producing a good or service. Different workers may also produce different goods or services.

economy of scale: falling average or unit costs as a firm increases its size or scale.

effective demand: the desire for a good or service backed by an ability to pay.

elasticity: the proportionate responsiveness of a second variable to an initial proportionate change in the first variable.

emissions trading: emissions trading systems allow policy-makers to set a pollution target, and then issue tradable permits corresponding to that amount. Companies that wish to pollute must hold permits equal to their emissions.

equilibrium: a state of rest or balance between opposing forces.

equity: fairness or justness.

excess demand: when consumers wish to buy more than firms wish to sell, with the price below the equilibrium price.

excess supply: when firms wish to sell more than consumers wish to buy, with the price above the equilibrium price.

exchange: specialisation and the division of labour mean that goods and services must be exchanged for each other. Money and the use of barter are mediums of exchange.

expenditure tax: a tax levied by the government on spending by consumers. The firms selling the good pay the tax to the government, but consumers indirectly pay via the resulting price rise.

externality: a public good, in the case of an external benefit, or a public bad, in the case of an external cost, that is 'dumped' on third parties outside the market.

finite resource: a resource, such as oil, which is scarce and runs out as it is used.

fiscal policy: government policy that uses the fiscal instruments of taxation, government spending and the government's budgetary position to achieve particular policy objectives.

free-rider: somebody who benefits from a good or service without paying for it.

good: a good yields utility, unlike a 'bad', which yields disutility.

government failure: occurs when government intervention in the economy is ineffective, or wasteful or damaging.

government transfers: a payment of money from a government to an individual for which no good or service is given in return.

immobility of labour: the inability of labour to move from one job to another, either for occupational reasons (e.g. the need for training) or for geographical reasons (e.g. the cost of moving to another part of the country).

incentive function: prices create incentives for consumers and firms to behave in certain ways.

income: a flow of money received (e.g. as a wage) from supplying labour.

income elasticity of demand: the proportionate change in demand for a good following an initial proportionate change in consumers' income.

increase in demand: a rightward shift of the demand curve.

increase in supply: a rightward shift of the supply curve.

inferior good: a good for which demand decreases as income rises.

information problem: this occurs when people make wrong decisions because they don't possess or they ignore relevant information. Very often they are *myopic* (short-sighted) about the future.

intervention price: a price at which a buffer stock agency starts to buy or sell a good, thereby adding to or depleting the buffer stock.

margin: refers to the last unit undertaken of an activity.

marginal benefit: the benefit resulting from the last unit of a good.

marginal cost: the cost of the last unit of a good.

market demand: the quantity of a good or service that all the consumers in a market are willing and able to buy.

market disequilibrium: when the market fails to clear. The market plans of consumers and firms are inconsistent with each other.

market equilibrium: when planned demand equals planned supply in the market.

market failure: a market completely failing to provide a good or service, or providing the wrong quantity (i.e. a quantity that leads to a misallocation of resources in the economy).

market supply: the quantity of a good or service that all the firms in a market are willing to sell.

merit good: a good, such as healthcare, for which the social benefits of consumption exceed the private benefits.

monopoly: a market dominated by one firm.

nationalisation: the state taking over firms or industries previously in the private sector.

natural monopoly: a market in which there is only room for one firm benefiting to the full from economies of scale.

normal good: a good for which demand increases as income rises.

normative statement: a statement of opinion based on a value judgement.

positive statement: a statement of fact, or one that can be scientifically tested.

price ceiling: a price *above* which it is illegal to trade. Price ceilings, or maximum legal prices, can distort markets by creating excess demand.

price elasticity of demand: the proportionate change in demand for a good following an initial proportionate change in the good's own price.

price elasticity of supply: the proportionate change in supply of a good following an initial proportionate change in the good's own price.

price floor: a price *below* which it is illegal to trade. Price floors, or minimum legal prices, can distort markets by creating excess supply.

private benefit maximisation: occurs when $MPC = MPB$.

private good: a good, such as an orange, that is excludable and rival.

privatisation: the state selling nationalised firms or industries to the private sector.

production: converts inputs or factor services into outputs of goods.

productive efficiency: occurs when a firm minimises average costs and produces at the lowest point on its average cost curve.

productive efficiency (for the whole economy): the whole economy is productively efficient when producing on its production possibility frontier.

productivity: output per unit of input (e.g. labour productivity is output per worker).

profit: the difference between total sales revenue and total costs of production.

progressive taxation: a progressive tax is where the tax rate increases as income rises. As a result, the rich pay a larger proportion of their income in tax than the poor.

public good: a good, such as a radio programme, that is non-excludable and non-rival.

pure monopoly: one firm only in a market.

rationing or **allocative function:** prices allocate scarce resources between competing uses.

regulation: involves the imposition of rules, controls and constraints, which restrict freedom of economic action in the market place.

renewable resource: a resource, such as timber, that with careful management can be renewed as it is used.

secondary market: a market that comes into existence when the primary market is not allowed to function properly.

signalling function: prices provide information to buyers and sellers.

social benefit: the total benefit of an activity, including the external benefit as well as the private benefit.

social benefit maximisation: occurs when *MSC* = *MSB*.

social cost: the total cost of an activity, including the external cost as well as the private cost.

specialisation: a worker only performing one task or a narrow range of tasks.

speculation: occurs when people buy or sell a good or service because they believe the price is going to rise or fall in the future. Successful speculation means people benefit from capital gains or avoid capital losses.

subsidy: a payment made by government, usually to producers, for each unit of the subsidised good that they produce. Consumers can also be subsidised: for example, bus passes given to children to enable them to travel on buses free or at a reduced price.

supply: the quantity of a good or service that firms plan to sell at given prices in a given period of time.

taxation: a tax is a compulsory levy imposed by the government or some other authority to pay for its activities. Taxes can be used to achieve other objectives, such as reduced consumption of demerit goods.

unit tax or **specific tax:** a tax levied on a unit of a good, irrespective of the good's price.

utility industry: an industry, such as the post, which delivers its service to millions of separate customers.

wealth: a stock of assets that a person or firm owns.

welfare benefits: transfers of money by the government to people in low income groups or with special needs (e.g. disabled people).

Unit 2

The national economy

Chapter 15

Introducing macroeconomics

This is the first chapter covering the macroeconomic topics in Unit 2. It is important to note that examination questions may be set on the national economies of countries other than the UK. For example, in past examinations, questions have required analysis of the French and Irish economies. On some occasions, questions have asked for a comparison of numerical data taken from a range of industrialised countries, such as European Union (EU) countries, Japan and the USA.

For the most part, however, questions are likely to be on the UK economy. If a question is set on a non-UK economy, the data in the question will provide all the necessary information about that economy.

Data-response questions usually test the skills of application, analysis and evaluation, rather than just the display of knowledge. Nevertheless, some knowledge of events that have taken place in the UK economy over the decade or so before your examination is required. Knowledge of the structure of overseas economies is not generally expected. However, the Unit 2 specification does require awareness of the fact that UK economic performance is influenced by the country's membership of the EU, and by external events in the international economy.

EXAM TIP

The Unit 2 specification states that 'Candidates should have a good knowledge of developments in the UK economy over the past 10 years.'

LEARNING OUTCOMES

This chapter will:
- review the difference between microeconomics and macroeconomics
- introduce different macroeconomic 'schools of thought', such as free-market economics and Keynesianism
- explain how the influences of free-market economics and Keynesian economics have changed over time
- introduce the main topics covered in the rest of the unit

The difference between microeconomics and macroeconomics

In Chapter 1, the difference between **microeconomics** and **macroeconomics** was briefly explained. This chapter revisits the difference, but approaches it in a different way. My starting point is three light bulb jokes about economists. The first joke highlights a key difference between microeconomics and macroeconomics, while the others introduce two opposing schools of thought, each with a very different view on how the macroeconomy functions. The first, and older, school is the free-market or neoclassical school. Free-market economists believe that economic problems can and should largely be solved at the microeconomic level and that government intervention in markets is generally not necessary. The second school is the Keynesian school, named after the economist John Maynard Keynes, who more or less invented **macroeconomics**. Keynesian economists often justify government intervention in the economy to achieve the government's macroeconomic objectives.

> **KEY TERM**
>
> **macroeconomics:** involves the study of the whole economy at the aggregate level.

> **EXAM TIP**
>
> At this stage, you should go back to Chapter 1 and re-read the brief explanation of the difference between microeconomics and macroeconomics, as well as the section on shifts of demand and the extension material in Chapter 3, where *ceteris paribus* is explained.

Joke 1

Question: How many economists does it take to change a light bulb?
Answer: Eight. One to screw it in and seven to hold everything else constant.

Joke 2

Question: How many free-market economists does it take to change a light bulb?
Answer: None. The invisible hand does it.

Joke 3

Question: How many Keynesian economists does it take to change a light bulb?
Answer: All of them. Changing the light bulb will generate employment, which will increase consumption, which will increase the demand for light bulbs, which will increase the need to change light bulbs...

> **KEY TERM**
>
> *ceteris paribus:* holding all other factors in the economy constant when examining one part of the economy. It is an important assumption in microeconomics, but not generally in macroeconomics.

So what message am I trying to convey with these light bulb jokes? The first joke reminds us of the *ceteris paribus* assumption, important to much of what we study in microeconomics.

By contrast, macroeconomics looks at the *whole economy*, or the economy *in aggregate*. This means that the *ceteris paribus* assumption seldom holds. For example, if wages are cut in large parts of the economy, we cannot assume there will be no effect on total spending or aggregate demand in the economy.

The second and third jokes relate to the two schools of economic thought introduced above. To understand macroeconomics with any degree of sophistication, it is important to appreciate how economists from different schools have held very different views on macroeconomic problems and on the type of government policy needed to reduce or solve the problems.

At the macroeconomic level, economists divide into **free-market** and **Keynesian economists**. Free-market economists generally believe that the economy is self-adjusting, with the market mechanism automatically

> **KEY TERMS**
>
> **free-market economists:** also known as neoclassical economists.
>
> **Keynesian economists:** followers of the economist John Maynard Keynes.

bringing about full employment and economic growth — providing that, at the microeconomic level, markets are allowed to function freely and are sufficiently competitive. Hence, the message conveyed by the second light bulb joke is that decentralised decision making and the market's *'invisible hand'* can achieve optimal resource allocation in a competitive market economy, without the need for government intervention in the economy.

The third light bulb joke, by contrast, gets to the heart of what Keynesian economics is all about. As I explain below, Keynes believed that in a modern economy, people may save too much and spend too little of their incomes. This means unemployment persists in the economy as long as people continue to spend too little.

Keynes's approach to the cause of large-scale persistent unemployment is illustrated in Figure 15.1. Keynes believed that too little spending and too much saving mean the economy produces at a point such as X, which lies inside the economy's production possibility frontier. By contrast, free-market economists (as illustrated in the second light bulb joke) believe that in competitive markets, the market mechanism automatically ensures the economy is on its production possibility frontier, producing at a point such as A or B. According to the free-market view, competitive market forces bring about full employment equilibrium in the economy (which occurs *on* the production possibility frontier). By contrast, Keynes argued that too little spending in the economy can result in an under-full employment equilibrium, at a point *inside* the production possibility frontier such as X.

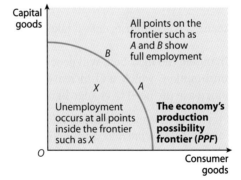

Figure 15.1 Using a production possibility curve diagram to show full employment and unemployment in the economy

Hence the Keynesian message in the third joke: if everybody (including Keynesian economists) were to change light bulbs, spending would increase in the economy (because new replacement bulbs have to be produced and then bought). The initial increase in spending would generate further increases, and so on until full employment is reached.

Don't worry too much if, on first reading, a lot of the information above seems difficult to understand. It has introduced the theme of competing schools of economic thought, which will now be put into a historical context, and will be returned to in some of the remaining chapters of this book. I hope when you re-read the commentary on the three light bulb jokes above, after you have completed the macroeconomic part of your course and just before the Unit 2 examination, the message will be clear.

Free-market and Keynesian economics and the history of macroeconomics

The interwar years and the Great Depression of the 1930s

To understand modern macroeconomics, we have to go back to the 1920s and 1930s, when the word 'macroeconomics' hardly existed. Economics was dominated by the free-market or neoclassical orthodoxy mentioned in the previous section. Free-market economists at this time believed that, in a competitive market economy, market forces would automatically deliver full employment and economic growth.

The problem was, however, that in the UK economy in the 1920s, and in the wider world economy (especially the USA) in the 1930s, free-market forces did *not* deliver full employment and economic growth. Instead, unregulated market forces produced economic stagnation and mass unemployment. The seminal event of the time was the **Great Depression**, which began around 1930 and lasted for several years. During the Great Depression, unemployment rose in 1933 to almost 25% in the USA, and in 1931 to 24% in the UK. Regional unemployment in towns such as Jarrow in northeast England rose to as high as 70%, although London, the southeast and the midlands fared much better.

Free-market economists responded to the Great Depression by arguing that markets were not to blame for persistent large-scale unemployment. Instead, they said that mass unemployment was caused by institutional and governmental factors that prevented markets from operating freely. In particular, they blamed trade unions for using monopoly power to prevent the wage cuts deemed necessary to price the unemployed into jobs.

In the 1920s and 1930s, free-market economists believed that persistent mass unemployment was caused by wage rates being too high. This explanation is illustrated in Figure 15.2, which shows the economy's aggregate labour market. The aggregate demand curve for labour (labelled AD_L) in Figure 15.2 shows how many workers all the employers in the economy are willing to hire at different real wage rates. Likewise, the aggregate supply curve of labour (labelled AS_L) shows how much labour all the economy's workers are willing to supply at different real wage rates.

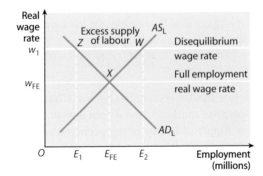

Figure 15.2 The free-market explanation of large-scale unemployment

CASE STUDY 15.1

The Great Depression in the 1930s

These days, a recession is defined in the UK (though not in the USA) as a fall in national output which lasts for at least 6 months. However, a depression (or slump) is a vaguer term, best thought of as a very deep and long recession. (According to an old joke, a downturn is when your neighbour loses his job, a recession is when you lose your own job, and a depression is when economists lose their jobs!)

The 1920s was a period of growing national prosperity in the USA. Nevertheless, the Great Depression, when it arrived in 1929–30, was steeper and more protracted in the USA than in other industrial countries. The US unemployment rate rose higher and remained higher longer than in any other Western country. US gross national product (GNP) fell by 9.4% in 1930 and the US unemployment rate climbed from 3.2% to 8.7%. In 1931, US GNP fell by another 8.5% and unemployment rose to 15.9%. But 1932 and 1933 were the worst years of the Great Depression. By 1932, GNP had fallen in the USA by 31% since 1929 and over 13 million Americans had lost their jobs. The US economy began the first stage of a long recovery in 1934: GNP rose by 7.7% and unemployment fell to 21.7%.

A soup kitchen in Chicago during the Great Depression

Follow-up questions

1 Find out how a recession is defined in the USA. See the article 'Economists who make the recession call' by Stephen Foley, 8 January 2008, www.independent.co.uk.
2 Research whether the UK economy entered the third 'dip' of a 'triple-dip' recession in 2013.

To repeat, in the 1920s, free-market economists believed that, provided labour markets were sufficiently competitive, market forces would deliver full employment through eliminating any excess supply of labour in the economy's aggregate labour market. Once the market-clearing wage of W_{FE} was achieved, full employment would occur at E_{FE}. At W_{FE}, the number of workers firms wished to hire exactly equals the number of workers who wished to work. The aggregate labour market would be in equilibrium: there would be no excess supply of labour, and hence no unemployment.

Suppose, however, that trade unions had restricted the supply of labour in order to fix the real wage rage at W_1, which was higher than W_{FE}. In this situation, E_2 workers wished to work, but there were only jobs available for E_1. As previously mentioned, free-market economists believed that if wage rates could be cut, the unemployed would be priced into jobs. However, labour market imperfections, notably the monopoly power of trade unions, prevented this from happening. In modern parlance, **wage rates were inflexible**, or **'sticky' downwards**. Thus, in the 1920s and 1930s, free-market economists believed that trade unions and excessive and inflexible wage rates were perhaps the most important cause of mass unemployment, and governments were not to blame for unemployment or for the Great Depression.

Keynes's explanation of mass unemployment and the Great Depression

In the late 1920s, John Maynard Keynes, who started his academic career as a free-market economist, began to change his view on the main cause of unemployment. In response to an accusation of inconsistency, Keynes is reported to have said, 'When the facts change, I change my mind — what do you do, sir?'

Whereas Keynes's predecessors explained large-scale mass unemployment and economic stagnation from the point of view of 'don't blame markets or the government for unemployment, blame trade unions', Keynes came to believe that 'if orthodox economic theory is inadequate, a better and more general theory is needed to explain mass unemployment'. Keynes completed his new theory in 1936 with the publication of *The General Theory of Employment, Interest and Money*, commonly referred to as Keynes's *General Theory*.

Keynes's *General Theory* marks the beginning of modern macroeconomics. For over a generation, until approximately 1979, 'Keynesian economics was macroeconomics' and 'macroeconomics was Keynesian economics'. In the years after the Second World War, **Keynesianism** became the new economic orthodoxy.

To capture the flavour of Keynes's view on how the economy works, read Case Study 15.2, which is adapted from a radio talk given by Keynes in 1934, entitled 'Poverty in Plenty'.

CASE STUDY 15.2

Keynes on 'Poverty in Plenty'

In 1934, in the depth of the Great Depression, and 2 years before he published his *General Theory*, John Maynard Keynes gave a radio talk in which he expressed his view on the causes of unemployment. Keynes's talk was one of a series, entitled 'Poverty in Plenty', in which a number of economists and public figures gave their views on the title theme. At this time, the UK unemployment rate was 16.7%. Keynes started by summarising the common ground between himself and the other contributors. He then outlined what he saw as the main difference between the various contributors, before arguing that, in his view, the economic system was not self-adjusting.

Is the economic system self-adjusting?

We must not regard the conditions of supply, our ability to produce, as the fundamental source of our troubles. It is the conditions of demand which our diagnosis must search and probe for explanation. All the contributors to these talks meet to this extent on common ground. But every one of us has a somewhat different explanation of what is wrong with demand, and, consequently, a different idea of the right remedy.

Though we all start out in the same direction, we soon part company into two main groups. On one side are those who believe that the existing economic system is, in the long run, a self-adjusting system, though with creaks and groans and jerks, and interrupted by time lags, outside interference and mistakes.

On the other side of the gulf are those who reject the idea that the existing economic system is, in any significant sense, self-adjusting. They believe that the failure of effective demand to reach the full potential of supply, in spite of human psychological demand being far from satisfied for the vast majority of individuals, is due to much more fundamental causes.

The strength of the self-adjusting school depends on it having behind it almost the whole body of organised economic thinking and doctrine of the last hundred years. Now, I range myself with the heretics on the other side of the gulf. There is, I am convinced, a fatal flaw in that part of the orthodox reasoning which deals with the theory of what determines the level of effective demand and the volume of aggregate employment. The system is not self-adjusting, and, without purposive direction, it is incapable of translating our actual poverty into our potential plenty.

Follow-up questions

1 What is meant by 'effective aggregate demand'?
2 Suggest why there may be too little effective aggregate demand in an economy.

Macroeconomics in the Keynesian era

The **Keynesian era** extended from the late 1940s and early 1950s to the late 1970s. During these decades, governments in the UK, the Netherlands and Scandinavia implemented Keynesian economic policies. Economic policy in the USA also eventually became Keynesian, with the Republican president, Richard Nixon, famously stating in 1971 that 'we are all Keynesians now'. As mentioned previously, the **Keynesian revolution** of the 1930s led to Keynesianism becoming the new orthodoxy, replacing the free-market economics of earlier years.

The Keynesian era covered the decades after Keynes's death in 1946, when economists and politicians who claimed to have inherited the mantle of the now-deceased British economist implemented policies they believed he would have supported.

Much more will be explained about Keynesian economics in the next few chapters. For the moment, at the risk of gross oversimplification, we will say that Keynesian economic policy centred on **managing the level of aggregate demand** in the economy, in order to prevent large-scale unemployment and inflation (a rising price level). For more than two decades after the late 1940s, UK governments used **fiscal policy** and sometimes **monetary policy** to increase aggregate demand. They did this to get rid of **demand-deficient unemployment**

> **KEY TERMS**
>
> **fiscal policy:** involves the use of taxation, public spending and the government's budgetary position to achieve the government's policy objectives.
>
> **monetary policy:** involves the use of interest rates to achieve the government's policy objectives.

(or **cyclical unemployment**), the type of unemployment that Keynes identified at the time of the Great Depression. Sometimes, however, expansionary policies created too much demand, which led to inflation. This meant the government had to reduce aggregate demand to relieve inflationary pressures in the economy.

The free-market counter-revolution

An economic orthodoxy can remain dominant and resistant to being replaced, as long as its theories appear to explain how the economy operates or functions, and as long as the policies based on those theories appear to work. If its theories fail to explain adequately the events taking place in the real economy, and if the policies based on those theories are ineffective or don't work at all, the orthodoxy becomes extremely vulnerable to attack.

This happened in the 1930s when free-market economics gave way to the Keynesian revolution. After the Second World War, Keynesianism dominated as long as Keynesian demand-management policies delivered full employment and economic growth, combined with a relatively stable price level. In the 1970s, the same fate befell Keynesian economics as had afflicted free-market economics 40 years earlier. As will be explained in the next chapter, in the 1970s there was simultaneous failure to achieve any of the standard objectives of macroeconomic policy, such as full employment and control of inflation. The 1970s became the decade of the **crisis in Keynesian economics**.

Perhaps not surprisingly, therefore, the failure of Keynesianism led to the **free-market counter-revolution**, or revival. In the 1970s and 1980s, an important part of the free-market revival was known as **monetarism**. Monetarists believe that inflation (or a rising price level) is caused by a prior increase in the money supply. It follows that if a government wishes to control inflation, it must first control the rate of growth of the money supply. In the **monetarist era**, monetary policy was elevated to become the main plank of macroeconomic policy. However, monetary policy was used not to manage aggregate demand (demand management was disparaged by the monetarists), but solely to control the rate of growth of the money supply, and thence the rate of inflation.

KEY TERM

monetarism: the belief that, as inflation is assumed to be caused by excessive growth of the money supply, monetary policy should be used to control its growth.

CASE STUDY 15.3

The following extract, adapted from a 1977 newspaper editorial, shows vividly how monetarism and free-market economics were replacing Keynesianism as the dominant economic orthodoxy in the 1970s and 1980s.

We are all monetarists now

From time to time a revolution in political ideas takes place. The trouble is that the process is so slow and so subtle that hardly anybody notices until it has happened. But if you can spot the thing immediately, it is worth noting and discussing. In the end, the country, indeed the world, is governed by ideas and hardly anything else.

In the management of the British economy for the last 20 years or so, the prevailing idea has been a doctrine called 'Keynesianism'. Most of us get a bit impatient when people start going on about various 'isms', but this particular one matters to you. If you have the misfortune to be out of work, if you are a housewife appalled by the constantly rising cost of living, or if you are angry when you look at your wage-packet or salary cheque and see how much has gone in tax, then you ought to know that all this is a product, not of chance or of the stars, but of an idea.

The big-spending, high-taxing governments we have had have largely created the inflation, unemployment and falling living standards that you now suffer. They did this because they thought Keynes was the 'Great Economist', and this was what he advised. Through unpleasant experience, Keynesianism has now been discredited and we are back to the old system of controlling the money supply, trying to hold back public spending and balancing the budget.

Follow-up questions

1 What is monetarism?

2 Why do monetarists believe that it is necessary to control the growth of the money supply?

Supply-side economics

To begin with, monetarism was perhaps the most important part of the free-market revival. However, the UK government largely abandoned monetarist policies in 1985, on the ground that they hadn't worked. The relationship between the growth of the money supply and the subsequent rise of the price level, which had appeared to be *stable* before monetarist policies were implemented, broke down *after* the UK government attempted to tightly control the growth of the money supply. On 18 October 1985, the *Financial Times* ran the headline 'Monetarism is dead — official' in response to the UK government's admission that targeting the money supply would no longer be practised in any meaningful way.

> **KEY TERM**
>
> **supply-side economics:** a branch of free-market economics arguing that government policy should be used to improve the competitiveness and efficiency of markets.

However, monetarism's alleged 'death' did not mean that free-market economists immediately reverted to Keynesianism. Instead, free-market theories continued to dominate the macroeconomic agenda, but were now rebranded as **supply-side theory**. These days, Keynesian demand-management policies are often called **demand-side policies**, to separate them from the **supply-side policies** advocated by free-market economists. Supply-side policies aim to improve national economic performance by creating competitive and more efficient markets. Arguably, for this reason, supply-side policies are more microeconomic than macroeconomic. Indeed, in the early days of supply-side economics, the UK government argued that a redefinition was needed of the respective roles of macroeconomic and microeconomic policies. The government argued that macro policy should be restricted to the limited role of controlling inflation, while micro policy would be used to promote growth and employment. This would be the new orthodoxy.

Where are we now?

From 2003 until 2008, when the UK enjoyed continuous economic growth, conflicts between free-market and Keynesian economists to some extent disappeared, or at least were downplayed. Members of both schools agreed about the importance of supply-side economics and the need at the macro level to control inflation — a need that to some extent was ignored during the Keynesian era. In the other direction, many free-market economists accepted the Keynesian argument that governments should manage the level of aggregate demand, but using monetary policy and not fiscal policy. Interest rates, the main instrument of modern monetary policy, were raised or lowered to try to achieve the inflation rate objective set by the government. Aggregate demand was allowed to expand (via monetary policy) so that there was just sufficient demand in the economy to absorb the extra output that successful supply-side policies enabled the economy to produce. During these years, demand-side policies were used to supplement supply-side policies.

In the 2 years following the onset of recession in 2008, in a period called the **fiscal stimulus**, there was a temporary revival in using Keynesian fiscal policy to manage aggregate demand. However, change of government in 2010 and the emergence of a completely new **sovereign debt** problem meant that the fiscal stimulus was quickly abandoned. In 2013, the UK is experiencing the opposite policy of **fiscal austerity** (**fiscal consolidation** or **fiscal restraint**). Instead of being increased or lowered, the Bank of England's interest rate (**Bank Rate**) has been kept at 0.5%, and at the time of writing (June 2013), there is some talk of replacing the monetary policy framework based on targeting a 2% inflation target with a completely new type of monetary policy. In a new monetary policy, economic growth and employment rather than inflation may be targeted.

> **KEY TERM**
>
> **sovereign debt:** the stock of accumulated government borrowing, often called the 'national debt'.

SUMMARY

- Modern macroeconomics came into existence between the two world wars.
- Free-market economists generally believe that, at the macro level, the economy is self-regulating or self-adjusting.
- John Maynard Keynes disputed this view.
- Keynes believed that an unregulated market economy can settle into an under-full employment equilibrium.
- Keynes also believed that large-scale unemployment is caused by deficient aggregate demand.
- The Keynesian revolution in the 1930s led to the Keynesian era in the post-Second World War years.
- The crisis in Keynesian economics in the 1970s led to the free-market counter-revolution in the next decade.
- Monetarism was an early feature of the renewed dominance of free-market economics.
- The decline of monetarism was followed by the growth of supply-side economics.
- After 1992, monetary policy was used to manage aggregate demand, with fiscal policy subordinated to monetary policy and primarily used as a supply-side policy.
- Despite a short-lived revival of demand-side fiscal policy from 2008 to 2010, monetary policy remains central to UK macroeconomic policy.

Exam-style questions

1 With the help of a production possibility diagram, explain one cause of unemployment.   (12 marks)

2 Explain how monetary policy is currently implemented in the UK.   (12 marks)

3 A few years ago a British chancellor of the exchequer claimed that his policies had eliminated the problem
of 'boom and bust' in the UK. Assess the extent to which this was true.   (25 marks)

4 'Mass unemployment and recessions are perhaps the most significant of all market failures.'
'Governments and not markets are responsible for mass unemployment and recessions.'
Evaluate these two statements.   (25 marks)

The objectives and instruments of macroeconomic policy

Chapter 16

A fruitful way of developing an understanding of how government activity affects the economy at the aggregate level is to approach the macroeconomic role of the government by distinguishing between macroeconomic policy objectives, policy instruments and policy indicators. This chapter provides an overview of what these concepts mean and the linkages between them. Later chapters will examine particular policy objectives such as full employment, economic growth and control of inflation, and the three main groups of policy instrument: monetary policy, fiscal policy and supply-side policy.

EXAM TIP

Examination questions are often set on particular policy objectives or policy instruments.

LEARNING OUTCOMES

This chapter will:
- distinguish between policy objectives and policy instruments
- outline the five main objectives of macroeconomic policy
- explain how the ranking of the policy objectives has changed over time
- discuss policy trade-offs and conflicts
- briefly explain each of the five main policy objectives
- explain how a 'policy indicator' differs from policy objectives and instruments

Policy objectives versus policy instruments

A **policy objective** is a target or goal that a government wishes to achieve or 'hit'. By contrast, a **policy instrument** is a tool, or set of tools, that the government uses to try to hit one or more of the government's policy objectives.

There are three main sets of policy instruments that UK governments have used in recent years to try to achieve their policy objectives: **monetary policy**, **fiscal policy** and **supply-side policy**. The rate of interest (the cost of borrowing money and the reward for lending money) is the main monetary policy instrument. Taxes, levels of government spending and the government's budgetary position are fiscal policy instruments. Supply-side policy instruments, which are often microeconomic rather than macroeconomic, centre on the methods the government uses to try to make individual markets and industries more competitive and efficient.

Since 1997, monetary policy has been implemented by the UK government's agent, the **Bank of England**, rather than by the government itself. The government sets the policy objective (currently in 2013, control of inflation) that the Bank of England has to

KEY TERMS

policy instrument: a tool or set of tools used to try to achieve a policy objective.

policy objective: a target or goal that policy-makers aim to 'hit'.

try to achieve. Fiscal policy is implemented by the government, through the government's finance ministry, the **Treasury**. The chancellor of the exchequer, who heads the Treasury, is the government minister who implements fiscal policy. These days, much of fiscal policy is an important part of supply-side policy. Supply-side policies are implemented by a number of government ministries or departments, the main one being the **Department for Business, Innovation and Skills**.

To find out more about the various policy instruments that the UK government uses to try to achieve its policy objectives, refer to Chapters 23 to 25.

A policy objective is a target or goal

The five main macroeconomic policy objectives

Since the Second World War, governments in mixed economies such as the UK have faced the same broad range of objectives. These are:

- to create and maintain full **employment** or low unemployment
- to achieve **economic growth** and improved living standards and levels of economic welfare
- to achieve an acceptable or **fair distribution of income and wealth** between regions and different income groups in society
- to limit or control **inflation**, or to achieve some measure of price stability
- to attain a satisfactory **balance of payments**, usually defined as the avoidance of an external deficit which might create an exchange rate crisis

EXAM TIP

Examiners may expect you to appreciate how Keynesian and free-market economists rank policy objectives in different ways.

Keynesian economists also tend to be interventionist, whereas free-market economists are non-interventionist, wishing to minimise government intervention in the economy.

How the ranking of the policy objectives has changed over time

The order in which the five main objectives of macroeconomic policy are listed above shows a broadly Keynesian ranking of priorities. Before the free-market counter-revolution in macroeconomics, Keynesian economists believed that economic policy should be used to achieve full employment, economic growth and a generally acceptable or fair distribution of income and wealth. For Keynesians, these were the prime policy objectives, which had to be achieved in order to increase human happiness and economic welfare — the ultimate policy objective. Keynesians regarded the fourth and fifth objectives as intermediate objectives or possibly constraints, in the sense that an unsatisfactory performance in controlling inflation or the balance of payments could prevent the attainment of full employment, growth and a satisfactory income distribution.

In the early 1980s, things changed. At the time, and partly in response to the fact that inflation had threatened to escalate out of control, free-market economists placed control of inflation in pole position, relegating full employment to a much lower economic priority. This was the era of monetarism, the period of a few years when UK macroeconomic policy revolved around controlling the growth of the money supply in order to control inflation.

Although monetarist policies lasted for only a few years, since the 'death of monetarism' in the mid-1980s, UK governments have continued to give much more attention to the need to control inflation than was the case in the Keynesian era. Indeed, in 1993, the Conservative chancellor Norman Lamont stated that high unemployment was a 'price well worth paying' for keeping inflation under control. This view was echoed in 1998 when, under a Labour government, the Governor of the Bank of England argued that 'job losses in the north were an acceptable price to pay for curbing inflation in the south'. However, free-market economists argue that, in order to maintain a high and sustainable level of employment, inflation must first be brought under control.

Trade-offs and policy conflicts

Economists often argue that it is difficult, if not impossible, to 'hit' all five macroeconomic objectives at the same time. Believing they can't achieve the impossible, policy makers often settle for the lesser goal of **'trading off' between policy objectives**. A trade-off exists when two or more desirable objectives are mutually exclusive. Because the government thinks it cannot achieve, for example, full employment and zero inflation, it aims for *less than full* employment combined with an *acceptably low* and sustainable rate of inflation.

In the Keynesian era, UK macro-policy was influenced and constrained by four significant **conflicts** between policy objectives. Governments often tried to resolve these conflicts by trading off between the competing policy objectives. The main conflicts were as follows:

- Between internal policy objectives of full employment and growth and the external objective of achieving a satisfactory balance of payments (or possibly supporting a particular exchange rate).

full employment and economic growth ← policy conflict and trade-off → satisfactory balance of payments or exchange rate

- Between achieving full employment and controlling inflation (this is the Phillips curve trade-off, which you will study at A2).

full employment and economic growth ← policy conflict and trade-off → control of inflation

- Between increasing the rate of economic growth and achieving a more equal distribution of income and wealth. During the Keynesian era, progressive taxation and transfers to the poor were used (as part of fiscal policy) to reduce inequalities

---

KEY TERMS

policy conflict: occurs when two policy objectives cannot both be achieved at the same time: the better the performance in achieving one objective, the worse the performance in achieving the other.

trade off between policy objectives: governments often do this because it may be impossible to achieve two or more objectives simultaneously. They aim for a satisfactory combination.

between rich and poor. In recent years, free-market supply-side economists have argued that such policies reduce entrepreneurial and personal incentives in labour markets, which make the economy less competitive and the growth rate slower. In the free-market view, greater inequalities are necessary to promote the conditions in which rapid and sustainable economic growth can take place.

economic growth ←— policy conflict and trade-off —→ greater income equality

■ Between higher living standards now and higher living standards in the *future*. In the short term, the easiest way to increase living standards is to boost consumption. However, this 'live now, pay later' approach means sacrificing saving and investment, which reduces economic growth.

current living standards ←— policy conflict and trade-off —→ future living standards

EXTENSION MATERIAL

Developing your understanding of policy objectives and policy instruments

At AS, you need only an elementary understanding of macroeconomic policy objectives and policy instruments. However, as you proceed through the 2-year course leading to the A-level qualification, you should develop a more sophisticated understanding of the two sets of concepts. Figure 16.1 illustrates what you may eventually learn.

Figure 16.1 The possible objectives and instruments of government economic policy

Figure 16.1 sets out some of the possible linkages between monetary policy, fiscal policy and supply-side policy instruments and the objectives they may be intended to 'hit'.

The left side of the flow chart shows the instruments and objectives of monetary policy, whereas the right side allows us to relate monetary policy to fiscal policy and supply-side policy. The left side shows control of inflation as an objective of monetary policy. However, control of inflation is best regarded as a penultimate policy objective, since improving economic welfare (shown at the top of the flow chart) should be regarded as the true ultimate policy objective.

At this stage of your course, you should not expect to understand all the nuances of the flow chart. Return to the figure towards the end of the AS course, or next year when you are studying A2 macroeconomics.

A closer look at the main policy objectives

Full employment

There are two definitions of full employment commonly used by economists and politicians. The first is often called the **Beveridge definition**. In 1944, a famous White Paper on employment policy, inspired by Keynes but largely written by William Beveridge (an economist at the London School of Economics, who later became Lord Beveridge), effectively committed postwar governments to achieving full employment. In the White Paper, Beveridge defined full employment as occurring when unemployment falls to 3% of the labour force.

EXAM TIP

In an exam, you can define full employment in either of the ways described here – but make sure your definition is precise.

During the 1950s and 1960s, UK unemployment always stayed below 3%, so full employment, according to Beveridge's definition, was achieved during the postwar Keynesian decades.

However, in the decades that followed, unemployment was above 3%. Unemployment rose rapidly in the two recessions that the UK suffered in the early 1980s and early 1990s, peaking at over 3 million workers unemployed in 1986, and again in 1993. Unemployment then fell in the late 1990s and early 2000s, as the UK recovered from recession and entered a boom. Unemployment fell below 5% in 2005, once again meeting Beveridge's definition of full employment (at 2.8%) in 2007. With the onset of recession in 2008, unemployment grew again, peaking in November 2011 at nearly 2.7 million (and an unemployment rate of 8.4%).

Partly because they regard Beveridge's 3% definition as too arbitrary and lacking any theoretical underpinning, free-market economists favour a second definition of full employment. For them, full employment occurs in the economy's aggregate labour market at the market-clearing real wage rate, where the number of workers willing to work equals the number of workers whom employers wish to hire. The implications of this way of defining unemployment will be developed in Chapter 20.

Economic growth and rising living standards

There isn't much point in achieving full employment if everybody with a job then experiences a very low standard of living. Thus, as well as aiming to reduce unemployment, a government must try to achieve an acceptable and sustainable rate of economic growth. Growth facilitates higher living standards, and usually also creates more jobs. As policy objectives, lower unemployment and economic growth generally go hand-in-hand, although some free-market economists argue that a certain level of unemployment is needed to create the supply-side conditions in which growth is best fostered.

CASE STUDY 16.1

UK GDP growth in recent years

To be a good economist, you need to undertake your own research. A good source to use at AS is the BBC News Economy Tracker webpage (www.bbc.co.uk). Besides providing data on GDP and growth, the Tracker webpage allows you to access up-to-date data on inflation, jobs, interest rates and house prices. The BBC News website also has an informative video clip on GDP: 'Q&A: What is GDP?'

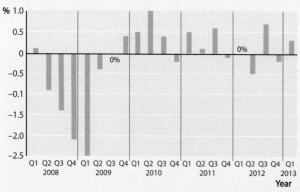

Figure 16.2 Quarterly changes in real UK GDP, Quarter 1 2008 to Quarter 1 2013

Source: ONS

Follow-up questions

1 Find out whether the UK economy suffered negative economic growth in any quarter between Quarter 1 2013 and the time when you are reading this book.
2 What are the benefits and costs of economic growth?

A fair distribution of income and wealth

As well as targeting full employment and an acceptable and sustainable rate of economic growth as policy objectives, most governments, especially those in countries where people vote, want to avoid unacceptably unfair or inequitable distribution of income and wealth. For example, most people would agree that a distribution in which 1% of the population received 99% of income, while the other 99% of the population earned hardly anything, is not politically acceptable. But as I first stated in Chapter 12, as soon as equitable considerations are introduced into economic analysis, normative judgements are made about what is a 'socially fair' distribution of income and wealth, and about what *ought* to happen in the economy. To recap on this, refer to the section in Chapter 12 on 'The distribution of income and wealth'. This describes the link between distributional issues and the role of markets in the economy, and also the link to market failure.

In a macroeconomic context, a possible conflict also exists between greater equality in the distribution of income and wealth and the policy objective of faster economic growth. Free-market economists argue that people must be incentivised for faster and sustained growth to be achieved. However, this may require greater income inequality to create the conditions in which people are prepared to take financial risks, knowing that if successful, they, rather than other people, will enjoy the fruits of their efforts.

EXAM TIP

Inequalities in the distribution of income and wealth can also be viewed as a form of market failure and tested as such in the Unit 1 exam.

CASE STUDY 16.2

What is inflation?

Inflation is a general rise in prices across the economy. This is distinct from a rise in the price of a particular good or service. Individual prices rise and fall all the time in a market economy, reflecting consumer choices and preferences, and changing costs. If the price of one item — say, a particular model of car — increases because demand for it is high, this is not inflation. Inflation occurs when most prices are rising by some degree across the whole economy.

In December 2012, the UK inflation rate was 2.7%, when measured by the consumer prices index (CPI) (see Chapter 21 to find out about the CPI). The inflation rate is a measure of the average change in prices across the economy over a specified period, usually a year (the annual rate of inflation). If the annual inflation rate measured in December 2012 was 2.7% (see Figure 16.3), then prices on average were 2.7% higher than they had been in December 2011. A typical basket of goods and services costing £100 in December 2011 would cost £102.70 in December 2012.

I have quoted the UK's inflation rate for December 2012 for an interesting reason. Chapter 21 explains how the UK government currently requires the Bank of England to keep the inflation rate between 1% above and 1% below a target rate of inflation set by the government of 2%. A glance at Figure 16.3 shows that from 2000 to 2008 inflation rose above the 3% ceiling only once, in March 2007. However, in 2008 and then again in 2011 there were two significant 'spikes' in the inflation rate, which rose on both occasions to well above 3%.

Any one individual price change may cause the measured rate of inflation to change, particularly if it is large and if the item has a significant weight in the price index. For example, large recent rises in the price of petrol raised the overall rate of inflation. However, unless the price of petrol continues to rise, the annual rate of inflation will eventually fall back again — providing the prices of other 'big ticket' items such as food do not rise by significantly more than the old (lower) rate of inflation.

Figure 16.3 Changes in the annual UK inflation rate, 2000–12

Source: ONS

Follow-up questions
1 Do you think that the CPI rate of inflation measures 'true' inflation as experienced by ordinary people?
2 What has happened to the UK rate of inflation since 2013?

Controlling inflation

People sometimes regard controlling inflation as an end in itself and believe that price stability (i.e. zero inflation) or a steady rate of inflation of, say 2%, is a 'good thing'. However, as will be explained in Chapter 21, under certain circumstances, inflation can yield benefits. For example, a steady but low rate of inflation may be associated with a climate of consumer and business optimism. If this is the case, then trying to achieve absolutely stable prices may be a bit like 'killing the goose that lays the golden egg'. The deflationary policies needed to remove inflation from the economic system completely may create economic stagnation and highly depressed economic conditions. It is better to live with a degree of inflation (albeit controlled) than to try to bleed inflation completely out of the economy.

To extend this argument a stage further, controlling inflation should be regarded not as an *ultimate* objective of macroeconomic policy, but as an *intermediate* objective, or a necessary condition that must be achieved in order to create the efficient and competitive markets that are required, in the long run, for the main policy objectives of full employment and sustained growth to be achieved. Even these don't form the *true* ultimate policy objective, increasing human happiness or economic welfare.

A steady but low rate of inflation could be viewed as the golden situation

A satisfactory balance of payments

As is the case with the word 'fair' in the context of a fair distribution of income, the word 'satisfactory' can be interpreted in different ways. People sometimes assume that a satisfactory balance of payments only occurs when the government achieves the biggest possible current account surplus (i.e. the value of exports exceeding the value of imports by the greatest amount). However, a country can only enjoy a trading surplus if at least one other country suffers a trading deficit. It is mathematically impossible for *all* countries to have a current account surplus at the same time. Therefore, most economists take the view that a 'satisfactory' balance of payments is a situation in which the current account is in equilibrium, or when there is a small surplus or a small but sustainable deficit.

The **current account of the balance of payments** contains two main items: the monetary value of **exports** (of both goods and services), and the monetary value of **imports**. If we ignore one or two other items in the current account, which are explained in Chapter 22, current account equilibrium occurs when the monetary value of exports equals the monetary value of imports. If the value of imports exceeds the value of exports, there is a **current account deficit**; if the value of imports is less than the value of exports, there is a **current account surplus**.

In the mid-1970s, huge current account deficits caused the UK to suffer two massive balance of payments crises. To try to reduce the deficits, UK governments had to contract or deflate the economy, which meant that unemployment grew and economic growth slowed down. Internal policy objectives were sacrificed in order to achieve the external objective of a satisfactory balance of payments. In recent years, however, the UK's current account deficit has been much larger, both in absolute size and as a ratio of UK output, without the newspapers being full of stories of balance of payments crises. A large payments deficit is no longer necessarily regarded as a problem, partly because modern governments are generally prepared to allow market forces to determine the exchange rate. By contrast, 30–40 years ago, a large balance of payments deficit forced the government to deflate the economy in order to support the exchange rate to which it was committed. This is explained in greater detail in Chapter 22.

CASE STUDY 16.3

The UK current account

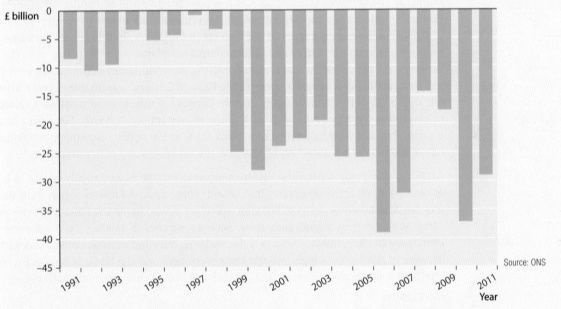

Figure 16.4 The current account of the UK balance of payments, 1991–2011

At AS, examination questions are set on the current account of the balance of payments, which, as noted, mainly records the value of trade in goods and services (exports minus imports).

Questions are not set directly on the other main part of the balance of payments, capital flows into and out of the UK. However, Chapters 22 and 23 explain how some knowledge of capital flows will help you to understand the link between monetary policy and changes in the current account of the balance of payments.

Figure 16.4 shows that the UK's current account has been in deficit in recent years, with the trade deficit rising to £39.1 billion in 2006. This was the highest ever recorded in *money* terms, but it only equalled 2.9% of GDP. The issues you have to consider centre on the extent to which a current account deficit poses problems for the UK economy, and the policies the government can and possibly ought to use to try to reduce the size of the deficit. These issues are explored in Chapter 22.

Follow-up questions

1 What is the difference between a 'budget deficit' and a 'balance of payments deficit'?
2 Research figures for the size of the UK balance of payments deficit since 2013.

Policy indicators

This chapter concludes with a short explanation of the difference between a **policy indicator** and policy *instruments* and *objectives*. Whereas a policy objective is a target or goal that a government wishes to 'hit', and a policy instrument is a tool used to achieve this end, a policy indicator simply provides the government with information about the state of the economy and/or whether current policy is on course to achieve the government's objectives.

KEY TERM

policy indicator: provides information about what is happening in the economy.

The **money supply** provides a good example of a policy indicator. In the monetarist era of the late 1970s and the early 1980s, the money supply (or stock of money circulating round the economy) was treated both as a policy objective and as a policy instrument. Under the influence of monetarist theory, governments attempted to control the rate of growth of the money supply in order to control inflation. In this sense, the money supply was the policy instrument, while control of inflation was the policy objective. However, for various technical reasons centring on what money is (for example, is it just cash, or are bank deposits money?), the Bank of England was unable to control the rate of growth of the money supply *directly*. Because of this, interest rates were raised or lowered to try to control the growth of the money supply *indirectly*. For a time, the Bank of England used its interest rate, Bank Rate, as the policy instrument, while the rate of growth of the money supply became the (intermediate) policy objective.

All this is now history. After the 'death' of monetarism, the money supply ceased to be either a policy objective or a policy instrument. These days, the money supply indicates whether or not there is plenty of liquidity (spending power) in the UK's financial system. Along with other economic indicators, such as surveys of business and consumer confidence and information about new houses being built and summer holidays booked, changes in the money supply provide the government and the Bank of England with information about what is happening, and what is likely to happen, in the UK economy.

SUMMARY

- A policy objective is a target or goal which a government aims to achieve or 'hit'.
- A policy instrument is a tool or set of tools used to try to achieve an objective or objectives.
- Policy instruments can be grouped under the headings of monetary policy, fiscal policy and supply-side policy.
- The main macroeconomic policy objectives are full employment, economic growth, a fair distribution of income and wealth, control of inflation and a satisfactory balance of payments on current account.
- Full employment and economic growth are the prime policy objectives, but many free-market and monetarist economists place control of inflation in pole position.
- Whatever the ranking of policy objectives, Keynesian or monetarist, improving economic welfare or human happiness is the ultimate policy objective.
- The main policy objectives and policy instruments are explained in more depth in later chapters.
- A policy indicator provides information about the state of the economy, and on how best policy instruments may be used to achieve particular policy objectives.

Exam-style questions

1 Explain how monetary and fiscal policy are (a) similar and (b) different.   (12 marks)

2 Explain **two** of the main conflicts affecting macroeconomic policy.   (12 marks)

3 Evaluate the view that a government should always aim for the biggest possible current account surplus.   (25 marks)

4 Do you agree that control of inflation should take precedence over reducing unemployment as a macroeconomic policy objective? Justify your answer.   (25 marks)

Chapter 17

Economic growth and the economic cycle

Chapter 16 explained how achieving a satisfactory, sustainable (and implicitly faster) rate of economic growth, along with other policy objectives such as reducing unemployment and controlling inflation, is an important target for governments. This chapter examines the nature of economic growth, both in the short run and in the long run, before explaining the ups and downs of economic growth in the various phases of the economic cycle.

LEARNING OUTCOMES

This chapter will:
- define economic growth and distinguish between short-run and long-run growth
- explain how economic growth is measured
- distinguish between the real and the nominal values of economic variables
- relate economic growth to capital, wealth and national income or output
- explain the causes of short-run and long-run economic growth
- explain the difference between economic growth and economic development
- relate economic growth to sustainability and the trade-off with environmental objectives
- explain the causes of the economic cycle and the phases of the cycle
- relate output gaps to the economic cycle and to the difference between actual and trend output

What is economic growth?

Economic growth is defined as the increase in the *potential* level of *real* output the economy can produce over a period of time: for example, a year. Strictly, this is **long-run economic growth**, which is not the same as **short-run economic growth** (both are illustrated in Figure 17.1). If the economy's production possibility frontier is PPF_1 initially, short-run economic growth is shown by the movement from point *C* *inside* the frontier to point *A* *on* the frontier. Long-run economic growth is shown by the outward movement of the frontier to PPF_2. The movement from point *A* to point *B* depicts long-run economic growth. Short-run growth makes use of spare capacity and takes up the slack in the economy, whereas long-run growth increases total productive capacity.

KEY TERM

economic growth: an increase in the economy's potential level of real output, and an outward movement of the economy's production possibility frontier.

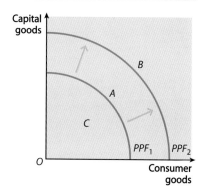

Figure 17.1 Short-run and long-run economic growth

How economic growth is measured

Economic growth is measured by the percentage annual increase in real national output. For example, a 3% growth rate means that the aggregate level of real output (actual goods and services) produced in the economy over the last year is 3% higher than it was when measured a year ago for the previous 12 months.

Real national output is the total of all the goods and services produced in an economy over a particular time period. As Case Study 17.1 explains, an increase in real national output can be calculated by subtracting the rate of inflation from the increase in nominal national output over the period in question.

CASE STUDY 17.1

Real and nominal national income or national output

It is important to avoid confusing *real* national income or output with *nominal* national income or output. (Nominal national output is also called *money* national output.)

The photograph shows a number of cheeses on display in a delicatessen in Oxfordshire. The cheeses contributed in a small way to the UK's real national output in 2012 — a contribution made even smaller because all the cheeses on display were imported.

Nominal national income or output is real national income or output multiplied by the average price

level for the year in question. Two of the cheeses on display in the Oxfordshire delicatessen were priced at £1.80 and £1.99 per 100 grams. Estimates for the level of UK nominal national output in 2012 were based on information about the prices charged for all goods produced in the UK, including cheeses sold by market stalls, delis and supermarkets. However, with imports, only the contribution to output added in the UK is included in the real and nominal values of UK national output.

While *nominal* national income rose by 3.41% in the UK in 2011, *real* national income rose by only 0.89%, the difference between the two reflecting the impact of the rate of inflation in 2011. It is the change in *real* income which measures the economy's rate of growth — the change in *nominal* income overstates the growth rate.

The approximate change in the real national income can be calculated by subtracting the rate of inflation from the rate of change of nominal national income.

Follow-up questions

1 Why do domestically produced cheeses such as British cheddar contribute more to UK national output than imported cheeses such as French brie?

2 Find out what has happened to real UK income since 2008 when the UK economy entered recession.

National output, national income and economic growth

Before exploring economic growth in more detail, I shall explain how long-term growth relates to the concepts of **national output** and **national income**.

Economists use the terms national output (also called national product) and national income interchangeably. To produce the flow of national output, the economy must possess a stock of physical capital goods (the **national capital stock**) and a **stock of human capital**.

> **KEY TERM**
>
> **national income** or **national output:** the *flow* of new output produced by the economy in a particular period (e.g. a year).

The national capital stock is part of the **stock of national wealth**, which comprises all physical assets owned by the nation's residents that have value. The national capital stock includes capital goods and raw materials, together with **social capital** such as the roads, hospitals and schools which are owned by the state. However, the national capital stock excludes consumer goods, which are a part of national *wealth* but not part of national *capital*. All capital is wealth, but not all wealth is capital.

> **EXAM TIP**
>
> Make sure you understand the difference between stocks and flows. The national capital stock is the stock of capital goods that has accumulated over time in the economy. By contrast, national income is the *flow* of new output produced by the stocks of physical and human capital.

Figure 17.2 shows how we can relate a country's national income or output (e.g. in 2016) to the national capital stock and the human capital stock. In the figure, national income in 2016 is shown as the area contained by the three rectangles *A*, *B* and *C*. I will now assume that at the beginning of 2016, the economy operates on its production possibility frontier. This means there is no unemployed labour, and the economy is working at full capacity to produce the flow of national income shown by *A* + *B* + *C*.

Figure 17.2 National income and the stocks of physical and human capital

However, part of the national capital stock wears out in the course of producing 2016's national income. Worn-out capital (or the **depreciation** of the national capital stock) reflects **capital consumption**. To maintain the size of the capital stock, so that (in the absence of population growth and technical progress) the stock is capable of producing exactly the same size of national income in 2017 as in 2016, part of 2016's national output must be replacement capital goods. The spending on replacement investment is shown by area *A*. If this investment doesn't take place, the national capital stock shrinks in size. **Negative economic growth** occurs and the economy's production possibility frontier shifts inward.

Positive economic growth generally requires that investment takes place, over and above the replacement investment shown by rectangle *A* in Figure 17.2. The extra investment needed to enlarge the capital stock is shown by rectangle *B*. This is called net investment. **Gross investment** (shown by *A* + *B*) is the sum of **replacement investment** and **net investment**. Only net investment increases the size of the capital stock, thereby facilitating long-run (positive) economic growth.

Rectangle *C* shows the fraction of national income available for consumption in 2016. As explained in the previous chapter, a decision to sacrifice *current* consumption in favour of a higher level of *future* consumption means that more of society's scarce resources go into investment or the production of capital goods, enabling the national capital stock to increase in size. However, in the short term, the easiest way to increase living standards is to boost current consumption. This 'live now, pay later' approach sacrifices saving and investment, which ultimately reduces long-term economic growth.

Gross national income and gross domestic product

Two of the most commonly used measures of national income or output are **gross national income (GNI)**, which used to be called 'gross national product' and **gross domestic product (GDP)**. Gross national income measures the total value of national income, including that generated in other countries. (UK residents and UK-based multinational companies (MNCs) receive profit and interest payments from the capital assets they own, but which are located overseas.) Likewise, overseas-owned MNCs such as IBM and Nissan receive profit from assets they own in the UK. The difference between inward and outward profit flows is called **net income from abroad**. Net income from abroad is included in GNI, but is excluded from GDP.

> **EXAM TIP**
>
> The specification states: 'candidates are *not* expected to have a detailed knowledge of the construction of national income accounts'. Nevertheless, data-response questions often include GDP data, so it is necessary to understand the concept.

CASE STUDY 17.2

GNI, GDP and living standards

Because it measures all the income available to spend in the UK, GNI is a better measure than GDP of the standard of living currently enjoyed by UK residents. However, GDP is a better measure of the productivity of industries located within the UK. As Table 17.1 shows, for the UK, net income from abroad is usually positive, reflecting the fact that the country has invested in and accumulated assets in other countries over time. As a result, UK GNI is generally larger than UK GDP. Unfortunately, for most developing countries, GDP usually exceeds GNI. Profit outflows and interest payments to developed world MNCs and banks explain why this is the case.

Table 17.1 UK gross national income, net income from abroad and gross domestic product, 2002–11 (£m)

	UK gross national income at market prices	UK net income from abroad	UK gross domestic product at market prices
2002	1,081,795	13,196	1,068,599
2003	1,150,765	14,169	1,136,596
2004	1,216,857	16,976	1,199,881
2005	1,283,217	20,507	1,262,710
2006	1,339,645	6,488	1,333,157
2007	1,429,346	17,227	1,412,119
2008	1,471,480	30,549	1,440,931
2009	1,419,028	17,165	1,401,863
2010	1,479,043	12,459	1,466,569
2011	1,531,327	15,174	1,516,153

Source: National Income Blue Book, 2012 (ONS)

Follow-up questions
1 What is the difference between gross national income (GNI) and gross domestic product (GDP)?
2 The data in Table 17.1 is measured at 'market prices'. How can *market price* data (*nominal* data) be turned into *real* data, for example to show real GDP?

Investment and technical progress: the two main factors leading to economic growth

Economic growth results from investment in new capital goods (physical capital), which enlarges the national capital stock, and investment in human beings (human capital). Although investment is an important factor in the growth process, it may not be as important as technical progress.

Until recently, economists had little to say about the causes of technical progress, treating it as 'manna from heaven' which falls upon the economy, triggering economic growth. However, an important relatively new theory, known as endogenous growth theory, incorporates the causes of technical progress into the theoretical explanation of the growth process. New growth theory suggests that governments can create supply-side conditions that favour investment and technical progress. These conditions include external economies for businesses, often in the form of infrastructure, and a judicial system which protects patents and other intellectual property rights, and which enforces the law of contract.

The difference between economic growth and economic development

Economic growth measures changes in the physical quantity of goods and services an economy actually produces, or has the potential to produce, but growth does not necessarily improve the economic welfare of all or most of the people living in a country. Economic development is a better indicator than economic growth of improved human happiness, and the ability to continue to improve happiness. **Economic development**, which includes the *quality* and not just the *quantity* of growth, is measured by:

- a general improvement in living standards that reduce poverty and human suffering
- greater access to resources such as food and housing required for basic human needs
- greater access to opportunities for human development: for example, through education and training
- environmental sustainability and regeneration, through reducing resource depletion and resource degradation

EXAM TIP

For the most part, AQA exam questions test knowledge of economic growth rather than knowledge of economic development.

Resource depletion occurs when finite resources such as oil are used up, and when soil fertility or fish stocks irreversibly decline. By contrast, **resource degradation** is best illustrated by pollution of air, water and land. To benefit people in the long run, growth (and development) must be sustainable.

Sustainable economic growth means the use of:
- renewable rather than non-renewable resources
- technologies that minimise pollution and other forms of resource degradation

The trade-off between faster economic growth and achieving environmental objectives

Governments continuously face a trade-off between the two policy objectives of maintaining and improving environmental quality, and maximising the economy's growth rate, measured by GDP growth.

Before explaining this trade-off, it is useful to identify three main components in standards of living and economic welfare:

standard of living	=	economic welfare derived from goods and services purchased in the market economy	+	economic welfare derived from public goods and merit goods collectively provided by the state	+	economic welfare derived from quality of life factors, including external benefits and intangibles minus external costs, and intangibles

GDP and GNI statistics are often used to measure standards of living and economic growth, but they usually only capture the first two of the components of the standard of living: the material goods and services. Intangible factors, the third element in people's living standards, are ignored. These intangible factors include the value that people place on leisure time and living close to work, and the externalities generated from the production and consumption of national income, which affect people's welfare and quality of life.

The environment provides us with many positive externalities which add to the quality of life, but also many negative externalities which do the opposite. Beautiful views, clean air, and the water-retaining and carbon dioxide-absorbing properties of forests provide examples of positive externalities (or external benefits). Conversely, traffic congestion, acid rain pollution, and rising sea levels and climate deterioration caused by global warming are examples of negative externalities (or external costs), which are likely to have growing adverse effects on the quality of life. If the pursuit of economic growth leads to the destruction of beautiful views and other external benefits conveyed by the environment, while simultaneously creating more pollution and congestion, there is a conflict between the government's growth objective and its environmental objectives.

EXAM TIP

This section of the chapter relates to the concept of negative externalities in the Unit 1 specification.

Insofar as externalities are taken into account in the measurement of GNP and GDP growth, what is in effect a welfare loss may be shown as an increase in national output, falsely indicating an apparent welfare gain. For example, the stresses and strains of producing an ever higher national output may not only lead to a loss of leisure time; it may make people ill more often, showing up in the national accounts as extra consumption of healthcare. Likewise, the extra time that motorists spend in traffic jams caused by increased traffic congestion apparently contributes to economic growth through increased expenditure on petrol and garage services.(Goods such as flood protection barriers and breathing masks, which fend off some of the adverse effects of a deteriorating environment, are sometimes called 'regrettables'.)

EXTENSION MATERIAL

The environment and the sustainability of economic growth

Over 40 years ago, the first oil crisis, in which the price of crude oil more than doubled, led to British people becoming aware of how the environment — in the guise of raw material and energy shortages — might severely limit a government's ability to achieve high employment levels and continuing economic growth.

Fuel shortages and increased energy prices drew people's attention to two publications of the new but fast-growing ecology or environmentalist movement. The first of these was a document called 'Blueprint for Survival', published in the January 1972 issue of the British journal *The Ecologist*. According to the authors:

> The principal defect of the industrial way of life with its ethos of expansion is that it is not sustainable. Its termination within the lifetime of someone born today is inevitable — unless it continues to be sustained for a while longer by an entrenched minority at the cost of imposing great suffering on the rest of mankind. Our task is to create a society which is sustainable and which will give the fullest possible satisfaction to its members. Such a society by definition would not depend on expansion but on stability.

The Limits to Growth: A Report for the Club of Rome's Project on the Predicament of Mankind, an influential book published a few months later in 1973, suggested that humanity would soon face a threefold dilemma: the impending exhaustion of the world's non-renewable natural resources, the world's pollution problem becoming so acute that the capacity for self-cleaning and regeneration is exhausted, and continued population growth leading to humankind destroying itself through sheer weight of numbers. One reviewer of this publication wrote:

> Man is heading for disaster if, overall, mankind does not learn to limit economic growth. That such a thesis would be unpopular with economists was to be expected. All their training, their research and their ethos has been concerned with ways in which the economy can be stimulated and expanded. Practically no economist has given thought to the problems of economic stability. For one thing stability is read as stagnation, and for another it is hard for an economist to find anyone to employ him who is interested in economic equilibrium. It has no appeal to governments, board chairmen, company presidents or even to used-car salesmen.

The authors of these two publications based much of their forecasts and predictions on the assumption of accelerating rates of population growth and resource use. This is known as exponential growth. Figure 17.3 illustrates the forecast made in 'Blueprint for Survival' of exponential growth in demand for crude oil or petroleum and exponential decline in petroleum reserves. The dashed lines show the total world oil reserves that the authors estimated would be available for extraction in 1975.

The forecasts of resource use and depletion made in *The Limits to Growth: A Report for the Club of Rome's Project on the Predicament of Mankind* were more sophisticated, but they were still based on the assumption of exponential rates of growth of use and depletion. In their most optimistic scenario, the authors argued that it might be possible to achieve a state of equilibrium — providing restrictions were placed on population growth and industrialisation, the two elements limiting growth which they argued are the principal causes of resource exhaustion and pollution.

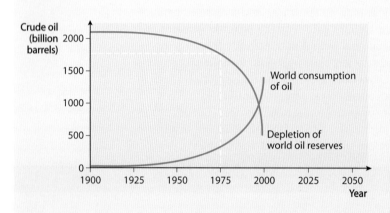

Figure 17.3 The 1970s gloomy prediction that exponential growth of oil consumption, matched by exponential depletion of known oil reserves, would lead to the world running out of oil by 2000

Fluctuations in economic activity and the economic cycle

Fluctuations in economic activity occur in two main ways: through **seasonal fluctuations**, and through **cyclical fluctuations** taking place over a number of years. Seasonal fluctuations are largely caused by changes in climate and weather. Examples include the effect of very cold winters closing down the building trade and seasonal employment in travel and tourism.

Cyclical fluctuations, which are longer than seasonal ones, divide into the **short economic cycle** (also called the **business cycle** and the **trade cycle**), which lasts for just a few years, and **long cycles** (or long waves), which arguably extend over approximately 60 years.

> **KEY TERM**
>
> **economic cycle:** the fluctuation of real output above and below the trend output line.

In an economic cycle, the economy's growth rate fluctuates considerably from year to year. Economic cycles, which can be between approximately 4 and 12 years long, are caused primarily by fluctuations in aggregate demand (the nature of aggregate demand is explained in the next chapter). In recent years, supply-side factors such as supply shocks hitting the economy have also been recognised as causes of economic cycles.

The causes of long cycles lie on the supply side of the economy. Significant improvements in technical progress cause firms to invest in new technology, which triggers a long period of boom. Electrification and the automobile have had this effect. In recent years, information and communication technology (ICT) may be having a similar effect, possibly creating a **new economy**. In the past, long booms have run out of steam when the innovating technology becomes fully used — until the next burst of technical activity creates another boom.

Trend output and actual output

Figure 17.4 shows two complete economic cycles, together with a line showing the economy's **trend output**, from which the economy's **long-term growth rate** can be calculated. **Actual** output rises and sometimes falls in the different phases of the economic cycle. **Short-term growth**, measured by the percentage change in real GDP over a 12-month period, also varies in the different phases of the economic cycle. In the cycle's upswing, growth is positive, but as Figure 17.4 shows, 'growth' becomes negative if and when a recession occurs in the cyclical downturn.

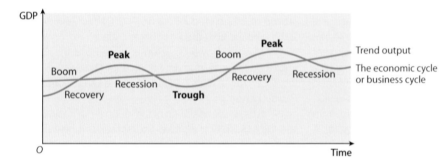

Figure 17.4 The phases of the economic cycle (or business cycle)

The economy's trend (or potential) growth rate is the rate at which output can grow, on a sustained basis, without putting upward or downward pressure on inflation. The trend growth rate is measured over a period covering more than one (and preferably several) economic cycles. Before 2000, the UK's trend growth rate was judged to be about 2.25% per year. At first sight, this growth rate appears low, especially when compared with higher trend growth rates in **newly-industrialising countries (NICs)** such as China. Nevertheless, the UK's trend growth rate was similar to the long-run growth rates of other developed economies in western Europe and North America. The absolute increase in real output delivered by a 2.25% growth rate may also exceed that delivered by a 10% growth rate in a much poorer country. Because of the compound interest effect, a 2.25% growth rate meant that average UK living standards doubled every generation or so. (The compound interest effect also explains why the trend output line in Figure 17.4 became steeper from year to year, moving along the line. For example, 2.25% of £1,000 billion is a larger annual increase in GDP than 2.25% of £800 billion.)

Recessions

A **recession** is defined in the UK as negative economic growth (or falling real GDP) for 6 months or more (i.e. two quarters or more). Before 2008, there had been two significant recessions in the UK since the 1970s. The first occurred between 1979 and 1981, and the second between 1990 and 1992. Both recessions (which raised unemployment to around 3 million) were followed by longer periods of recovery and boom in the rest of the 1980s and 1990s, in the latter case extending into the early 2000s.

KEY TERM

recession: a fall in real output for 6 months or more.

The alphabet of recessions and the disappearing 'double-dip' recession

To make economics as interesting as possible, journalists like to use slang. This is certainly true when they cover recessions, particularly when predicting the length and depth of a recession that might occur in the future.

In recent years it had become fashionable to write about V-shaped, U-shaped and W-shaped recessions. A V-shaped recession can be described as 'quickly in, quickly out', in the sense that recovery occurs soon after the recession starts. A V-shaped recession is really a 'blip' in an otherwise continuing growth process. A W-shaped recession, or 'double-dip' recession, describes a situation in which an economy appears to be recovering from recession, but is quickly dragged into another downturn. A U-shaped recession is long, deep and nasty: for example, the recessions suffered by the UK at the beginning of the 1980s and 1990s. In the 1990s, Japan experienced what was described as an L-shaped recession — in the sense that at the time Japan appeared to be going through a never-ending recession.

If you look back to Figure 16.2 on page 174, you will see that zero growth occurred in the first quarter of 2012. During January, February and March in 2012 growth was neither positive nor negative. Why is this important? The answer lies in the fact that before revised data was published by the Office for National Statistics (ONS) (i.e. the data in Figure 16.2), official data showed negative growth in Quarter 1 2012. Given that negative growth also occurred in Quarter 4 2011 and Quarter 2 2012, Britain appeared to have suffered a 'double-dip' recession. However, when in June 2013 the ONS published the new zero growth data for Quarter 1 2012, the BBC ran a headline 'UK Double-Dip Recession Revised Away'.

With the disappearance of the 'double-dip' recession and the possibility of a 'triple-dip' recession, a new slang term has come into use. The UK economy is said to be 'flat-lining' when growth is slightly positive (around 1% on an annual basis), but insufficient to constitute a proper economic recovery. Economists and journalists also talk about 'hard' and 'soft' landings. A 'hard landing' is a drop into a deep recession. By contrast, when predicting a 'soft landing', journalists believe that growth will slow down but just about remain positive, or, if a recession occurs, the downturn will be short and mild.

Follow-up questions
1 What is the official definition of a recession in the UK?
2 Outline what has happened to economic growth in the UK since 2013.

Recent UK economic cycles

Figure 17.5 illustrates how the UK economy performed between 2002 and the final quarter of 2012. The first half of the 11-year period, from 2002 to 2007, shows the tail-end of a long economic boom that had started in the 1990s. Despite continuous economic growth, mild economic cycles could still be identified.

The UK government defines economic cycles as beginning and ending when there are no output gaps. According to this definition, even in a period of continuous economic growth, mild economic cycles still occur. Although there is a downswing in economic activity, there is no recession.

However, as the years from 2008 to 2012 show, the mild cycles of most of the 1990s and the early 2000s ended in 2008. A recession, which arguably was the longest and deepest since the Great Depression of the 1930s, hit the UK economy (and many other economies throughout the world). At the time of writing (in March 2013), there is some evidence that recovery may be occurring. Some commentators believe the economy is entering a 'growth recession' — a period of very weak growth or possibly stagnant output, and high unemployment, that feels very much like a recession.

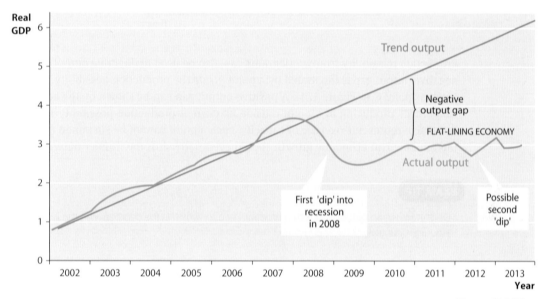

Figure 17.5 UK economic cycles and the current negative output gap, 2002–13

Source: ONS

Output gaps

If the economy's *actual* level of output were always to equal *trend* output, there would be no **output gaps**. (In this situation, there would also be no economic cycles.) An output gap measures the difference between the level of actual output or real GDP that the economy is producing and the trend output line above or below the level of actual output. As Figure 17.6 shows, output gaps can be negative or positive. Negative output gaps occur when actual output is *below* the trend output line. The vertical line drawn from point *A* to point *B* illustrates a negative output gap. As well as occurring in the cycle's downturn, negative output gaps can occur in the recovery phase of the economic cycle when output is growing, but the level of output is still *below* the trend output line. (Figure 17.5 also illustrates a negative output gap.) By contrast, positive output gaps occur when actual output is *above* the output line, both in the cycle's boom phase and when the downturn has started, but the level of output still lies *above* the trend output line. The vertical line drawn from point *C* to point *D* depicts a positive output gap.

> **KEY TERM**
>
> **output gap:** the difference between actual output and the trend output line.

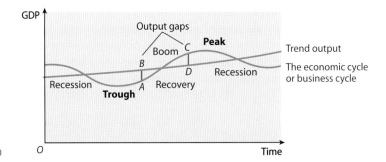

Figure 17.6
A negative and a
positive output gap

Production possibility frontier diagrams can also be used to illustrate output gaps. A negative output gap is illustrated by a point *inside* the production possibility frontier (such as point *C* in Figure 17.1). A positive output gap can be shown by the economy *temporarily* producing at a point outside its current production possibility frontier. Because it represents overuse of capacity, such a point cannot be sustained for long, though long-run economic growth should eventually shift the frontier outwards.

EXAM TIP

Don't confuse an output gap with a productivity gap, which is the gap between the levels of labour productivity of two countries.

Some explanations of the economic cycle

In the 1930s, John Maynard Keynes argued that economic recessions are caused by fluctuations in aggregate demand, which are caused by consumer and business confidence giving way to pessimism, and vice versa. However, it is now recognised that supply-side factors can also trigger economic cycles. Edward Prescott and Finn Kydland, the 2004 Nobel Laureates in economics, have developed a theory of 'real business cycles', which argues that changes in technology on the supply side of the economy might be as important as changes in aggregate demand in explaining economic cycles. Other factors that may cause or contribute to economic cycles include:

- **The role of speculative bubbles.** Rapid economic growth leads to a rapid rise and speculative bubble in asset prices. When people realise that house prices and/or share prices rise far above the assets' real values, asset selling replaces asset buying. This causes the speculative bubble to burst, which in turn destroys consumer and/or business confidence. People stop spending and the economy falls into recession.
- **Political business cycle theory.** In democratic countries, general elections usually have to take place every 4 or 5 years. As an election approaches, the political party in power may attempt to 'buy votes' by engineering a pre-election boom. After the election, the party in power deflates aggregate demand to prevent the economy from overheating, but when the next general election approaches, demand is once again increased.

■ **Outside shocks hitting the economy.** These divide into 'demand shocks', which affect aggregate demand, and 'supply shocks', which impact on aggregate supply. In some cases, an outside shock hitting the economy may affect both aggregate demand and aggregate supply. Thus, the outbreak of a war in the Middle East may affect demand by causing a sudden collapse in consumer and business confidence, and aggregate supply via its effect on the supply and price of crude oil.

EXTENSION MATERIAL

Other explanations of the economic cycle

At AS, it is a good idea to stick to learning two or three simple explanations of the economic cycle. However, there are other explanations that could give depth to your answers at A2:

■ **Climatic cycles.** Stanley Jevons, a nineteenth-century neoclassical economist, was one of the first economists to recognise the economic cycle. Perhaps taking note of the Bible's reference to '7 years of plenty' followed by '7 years of famine', Jevons believed a connection exists between the timing of economic crises and the solar cycle. Variations in sunspots affect the power of the sun's rays, influencing the quality of harvests and thus the price of grain, which, in turn, affects business confidence and gives rise to trade cycles.

Climate changes can effect the economic cycle

Although Jevons's sunspot theory was never widely accepted, there is no doubt that climate changes affect economic activity. The effect named 'El Niño' has renewed interest in Jevons's theory. This is a severe atmospheric and oceanic disturbance in the Pacific Ocean, occurring every 7–14 years. The disturbance leads to a fall in the number of plankton, upsetting the entire ocean food chain and devastating the fishing industry. The effect leads to a complete reversal of trade winds, bringing torrential rain, flooding and mud slides to the otherwise dry Pacific coastal areas of countries such as Chile and Peru. By contrast, droughts occur in much of Asia and in areas of Africa and central North America. Usually, the effect is quite weak, and in any case, any climatic disturbance in the south Pacific is often wrongly attributed to El Niño.

■ **Changes in inventories.** Besides investing in fixed capital, firms also invest in stocks of raw materials, and in stocks of finished goods waiting to be sold. This type of investment is called **inventory investment** or **stock-building**. Although this accounts for less than 1% of GDP in a typical year, swings in inventories are often the single most important determinant of recessions. Firms hold stocks of raw materials and finished goods in order to smooth production to cope with swings in demand. However, paradoxically, changes in stocks tend to trigger and exacerbate economic cycles. Stocks of unsold finished goods build up when firms over-anticipate demand for finished goods. As the stocks accumulate, firms are forced to cut production by more than the original fall in demand. The resultant destocking turns a slowdown into a recession. In the USA, swings in inventory investment account for about half of the fall in GDP in recent recessions. Destocking has also made UK recessions worse.

■ **Marxist theory.** Marxist economists explain economic cycles as part of a restructuring process that increases the rate of profit in capitalist economies. Under normal production conditions, a fall in the rate of profit caused by competitive pressure threatens to bankrupt weaker capitalist firms. Marxists believe that recessions create conditions in which stronger firms either take over weaker competitors, or buy at rock-bottom prices the assets of rivals that have been forced out of business. Either way, restructuring by takeover or bankruptcy means that the 'fittest' capitalist firms survive. In Marxist analysis, economic cycles are deemed necessary for the regeneration and survival of capitalism.

■ **Multiplier/accelerator interaction.** Keynesian economists have argued that business cycles may be caused by the interaction of two dynamic processes: the multiplier process, through which an increase in investment leads to multiple increases in national income; and the accelerator, through which the increase in income induces a change in the level of investment. (The multiplier and accelerator are explained more fully in Chapter 24 (the multiplier) and Chapter 18 (the accelerator).)

Stabilising the economic cycle

Demand management policies can be used to try to reduce fluctuations in the economic cycle. In the Keynesian era, fiscal policy was used in this way in the UK. However, during the monetarist era, in the late 1970s and early 1980s, demand management was abandoned. Arguably, this deepened and lengthened the recession that the UK suffered at the beginning of the 1980s.

Since the end of the 1992 recession, monetary policy has been used successfully to stabilise the economic cycle. In a boom, when the economy is overheating, the Bank of England raises Bank Rate to contract or deflate aggregate demand. By contrast, in a downturn the Bank of England cuts Bank Rate to reflate or boost aggregate demand.

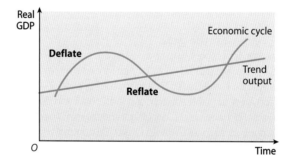

Figure 17.7 Getting the timing right when stabilising the economic cycle

Successful stabilisation of the economic cycle requires accurate timing. If monetary policy is used to stabilise the economic cycle, interest rates should be raised *before* output would otherwise peak in the boom phase of the economic cycle. Likewise, interest rates should be cut *before* output bottoms out in the downturn that follows.

The danger is that bad timing will destabilise the economic cycle and make the fluctuations more volatile. The deep recession illustrated in Figure 17.5 may have been caused in part by 'bad timing'. The UK government used contractionary fiscal policy in order to cut its budget deficit. According to Keynesian theory, expansionary fiscal policy should have been used to 'spend the economy out of recession'.

SUMMARY

- Long-run economic growth is an increase in an economy's potential level of output, whereas short-term economic growth is a movement from a point inside the economy's production possibility frontier to a point on the frontier.
- Economic growth is measured as a change in *real* output rather than as a change in *nominal* output.
- National income or output is the *flow* of new output produced by an economy in a year.
- Investment and technical progress are two of the causes of economic growth.
- The economic cycle or business cycle reflects actual output fluctuating around trend output.
- Economic cycles are usually caused by changes in aggregate demand, though supply-side factors can also cause recessions.
- A recession occurs in the UK when real national output falls for 6 months (two quarters) or more.
- An output gap is the difference between actual output and the trend output.

Exam-style questions

1 Explain the difference between GNI and GDP. (12 marks)

2 Explain **two** benefits and **two** costs of economic growth. (12 marks)

3 'Some economists argue that recessions are necessary for restructuring the economy'.
Evaluate this view. (25 marks)

4 Evaluate **three** policies the government could use to increase the economy's long-term rate of growth. (25 marks)

Chapter 18

Aggregate demand and the circular flow of income

Aggregate demand has been mentioned, in previous chapters, without explaining in any detail what the concept means. This chapter starts by defining aggregate demand, before focusing on two of its components, consumption and investment, and relating both to the nature of saving. The coverage of investment provides a brief explanation of the accelerator concept. The last part of the chapter links aggregate demand to the circular flow model of the macroeconomy and to the multiplier process, through which a change in aggregate demand leads to a larger decrease or increase in national income.

LEARNING OUTCOMES

This chapter will:

- explain the meaning of aggregate demand
- introduce the aggregate demand equation and the components of aggregate demand
- explain the determinants of the aggregate levels of consumption and saving in the economy
- briefly explain the personal saving ratio and the household saving ratio
- explain the determinants of the aggregate level of investment in the economy
- link investment to the concept of the accelerator
- relate aggregate demand to the circular flow of income in the economy
- explain the equilibrium level of national income in the context of the circular flow model

The meaning of aggregate demand

Aggregate demand comprises total planned spending on goods and services produced by the economy. (The closely related concept of **national expenditure** measures realised or actual spending, which has already taken place.) Four types of spending are included in aggregate demand, each type originating in a different sector of the economy: households, firms, the government sector and the overseas sector. The four sources of aggregate demand are shown in the following equation and identity:

KEY TERM

aggregate demand: the total planned spending on real output produced within the economy.

$$\text{aggregate demand} = \text{consumption} + \text{investment} + \text{government spending} + \text{net export demand}$$

or:

$$AD = C + I + G + (X - M)$$

where C, I, G, X and M are the symbols used respectively for consumption, investment, government spending, and net export demand (i.e. exports minus imports).

Aggregate demand is a macroeconomic example of an *ex ante* concept: it is a measure of what people plan or intend to do.

The components of aggregate demand

Consumption, **investment**, **government spending** and **net export demand** (spending on UK exports by residents of other countries minus spending on imports by UK residents) form the components of aggregate demand. If any of the components changes, aggregate demand increases or decreases. The next sections of this chapter examine two of the components of aggregate demand, consumption and investment, and their relationship to saving. The remaining components of aggregate demand, government spending and net export demand, are explained in Chapters 24 and 22.

Aggregate consumption and saving

Aggregate **consumption** is spending by all the households in the economy on consumer goods and services produced within the economy. Aggregate consumption does not include spending by households on imports, which are part of the goods and services produced in other countries.

If we assume a **closed economy** — pretending that there are no exports or imports — and that there is no taxation, then at any level of income, households can only do two things with their income: spend it or not spend it. Spending income is consumption, whereas not spending income is saving.

KEY TERMS

consumption: total planned spending by households on real output produced within the economy.

investment: total planned spending by firms on real output produced within the economy.

saving: income which is not spent.

The difference between saving and investment

Economists make a clear separation between **saving** and **investment**, even though in everyday language the two terms are often used interchangeably. Whereas saving is simply income that is not spent on consumption, investment is spending by firms on capital goods such as machines and office equipment. Investment also includes spending by firms on raw materials and energy.

It is important not to confuse consumption, saving and investment.

As a simplification, economists often assume that households make saving decisions, while firms make investment decisions. There are, however, exceptions to this rule. An important example occurs when a firm makes a decision to plough back retained profits and spend them on capital goods, rather than to distribute them as income to the owners of the business. In this situation, the firm is simultaneously saving and investing. If a business were simply to store these profits as a cash reserve — usually on deposit in a bank — then the firm would only be saving and not investing.

The determinants of consumption and household saving

Whenever members of households make decisions about whether or not to spend on consumer goods, they are simultaneously deciding whether or not to save. A determinant of consumption is also a determinant of household saving. In the next sub-sections, I explain a number of factors influencing consumption and saving. These are: **interest rates** (the reward for saving), the **level of income, expected future income, wealth, consumer confidence** and the **availability of credit**.

> **KEY TERM**
>
> **interest rate:** the reward for lending savings to somebody else (e.g. a bank) and the cost of borrowing.

Interest rates

Before Keynes, economists generally gave little attention to explaining how the level of aggregate consumption spending is determined in the economy. Some attention was, however, given to the determination of saving. Economists assumed that interest rates are the main determinant of saving. The rate of interest rewards savers for sacrificing current consumption, and the higher the rate of interest, the greater the reward. Thus, at any particular level of income, the amount saved will increase as the real rate of interest rises and the amount consumed will fall.

The level of income

In his *General Theory*, Keynes explained his theory of aggregate consumption in the following way:

> The fundamental psychological law, upon which we are entitled to depend with great confidence… is that men are disposed, as a rule and on average, to increase their consumption as their income increases, but not by as much as the increase in their income.

Keynes believed that, although aggregate planned consumption rises as income rises, it rises at a slower rate than income, so that at high levels of income planned consumption is less than income, and planned saving is positive.

EXTENSION MATERIAL

Keynes's theory of consumption and saving

In the 1930s, Keynes argued that interest rates have little effect on aggregate saving and consumption decisions, although they do affect how people move their savings: for example, between a bank and a building society. During the Great Depression, Keynes doubted whether a fall in interest rates could allow market forces to adjust automatically to eliminate the deficient demand plaguing the world's depressed economies. This caused Keynes to focus on the level of income as the main determinant of consumption and saving decisions.

In contrast to his predecessors, Keynes argued that the level of income (Y) is the most important single determinant of consumption: consumption is largely a function of the level of income. Using functional notation, we may state the Keynesian consumption theory in the following equation:

$C = f(Y)$

Autonomous consumption and income-induced consumption

The equation $C = f(Y)$ is general, telling us no more than that consumption is assumed to be determined mainly by income, and is some (as yet) unspecified function of the level of income. We can write the consumption function in more detail as:

$$C = a + cY$$

Written in this way, the equation for the consumption function shows aggregate consumption as comprising two elements: autonomous consumption and income-induced consumption.

Figure 18.1 Keynes's theory of consumption

Autonomous consumption (represented by the symbol a) is the part of total consumption which is unaffected by the level of income: that is, it is constant at all levels of income. The value of autonomous consumption is thus determined by influences on income other than the level of income. These influences will include the rate of interest (which has already been covered) and others such as wealth and the availability of credit (which will be discussed shortly).

Income-induced consumption is measured by (cY), c being the slope of the consumption function. As the name suggests, income-induced consumption is the part of consumption that varies with the level of income.

If consumption increases as incomes rise, but at a *slower* rate than income, it follows that household saving also increases as incomes rise, but at a *faster* rate than income.

Saving can be positive or negative. People on very low incomes borrow, or dissave, in order to spend more than their incomes. By contrast, rich people spend less than their incomes, even though their total spending is greater than that of the poor. The rich spend more and save more than the poor, and the rich are positive savers.

Expected future income and the 'life-cycle' theory of consumption

The Keynesian consumption theory explained above is sometimes also called the **'absolute income' consumption theory** because it assumes that the most important influence on consumption is the *current* level of income. However, the current level of income in a particular year may have much less influence on a person's planned consumption than some notion of 'expected income' over a much longer time period, perhaps extending over the individual's remaining lifetime or life cycle.

EXAM TIP

You should appreciate that people's economic behaviour is influenced by their expectations of what might happen in the future.

In order to understand the **'life-cycle' theory**, which is illustrated in Figure 18.2, it is useful to distinguish between two different types of saving: 'non-contractual' and 'contractual' saving. **Non-contractual saving** takes place when a person sets income aside: for example, in a building society deposit. Such saving is usually short term:

for example, saving to pay for a summer holiday. **Contractual saving**, by contrast, occurs when an individual makes a contract to save regularly with a financial institution such as a pension fund. This type of saving is usually undertaken with a long-term motive in mind. Many people sign savings contracts, especially early in their working lives, to finance a house purchase, and then continue to save to finance retirement or to protect dependants against the financial problems that would result from the saver's early death. Thus, with contractual saving, saving takes place at regular intervals over a number of years, to be followed in later years by dissaving when a house is purchased or on retirement.

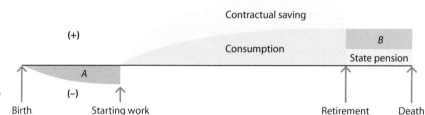

Figure 18.2 The life-cycle theory of consumption

People therefore plan their contractual savings on the basis of a long-term view of their expected lifetime or permanent income, and of likely spending plans over the remaining length of an expected life cycle. Temporary fluctuations in yearly income generally have little effect on the contractual savings that are regularly contributed to pension schemes and to the purchase of life insurance policies.

Wealth

The *stock* of personal wealth, as well as the *flow* of income, influences consumption and saving decisions. In countries such as the UK and the USA, houses and shares are the two main forms of wealth asset that people own. An increase in house prices usually causes home-owners to consume more and to save less from their current flow of income, partly because the wealth increase 'does their saving for them'. The same is true when share prices rise, though the effect is less noticeable in the UK, where houses rather than shares are the main household wealth asset. Rising house prices induce a feel-good factor among owner-occupiers of houses, which leads to a consumer spending spree in the shops. Conversely, falling house prices have the opposite effect, increasing uncertainty and precautionary saving via a 'feel-bad' factor.

The stock market crash in 2000, which centred on the collapse of the share prices of dot.com and high-tech companies, reduced the wealth of shareholders, and thence their consumption. In the summer of 2007, share prices also fell at the time of a financial crisis in the USA, resulting from US banks lending

> **EXAM TIP**
>
> Make sure you don't confuse *wealth*, which is a stock, with *income*, which is a flow.

> **KEY TERM**
>
> **wealth:** the stock of assets, or things that have value, which people own.

unwisely to poorer American families to finance house purchase (these are known as sub-prime loans). In 2008, falling house and share prices, accompanied by a collapse in consumer and business confidence, ushered in recession, in the USA and then in other countries such as the UK.

CASE STUDY 18.1

'Credit crunch' and recession

The financial crisis which hit the world economy in 2007 started in the US housing market where banks had lent money to sub-prime borrowers. When these borrowers couldn't repay their loans, or even the interest on them, the banks were left with bad debts, as were other financial institutions that had bought 'packages' of bad debt from the banks.

This infected the entire financial system and meant that banks stopped lending to each other — creating the credit crunch. The first UK bank to be affected by the seizing up of financial markets was Northern Rock, which had to be rescued by the British government. A lack of mortgages meant the market began to stagnate and the properties that did change hands went for less than they would have done a few months previously. This increased the amount of negative equity in the economy.

Follow-up questions

1 Explain the underlined terms: sub-prime borrowers; credit crunch; negative equity.
2 Find out about how the UK housing market has fared since 2012.

Consumer confidence

The state of consumer confidence is closely linked to people's views on expected income and to changes in personal wealth. When consumer optimism increases, households generally spend more and save less, whereas a fall in optimism (or a growth in pessimism) has the opposite effect.

Governments try to boost consumer (and business) optimism to ward off the fear of a collapse in confidence by 'talking the economy up' and by trying to enhance the credibility of government economic policy. If the government is optimistic about the future, and people believe there are good grounds for this optimism, then the general public will be optimistic and confident about the future. However, if people believe the government is pursuing the wrong policies, or if an adverse economic shock hits the economy in a way that the government can't control, confidence can quickly dissipate.

The availability of credit

Besides the rate of interest, other aspects of monetary policy, such as controls on bank lending and hire-purchase controls, affect consumption. If credit is available easily and cheaply, consumption increases as people supplement current income by borrowing on credit created by the banking system. Conversely, a tight monetary policy reduces consumption. The financial crisis that occurred in 2007 and 2008, which arose from bad debts in the US sub-prime market, had this effect in the UK and the USA. In the credit crunch, interest rates rose and the supply of credit dried up, with banks refusing to supply applicants with new credit cards or mortgages.

Other influences on consumption and saving

The distribution of income

Rich people save a greater proportion of their income than the poor. Redistribution of income from rich to poor therefore increases consumption and reduces saving.

Expectations of future inflation

Uncertainty caused by fears of rising inflation increases precautionary saving and reduces consumption. It may also, however, have the opposite effect. Households may decide to bring forward consumption decisions by spending now on consumer durables such as cars or television sets, thereby avoiding expected future price increases. People may also decide to borrow to finance the purchase of houses if they expect property prices to appreciate at a rate faster than general inflation. In this situation, and particularly if the real rate of interest is low or negative, people often decide to buy land, property and other physical assets such as fine art and antiques as a 'hedge' against inflation, in preference to saving through the purchase of financial assets.

Speculative demand for housing occurs because house prices rise faster than general inflation

The personal saving ratio and the household saving ratio

The personal saving ratio measures the *actual* or *realised* saving of the personal sector as a ratio of total personal sector disposal income:

$$\text{personal saving ratio} = \frac{\text{realised or actual personal saving}}{\text{personal disposable income}}$$

The household saving ratio is used in a similar way. It measures households' realised saving as a ratio of their disposable income. However, the personal saving ratio and the household saving ratio are not the same. The personal sector is more than just households, including unincorporated businesses such as partnerships and charitable organisations such as independent schools.

Economists and the government are interested in how much of their incomes people *plan* to save and to consume in the near future, as this provides important information about what lies ahead for the state of aggregate demand. Because it is difficult to measure people's plans accurately, the personal saving ratio calculated for the most recent past period is generally used as an indicator of what people wish to do in the future.

CASE STUDY 18.2

Changes in the UK household saving ratio

Figure 18.3 shows that the UK household saving ratio fell rapidly, though with some volatility, between the end of 1996 and early 2008, bottoming out around zero per cent, just before the beginning of recession. (Negative saving occurs if people borrow more than they save. This is called dissaving.) As Figure 18.3 shows, after early 2008 the household savings ratio recovered to around 8% in 2009 and 2012.

One of the factors affecting household savings is people's uncertainty about the future. People who fear job losses, or who expect to suffer a fall in future income, are likely to save more for essentially precautionary reasons. They want a 'nest egg' to protect themselves from the loss of future income. This means that savings ratios generally rise in recessions, unless overridden by other factors such as the need to borrow more so as to maintain spending levels and current standards of living and lifestyles.

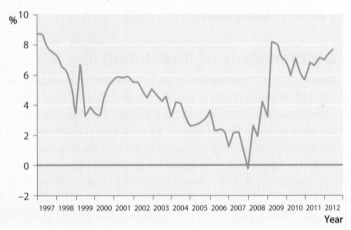

Figure 18.3 Changes in the UK household saving ratio, 1997–2012

Source: ONS

Follow-up questions

1 How have very low interest rates affected the saving ratio?

2 Research what has happened to UK savings ratios since 2012.

Investment

Investment is the second of the components of aggregate demand covered in this chapter. In everyday speech, investment is often used to describe a situation in which a person 'invests' in stocks or shares, paintings or antiques. In economic theory, the term has the narrower and more specific meaning explained earlier in this chapter. In the aggregate demand equation, investment is *planned* demand for capital goods, which must not be confused with demand for financial assets such as shares and bonds. The latter is called financial investment, but is not the same as demand for physical capital needed for the production of other goods and services. Finally, by providing or improving education and training, firms and the government can invest in human capital.

It is important to remember that capital is a *stock* concept, but investment is a *flow*. We can measure the national capital stock at any particular point of time. It represents the total of all the nation's capital goods, of all types, which are still in existence and capable of production. By contrast, we measure the flow of investment over a period, usually a year. A country's **gross investment** includes two parts: **replacement investment** (to make good depreciation or capital consumption), which simply maintains the size of the existing capital stock by replacing worn-out capital, and **net investment**, which adds to the capital stock, thereby increasing productive potential. Along with **technical progress**, net investment is one of the engines of economic growth.

Investment in physical capital goods can be of two types:

- **investment in fixed capital**, such as new factories or plant, and social capital such as roads and socially owned hospitals
- **inventory investment** in stocks of raw materials or variable capital

Determinants of investment in fixed capital

Entrepreneurs' expectations of an investment's *future* yield or rate of return and the cost of borrowing funds to finance the purchase of capital goods are two of the main determinants of investment in fixed capital. Suppose that a firm expects an investment to yield a return of 8% on average for each year of the investment's expected future life. If the cost of borrowing the funds to finance the investment (i.e. the rate of interest) is 6%, the investment is worthwhile, since it is expected to be profitable. An expected rate of return of only 4% would render the investment unprofitable.

EXTENSION MATERIAL

The marginal efficiency of capital

The expected future rate of return of capital and the rate of interest or cost of borrowing are part of a theory of investment first explained by John Maynard Keynes in his marginal efficiency of capital theory (part of his General Theory) of 1936.

At any point in time, there are thousands of *potential* investment projects not yet undertaken in the economy. Each potential project has its own expected future income stream and expected future rate of return, represented in Figure 18.4 by the symbol i. If the expected future productivity were to be calculated for each and every possible capital project available to all the business enterprises in the economy, we could, in principle, rank the investments in descending order of expected future yields. Plotted on a graph, the resulting curve is called the **marginal efficiency of capital curve**. This is the downward-sloping line in Figure 18.4.

Taking the rate of interest as given at r_1, the equilibrium level of aggregate investment (I_1) is determined on the graph at the point where the marginal efficiency of capital equals the cost of borrowing. This is where $i = r$. The investment I_1 is the marginal investment. This investment is expected to be only just worthwhile, since the value of its future returns is expected to match exactly the cost of borrowing the funds to finance the investment. However, all investments to the left of I_1 in the graph are supra-marginal or worthwhile. For them, $i > r$. Investments to the right of I_1 are sub-marginal and should not be undertaken. Future returns are expected to be less than the interest payments needed to finance the investments.

In his *General Theory*, Keynes introduced the colourful term: businessmen's 'animal spirits'. In Keynes's view, businessmen and women are extremely jittery creatures, whose expectations of an uncertain future constantly change. If expectations and 'animal spirits' collapse, the *MEC* curve shifts significantly to the left, investment in turn collapses, aggregate demand falls, and recession ensues.

Figure 18.4 The marginal efficiency of capital theory

Other determinants of investment, besides expected future rates of return and the rate of interest, include the relative prices of capital and labour, the nature of technical progress, the adequacy of financial institutions in the supply of investment funds and the impact of government policies and activities on investment by the private sector.

When the price of capital rises (for example, when the prices of capital goods or rates of interest rise), in the long run firms adopt more labour-intensive methods of production, substituting labour for capital. A decrease in the relative prices of capital goods has the opposite effect. If the price of capital goods or interest rates fall, firms switch to capital-intensive methods of production, so investment increases.

Technical progress can make machinery obsolete or out-of-date. When this happens, a machine's business life becomes shorter than its technical life: that is, the number of years before the machine wears out. A sudden burst of technical progress may cause firms to replace capital goods early, long before the end of the equipment's technical life.

> **KEY TERM**
>
> **technical progress:** improvements in methods of production resulting from invention, innovation and research and development. It often leads to the production of new types of goods and better-quality goods.

Many investments in fixed capital goods are long-term investments that yield most of their expected income several years into the future. These investments may be difficult to finance because of the inadequacy of the financial institutions that provide investment funds. Banks have been criticised for favouring short-term investments and being reluctant to provide the finance for long-term investments. Likewise, the stock market may favour short-termism over long-termism, although in recent years, the growth of private equity finance has emerged to provide an important source of medium- to longer-term finance.

Governments can also provide funds for firms to borrow to finance investment projects. Arguably, however, when choosing whether to invest in or support investment projects, governments may be better at 'picking losers' than 'picking winners'. In the past, UK governments have sometimes provided investment funds to rescue jobs in loss-making and uncompetitive industries that ought to be allowed to continue their decline. Government ministers and their civil servants may make bad investment decisions because, unlike entrepreneurs, they don't face the risk of being bankrupted as a result of poor decision making.

The accelerator theory of investment

The **accelerator theory** stems from a simple and mechanical assumption that firms wish to keep a relatively fixed ratio, known as the **capital–output ratio**, between the output they are currently producing and their existing stock of fixed capital assets. If output grows by a constant amount each year, firms invest in exactly the same amount of new capital each year to enlarge their capital stock so as to maintain the desired capital–output ratio. From year to year, the level of investment is therefore constant. When the rate of growth of output accelerates, investment also increases as firms take action to enlarge the stock of capital to a level sufficient to maintain the desired capital–output ratio. When the rate of growth of output decelerates, investment declines.

> **KEY TERMS**
>
> **accelerator:** a change in the level of investment in new capital goods induced by a change in national income or output. The size of the accelerator depends on the economy's capital–output ratio.
>
> **capital–output ratio:** the ratio between the output that firms are currently producing and their existing stock of fixed capital assets.

EXTENSION MATERIAL

A numerical example of the accelerator

To illustrate the accelerator principle, I will that assume the economy's capital–output ratio is 4:1, or simply 4. This means that 4 units of capital are required to produce 1 unit of output. I will also assume that the level of *current* net investment in fixed capital depends on the change in income or output in the *previous* year:

$$I = v(\Delta Y)$$

or $I_t = v(Y_t - Y_{t-1})$

where I_t is net investment this year, Y is current national income, Y_{t-1} is national income last year and v is the capital–output ratio. The capital–output ratio, v, is also known as the accelerator coefficient, or simply as the accelerator. I shall also assume no replacement investment is needed, and that the average capital–output ratio in the economy stays at 4.

Given these assumptions, consider the following numerical example of the accelerator principle.

Table 18.1 The accelerator: an example

Year	Net investment		Current income		Last year's income
$t = 2013$	£40bn	=	4 × (£100bn	–	£90bn)
$t = 2014$	£40bn	=	4 × (£110bn	–	£100bn)
$t = 2015$	£80bn	=	4 × (£130bn	–	£110bn)
$t = 2016$	£40bn	=	4 × (£140bn	–	£130bn)

In each of the years from 2013 to 2016, national income grows. Between 2012 (the year preceding the data in the table) and 2013, income grows by £10 billion. Via the capital–output ratio, the £10 billion income growth induces net investment of £40 billion in 2013. The size of the capital stock increases by £40 billion, which enables the desired capital–output ratio to be maintained at the now higher level of income. In the second row, income continues to grow by £10 billion, so investment in 2014 remains at £40 billion. However, the next year is different. In 2015, shown in the third row, the growth of income accelerates, doubling from £10 billion to £20 billion. Investment also doubles from £40 billion to £80 billion to maintain the value of the capital–output ratio. Thus, a £20 billion *increase* in income induces a £80 billion *increase* in investment. But in the fourth row, the growth of income falls back to £10 billion in 2016. Although income is still growing, net investment falls back to £40 billion.

This example shows how the accelerator gets its name. The data show the rate of growth of income and output determining whether investment grows, falls or remains at a constant level. In summary:
- If income grows by the same amount each year, net investment is constant.
- If income growth speeds up or *accelerates*, net investment increases.
- If income growth slows down or *decelerates*, net investment declines.

As firms adjust the stock of capital to the desired level, relatively slight changes in the rate of growth of income or output cause large absolute rises and falls in investment. You can use the accelerator to explain why investment in capital goods is a more volatile or unstable component of aggregate demand than consumption.

The circular flow of income and aggregate demand

The first version of the circular flow model, illustrated in Figures 18.5 and 18.6, is based on the simplifying assumption that there are just two sets of economic agents in the economy: households and firms (pretending that the government and foreign trade don't exist). Figures 18.5 and 18.6 assume a two-sector economy, or a closed economy with no government sector. The dashed flow lines in the figures show the real flows occurring in the economy between households and firms. Households supply labour and other factor services in exchange for goods and services produced by the firms. These *real flows* generate money flows of income and expenditure, shown by the solid flow lines.

> **EXAM TIP**
>
> Refresh your memory on the difference between real and nominal or money flows taking place in the economy.

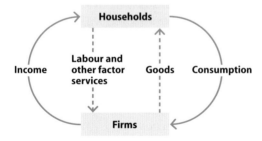

Figure 18.5 A simplified circular flow diagram of a two-sector economy

Aggregate demand in this simplified economy is represented by the equation:

$$AD = C + I$$

There is no saving, but also no investment by firms. All the income received by households (shown by the left-hand flow curve of the diagram) is spent on consumption (shown by the right-hand flow curve). **Deficient aggregate demand** (and likewise **excess aggregate demand**) cannot occur in this economy — as long as the assumption that all income is spent on consumption holds. At the current price level, spending is just sufficient to purchase the real output produced.

> **EXAM TIP**
>
> The circular flow model is one of the two macroeconomic models of how the economy works that you need to know. The second model, the *AD/AS* model, is explained in Chapter 19.

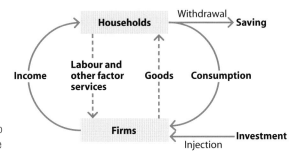

Figure 18.6 Introducing saving and investment into the circular flow of income

Figure 18.6 is more realistic than Figure 18.5, because it shows households saving as well as consuming, and firms investing in capital goods. When households save part of their incomes, people are spending less than their incomes. Saving, which is an example of a **leakage** or **withdrawal from the circular flow of income**, is depicted by the upper of the two horizontal arrows in Figure 18.6. The lower of the two horizontal arrows shows investment, or spending by firms on raw materials, machinery and other capital goods, which is an **injection of demand** into the economy.

> **EXAM TIP**
>
> It is important to understand the difference between leakages or withdrawals from the circular flow of income and injections into the flow.

The equilibrium level of national income

If planned saving (or the planned *withdrawal* of spending) equals planned investment (or the planned *injection* of spending into the flow), **national income is in equilibrium**, tending neither to rise nor to fall. However, if the withdrawal exceeds the injection, the resulting net leakage of spending from the circular flow causes output and income to fall.

> **KEY TERM**
>
> **equilibrium national income:** the level of income at which withdrawals from the circular flow of income equal injections into the flow. In a two-sector model of the economy, national income is in equilibrium when $S = I$.

Savings can be hoarded, or the funds being saved can be lent for others to spend. Hoarding — for example, keeping money under the mattress — means that a fraction of income is not spent. However, if all savings are lent, via financial intermediaries such as banks, for firms and other consumers to spend, planned saving may end up equalling planned investment. With this outcome, national income remains in equilibrium and there is no reason why the level of income should fall.

In the two-sector circular flow model, national income is in equilibrium when:

planned saving = planned investment

or:

$S = I$

However, because households and firms have different motives for making their respective saving and investment decisions, there is no reason why, initially, household saving should exactly equal the amount firms plan to spend on capital goods (i.e. investment). Let us consider a situation in which planned saving is greater than planned investment ($S > I$). In this situation, the national income or output circulating round the economy is in disequilibrium, with leakages out of the system exceeding injections of spending into the flow of income.

Keynes and deficient aggregate demand

If planned saving by households exceeds planned investment by firms, there is a danger that deficient aggregate demand may cause the economy to sink into a recession. In the 1930s, during the Great Depression, John Maynard Keynes argued that if household savings are not lent to finance spending by others, particularly investment by firms, the level of income or output circulating round the economy falls. This reduces saving, until planned saving equals planned investment and equilibrium is restored, albeit at a significantly lower level of national income. The economy ends up in recession.

EXAM TIP

Whether or not deficient aggregate demand exists in the economy, except temporarily, is one of the issues separating Keynesian and free-market economists.

The free-market view of deficient aggregate demand

Keynes's opponents believed that deficient aggregate demand only exists as a *temporary* and self-correcting phenomenon. They argued that when deficient aggregate demand occurs, the rate of interest, rather than the level of income or output, falls, quickly restoring equality between saving and investment intentions. When interest rates fall, people save less because saving becomes less attractive. At the same time, firms invest more in new capital goods because the cost of borrowing has fallen.

Keynes agreed that a fall in interest rates can bring about equality between saving and investment but he believed the process to be slow. In the very long run it may work, but, in Keynes's memorable phrase, 'in the long run we are all dead'. Keynes argued that when planned leakages of demand from the circular flow of income exceed planned injections of demand into the flow, the level of income or output falls to restore equilibrium. According to Keynes, deficient aggregate demand is the cause of recessions.

Introducing the government sector and the overseas sector into the circular flow model

Figure 18.7 illustrates a four-sector model of the economy, incorporating the full aggregate demand equation introduced at the beginning of the chapter:

$$AD = C + I + G + (X - M)$$

I have now extended the circular flow model to show an **open economy** with a government sector. The government and overseas sectors have been added to the two demand sectors, households and firms, included in the simplified, circular flow model.

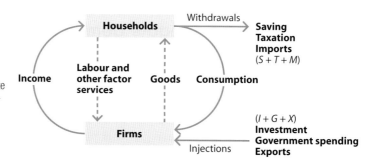

Figure 18.7 The components of aggregate demand and the circular flow of income in an open economy with a government sector

To recap, in the two-sector circular flow model, national income is in equilibrium when:

planned saving = planned investment

or:

$S = I$

In the extended circular flow model, national income is in equilibrium, tending neither to rise nor to fall, when:

saving + taxation + imports = investment + government spending + exports

or:

$S + T + M = I + G + X$

> **KEY TERMS**
>
> **closed economy:** an economy with no international trade.
>
> **open economy:** an economy with exports and imports.

However, whenever:

$$S + T + M > I + G + X$$

a net leakage of demand out of the circular flow occurs, which in Keynesian analysis causes the equilibrium level of national income to fall.

If:

$$S + T + M < I + G + X$$

a net injection of demand into the circular flow occurs, which for Keynesians causes the equilibrium level of national income to rise.

SUMMARY

- Aggregate demand is total *planned* spending on real output of all the economic agents in the economy.
- Consumption by households and investment by firms are two components of aggregate demand.
- Saving, or income which is not consumed, must not be confused with investment.
- Consumption and saving are determined by the same factors.
- Aggregate consumption and saving are determined by the rate of interest, the levels of current and future income, wealth, consumer confidence and the availability of credit.
- The household savings ratio measures *realised* saving as a ratio of household income.
- Investment is determined by factors such as the rate of interest, expected returns on capital, technical progress, the availability of finance, and the accelerator.
- The nature of aggregate demand can be illustrated in a circular flow model of the economy.
- The circular flow model can illustrate injections into and leakages from income circulating round the economy and equilibrium national income.

Exam-style questions

1 Explain how changes in the rate of interest affect consumption and saving. (12 marks)

2 Explain the meaning of the circular flow of income. (12 marks)

3 Do you agree that recessions are always caused by a collapse in aggregate demand? Justify your answer. (25 marks)

4 'Lending your savings to a bank is always good; hoarding your savings by keeping them in a safe is always bad.' Discuss the extent to which you agree or disagree with this view. (25 marks)

Chapter 19

The aggregate demand and aggregate supply macroeconomic model

Chapter 18 introduced the concept of aggregate demand, and explained the determinants of two of the components of aggregate demand: consumption and investment. That chapter also related aggregate demand to the circular flow of income, and explained that when injections of spending into the circular flow equal leakages or withdrawals from the flow, national income is in equilibrium. This chapter extends the analysis to aggregate supply, and examines the interaction of aggregate demand and supply in the AD/AS macroeconomic model of the economy.

··

LEARNING OUTCOMES

This chapter will:

- introduce the *AD/AS* model and use the model to explain macroeconomic equilibrium
- distinguish between macroeconomic equilibrium and microeconomic equilibrium
- relate *AD* curves to the explanation of aggregate demand provided in Chapter 18
- explain the meaning of aggregate supply
- explain the slope of the short-run aggregate supply (*SRAS*) curve and discuss its significance
- distinguish between increases and decreases in aggregate demand and aggregate supply and adjustments or movements along *AD* and *AS* curves in response to changes in the price level
- introduce the long-run aggregate supply (*LRAS*) curve
- explain how the vertical free-market *LRAS* curve differs from the Keynesian *LRAS* curve

Introducing the *AD/AS* macroeconomic model of the economy

In recent years, the *AD/AS* model has become the preferred theoretical framework for the investigation of macroeconomic issues. The model is particularly useful for analysing the effect of an increase in aggregate demand on the economy. It does this by addressing the following question: will expansionary fiscal policy and/or monetary policy increase real output and jobs (i.e. will the policy be **reflationary**), or will the price level increase instead (i.e. will the policy be **inflationary**)? The answer to this key macroeconomic question depends on the shape of the aggregate supply (*AS*) curve, in the short run and the long run.

Macroeconomic equilibrium

Macroeconomic equilibrium occurs in an economy's aggregate goods market when the aggregate demand for real output equals the aggregate supply of real output: that is, where *AD* = *AS*. At this point, households,

KEY TERM

macroeconomic equilibrium: the level of real national output at which *AD* = *AS* or at which planned injections into the circular flow of income equal planned withdrawals from the flow.

firms, the government and the overseas sector plan to spend in real terms within the economy an amount exactly equal to the level of real output that firms are willing to produce. In Figure 19.1, macroeconomic equilibrium occurs at point X, where the AD curve intersects the AS curve. The equilibrium level of real output is y_1, and the equilibrium price level is P_1.

Figure 19.1 Macroeconomic equilibrium

EXAM TIP

A common mistake students make when answering examination questions is to confuse macroeconomic equilibrium and microeconomic equilibrium. When this confusion occurs, examiners cannot give candidates the full marks that would be available for a correct and relevant diagram. Macroeconomic equilibrium relates to the whole economy, or the economy in aggregate. Microeconomic equilibrium occurs in a particular market within the economy, under the assumption that everything else in the economy is held fixed (the *ceteris paribus* assumption).

EXTENSION MATERIAL

Building and using economic models

This chapter introduces you to the *AD/AS* macroeconomic model. Model building is one of the most fundamental analytical techniques used by economists. Economic theory is based on developing economic models which describe particular aspects of the economic behaviour of individuals, groups of individuals and, in a macro context, the whole economy.

A model is a small-scale replica of real-world phenomena, often incorporating a number of simplifications. An economic model simplifies the real world in such a way that the essential features of an economic relationship or set of relationships are explained using diagrams, words and often algebra. Models are used by economists, first, to understand and explain the working of the economy, and second, to predict what might happen in the future.

A good economic model simplifies reality sufficiently to allow important and often otherwise obscure economic relationships to be studied, away from irrelevant detail or 'background noise'. The danger is that reality can be oversimplified, with the resulting model failing to reflect in a useful way the world it seeks to explain. Economic modelling involves the art of making strong assumptions about human behaviour so as to concentrate attention and analysis on key economic relationships in a clear and tractable way, while avoiding an excessive oversimplification of the problem or relationship to be explained.

The ultimate purpose of model building is to derive predictions about economic behaviour, such as the prediction of demand theory that demand will increase when price falls. Economic controversy often exists when models generate conflicting predictions about what will happen in a given set of circumstances. For example, a model of the labour market which predicts that the supply of labour increases as wages rise carries the policy-making implication that a cut in income tax, being equivalent to a wage rise, creates an incentive to effort and hard work. Under alternative assumptions, the model could predict the opposite: that, as wages rise, workers begin to prefer leisure to work and react to the tax cut by working less.

It may often be possible to accept or dismiss a model of economic behaviour on the basis of common sense or casual observation of the world around us. Economists now usually go further, using sophisticated statistical tests to evaluate empirically the model's predictions. Good economic models or theories survive the process of empirical testing (which is part of a branch of the subject called 'econometrics'), whereas models or theories shown to be at odds with observed behaviour must be revised or discarded.

This globe is a small-scale replica of the Earth

Aggregate demand

EXAM TIP

The slope of the *AD* curve tells us what happens to aggregate demand when the price level changes. Don't make the mistake of asserting that a change in the price level shifts the *AD* curve.

The **aggregate demand** (*AD*) curve illustrated in Figure 19.1 shows the total quantities of real output that all economic agents — households, firms, the government and the overseas sector — *plan* to purchase *at different price levels* within the economy, when all the

KEY TERM

aggregate demand: the total planned spending on real output produced within the economy.

factors influencing aggregate demand, other than the price level, are held constant. If any of the determinants of aggregate demand change (apart from the price level), the *AD* curve shifts right or left, depending on whether there has been an increase or a decrease in aggregate demand. For example, an increase in consumer or business confidence shifts the *AD* curve right, via the effect on consumption or investment. Likewise, expansionary monetary policy and expansionary fiscal policy both shift the *AD* curve right. Contractionary monetary or fiscal policy, or a collapse in consumer or business confidence, shift the *AD* curve left.

Demand can also originate in the overseas sector of the economy. Spending by residents of other countries on UK output (i.e. exports) is an injection into the circular flow of UK income. Conversely, spending by UK residents on goods produced in other countries (i.e. imports) is demand for their output rather than demand for UK output. Imports are a withdrawal or leakage from the circular flow of UK income. Thus, net export demand (exports minus imports or $X - M$) is a component of aggregate demand. If exports increase, the AD curve shifts right, but if imports increase, it shifts left.

EXTENSION MATERIAL

Explaining the shape of the *AD* curve

At AS, you must understand that the AD curve slopes down to the right, showing that all the economic agents in the economy *plan* to demand more real output as the average price level falls. You are unlikely to be asked to explain why an AD curve slopes down, but the explanations are useful to know.

A number of factors explain the slope of the AD curve, as distinct from a shift of the curve.

One explanation lies in a **wealth effect** or real balance effect. Assuming a given *nominal* stock of money (or money supply) in the economy, a decrease in the price level increases people's *real* money balances: that is, the same amount of money buys more goods and services. Because money is a part of people's wealth, an increase in real money balances makes people wealthier. As was explained in Chapter 18, when wealth increases, consumption also increases, which means that the demand for real output increases following a fall in the price level.

Figure 19.2 Aggregate demand for real output expands from y_1 to y_2, following a fall in the average price level from P_1 to P_2

The increase in real money balances also means that the real money supply has increased, relative to people's demand or desire to hold money: for example, in cash or in bank deposits. Basic supply and demand analysis tells us that when the supply of any commodity increases relative to demand for the commodity, its price tends to fall. Now, the rate of interest is the price of money. The increase in the supply of real money balances relative to demand reduces real interest rates, which leads to higher levels of consumption and investment.

A third factor relates to exports and imports. When the domestic price level falls (and assuming the exchange rate remains unchanged), demand increases for the country's exports. At the same time, consumers buy domestically produced goods instead of imports because the latter have become relatively more expensive.

Aggregate supply

Just as the AD curve shows the total quantities of real output that economic agents plan to purchase at different levels of domestic prices, so the AS curve shows the quantities of real output that businesses plan to produce and sell at different price levels.

> **KEY TERM**
>
> **aggregate supply:** the level of real national output that producers are prepared to supply at different average price levels.

The position of the *AS* curve

As is the case with the AD curve, if one of the factors determining the position of the AS curve changes, the curve shifts right or left.

The factors determining the position of the AS curve are virtually the same as those fixing the position of a market supply curve in a particular microeconomic market, such as those studied in Chapter 4. The main determinants are costs of production, taxes firms have to pay, technology, productivity, attitudes, enterprise, factor mobility, economic incentives facing workers and firms, and the institutional structure of the economy.

To take an example, if costs of production increase at all levels of real output, the *AS* curve shifts leftward. A fall in costs of production shifts the *AS* curve rightward.

Explaining the shape of the short-run *AS* curve

While it is seldom necessary at AS for students to explain the shape and slope of the *AD* curve, this is not true for the *AS* curve, because there are two aggregate supply curves: the **short-run aggregate supply (SRAS)** curve and the **long-run aggregate supply (LRAS)** curve.

EXAM TIP

You must know the difference between short-run and long-run *AS* curves, and the different contexts in which to use the curves to analyse economic problems and issues.

The *AS* curve drawn in Figure 19.1 is an *SRAS* curve, even though it is not labelled as such: at the beginning of the chapter, it was more important to introduce you to aggregate supply than to distinguish between the short run and the long run.

Nowadays, there is general agreement that, in the short run, *AS* curves slope upward. An upward-sloping *SRAS* curve is illustrated in Figure 19.3.

The upward-slope of the *SRAS* curve is explained by two microeconomic assumptions about the nature of firms:
- all firms aim to maximise profits
- in the short run, the cost of producing extra units of output increases as firms produce more output

At the average price level P_1 in Figure 19.3, the level of real output that all the economy's firms are willing to produce and sell is y_1. To persuade the firms it is in their interest to produce the larger output of y_2, the price level must rise. This

Figure 19.3 An upward-sloping *SRAS* curve

is because higher prices are needed to create the higher sales revenues needed to offset the higher production costs that firms incur as they increase output, so that profits do not fall. In Figure 19.3, the average price level has to rise to P_2 in order to create conditions in which profit-maximising firms are willing and able to supply more output. If the prices that firms could charge were not to rise, it would not be profitable to increase supply. Without a higher price level, profit-maximising firms, taken in aggregate, will not voluntarily increase the supply of real output.

The slope of the *SRAS* curve

At AS you need to know that in the short run the cost of producing an extra unit of output increases as more output is produced. At A2 you will learn about an important economic 'law' known as the **law of diminishing returns**.

In the short run, firms cannot change some of the capital equipment they use: for example, buildings and machines. These are examples of **fixed capital**, which, as the name indicates, comprises capital goods that cannot be added to or reduced in size in the short run. It follows that the only way firms can increase output in the short run is by adding increasing numbers of variable factors of production to their fixed capital assets.

Figure 19.4 A linear *SRAS* curve

Labour is usually classified as a **variable factor of production**. However, as more workers are added to a fixed quantity of capital, a point is reached beyond which extra workers add less to total output than previous workers added to the firms' labour forces. This results in diminishing returns to labour.

At any given money wage rate paid to workers, diminishing returns to labour mean that in the short run, the cost of hiring more workers increases at a faster rate than output. This raises the cost of producing extra units of output.

This brings us back to the shape of the *SRAS* curve. The *SRAS* curve slopes upward because profit-maximising firms only produce more output if prices rise to compensate them for the rising average costs of production that the firms suffer as their output increases.

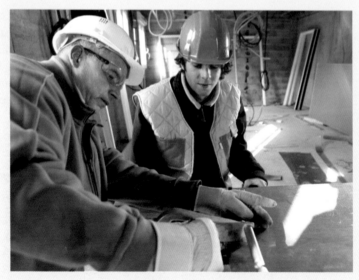

Labour is a variable factor of production

Different textbooks and teachers hold different views on the shape and slope of the *SRAS* curve. As a result, the explanations in this chapter may differ from those you come across elsewhere. Some textbooks assume that the *SRAS* curve is linear (an upward-sloping straight line, as in Figure 19.4).

In an AQA exam, it does not matter whether you draw a curved (Figure 19.3) or linear (Figure 19.4) *SRAS* curve. However, you will lose marks if you confuse an *SRAS* with an *AD* curve, or if you confuse the short-run aggregate supply curve with a long-run aggregate supply (*LRAS*) curve.

Increases and decreases in aggregate demand or aggregate supply

Increases and decreases in aggregate demand refer respectively to shifts of the *AD* curve to the left and the right. Likewise, increases and decreases of aggregate supply refer to similar shifts of the *SRAS* curve.

In microeconomics, exam candidates often confuse an increase or decrease in demand (or supply) with the resulting expansion or contraction along the curve that hasn't shifted. Similar mistakes are made in macroeconomic exams, when, for example, a candidate confuses a decrease in *AD* with the resulting contraction of aggregate supply.

A shift of the *AD* curve, such as that illustrated in Figure 19.5(a), must not be confused with the adjustment that follows along the *SRAS* curve. In this case, the adjustment is called an *expansion* or *extension* of aggregate supply.

Figure 19.5(b) shows a shift of the *SRAS* curve to the left, followed by a movement or adjustment up the *AD* curve. This time, the adjustment is called a *contraction* of aggregate demand. Other possibilities not shown in the diagram are a decrease in aggregate demand (or shift of the *AD* curve to the left) followed by a contraction of aggregate supply, and an increase in aggregate supply (shift of the *SRAS* curve to the right) followed by an expansion or extension of aggregate demand. As a practice exercise, try drawing diagrams to illustrate these events.

Figure 19.5 Shifts of, and adjustment along, *AD* and *AS* curves

Applying the *AD/AS* macroeconomic model in the short run

At the beginning of the chapter, it was stated that the *AD/AS* macroeconomic model of the economy is particularly useful for analysing the effect of an increase in aggregate demand on the economy. This proposition will now be illustrated with the aid of Figure 19.6, which shows an upward-sloping *SRAS* curve, together with a number of *AD* curves.

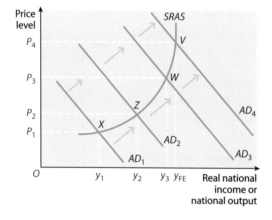

Figure 19.6 The effect of a rightward shift of *AD* on the economy

Figure 19.6 tells us that, with an upward-sloping *SRAS* curve, an increase in aggregate demand simultaneously **reflates** real output and creates jobs, and **inflates** the price level. The extent to which the demand increase is reflationary or inflationary depends on the steepness of the *SRAS* curve to the right of the initial macroeconomic equilibrium. Suppose that macroeconomic equilibrium initially is at point X in Figure 19.6, with the aggregate demand curve in position AD_1. In this situation, which depicts a recessionary economy suffering significant demand deficiency, an increase in aggregate demand to AD_2 increases both real output and the price level. The increase in aggregate demand simultaneously reflates and inflates the economy, though the reflationary effect is greater as long as the *SRAS* curve is gently sloped. Real output and the price level both increase, respectively to y_2 and P_2, to bring about a new macroeconomic equilibrium at point Z.

KEY TERMS

inflation: a persistent or continuing rise in the average price level.

reflation: an increase in the level of real output following an increase in aggregate demand.

However, as the *SRAS* curve becomes steeper, any further increase in aggregate demand — for example, to AD_3 — is more inflationary than reflationary. The increase in aggregate demand to AD_3 moves macroeconomic equilibrium to point W. Real output has increased to y_3, and the price level has risen to P_3.

Thus, for any given shift of the *AD* curve to the right along an ever-steeper *SRAS* curve, the reflationary effect of the increase in demand becomes smaller and the inflationary effect becomes greater, particularly as the economy approaches full employment. The shift of the *AD* curve to the right from AD_3 to AD_4 illustrates this. Following the move from AD_3 to AD_4, the new macroeconomic equilibrium occurs at point V. Real output is now the full employment level of output (y_{FE}). Figure 19.6 shows that any further increase in aggregate demand to the right of AD_4 solely causes inflation. As the economy is producing at full capacity (being on its production possibility frontier), real output cannot increase any further, except perhaps temporarily.

The difference between long-run and short-run aggregate supply

The aggregate supply curves considered so far in this chapter are short-run *AS* curves. The analysis will now be extended to explain the economy's long-run aggregate supply (*LRAS*) curve. Many economists believe that the *LRAS* curve is vertical, as illustrated in Figure 19.7.

Figure 19.7 The vertical long-run aggregate supply curve

In the short run, the aggregate supply or real output depends on the average price level in the economy. Other things remaining constant, firms are only prepared to supply more output if the price level rises. However, in the long run, aggregate supply is *not* influenced by the price level. Long-run supply reflects the economy's production potential. It is the maximum level of output that the economy can produce when the economy is on its production possibility frontier.

Producing on the production possibility frontier means that the labour force is fully employed. Thus, the vertical *LRAS* curve in Figure 19.7 is located immediately above the full-employment level of output (y_{FE}), which is the maximum level of physical output that the economy can produce. As Figure 19.7 shows, once the economy produces the full-employment level of real output, an increase in aggregate demand from AD_1 to AD_2 increases the price level from P_1 to P_2, but real output remains unchanged.

Figure 19.8 brings together the *SRAS* curve and the *LRAS* curve on the same graph. The *SRAS* curve merges into the *LRAS* curve at the point at which the *SRAS* curve becomes vertical.

Figure 19.8 Bringing the *SRAS* and *LRAS* curves together

EXTENSION MATERIAL

Producing to the right of the full-employment level of real output

If you refer to the section covering output gaps in Chapter 17, you will see that the economy can temporarily produce at a point *outside* its current production possibility frontier. However, because this represents overuse of capacity, such a point cannot be sustained for long.

In the context of the *AD/AS* model, this means that the economy can produce *temporarily* in a position to the right of the *LRAS* curve and above the full-employment level of output: for example, at point *W* in Figure 19.9. Note that in this diagram the *SRAS* curve extends to the right of the full-employment level of output (y_{FE}), without becoming vertical at point *X*. For a short period, output can rise above y_{FE} to y_1, but as the arrow at the bottom of the figure shows, eventually output falls back to the full-employment level.

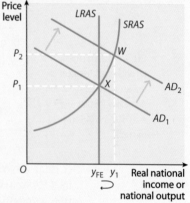

Figure 19.9 A temporary increase in output above the full-employment level of output

The position of the *LRAS* curve, shifts of the *LRAS* curve, and economic growth

The position of the LRAS curve is determined by the same factors that determine the position of the economy's production possibility frontier: the quantities of capital and labour and other factors of production in the economy, and technical progress.

> **EXAM TIP**
>
> Examination questions often ask candidates to discuss the effects of increased productivity and/or investment in human capital on long-run aggregate supply.

Chapter 17 explained how an *increase* in the quantity of available factors of production, and improvements in technology that increase the productivity of labour, capital or land, shift the economy's production possibility frontier outwards. For the same reasons, the economy's *LRAS* curve shifts right. The shifts of the production possibility frontier and the *LRAS* curve to the right are both illustrated in Figure 19.10.

EXAM TIP

You can illustrate long-term economic growth by shifting the *LRAS* curve right, by shifting the economy's production possibility frontier right, or by drawing a diagram to show the economy's trend growth rate.

Figure 19.10 Linking an outward movement of the economy's production possibility frontier to a shift of the *LRAS* curve to the right

A final way of bringing together the economy's production possibility frontier and its *LRAS* curve is by relating both to the process of economic growth. Remember that economic growth (long run) involves an outward movement of the economy's production possibility frontier. This is shown in Figure 19.10(a). Meanwhile, Figure 19.10(b) depicts economic growth in terms of a shift of the economy's *LRAS* curve to the right. The shift from $LRAS_1$ to $LRAS_2$ increases the full-employment level of real output, from y_{FE1} to y_{FE2}.

Free-market and Keynesian long-run aggregate supply curves

The AQA Unit 2 specification states that 'emphasis should be given to the assumption that the *LRAS* curve is vertical but candidates should also have an understanding of the Keynesian curve'.

The vertical *LRAS* curve described in this chapter is sometimes called the free-market *LRAS* curve. This label reflects the view commonly expressed by free-market economists that, provided markets function competitively and efficiently, the economy always operates at or close to full capacity. In the short run, real output is influenced by the average price level, but in the long run, aggregate supply is determined by maximum production capacity (though as the extension material on page 221 explains, an economy can *temporarily* produce above full capacity, when there is a positive output gap).

Most modern Keynesians agree that the *LRAS* curve is vertical. However, in the past, some Keynesians have been associated with a different *LRAS* curve, illustrated in Figure 19.11. This curve is derived from Keynes's own views on how the economy operates.

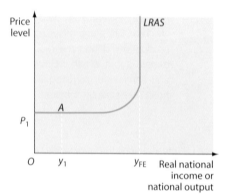

Figure 19.11 The Keynesian *LRAS* curve

The Keynesian *LRAS* curve is based on Keynes's explanation of the Great Depression in the UK and US economies in the 1930s. Keynes argued that a depressed economy can settle into an under-full employment equilibrium, shown for example by point *A* on the horizontal section of the *LRAS* curve. At point *A* in Figure 19.11, the level of real national output is y_1. Keynes argued that without purposeful intervention by the government, an economy could display more or less permanent demand-deficiency. Market forces would fail to adjust automatically and achieve full employment. If the government could shift *AD* to the right along the horizontal section of the *LRAS* curve (mainly through expansionary fiscal policy), the existence of huge amounts of spare capacity would lead, in Keynes's view, to a growth in real output (and employment), without an increase in the price level.

EXAM TIP

Some economists do not believe that the *LRAS* curve shown in Figure 19.11 is a *long-run AS* curve. They argue that the curve is just an exaggerated version of the *short-run AS* curve illustrated in Figure 19.6, with a longer and more pronounced horizontal section.

Be that as it may, at AS you should assume that the *LRAS* curve is vertical, with its position determined by the full-capacity and full-employment level of output, but understand that there is a second 'Keynesian' version of the curve.

Examination questions at AS will not require detailed explanation of either of the two *LRAS* curves.

CASE STUDY 19.1

Applying *AD/AS* analysis to the UK economy

Unit 2 data-response examination questions usually include information about the state of a national economy (not necessarily the UK). Below is some information about the UK economy in 2012 and earlier years. Think how you might use *AD/AS* diagrams and analysis to answer the questions that follow.

Average earnings rise by 1.4% to £26,500, says ONS

The average annual earnings of full-time workers in the UK rose by 1.4% to £26,500 in the year to April 2012. The figures have been published by the Office for National Statistics (ONS) in its annual survey of hours and earnings.

There was a cut in the real value of pay, however, as inflation was higher during the same period, at 3.5%. And the ONS data also reveal that inflation has outstripped the rise in average pay for the past 12 years. The survey results show that since April 2000, average annual pay for full-time workers has risen by 40%, from £18,848 to £26,500. In that time, inflation, as measured by changes in the retail prices index, has gone up by 43%.

The ONS has also reported a fall in UK labour productivity during the recession. This has prompted a debate about whether Britain's ability to produce goods and services at anything like its pre-recession level has been permanently impaired.

Source: ONS, 2012

Follow-up questions

1 Using an *AD/AS* diagram, explain possible effects on UK real national output of falling real incomes in 2012 and in earlier years.
2 How might recent changes in UK productivity have affected the position of the UK's *LRAS* curve?

SUMMARY

- The *AD/AS* model can be used to show macroeconomic equilibrium in the economy.
- Don't confuse macroeconomic equilibrium and microeconomic equilibrium.
- Make sure you can relate the *AD* curve to the explanation of aggregate demand in Chapter 18.
- The *AD* curve shows total planned spending on real national output at different price levels.
- Likewise, the *SRAS* curve shows how much output producers are prepared to supply at different price levels.
- It is important to distinguish between a *shift* of an *AD* or *AS* curve and the resulting *adjustment* along the curve that doesn't shift.
- A shift of the *AD* curve to the right is known as an increase in aggregate demand.
- The resulting movement up the *SRAS* curve is known as an expansion or extension of aggregate supply.
- Similar labelling is used with respect to other shifts of, and adjustments along, the *AD* and *SRAS* curves.
- The *LRAS* curve, which should not be confused with *SRAS* curves, is vertical because it is determined by the maximum potential output that the economy can produce.
- The economy can produce to the left of the *LRAS* curve, in which case there is unused capacity and unemployment, *temporarily* to the right of the *LRAS* curve, or above the potential level of output.
- A rightward movement of the *LRAS* curve illustrates long-term economic growth.
- Some Keynesian economists have argued that the *LRAS* curve is horizontal to the left of the full-employment level of real output, becoming vertical at the full-employment level of output.

Exam-style questions

1 Explain the shape of the aggregate demand curve. (12 marks)

2 Considering only the *SRAS* curve and not the *LRAS* curve, explain how an increase in aggregate demand may affect output and the price level. (12 marks)

3 Evaluate the view that unemployment can always be eliminated by increasing aggregate demand. (25 marks)

4 With the help of *AD/AS* analysis, discuss how demand-side and supply-side policies might be used to improve UK macroeconomic performance. (25 marks)

Chapter 20

Full employment and unemployment

In Chapter 16 it was shown how achieving full employment, or at least reducing the level and rate of unemployment, is arguably one of the government's two main policy objectives — the other being an acceptable and sustainable rate of long-term economic growth. Full employment was defined using Lord Beveridge's approach, set out in the 1944 White Paper on Employment Policy. Beveridge stated that an economy with 3% unemployment is more or less fully employed.

Having explained the two ways in which unemployment is measured in the UK, this chapter offers an alternative definition of full employment, in terms of the aggregate demand for, and the aggregate supply of, labour. It surveys the main causes of unemployment, and the government policies appropriate to reduce unemployment. The chapter concludes by considering the costs of unemployment, for the economy as a whole and for the unemployed and their families.

LEARNING OUTCOMES

This chapter will:
- explain how unemployment is measured in the UK
- define full employment
- illustrate full employment on a graph showing the economy's aggregate labour market
- explain the main causes of unemployment
- discuss the government policies appropriate for reducing unemployment
- assess the costs of unemployment, both for individuals and for the wider economy

How unemployment is measured in the UK

Unemployment is officially measured or estimated by the UK government in two ways: through the use of the claimant count and the Labour Force Survey.

The claimant count

Until quite recently, the main measure of unemployment officially used in the UK was the monthly **claimant count**. This is a by-product of the administrative system for paying unemployment-related benefits. The Jobseeker's Allowance, which until 2013 was the main employment-related benefit, is currently being merged into a new Universal Credit.

Many economists believe that the claimant count provides an inaccurate measure of true unemployment. Free-market economists, in particular, argue that the claimant count overstates unemployment because many claimants are either (a) not genuinely looking for work, or (b) not genuinely unemployed because they work in undeclared jobs in the underground or informal economy.

EXAM TIP

Exam questions might be set on how unemployment is measured in the UK. You must also be able to interpret claimant count or Labour Force Survey data.

In other respects, however, the claimant count understates true unemployment. The toughening up of eligibility requirements or tests for the availability for work in the 1980s and early 1990s reduced the claimant count without reducing unemployment. Various groups of unemployed, such as young workers on government training schemes and unemployed workers approaching retirement (who were reclassified as 'early retired'), have also been removed from the register, even though some of them would like full-time jobs.

The Labour Force Survey

The UK government now recognises a second measure of unemployment, based on the **Labour Force Survey** (LFS) of households. The LFS method uses standard, internationally recognised definitions recommended by the International Labour Organisation (ILO). It is a quarterly survey of 60,000 households that counts people as unemployed if they are actively seeking work (they have been looking for a job in the last 4 weeks) and have not had a job during the week in question.

KEY TERMS

claimant count: the method of measuring unemployment according to those people who are claiming unemployment-related benefits.

Labour Force Survey: a quarterly sample survey of households in the UK. Its purpose is to provide information on the UK labour market. The survey seeks information on respondents' personal circumstances and their labour market status during a period of 1–4 weeks.

When the LFS method of measuring unemployment is used, the unemployment total is significantly larger than the claimant count total. One of the reasons for this stems from the fact that many people without jobs who are actively looking for work are not registered as unemployed at Job Centres. Take the example of a family in which the father is employed full time, but the mother stays at home bringing up the couple's children. When their youngest child becomes a teenager, the mother decides to look for a job that allows her to take time off during school holidays or if her children are ill. Because such jobs are few and far between, the mother is prepared to wait until such a vacancy appears. As she is actively looking for work but not claiming benefit, the mother is unemployed according to the LFS measure of unemployment, but not according to the claimant count.

Although the LFS measure is higher than the claimant count, both measures may understate true unemployment because they ignore 'discouraged workers' — people who have given up hope of finding a job even though they would take one if it were offered — and roughly half a million people who are classified as 'economically inactive'.

CASE STUDY 20.1

How unemployment has changed in the UK

Figure 20.1 shows how UK unemployment, measured by both the LFS method and the claimant count, changed between 1992 and 2013. According to both measures, unemployment peaked at around 3 million at the end of 1992, just after the end of the deep recession that hit the UK in 1990. In the years of recovery and boom which followed, unemployment fell almost continuously to bottom out at 1.62 million (LFS) and 790,000 (claimant count) early in 2008. By the early 2000s, many communities in the UK, particularly in southeast England, could be said to be fully employed. However, other regions in the north and west of the UK were not so fortunate, and there were continuing pockets of unemployment in parts of London such as Hackney. By early 2008, recession was again looming, and with it a severe growth in unemployment, which peaked at 2.68 million, measured by the LFS, in November 2011.

The LFS measure is higher than the claimant count

Figure 20.1 LFS unemployment and the claimant count in the UK, 1992–2013

Source: ONS

Follow-up questions

1 Compare the changes in the LFS and the claimant count measures of unemployment over the period shown by the data in Figure 20.1.

2 Research how both measures of UK unemployment have changed over the period since 2013.

Making sense of employment and unemployment data

Some of the points to note about recent changes in employment and unemployment in the UK economy are as follows:

- The employment and unemployment data show the impact of recession on the UK economy.
- Much of the increase in employment in the 1990s and pre-2008 years resulted from growth of the public sector. However, since the recession, there have been swingeing cuts in public sector employment. The coalition government hoped that this would 'make room' for a growth in private sector employment. To a limited extent this happened, but the even greater cuts in public sector spending expected from 2013 onward may lead to a significant increase in overall unemployment.
- The figures also reflect a more deep-seated and perhaps intractable feature of British society: the gap between households in which every adult works, apart from those still in education or retired; and those in which nobody works, but people live on welfare benefits instead.
- In some years, both unemployment and employment were growing. This can happen when the number of people available for work grows faster than the number of jobs. Immigration of workers from central Europe provides part of the explanation for this.
- Unemployment is a lagged economic indicator. When the economy enters recession, employers often delay sacking workers for as long as they can. They decide to 'hoard' skilled workers, who might be difficult to rehire if the recession is short and the economy recovers quickly. Labour hoarding creates over-capacity at the beginning of a recession, which then results in a fall in labour productivity (output per worker).
- At the start of an economic upturn, firms may delay taking on new workers, preferring instead to squeeze more overtime from their labour force, at least until they can be sure the recovery is more than a mere 'blip'. This was certainly the case in the 1990s. However, the labour market behaved differently in 2012 and 2013. In the final quarter of 2012 employment was growing even though output was falling.
- Part-time and casualised employment has been growing as a percentage of total employment. Over half of newly created jobs have been part time. The number of people working part time because they can't find a full-time job has increased. Thousands of people now work on 'zero hours' contracts where work is dependent on employer need and where the absence of work results in an unpaid 'day off' rather than the person being regarded as unemployed.
- Youth unemployment has generally been growing. The number of 16–24-year-olds not in full-time education and looking for work was over a million in 2013, climbing to at least 20.3% of the youth labour force. For workers in general, there has also been a significant increase in 'economic inactivity' — a category which includes those who have simply given up looking for employment.
- The number of unemployed women has grown faster than male joblessness. This reflects the greater number of women in the workforce and the impact of public sector cuts, where a higher proportion of jobs are done by women.

The meaning of full employment

Full employment does not necessarily mean that every single member of the working population is in work. Rather, it is a situation in which the number of people wishing to work at the going market real wage rate equals the number of workers whom employers wish to hire at this real wage rate. Figure 20.2 reflects the free-market view that full employment occurs at the level of employment E_{FE}, where the aggregate demand for labour equals the aggregate supply of labour at real wage rate W_{FE}.

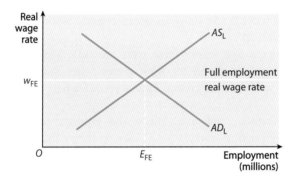

Figure 20.2 Full employment in the economy

EXTENSION MATERIAL

Equilibrium employment and unemployment

At AS, it is not necessary to understand the meaning of equilibrium employment and unemployment, but the concepts will be useful at A2. In Figure 20.2, the full-employment level of employment E_{FE} occurs when the economy's aggregate labour market is in equilibrium. Free-market economists also call this the natural level of employment.

At first sight, Figure 20.2 suggests that there is *no* unemployment when labour market equilibrium occurs, but as Figure 20.3 shows, this is not the case. There can be unemployment in the economy even when the aggregate labour market clears.

Frictional and structural unemployment (which are explained on pages 231–34) are the two forms of equilibrium unemployment. In Figure 20.3, the AS_{LN} curve shows *all* the workers available for work, and not just those willing to work at different real wage rates. The AS_{LN} curve is located to the right of the AS_L curve. Although full employment occurs at

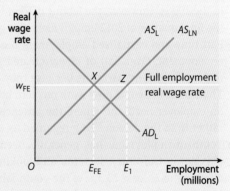

Figure 20.3 Equilibrium unemployment

E_{FE}, depicted where the AD_L and AS_L curves intersect at point X, equilibrium unemployment is measured by the distance from X to Z, or E_1 minus E_{FE}. Free-market economists call the equilibrium level of unemployment the natural level of unemployment.

The causes of unemployment

Full employment does not necessarily mean that every member of the working population is in work. Rather, as I have stated, it means a situation in which the number of people wishing to work at the going market real wage rate equals the number of workers whom employers wish to hire at this real wage rate.

However, even this definition needs qualifying since, in a dynamic economy, change is constantly taking place, with some industries declining and others growing. Workers moving between jobs may decide to take a break between the two employments. This is called **frictional unemployment**. As new products are developed and demand and cost conditions change, firms demand more of some labour skills while the demand for other types of labour declines. This leads to **structural unemployment**.

> **KEY TERM**
>
> **frictional unemployment:** voluntary unemployment, occurring when a worker switches between jobs.

Frictional unemployment

Frictional unemployment, also known as **transitional unemployment**, is essentially 'between jobs' unemployment. As its name suggests, this type of unemployment results from frictions in the labour market which create a delay, or time-lag, during which a worker is unemployed when moving from one job to another. Note that the definition of frictional unemployment assumes that a job vacancy exists and that a friction in the job market, caused by the immobility of labour, prevents an unemployed worker from filling the vacancy. It follows that the number of unfilled job vacancies existent in the economy can be used as a measure of the level of frictional unemployment.

Among the causes of frictional unemployment are geographical and occupational immobilities of labour, which prevent workers who are laid off from immediately filling job vacancies.

> **EXAM TIP**
>
> Do not confuse the *causes* and *effects* of unemployment.

The **geographical immobility of labour** is caused by factors such as family ties and local friendships discouraging people from moving to other parts of the country, ignorance about whether job vacancies exist in other parts of the country, and above all, the cost of moving and difficulties of obtaining housing.

The **occupational immobility of labour** results from difficulties in training for jobs that require different skills, the effects of restrictive practices such as a requirement that new workers must possess unnecessary qualifications, and race, gender and age discrimination in labour markets.

The **search theory of unemployment** also helps to explain frictional unemployment. Consider the situation illustrated in Figure 20.4. A worker earning £1,000 a week in a skilled professional occupation loses her job. Although no vacancies apparently exist at present in her current line of work, there are plenty of vacancies for low-skilled office workers earning around £300 a week. Given this information, if on the day of her job loss, the newly unemployed worker sets the weekly wage she aspires to at £1,000, she will *choose* to be unemployed, at least to start with, because she doesn't wish to fill a lower-paid vacancy. The lower weekly wage on offer, and perhaps poorer conditions of work and status associated with the lower-paid job, fail to meet her aspirations. She may also realise that she possesses imperfect information about the state of the job market. This means she needs to search the labour market to find out whether better-paid and higher-status vacancies exist, but which she does not know about currently.

Figure 20.4 Search theory and frictional unemployment

Approached in this way, frictional unemployment can be viewed as a *voluntary* search period in which newly unemployed workers scan the labour market, searching for vacancies which meet their aspirations.

There are a number of ways in which a voluntary search period can end. First, in the example described above, the woman may eventually learn of a vacancy for which she is qualified, and which meets her initial aspiration. Indeed, the vacancy might have been there all the time but, until she searched the job market, she was unaware of its existence. Second, the vacancy may have arisen during her search period, perhaps because of a general improvement in the condition of labour markets. Third, she may end her voluntary unemployment if she decides, on the basis of her lack of success in getting a job, that her initial aspirations were unrealistically high and that she must settle for a lower-paid, less attractive job.

Long search periods, which increase the amount of frictional unemployment in the economy, result in part from the welfare benefit system. Without the receipt of welfare benefits, search periods would have to be financed by running down stocks of saving, or through the charity of family and friends. In this situation, the threat of poverty creates an incentive to search the job market more vigorously and to reduce the aspirational wage levels of the unemployed.

The availability of a state safety net provided by unemployment benefits and other income-related welfare benefits, together in some cases with redundancy payments, enable unemployed workers to finance long voluntary search periods. Because of this, many free-market economists support a reduction in the real value of unemployment benefits, together with restricting benefits to those who can prove they are genuinely looking for work. Free-market economists believe these policies create incentives for the unemployed to reduce aspirations quickly, which shortens search periods.

EXTENSION MATERIAL

The replacement ratio

The replacement ratio is a factor influencing the length of periods of voluntary frictional unemployment. It is defined in the following equation:

$$\text{replacement ratio} = \frac{\text{disposable income out of work}}{\text{disposable income in work}}$$

The size of the replacement ratio is largely determined by the level of welfare benefits claimable when unemployed, relative to income after taxation and receipt of benefits when in work. A replacement ratio of 100% means that a worker is no better off in work than out of work and living off the state. Even for low-paid workers, replacement ratios are seldom as high as 100%. Nonetheless, high replacement ratios approaching 100% destroy the incentive to work, at least in the 'official' or formal economy. For people with poor job prospects, high replacement ratios create an **unemployment trap**. Those caught in the unemployment trap are out of work — at least in terms of officially declared employment. The trap contains unwaged social security claimants who 'choose' unemployment over paid work because they are better-off out of work and living on benefits than in low-paid jobs paying income tax and National Insurance Contributions (NIC) and losing some or all of their right to claim means-tested benefits.

In Figure 20.4, for a worker earning £300 a week, points A and B could be used to calculate the replacement ratio. Point A shows the weekly wage (although income tax and receipt of any benefits available to the worker in work also need to be taken into account to calculate weekly disposable income). Point B shows the level of welfare benefit claimable when out of work.

Structural unemployment

Structural unemployment results from the structural decline of industries which are unable to compete or adapt in the face of changing demand or new products, and the emergence of more efficient competitors in other countries. Structural unemployment is also caused by changing skill requirements as industries change ways of producing their products. In the latter case, the structural unemployment is often called **technological unemployment**. Technological unemployment results from the successful growth of new industries using labour-saving technology such as **automation**.

KEY TERM

structural unemployment: unemployment caused by structural change in the economy: for example, when industries decline without being replaced by new industries.

In contrast to **mechanisation** (workers operating machines), which has usually increased the overall demand for labour, automation can lessen the demand for labour because it means that machines (such as robots) rather than humans operate other machines. Whereas the growth of mechanised industry increases employment, automation of production can lead to the shedding of labour, even when industry output is expanding.

The growth of international competition has been a particularly important cause of structural unemployment. During the post-Second World War era from the 1950s to the 1970s, structural unemployment in the UK was regionally concentrated in areas where nineteenth-century staple industries such as textiles and shipbuilding were suffering structural decline. This regional unemployment, caused by the decline of 'sunset industries', was more than offset by the growth of employment elsewhere in the UK in 'sunrise industries'. However, in the severe recessions of the 1980s and 1990s, and also in the 2008 recession, structural unemployment

Automation can lead to technological unemployment

affected almost all regions in the UK as the de-industrialisation process spread across the manufacturing base.

Although manufacturing output grew in the 'boom' years before the 2008 recession, employment in manufacturing industries often fell. Recession and the growth of cyclical unemployment caused a further fall in manufacturing employment. However, there is a danger of exaggerating the growth of unemployment in manufacturing employment, because many activities, ranging from cleaning to IT maintenance, which were previously undertaken 'in house' by manufacturing firms, have been out-sourced to external service sector providers. Structural unemployment has occurred within the service sector as well as in manufacturing industries. For example, increasing use of ICT, automated services and the internet has meant that total employment has fallen in the travel agency industry. Call centre employment has grown significantly in recent years, though much of this growth has been in low-wage economies such as India. However, a decline has been forecast, partly because companies employ automated communication software rather than human beings to provide customer service and answer telephone and internet queries.

Casual and seasonal unemployment

Casual unemployment is a special case of frictional unemployment, which occurs when workers are laid off on a short-term basis in trades such as tourism, agriculture, catering and building. When casual unemployment results from regular fluctuations in weather conditions or demand, it is called **seasonal unemployment**.

Cyclical, Keynesian or demand-deficient unemployment

The possibility of **demand-deficient unemployment** was introduced in Chapter 15. Keynes — but not his opponents — believed that deficient aggregate demand was a major cause of persistent mass unemployment between the First and Second

World Wars. Free-market economists generally agree that temporary unemployment (called **cyclical unemployment**) may be caused by a lack of demand in the downswing of the economic cycle. However, Keynes went further, arguing that the economy could settle into an under-full employment equilibrium, caused by a continuing lack of effective aggregate demand. In contrast to frictional unemployment, which is voluntary, Keynes believed that cyclical unemployment is involuntary: that is, not caused by the workers themselves. As a result, the unemployed should not be blamed for their idleness.

Figure 20.5 illustrates cyclical unemployment in the context of the economy's AD/AS diagram. A collapse in business and consumer confidence causes the AD curve to shift left from AD_1 to AD_2. If goods and labour markets are competitive, the average price level should then fall from P_1 to P_2. If this happens, real output only falls from y_1 to y_2.

Figure 20.5 Cyclical unemployment caused by a shift of aggregate demand to the left

Figure 20.6 Cyclical unemployment and the economy's production possibility frontier

However, price (and wage) stickiness (or inflexibility) can prevent this happening. If prices (and wages) don't fall, real output falls to y_3 rather than y_2. Deficient aggregate demand, shown by the distance between points X and Z, leads to severe cyclical unemployment.

Figure 20.6, which shows the economy's production possibility frontier (*PPF*), illustrates another way of showing cyclical unemployment. All points on the production possibility frontier, including point X, show the economy using all its productive capacity, including labour. There is no demand deficiency and thus no cyclical unemployment. By contrast, deficient aggregate demand can lead to the economy producing inside its production possibility frontier: for example, at point Z. When this is the case, cyclical unemployment exists in the economy.

EXAM TIP

This is an example of applying AD/AS analysis to illustrate an important aspect of macroeconomics. There are many other economic problems and issues that can be analysed in similar ways.

EXAM TIP

This is another example of how to use a production possibility curve diagram to illustrate your point. Remember its other applications: scarcity, opportunity cost, choice, productive efficiency and economic growth.

Other causes of unemployment

The AQA specification requires knowledge of cyclical, frictional, seasonal and structural unemployment. Unemployment can, however, have causes other than those that lead to the four types of unemployment listed in the AS specification. It is useful, though not essential, to be aware of some of these other causes, particularly if you intend to study economics at A2.

Classical or real-wage unemployment

Before the Keynesian era, economists believed that a large part of the high level of unemployment in the 1920s and 1930s was caused by excessively high real wages in labour markets, which were insufficiently competitive for market forces to eliminate the problem. In recent years, the view that a large part of modern unemployment in the UK, especially youth unemployment, has been caused by too high a level of real wages has been revived by free-market and supply-side economists.

Figure 20.7 Classical or real-wage unemployment

Figure 20.7 is similar to Figure 20.2, except that it is now assumed that the average real wage rate in the economy is w_1 rather than w_{FE}. At this wage, employers wish to hire E_1 workers, but a greater number of workers (E_2) wish to supply their labour. This results in an excess supply of labour in the labour market. The pre-Keynesians believed that, as long as the labour market was competitive, this classical or real-wage unemployment could only be temporary. Market forces operating in the labour market would cure the problem, bidding down the real wage rate to w_{FE} to get rid of excess supply of labour. Full employment would be restored when the number of workers willing to work equalled the number whom firms wished to hire.

Suppose labour market rigidity, perhaps caused by trade unions, prevents the real wage rate falling below w_1. In this situation, the market mechanism fails to work properly, the excess supply of labour persists, and real-wage or classical unemployment occurs. Using modern terminology, unemployment is caused by wage stickiness or wage inflexibility.

Hysteresis

Hysteresis is the destruction of productive capacity and job skills in a deep recession. When the economy recovers, productive capacity is no longer there, so demand has to be met by imports. Hysteresis tends to blur the distinction between cyclical and structural unemployment. In a prolonged recession, members of the labour force, who were initially cyclically unemployed, drift into becoming structurally unemployed.

'Insider/outsider' unemployment

The 'insider/outsider' theory of unemployment argues that trade union members are 'insiders' in the labour market, while the unemployed, especially those who allowed their union membership to lapse on losing their jobs, are 'outsiders'. The theory is based on the assumption that unionised workers enjoy higher wages than non-unionised ones. Unions may care only about the employment prospects of their members who are currently employed (the insiders), and may not really care about the outsiders. The 'insider/outsider' theory suggests that unions may be prepared to push for higher real wages even when unemployment is high, basically because they are unconcerned about unemployment among 'outsiders'.

Queuing unemployment

Queuing unemployment occurs when unemployed workers reject lower-paid jobs in the non-unionised sector of the economy, in the hope that a better-paid unionised job will arise. Continuous turnover in the labour market also contributes to queuing. Every week, some employees retire or leave the labour force, others switch jobs, while simultaneously new jobs are created. Waiting for a suitable vacancy may be a sensible strategy. In this second interpretation, queuing unemployment is closely related to the search theory of voluntary frictional unemployment, explained earlier in the chapter.

Government policies to reduce unemployment

When governments intervene to reduce unemployment, the appropriate policy depends on identifying correctly the underlying cause of unemployment. For example, if unemployment is incorrectly diagnosed in terms of demand deficiency, when the true cause is structural, a policy of fiscal or monetary expansion to stimulate aggregate demand will be ineffective and inappropriate. Indeed, reflation of demand in such circumstances would probably create excess demand, which raises the price level in a demand-pull inflation, with no lasting beneficial effects on employment.

Governments can try to reduce frictional unemployment by improving the geographical and occupational mobility of labour, and by reducing workers' search periods between jobs. Geographical mobility can be improved by making it easier for families to move house from one region to another. However, the widening difference in house prices between south and north are in fact increasing the geographical immobility of labour.

The introduction of the Jobseeker's Allowance in 1996 (now being merged into the Universal Credit) was an attempt to reduce search periods between jobs. Because the allowance can only be claimed for the first few months of unemployment, it creates an incentive for the newly unemployed to accept lower wage rates and to speed up the search for vacancies that meet their (now reduced) aspirations. However, the only really effective way to reduce frictional and structural unemployment is to achieve successful economic growth, which increases firms' demand for new employees.

Governments can improve the occupational mobility of labour by providing retraining schemes and introducing laws to ban professional and trade union restrictive practices that prevent workers moving between jobs. Government retraining schemes are usually less effective than those run by private sector firms. But a problem is that employers in trades such as plumbing often prefer to free-ride, by poaching workers from the few employers who do train their workers. As a result of this market failure, too few workers end up being trained.

Supply-side policies which try to improve the competitiveness and efficiency of markets are now used to reduce frictional and structural unemployment. In the past, deindustrialisation, or the decline of manufacturing industries, together with coal mining and fishing, led to large-scale structural unemployment, concentrated in regions of decline such as coal fields and areas previously dominated by heavy industry.

Many traditional manufacturing industries and the coal industry have now largely disappeared, so there is less scope for further structural decline in these activities. The supply-side reforms of the 1980s and 1990s also created conditions in which service industries grew to replace manufacturing. As a result, more workers were able to move from declining industries into growing ones. However, as the recent and current financial services crisis shows, service industries such as banking have themselves become vulnerable to structural decline and to overseas location.

Unemployment and supply-side economics

It is now widely agreed, by Keynesians as well as by free-market economists, that the cause of much modern unemployment in countries such as the UK lies on the supply side of the economy rather than on the demand side. There is much disagreement, however, on the appropriate policies to improve supply-side performance.

Free-market economists argue that poor supply-side performance is the legacy of government interventionism in the Keynesian era in the 1960s and 1970s. Supply-side economists argue that to cut frictional, structural and real-wage unemployment, the state's economic role should be reduced rather than extended. Obeying the dictum, 'markets and not governments create full employment', the government's role should be to create the conditions, in which the market mechanism and private enterprise can function properly, by controlling inflation, promoting competitive markets and maintaining the rule of law and social order. Supply-side economists see the government, not as a *provider*, but as an *enabler*, setting markets free, encouraging competition, fostering private enterprise and the entrepreneurial spirit, and thereby creating an enterprise culture in which the price mechanism, and not the government, delivers economic growth and reduces unemployment.

Many Keynesian economists disagree. They believe that markets are prone to market failure and that unemployment is the result of a massive market failure. The failure can only be cured by interventionist policies to modify the market and make it function better.

The costs and consequences of unemployment for the whole economy

Unemployment is bad for the economy as a whole, largely through the waste of human capital. When workers are unemployed, not all the economy's productive resources are used to produce output, which, if produced, could add to the material standards of living and economic welfare of the whole population. Instead, the economy produces inside its production possibility frontier and fails to operate to its potential.

Unemployment is also one of the factors that reduce an economy's international competitiveness. High unemployment can reduce incentives for firms to invest in new state-of-the-art technologies that generally lead to increased export competitiveness. The under-investment associated with high unemployment also results from a reduced need to invest in capital-intensive technologies when there are plenty of unemployed workers who are not only available, but cheap to hire. In these circumstances, employers continue to use labour-intensive but antiquated technologies, particularly when high unemployment accompanies a stagnant economy, low profits and a climate of business pessimism.

Under-investment can also be caused by the higher business taxes that firms may have to pay to help finance the welfare benefits paid to unemployed workers.

While it is true that the Jobseeker's Allowance could only be claimed in the first months of unemployment, in the UK the state continued to pay Income Support to families in which there is no wage earner, in order to save family members, particularly children, from the effects of absolute poverty. However, in 2013, with the introduction of the Universal Credit the coalition government introduced a **benefit cap**, which limits to £26,000 a year all the benefits an out-of-work family can receive. The government justified the 'cap' on the ground that families living solely on benefits should not receive welfare payments higher than the earnings of low-paid wage earners.

Economies are particularly badly affected by long-term unemployment. A worker may become effectively unemployable the longer the period that he or she is out of work: for example, because of the erosion of job skills and work habits. Long-term unemployment is also made worse by the fact that employers, who might otherwise hire and retrain workers who have been economically inactive for several years, perceive that workers with more recent job experience present fewer risks and are more employable. When inactive workers are seen as unemployable, the economy begins to behave as if it is on its production possibility frontier, even though there are plenty of unemployed workers notionally available for work. An increase in aggregate demand can then lead to inflation rather than to an increase in output and jobs.

Nevertheless, despite the disadvantages of high unemployment for the economy, many free-market economists believe a certain amount of unemployment is necessary to make the economy function better. In particular, by providing downward pressure on wage rates, unemployment can reduce inflation. Unemployment also contributes to a widening of income differentials between better-paid and low-paid workers. Some free-market economists argue that this is a good thing, believing that differences in pay are needed to promote incentives, which then create the supply-side conditions in which the economy can prosper.

The costs and consequences of unemployment for the unemployed and their families

Unemployment is obviously bad for the unemployed themselves and for their families, largely because of the way in which the low incomes that accompany unemployment lead to low standards of living. However, the costs of unemployment for the unemployed go further than this. Apart from situations in which the unemployed enjoy having 24 hours of leisure time each and every day, or when the so-called 'unemployed' are engaged in black economy activity, unemployment destroys hope in the future. The unemployed become marginalised from normal economic and human activity, and their self-esteem is reduced. Families suffer increased health risks, greater stress, a reduction in the quality of diet, and an increased risk of marital break-up and social exclusion caused by loss of work and income.

SUMMARY

- In the UK, unemployment is measured by the claimant count and through the Labour Force Survey.
- UK unemployment is much higher when measured by the LFS.
- People may be employed, unemployed or economically inactive.
- Full employment exists when the number of workers whom firms wish to hire equals the number of workers wanting to work.
- AS exam questions may test knowledge of frictional, structural, cyclical and seasonal unemployment.
- Frictional unemployment is transitional and 'between jobs' unemployment. It is also voluntary.
- Structural unemployment results from the structural decline of industries and from changes in required job skills.
- Cyclical unemployment is also known as Keynesian and demand-deficient unemployment.
- Keynesian economists argue that cyclical unemployment is involuntary, which means that it is not the fault of the unemployed themselves.
- Policies to reduce unemployment will only be effective if the causes of unemployment are correctly diagnosed.
- The costs of unemployment fall on the whole economy and on the unemployed and their families.

Exam-style questions

1 Explain the difference between frictional and structural unemployment.   (12 marks)

2 Explain why it is important to identify correctly the cause of unemployment.   (12 marks)

3 Do you agree that it is more important to reduce unemployment than to reduce inflation? Justify your answer.   (25 marks)

4 Evaluate the view that a certain amount of unemployment is necessary in order to make the economy function better.   (25 marks)

Price stability and inflation

For three decades from the 1960s to the early 1990s, unacceptably high rates of inflation were perhaps the most serious problem facing UK governments. The inflation rate crept up in the 1960s, before accelerating in the early 1970s to over 15% in each year between 1974 and 1977. Inflation peaked at its highest rate in modern UK history in the mid-1970s, when it hit 25–26%. A further surge, which took inflation to above 18% in 1980, ushered in the modern era in which, at least until 2008, control of inflation became arguably the most important single macroeconomic policy objective.

In 2008, the economic climate changed when inflation as well as recession both hit the UK economy. Inflation had been more or less under control from around 1993 until 2008. However, in 2008 and then again in 2011, rising prices of commodities, ranging from crude oil to copper and wheat, together with the rising prices of manufactured goods produced in China, led to relatively severe bouts of imported inflation. Despite the recession, and because of its imported nature, UK inflation had become difficult to control.

LEARNING OUTCOMES

This chapter will:

- review the meaning of inflation and related concepts such as deflation and reflation
- describe how inflation is measured
- compare changes in the rate of inflation for goods with changes in the rate of inflation for services
- introduce the main theories of inflation
- apply *AD/AS* analysis to the two main theories of inflation: demand-pull and cost-push
- discuss the benefits and costs of inflation

The meaning of inflation

Inflation is best defined as a persistent or continuing rise in the price level, or as a fall in the value of money. **Deflation** is the opposite, a persistent tendency for the price level to fall, which involves a rise in the value of money. However, because the *overall* price level has seldom fallen in western industrialised countries since the 1930s, the term 'deflation' is usually applied in a looser way to describe a reduction in aggregate demand and levels of economic activity, output and employment. A **deflationary policy** (also known as a *disinflationary* policy) involves using fiscal and/or monetary policy to reduce aggregate demand. Likewise, **reflation** refers to an increase in economic activity and output, and a **reflationary policy** stimulates aggregate demand. When caused by excess spending in the economy, it is useful to think of inflation as 'reflation gone wrong', with an increase in aggregate demand stimulating the price level rather than real output and employment.

KEY TERMS

deflation: a persistent or continuing fall in the average price level.

inflation: a persistent or continuing rise in the average price level.

reflation: an increase in the level of real output following an increase in aggregate demand.

The measurement of inflation

Until 2003, the rate of inflation was measured in the UK by changes in the **retail prices index (RPI)**. The government still uses the RPI for this purpose, but the **consumer prices index (CPI)** has now become the main measure of inflation. The CPI is based on the method of measuring the price level used in the European Union. As will be explained in greater detail in Chapter 23, UK monetary policy has aimed to hit an inflation rate target of 2%, measured by the CPI.

Each month, the prices of all the goods in the national 'shopping basket' are recorded at hundreds of supermarkets, shops and other retail outlets, so that the price index for that month can be calculated. Twelve months earlier, the price index will have been calculated for the same month in that year. The inflation rate covering the 12-month period between these two dates can therefore be calculated using one of the following formulae:

CPI formula

$$\frac{\text{later date CPI} - \text{earlier date CPI}}{\text{earlier date CPI}} \times 100$$

RPI formula

$$\frac{\text{later date RPI} - \text{earlier date RPI}}{\text{earlier date RPI}} \times 100$$

Using these formulae, the annual rate of inflation measured by the CPI was 2.7% for the year ending December 2012. By contrast, the inflation rate measured by the RPI was higher, at 3.1%.

Why the CPI and the RPI may fail to measure the true rate of inflation

A price index can never provide a completely accurate measure of the price level, the cost of living, or the rate of inflation. There are a number of reasons for this. The representative sample of goods in the national shopping basket is never fully representative of all income groups and types of household in the economy. Different income groups and households buy different goods and services, so some will experience higher inflation rates than others. Because it is difficult to accommodate improvements in the quality of goods in a price index, price indices may also tend to slightly overstate the true rate of inflation. In the case of the CPI, however, this may be countered by the exclusion from the index of 'big ticket' high-inflation items such as mortgage costs and the council tax. The way in which goods in the sample are weighted may also be inaccurate, and it is possible that junior government employees who collect raw data that go into the construction of the index may not record prices accurately.

The RPI, the CPI and 'index linking'

In the early days of the RPI, approximately 50 years ago, its main purpose was measurement of the cost of living and the rate of inflation. However, the RPI came to be used in another way: for **index linking** rates of increase in welfare benefits: for example, the state pension and unemployment benefits. The rates at which welfare benefits were paid (and some public sector pay) increased each year in line with annual changes in the RPI.

Used in this way, a significant problem arises when the RPI understates the true rate of inflation, particularly the rate experienced by pensioners and the unemployed. In this situation, the *money* incomes of pensioners and benefit claimants rise at exactly the same rate as the RPI, but by less than the true rate of inflation affecting them. If, at the same time, the incomes of employed people keep up with or exceed the RPI rate of inflation, people on index-linked benefits or pay become *relatively* poorer. The opposite is true when index-linked benefits rise faster than average pay.

Recently, to reduce the cost of welfare payments, which are by far the largest item in central government spending, the government switched their index linking away from the RPI to the CPI. The CPI usually rises at a slower rate than the RPI because it does not take into account changes in housing costs.

CASE STUDY 21.1

Measuring inflation: changes to CPI and RPI shopping baskets

The contents of the CPI and RPI baskets of goods and services and their weights are updated annually. This is important in helping to avoid potential biases that might otherwise develop over time — for example, due to the development of entirely new goods and services, or the tendency for consumers to move away from buying goods and services which have risen relatively rapidly in price.

In principle, the basket should contain all consumer goods and services purchased by households, and the prices measured in every shop or outlet that supplies them. In practice, both the CPI and RPI are calculated by collecting a sample of prices for a selection of representative goods and services in a range of UK retail locations. Currently, around 180,000 separate price quotations are used every month in compiling the indices, covering approaching 700 representative consumer goods and services for which prices are collected in around 150 areas throughout the UK.

The ONS collects information on a 'shopping basket'

There are some individual goods and services where typical household spending is so large that they merit inclusion in the basket in their own right: examples include petrol, and electricity and gas supply. However, it would be both impractical and unnecessary to measure price changes of every item bought by every household in compiling the CPI and RPI.

More commonly, a sample of specific goods and services has to be selected that gives a reliable measure of price movements for a broader range of similar items. Changes to the basket reflect evolving consumer tastes and considerations such as practical experience in collecting prices.

In 2012, baby wipes were introduced to represent 'cleansers on the go'. Bundled communication packages comprising telephone services, internet access and television subscriptions were also included for the first time, as were tablet computers (such as the iPad and Samsung Galaxy Tab) and teenage fiction books. Other products were added to widen the range of goods in a particular category, such as soft continental cheese to the dairy product category and cans of stout to the beer category. Subscription to cable television has been removed but it is still covered as part of the bundled communication package.

Source: ONS, accessed March 2013

Follow-up questions
1 What is meant by 'weighting' in the construction of a price index such as the CPI?
2 Why may changes in a price index such as the CPI or the RPI not provide an accurate measure of the rate of inflation, especially the inflation rate affecting pensioners?

CASE STUDY 21.2

The state pension and pensioners' costs of living

The annual change in the CPI inflation rate, measured in September, is currently used to determine the following year's benefit increases. CPI inflation was at its lowest for 3 years at 2.2% in September 2012, but is currently rising towards 3% or more.

Under a government guarantee introduced when the decision was made to change the index-linking of the state pension, pensions must rise each year by at least 2.5%. For 2013, this is £2.69 a week. But if the RPI inflation rate were still to be used, pensions would increase by 2.6%, or £2.80, in April 2013.

The director-general of Saga recently said that because old people's rate of inflation is significantly higher than the inflation rate measured by both the RPI and the CPI, pensioners' spending power has already been squeezed more tightly than that of the population generally. She said the real value of the pension is likely to fall even further behind in future years, despite state pension increases.

Source: adapted from news reports, March 2013

Follow-up questions
1 Why is the rate of inflation suffered by pensioners higher than RPI or CPI inflation?
2 Suggest reasons why pensioners experience a higher rate of inflation than students living with their parents.

Recent changes in the RPI and the CPI inflation rates

As Figure 21.1 shows, there have been a number of ups and downs in the UK inflation rate during recent years. In 2008, the inflation rate rose to approximately 5%. Very high oil prices drove up transport costs, which then fed into higher retail prices of products in the shops and into higher household energy bills. High oil price rises also made food more expensive, via the effect on fertiliser prices and on the fuel used by farmers to power their tractors. Droughts, rising demand from emerging economies

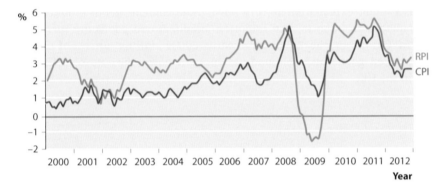

Figure 21.1 Annual percentage RPI and CPI inflation rates, 2000–12

Source: ONS, March 2013

and land being used to produce biofuel, together with a fall in the exchange rate, also contributed to higher import prices.

But a year later in 2009, the CPI annual inflation rate had fallen to about 1%, while the RPI inflation rate was negative. Almost zero inflation, or deflation (depending on which price index was used to measure changing price), was caused by a dramatic fall in the price of oil in just 6 months and by the collapse in aggregate demand as recession hit the UK economy. Another contributing factor in the UK was a temporary cut in the VAT rate from 17.5% to 15%, introduced to try to kick-start aggregate demand.

However, the VAT rate was raised back to 17.5% at the beginning of 2010, before increasing again to 20% in 2011. Rapidly rising energy prices, transport prices and food prices soon led to a return to strongly positive inflation. By September 2011, the CPI inflation rate was again at its 2008 peak of 5.2%. The RPI inflation rate was even higher, at 5.6%. In 2011 and 2012, both inflation rates steadily dropped, but the CPI rate stubbornly refused to fall to the 2% target.

The Bank of England (and the government) still hope to achieve the 2% target, believing that lower oil and import prices will do the trick. However, critics say that the methods used to try to reduce the inflation rate to 2% lack credibility and that the Bank of England has 'shot its bolt'. I shall explore this issue in Chapter 23 which links the control of inflation to monetary policy.

Comparing the rates of inflation for goods and services

Figure 21.2 shows the rates of inflation for goods and services in the UK from 1997 until the end of 2011. The graph divides into two distinct periods. In the earlier years, the inflation rate for services was significantly higher than the inflation rate for goods. From early 1999 until the end of 2005, goods experienced price deflation while the rate of inflation for services was positive — as it has always been, at least in living memory.

There is a simple explanation for this. Most, though not all, goods produced in the UK compete with imports, and imported manufactured goods are increasingly made in China. In the 1990s and early 2000s, falling prices of imported manufactured goods and commodities brought down the rate of inflation for goods in the UK.

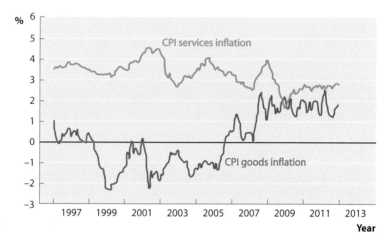

Figure 21.2 The rates of inflation for goods and service, 1997–2012

Source: ONS and Bank of England

Unlike goods, many, though not all, services do not have to compete with imports. Services such as hair cuts, car servicing and restaurant meals are sold in the 'sheltered', or non-internationally traded, economy. By contrast, goods such as cars and food are generally sold in the open, or internationally traded, economy. Service provision also tends to be labour intensive, and thus less able to benefit from the productivity increases which reduce costs in the manufacturing industry. Note also that, with increasing real incomes, people tend to spend more of their incomes on services and a smaller proportion on manufactured goods.

Since 2005, as noted earlier, the prices of many goods, especially commodities and sources of energy such as wheat, copper and oil, have risen rapidly. Rising goods and services prices help to explain why overall inflation remains above the government's 2% target.

The causes of inflation

There are two basic causes of inflation: excess aggregate demand in the economy, and a general rise in costs of production. The former gives rise to demand-pull inflation (or demand inflation), while the latter is called cost-push inflation (or cost inflation).

EXAM TIP

Don't confuse the *causes* of inflation with the *effects* of inflation.

As the names imply, demand-pull inflation locates the cause of inflation in the demand side of the economy, whereas cost-push inflation has supply-side causes.

Demand-pull inflation

Demand-pull inflation is caused by an increase in aggregate demand. Following the shift of the aggregate demand curve to the right, the price level has to rise to persuade firms to produce more output to meet the extra demand.

KEY TERM

demand-pull inflation: a rising price level caused by an increase in aggregate demand, shown by a shift of the AD curve to the right.

Demand inflation also occurs when the economy is on its production possibility frontier (and also producing at a point on the vertical LRAS curve). In this situation, an increase in aggregate demand creates excess demand that cannot be met in the short run by an increase in output (except through a temporary increase in output above the potential level of output). Excess aggregate demand pulls up the price level.

EXAM TIP

Investment spending and government spending on capital goods shift the LRAS curve to the right. In the long run, a shift of the LRAS curve to the right can offset demand-pull inflationary pressures.

The equation summarising the different elements of aggregate demand is:

$$AD = C + I + G + (X - M)$$

An increase in any of the components of aggregate demand, C, I, G or $(X - M)$, can lead to demand-pull inflation. Increases in consumption spending (C) by households or current government spending (G) on public sector pay and welfare benefits are particularly likely to pull up the price level.

Using AD/AS diagrams to illustrate demand-pull inflation

Aggregate demand/aggregate supply (AD/AS) diagrams can illustrate the main features of demand-pull and cost-push inflation. Figure 21.3 illustrates demand-pull inflation.

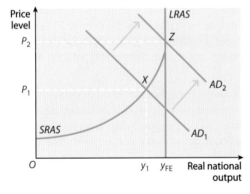

Figure 21.3 Demand-pull inflation illustrated by an AD/AS diagram

The figure assumes that macroeconomic equilibrium is initially at point X. The AD curve is in the position AD_1; real output is at level y_1 and the price level is P_1. Given this initial situation, any event that shifts the AD curve to the right — for example, to AD_2 — causes the price level to rise, in this case to P_2. In this example, real income increases to its full-employment level at y_{FE}. At the price level P_1, the economy's firms are only prepared to produce an output of y_1. This means that a higher price level is needed to create the conditions in which firms increase output from y_1 to y_{FE}.

> **EXAM TIP**
>
> As Chapter 19 explains, an economy may be able to produce *temporarily* above its production potential and to the right of the *LRAS* curve, but this level of output cannot be sustained.

Figure 21.3 shows an economy initially close to full employment, and eventually at full employment, once the *AD* curve has shifted right to AD_2. Following the increase in aggregate demand, macroeconomic equilibrium is at point Z, with the economy also on its long-run aggregate supply (*LRAS*) curve. This means the economy is producing at full capacity, so any further shift of aggregate demand to the right would result solely in demand-pull inflation, with no increase in real output (except on a temporary basis).

Contrast this outcome with what would happen had the *AD* curve initially been located substantially to the left of AD_1, with the economy in deep recession, suffering demand-deficient or cyclical unemployment. In this situation, a shift of aggregate demand to the right would increase output and employment, but with relatively little effect on inflation. Arguably, the adverse effect of a rising price level would be less significant than the boost to output and employment brought about by an increase in aggregate demand. However, as the increasing slope of the *SRAS* curve suggests, as the *AD* curve shifts right and moves closer to the *LRAS* curve, increasingly, the reflation of real output (and employment) gives way to demand-pull inflation.

EXTENSION MATERIAL

Monetarist and Keynesian demand-pull inflation

The monetarist theory of inflation

In the late 1970s and the early 1980s, a group of generally pro-free-market economists became known as monetarists.

Monetarists argue that inflation is caused by excess demand pulling up the price level, but they go one stage further by arguing that excess aggregate demand for output is caused by a prior increase in the money supply. To quote the leading monetarist economist Milton Friedman, many monetarists believe that 'inflation is always and everywhere a monetary phenomenon'.

The oldest theory of inflation, the quantity theory of money, lies at the heart of the monetarist theory of inflation. According to the quantity theory, the government creates or condones an expansion of the money supply greater than the increase in real national output. As a result, households and firms hold excess money balances which, when spent, pull up the price level — given the assumption that real output does not expand in line with the increase in spending power.

The Keynesian demand-pull theory of inflation

The quantity theory of money and the Keynesian demand-pull theory are both *demand* theories of inflation, which locate the cause of inflation in excess demand for goods and services. The difference between the two lies in the underlying cause of aggregate demand increasing. Monetarists locate the cause in excess growth of the money supply. Keynesians locate the 'engine of inflation' firmly in the real economy, in behavioural factors that cause the planned expenditure of economic agents (households, firms, the government and the overseas sectors) to exceed the quantity of output which the economy was capable of producing.

However, the two demand-pull theories may not be as different as they appear at first sight. In both theories, the *ultimate* cause of inflation may lie with the government. In the monetarist theory, financing the government's budget deficit causes monetary expansion which triggers, and then sustains, demand-pull inflation. In the Keynesian theory, a budget deficit is increasingly viewed as the most important single cause of excess demand.

Cost-push inflation

During the Keynesian era in the 1960s and 1970s, the rate of inflation increased even when there was no evidence of excess demand in the economy. This led to the development of the **cost-push theory of inflation**. Cost theories of inflation locate the cause of inflation in structural and institutional conditions on the supply side of the economy, particularly in the labour market and the wage-bargaining process.

Causes of cost-push inflation

Cost-push theories generally argue that the growth of monopoly power in the economy's labour market and in its markets for goods and services is responsible for inflation. In labour markets, growing trade union strength in the Keynesian era enabled trade unions to bargain for money-wage increases in excess of any rise in labour productivity. Monopoly firms were prepared to pay these wage increases, partly because of the costs of disrupting production, and partly because they believed that they could pass on the increasing costs as price rises when they sold output in the markets for their goods.

Using AD/AS diagrams to illustrate cost-push inflation

The *AD/AS* diagram in Figure 21.4 illustrates cost-push inflation. Once again (as is the case in Figure 21.3, which illustrates demand-pull inflation), macroeconomic equilibrium is at point X, with real output and the price level respectively at y_1 and P_1. In this case, the money costs of production that firms incur when they produce output rise: for example, because money wages or the price of imported raw materials increase. The increase in production costs causes the *SRAS* curve to shift left and up from $SRAS_1$ to $SRAS_2$.

Figure 21.4 Cost-push inflation illustrated on an *AD/AS* diagram

As a result of the shift of the *SRAS* curve to the left, the price level increases to P_2, but higher production costs have reduced the equilibrium level of output that firms are willing to produce to y_2. The new macroeconomic equilibrium is at point Z.

Cost-push inflation and the danger of 'stagflation'

An increase in business costs, which leads to the shift of the *SRAS* curve to the left and the consequent increase in the price level, also causes the level of real output to fall, or at least for its rate of growth to slow down. In the 1970s, when cost-push inflation was rampant in the UK, the combination of rising prices and falling output became known as 'stagflation' or 'slumpflation'. Stagflation was one of the factors that led to free-market policies replacing the Keynesian policies of demand management and intervention in markets.

In the 2008 recession, stagflation returned to haunt the UK economy and its policy-makers.

In 2003, the governor of the Bank of England had coined the term 'NICE-ness' to describe the benign years of continuing economic growth, falling unemployment and low inflation that benefited the UK during most of the 1990s and the early 2000s. (The acronym 'NICE' stands for non-inflationary, consistently expansionary.)

As the first decade of the twenty-first century reached its end, economists worried that 'NICE-ness' had given way to the 'VILE' decade: namely, 'volatile inflation, less expansionary'.

CASE STUDY 21.3

What does the future hold?

The rapid growth of India and China is having a major impact on the UK economy. In the past, goods made in China helped to keep UK inflation down. We have been able to buy cheap household goods and other manufactured products at far lower prices than if they had been produced in the Western economies. But now that has all changed. The spectacular growth of the emerging markets of the world is putting excessive demands on oil and gas reserves as well as on most other commodities. This is having a direct knock-on effect on the prices of almost everything we buy in our supermarkets. We are now in a permanent state of high oil and energy prices.

The Western world has had it very good up to now. The economic growth of the UK, Europe and the USA has been underwritten by cheap energy, commodity and food prices. But the global economy has now entered a 'perfect storm' where the growth of the emerging markets, climate change, population increases and the peaking of oil production are forcing us to have a serious rethink about the future.

Follow-up questions

1 Explain **two** reasons why events in the global economy have partially caused the stagflation that the UK has recently experienced.
2 Explain how cost-push inflation contributes to stagflation.

The benefits and costs of inflation

Inflation can have serious adverse effects or costs, and the seriousness of the adverse effects depends on whether inflation is anticipated or unanticipated. If inflation could be anticipated with complete certainty, it would pose few problems. Households and firms would simply build the expected rate of inflation into their economic decisions, which would not be distorted by wrong guesses.

EXAM TIP

You should discuss the benefits and costs of inflation when explaining the *effects* of inflation on the economy.

When inflation is relatively low, with little variation from year to year, it is relatively easy to anticipate next year's inflation rate. Indeed, creeping inflation, which is associated with growing markets, healthy profits and a general climate of business optimism, 'greases the wheels' of the economy. Viewed in this way, a low rate of inflation — and not absolute price stability or zero inflation — may be a necessary side-effect or cost of expansionary policies to reduce unemployment.

However, some free-market economists argue that inflation acts like 'sand in the wheels' of the economy, making it less efficient and competitive. If the 'sand-in-the-wheels' effect is stronger than the 'greasing-the-wheels' effect, the costs or disadvantages of inflation exceed the benefits or advantages.

A low but stable inflation rate may also be necessary to make labour markets function efficiently. Even if average real wage rates are rising, there will be some labour markets in which real wages must fall in order to maintain a low rate of unemployment. When prices are completely stable (i.e. when the inflation rate is zero), to cut real wage rates, nominal wage rates have to fall. To save jobs, workers may be willing to accept falling real wages caused by money-wage rates rising at a slower rate than inflation. However, workers are much less willing to accept cuts in money-wage rates. Thus, with zero inflation, the changes required in relative real-wage rates, which are needed to make labour markets function efficiently, fail to take place. Labour markets function best when inflation is low but stable. By contrast, absolute price stability produces wage stickiness, which results in unnecessarily high unemployment.

Some of the costs or disadvantages of inflation are:

- **Distributional effects.** Weaker social groups in society, living on fixed incomes, lose, while those in strong bargaining positions gain. Also, with rapid inflation, real rates of interest may be negative. In this situation, lenders are really paying borrowers for the doubtful privilege of lending to them, and inflation acts as a hidden tax, redistributing income and wealth from lenders to borrowers.
- **Distortion of normal economic behaviour.** Inflation can distort consumer behaviour by causing households to bring forward purchases and hoard goods if they expect the rate of inflation to accelerate. Similarly, firms may divert funds out of productive investment in fixed investment projects into unproductive commodity hoarding and speculation. People are affected by **inflationary noise**. This occurs when changes in relative prices (i.e. a rise or fall in the price of *one* good) is confused with a change in the *general* price level or inflation.
- **Breakdown in the functions of money.** In a severe inflation, money becomes less useful and efficient as a medium of exchange and store of value. In the most extreme form of inflation, a hyperinflation in which the rate of inflation accelerates to a minimum of several hundred per cent a year, less efficient barter replaces money and imposes extra costs on most transactions.
- **International uncompetitiveness.** When inflation is higher than in competitor countries, exports increase in price, putting pressure on a fixed exchange rate. With a floating exchange rate, the exchange rate falls to restore competitiveness, but rising import prices may fuel a further bout of inflation.

■ **Shoe leather and menu costs.** Consumers incur shoe leather costs, spending time and effort shopping around and checking which prices have or have not risen. By contrast, menu costs are incurred by firms having to adjust price lists more often.

Should a government aim for complete price stability or for a low rate of inflation?

Achieving a completely stable price level and controlling inflation are not necessarily the same thing. A completely stable price level means that the percentage rate of inflation must be zero. By contrast, controlling the rate of inflation usually means achieving a rate of 2% in the UK. The reason why the UK government aims to achieve a low, but not a zero, rate of inflation is the greasing-the-wheels argument which was explained earlier. A low but stable rate of inflation may be necessary for markets to function properly. It is also possible that zero inflation may slip quickly into deflation: that is, a falling price level. However, when prices are falling and people believe tomorrow to be a better day than today for spending, falling aggregate demand may lead to recession.

EXAM TIP

Students often wrongly assume that controlling inflation and achieving complete price stability always mean the same thing.

Why it is important to diagnose correctly the causes of inflation

Just as a government must correctly diagnose the cause or causes of unemployment when implementing policies to reduce the level of unemployment, so it (and its central bank) must first determine whether inflation is caused by excess demand or by cost-push factors when deciding on the appropriate policies to reduce or control inflation.

The Bank of England has tended to assume that UK inflation has been caused by excess aggregate demand. The increase in aggregate demand that occurred in the 1990s and early 2000s was accompanied by an absence of cost-push inflationary pressure. This was partly due to the success of the supply-side policies implemented in the 1980s and 1990s. These policies improved labour market flexibility: for example, through attacking the power of trade unions. The economy also benefited from the benign effect of globalisation, which at the time reduced the prices of imported manufactured goods.

As long as the assumption holds that inflation is caused primarily by excess aggregate demand, **raising or lowering interest rates** (i.e. **monetary policy**) remains an appropriate policy for controlling inflation. The fact that interest rate policy kept the rate of inflation within the government's target range in virtually every month between 1997 and 2007 gave further support to the view that UK inflation had been primarily of the demand-pull kind.

However, cost-push inflationary pressures have now become much more significant, particularly those stemming from the increased prices of imported energy and commodities such as copper. In this situation, raising interest rates to reduce aggregate demand can be an ineffective policy for tackling cost-push inflation, unless it is argued that the economy should suffer a severe recession in order to reduce the demand for imported oil, gas and industrial raw materials. If this view is correct, UK governments now have to face up to the fact that they lack the tools, apart from interest rates (and other monetary instruments which are discussed in Chapter 23), for controlling the rate of inflation.

EXTENSION MATERIAL

Inflationary expectations and the psychology of inflation

Inflationary expectations

It is now widely accepted by economists that people's expectations of *future* inflation can affect the *current* rate of inflation. Along with the quantity theory of money, expectations of future inflation are an important part of the monetarist theory of inflation. The leading monetarist Milton Friedman was one of the first economists to draw attention to the role of expectations in the inflationary process.

Theories of expectation formation are complicated. However, the central idea is simple: if people expect that the rate of inflation next year is going to be high, they will behave in an inflationary way now, and their behaviour will deliver high inflation next year. Trade unions and workers bargain for higher wages, and their employers then raise prices, in anticipation of tomorrow's higher expected inflation rate. Workers and firms try to 'get their retaliation in first', to avoid being left behind when the inflation rate they are expecting eventually materialises.

Likewise, when people expect the inflation rate to fall, they behave in a way that enables low inflation to be achieved. Governments therefore try to 'talk down' the rate of inflation by convincing people that government policies are credible and that the government (and its central bank) know how to reduce inflation. The UK government's decision to make the Bank of England operationally independent in 1997 was part of an attempt to convince people (and financial markets) of the credibility of government policies and of its determination to keep the rate of inflation low. More recently, however, the on-going failure to hit the 2% target has eroded this credibility.

The psychology of inflation

One of the factors that has made inflation difficult to control in the UK has been the existence, built up over decades, of an 'inflation psychology'. Over the years, many groups in British society, including house owners, wage earners in strong bargaining positions, and also governments, have done extremely well out of inflation. Home owners with large mortgages, and also the government, have a vested interest in allowing inflation to continue in order to reduce

Homeowners expect to do well out of inflation

the real value of their accumulated debt. (Indeed, home owners do even better when house price inflation exceeds the general rate of inflation. In this situation, the real value of houses increases while the real value of mortgages falls.) Between 1997 and 2007, UK governments successfully cut through much of this inflation psychology by convincing people that inflation would remain low and around the target inflation rate of 2%. Because of this benign effect on people's behaviour and their expectations, it became much easier to control inflation. However, even in these years, some economists argued that circumstances could change quickly for the worse, and that inflationary dangers should be regarded as dormant rather than dead. Since 2008, inflation has indeed raised its ugly head once again.

- Inflation is a continuing or persistent rise in the average price level.
- In the UK, the retail prices index (RPI) and the consumer prices index (CPI) are used for measuring inflation.
- The CPI is now used for the indexation of welfare benefits, as well as for setting the inflation rate target.
- It is useful to distinguish between the rates of inflation for services and for goods.
- It is important to distinguish between demand-pull and cost-push inflation.
- Demand-pull inflation results from the fact that, when aggregate demand increases, firms are only prepared to produce and supply more output if prices increase.
- Cost-push inflation results from higher costs of production experienced by businesses.
- Demand-pull inflation and cost-push inflation can both be illustrated on *AD/AS* diagrams.
- Whether the benefits of inflation exceed the costs of inflation depends on the rate of inflation, its stability and whether the rate of inflation can be anticipated correctly.
- It is important to diagnose correctly the cause(s) of inflation when selecting policies to reduce the rate of inflation.

Exam-style questions

1 Explain the difference between deflation and disinflation. (12 marks)

2 With the help of an *AD/AS* diagram, explain the difference between demand-pull and cost-push inflation. (12 marks)

3 Do you agree that the UK government should aim for a low and stable rate of inflation rather than for a completely stable price level? Justify your answer. (25 marks)

4 Assess whether the costs of inflation exceed any benefits. (25 marks)

The balance of payments

Chapter 22

Whenever international trade takes place between countries, payment must eventually be made in a currency acceptable to the country from which the goods and services have been purchased. The balance of payments is the part of the national accounts which attempts to measure all the currency flows into and out of the economy within a particular month, quarter or year. However, the balance of payments is only an estimate of the currency flows. Activities such as smuggling and money laundering mean that the balance of payments accounts are never completely accurate.

LEARNING OUTCOMES

This chapter will:

- advise on what you need to know about the current account of the balance of payments
- explain the main items in the current account: exports and imports
- describe how investment income provides a link between capital flows and the current account
- apply *AD/AS* analysis to the current account
- consider whether current account deficits and surpluses pose problems for countries

The current account of the balance of payments and capital flows

The balance of payments accounts are the official record published by the government of all the currency flows into and out of the country. There are two main parts to the balance of payments: the **current account** and **capital flows**. The current account, which includes exports and imports, is so called because it measures income generated in the current time period flowing into and out of the economy.

KEY TERM

current account: the part of the balance of payments measuring payments for exports and imports, investment income and transfers.

EXAM TIP

While you are not expected to have a detailed knowledge of the construction of the current account of the balance of payments accounts, you must display basic knowledge.

By contrast, capital flows occur when residents of one country acquire capital assets such as factories, shopping malls, and property such as office blocks located in other countries. For example, Sir Philip Greene's Arcadia Group has recently invested in Topshop and Topman stores in the USA. The payments made when purchasing US stores were a capital outflow. By contrast, the payments made several years ago by Toyota when building car plants in Derbyshire were a capital inflow from Japan to the UK. Arcadia's investment is an example of **outward investment** from the UK. Toyota's investment is an example of **foreign direct investment (FDI)** into the UK.

What you need to know about the balance of payments

The Unit 2 examination does not require knowledge of capital flows, which are an A2 topic. Knowledge is, however, required of the different items in the current account of the balance of payments, especially exports and imports. In addition, there are two specification topics for which some knowledge of capital flows is useful. The first is a non-trade item in the current account, labelled 'income', with 'investment income' its main component.

> **EXAM TIP**
>
> Although examination questions will only be set on the current account of the balance of payments, some knowledge of capital flows is useful: for example, knowledge of how capital flows affect the exchange rate and monetary policy.

The second topic is monetary policy. Some knowledge of capital flows helps when developing an understanding of the link between interest rates (the main monetary policy instrument) and the exchange rate, which in the UK is the price at which the pound exchanges for other currencies such as the dollar and the euro.

Exports and imports and the current account

The main items in the current account that generate currency flows between countries are **exports** and **imports**. Exports occur when people living in the rest of the world buy goods and services produced in the UK. Overseas residents buy pounds in order to finance the purchase of UK exports. Currency flows into the UK in payment for the goods and services that are flowing out.

> **KEY TERMS**
>
> **export:** a domestically produced good or service sold to residents of other countries.
>
> **import:** a good or service produced in another country and sold to residents of this country.

In the case of imports, both the trade and currency flows are reversed. UK residents sell pounds and buy foreign currencies in order to finance the purchase of goods and services that other countries produce. Goods and services flow into the UK, while currency flows out to pay for the imports.

Non-trade items in the current account

Exports and imports generate *trade-related* currency flows. There are also two significant *non-trade* items in the current account. These are **investment income** (which has already been mentioned) and **transfers**.

> **EXAM TIP**
>
> Data-response questions may include data on income and transfers, and knowledge of these non-trade items may be tested in objective test questions.

To explain investment income (which is the major part of the item 'income' in the current account), I will return to the earlier example of Arcadia investing in US clothing stores. Since Arcadia is a business and not a charity, its main aim is to make a profit. The outward flow of capital that occurred when Arcadia expanded overseas generates profit, which flows back each year to Arcadia and its parent company, which is also owned by Sir Philip Greene. Greene benefits from the inward flow of profit. Provided the US clothing stores continue to be successful, profit flows each year from Arcadia's subsidiary business in the USA to the company's UK headquarters. This profit contributes to UK investment income (a *current* account item), whereas the investment that created the ability to make the profit in the USA was a *capital* outflow in the years in which the investment took place.

The Topshop store in New York, part of the Arcadia Group

Interest payments flowing between countries are another form of investment income. For example, UK residents depositing money in offshore bank deposits in other countries (a capital *outflow*) receive interest payments (an investment income *inflow*) in subsequent years. At the same time, profit and interest payments flow in the opposite direction, out of the UK to the overseas owners of physical and financial assets located in the UK. The outward income flow includes profits paid to Japanese and US multinational companies operating in the UK and interest payments to overseas owners of deposits in UK banks. **Net investment income** is the difference between these inward and outward profit flows.

Transfers form the second non-trade item in the balance of payments on current account. Examples of *outward* transfers from the UK include British aid donated to developing countries, Britain's contribution to the European Union budget, and income sent overseas by migrant workers to their families living in the countries of origin, such as Poland and Bangladesh. An *inward* transfer would be money paid by rich American parents to support the lifestyle of their children studying at British universities.

The importance of the current account

The current account is usually regarded as the most important part of the balance of payments because it reflects the economy's international competitiveness and the extent to which the country is living within its means. If the currency outflows in the current account exceed the currency inflows, there is a **current account deficit**. If receipts exceed payments, there is a **current account surplus**.

Many people think that a current account deficit is bad for the country, whereas a surplus is a source of national pride. While there is a lot of truth in this view, there are circumstances in which a deficit can be good for the economy and a surplus bad. Arguments for and against current account deficits and surpluses will be explained later in the chapter.

KEY TERMS

balance of trade in goods: the part of the current account measuring payments for exports and imports of goods. It is sometimes called the 'balance of visible trade'.

current account deficit: occurs when currency outflows in the current account exceed currency inflows. It is often shortened to 'exports less than imports $(X < M)$'.

current account surplus: occurs when currency inflows in the current account exceed currency outflows. It is often shortened to 'exports exceeding imports $(X > M)$'.

The balance of trade in goods

The UK's **balance of trade in goods** for 2011 is shown in Table 22.1, along with the other items in the UK's balance of payments on current account. A plus sign (+) indicates a credit item (currency flowing into the UK), and a minus sign (−) indicates a debit item (currency flowing out of the UK). The balance of trade in goods is sometimes called the balance of visible trade, and the balance of trade in services is part of the balance of invisible trade.

EXAM TIP

You must avoid confusing the balance of trade in goods with the whole of the current account, and the current account with the balance of payments as a whole.

Table 22.1 The UK balance of payments on current account, 2011 (£ billions)

The current account (*mostly trade flows*)	
Balance of trade in goods	−100.343
Balance of trade in services	+76.380
Net income flows	+17.133
Net current transfers	−22.216
Balance of payments on the current account	−29.046

Source: 2012 Pink Book, ONS

The balance of trade in goods shows the extent to which the value of exports of goods exceeds the value of imports, and vice versa. Table 22.1 does not indicate the absolute levels of exports and imports, which were respectively £298.987 billion and £399.330 billion in 2011. The balance of trade in goods was therefore in deficit to the tune of £100.343 billion. This figure is shown in the top row of Table 22.1.

The balance of trade in goods can also be disaggregated (broken up) into different forms of trade in goods, such as the balances of trade in manufactured goods and non-manufactured goods. Some of the different ways of disaggregating the balance of trade in goods on this basis are shown in Table 22.2.

Table 22.2 Selected items from the UK balance of trade in goods, 2011 (£ billions)

Balance of trade in food, drinks and tobacco	−17.971
Balance of trade in raw materials	−2.911
Balance of trade in oil	−11.492
Balance of trade in manufactured goods	−50.455
Balance of trade in automobiles	−1.041
Balance of trade in all goods	−100.343

Source: 2012 Pink Book, ONS

EXAM TIP

Make sure you have some knowledge of the balances of trade in items such as manufactured goods, oil and automobiles, which may appear in a data-response question.

Table 22.2 shows that the UK is a net importer of primary products (food and raw materials), and had also by 2011 become a large net importer of oil. Up until 2005, the UK enjoyed a balance of trade surplus in oil, as a result of the development of the North Sea oil and gas fields in the 1970s and 1980s. However, depletion of these fields means that the UK now imports much of the energy it uses, including coal and natural gas as well as oil.

The balance of payments deficit in manufactured goods is significant. Apart from the periods during and immediately following the First and Second World Wars, for over 200 years Britain was a net exporter of manufactured goods. In the mid-nineteenth century, Britain was the 'workshop of the world'.

This has now changed. In the early 1980s, the UK became a net importer of manufactured goods. The manufactured goods deficit is now huge, reflecting loss of competitiveness, the resulting deindustrialisation of the UK, and the fact that most manufactured goods are now produced in the newly industrialised countries (NICs) of Asia, and particularly China.

The balance of trade in automobiles, shown in Table 22.2, is a partial exception to the decline of manufactured exports and the growth of manufactured imports. As Case Study 22.1 indicates, the trade balance for automobiles moved toward surplus in

CASE STUDY 22.1

In 2012 the UK became a net exporter of cars once again

Rising exports to new markets such as Russia and China will increase the number of cars built in British factories in 2012 by 9%. The Society of Motor Manufacturers and Traders (SMMT) predicts that UK car manufacturing will continue to rise at the same rate for at least the next 4 years.

Eight out of ten cars currently built in the UK end up on foreign roads. British-made cars are now sold in more than 170 countries. And for the first time for many years, the UK is making more money from exporting cars than it spends on importing them. Jaguar Land Rover recorded its highest ever annual sales in 2012 with a 76% growth in China.

Dr Peter Wells of Cardiff University says: 'Overall, we're doing fantastically well at a bleak time for car manufacturing around the world. Prestige brands such as Jaguar seem to have come through better than we expected, while other companies have sought out new markets. In the Middle East and Africa, there's an appreciation of British culture and heritage. On its own, British-ness is not enough to sell cars but underpinned by quality and performance it gives us an edge. In China and Russia there are individuals with significant wealth who want British-made cars.'

Follow-up questions

1 'The recent success of the UK car industry reflects increased price and quality competitiveness.' Explain this statement.

2 How might the UK's membership of the European Union have helped the growth of the British car industry?

2012, despite being in deficit in 2011. A large number of cars continue to be manufactured in the UK, albeit in the Japanese-owned plants created by foreign direct investment in the late 1980s and the 1990s. The UK plants owned by Nissan, Toyota and Honda are modern, incorporating state-of-the-art technology, and labour productivity is high. Following the closure of MG Rover's plants in 2005, the deindustrialisation of the UK car industry has for the moment come to an end. However, ownership of Jaguar and Land Rover has moved to India, raising fears that production may also eventually move there.

The balance of trade in services

The decline of manufacturing and the growth of service industries mean that the UK now has a post-industrial and service sector economy. This is reflected in the **balance of trade in services** shown in Table 22.3.

Table 22.3 Selected items from the UK balance of trade in services, 2011 (£ billions)

Balance of trade in transport	+3.169
Balance of trade in travel	−9.942
Balance of trade in communications	+1.761
Balance of trade in insurance	+8.013
Balance of trade in financial services	+38.663
Balance of trade in computer and information services	+5.174
Balance of trade in all services	+76.380

Source: 2012 Pink Book, ONS

KEY TERM

balance of trade in services: the part of the current account measuring payments for exports and imports of services. It is sometimes called the 'balance of invisible trade', though the two terms are not strictly identical.

You should appreciate the significance of exports of financial services to the UK economy.

CASE STUDY 22.2

The UK financial services industry

The financial services sector is a significant contributor to UK income and employment. Over a million people in Britain are employed in financial services, of which two-thirds are based outside London. Financial services is also one of the largest export industries in the UK.

The financial crisis that began in the summer of 2007 has, however, highlighted the need for a more resilient and sustainable financial services industry to support the broader economy. In addition to being an important part of the economy in its own right, the financial services sector provides essential credit and financial services to businesses and households.

During the period after 2000 the expansion of the financial sector was a significant influence on the growth rate of the economy overall. But the recent growth of the sector was reversed in the recession, reducing GDP permanently by about 1.9%. The country will suffer a further loss of income as a result of the losses that banks have made, giving a total fall in national income of about 2.4%, and reducing government revenue by about 1% of GDP.

Follow-up questions

1 Explain **two** reasons for the decline of the UK financial services industry after 2007.
2 'The growth of the financial services industry has led to an unbalanced economy.' How might the UK economy be 'rebalanced'?

Whereas most manufactured goods are internationally tradable, the same is not generally true for services such as retailing, education and the provision of healthcare. As stated earlier, services such as these are produced and consumed in the non-internationally traded economy, or *sheltered* economy. However, many services which were previously produced within the UK are now being imported. This is an important part of the **globalisation** process.

UK companies, which used to produce services 'in-house', now outsource or buy in the services from outside suppliers, often located in countries with cheap labour. UK-based companies are locating 'back-office' service activities overseas, including many financial and ICT-related services. Many call centres providing customer services and direct marketing services have moved to India.

Nevertheless, as Table 22.3 shows, the UK is still a significant net exporter of financial, insurance and ICT services. These industries illustrate the UK's competitive advantage in service sector industries, though the picture is not as rosy in industries such as travel and tourism, where Britons now spend much more in other countries than overseas residents spend in the UK.

'Balance', equilibrium and disequilibrium in the balance of payments

It is important to avoid confusing balance of payments *equilibrium* with the balance of payments *'balancing'*. Balance of payments equilibrium occurs when the current account more or less balances over a period of years, and is perfectly compatible with occurrence of short-term current account deficits and surpluses. Fundamental disequilibrium exists when there is a persistent tendency for payments for imports to be significantly greater or less than payments for exports over a period of years.

The balance of payments is a balance sheet and, like all balance sheets, must balance in the sense that all items must sum to zero.

In practice, however, the estimates of the items in the balance of payments never sum to zero. This is simply because trade flows, and most of the other items in the balance of payments, are inaccurately measured and recorded. For example, a drug dealer flying a light aircraft into a remote landing strip in Essex is hardly likely to declare the value of the cocaine he is illegally importing. Hence, a balancing item (labelled as 'net errors and omissions') is included as a 'mistakes item' to make the balance of payments sum to zero.

The statisticians who construct the UK balance of payments use a continuous revision method of measurement. When the estimates of the balance of payments for a particular year are first published soon after the end of the year in question, the balancing item is usually large. In this situation, the estimated figures should not be trusted completely. However, in subsequent months and years, the balancing item usually decreases. In the light of new and previously unavailable information, the statisticians whittle away the balancing item, allocating it to one or more of the real trade, investment income, or capital flows in the balance of payments.

Applying AD/AS analysis to the current account of the balance of payments

In Chapter 18, the meaning of aggregate demand in the economy was explained, together with the aggregate demand equation: $AD = C + I + G + (X - M)$. Chapter 19 explained how, in an *AD/AS* graph, an increase in *any* of the components of aggregate demand (C, I, G or $(X - M)$) causes the aggregate demand (AD) curve to shift rightward, leading to a new macroeconomic equilibrium.

AD/AS analysis will now be used to explain how a change in net exports, or $(X - M)$, affects the national economy. As explained earlier, the current account includes non-trade items (income and transfers) as well as exports and imports. However, for the rest of this section, it will be assumed that exports and imports are the only two items in the current accounts of the balance of payments. Given this simplifying assumption, there is a current account surplus when net exports are positive (i.e. $X > M$), and a current account deficit when net exports are negative (i.e. $X < M$).

Exports are an injection of spending into the circular flow of income, whereas imports are a leakage or withdrawal of spending from the flow (refer to Figure 18.7 in Chapter 18, and to the accompanying explanation of the circular flow diagram).

Suppose initially that $X = M$, which means there is neither a surplus nor a deficit in the current account. Note also that in this situation, given the assumption of no non-trade flows in the current account, foreign trade injections into the circular flow of income exactly equal foreign trade withdrawals from the flow. When $X = M$, the current account has a neutral effect on the state of aggregate demand and on the circular flow of income.

However, at the next stage, overseas demand for British exports increases, but UK demand for imports remains unchanged. This means there is a net injection of spending into the circular flow of income. The current account moves into surplus, with $X > M$.

In the AD/AS diagram in Figure 22.1, the increase in exports shifts the AD curve to the right. What happens next in the economy depends on the shape and slope of the SRAS curve around the initial point of macroeconomic equilibrium. In Figure 22.1, macroeconomic equilibrium is initially at point X, which shows the economy in deep recession, suffering from deficient aggregate demand. In this situation, any event that increases aggregate demand increases the level of real output in the economy and causes demand-deficient unemployment to fall. An increase in exports is just such an event, shifting the AD curve from AD_1 to AD_2. This causes real output to rise from y_1 to y_2, though at the cost of some inflation, since the price level rises from P_1 to P_2.

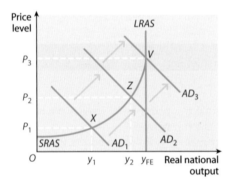

Figure 22.1 How an increase in exports can affect the national economy

Following the rightward shift of the aggregate demand curve to AD_2, macroeconomic equilibrium is now shown at point Z. As the SRAS curve becomes steeper, moving up the curve, the diagram tells us that the main effect of a further shift of the AD curve from AD_2 to AD_3 falls on the price level rather than on output and jobs. Output increases, from y_2 to y_{FE}, but the price level also increases to P_3. As full employment approaches, export demand becomes *inflationary* rather than *reflationary*.

Nevertheless, in this situation, the growth in export demand eliminates the demand deficiency previously existent in the economy. The economy ends up on its long-run aggregate supply (LRAS) curve, with macroeconomic equilibrium at point V.

At point V, what happens next in the economy depends on assumptions made about the nature of short-run and long-run aggregate supply. In Figure 22.1, when the economy produces on the vertical LRAS curve, any further increase in the demand for exports leads only to the price level rising above P_3, without any sustained increase in real output. However, there is another possibility. Foreign demand for a country's exports may be a response to favourable supply-side conditions in the domestic economy which shift the *LRAS* curve to the right. This means the economy can produce and supply the goods needed to meet the increase in export demand without generating inflation. This is the desired result of **export-led growth**. The German and Japanese economies enjoyed export-led growth from the 1960s to the 1980s, and China is now enjoying similar benefits. However, the world-wide growth of demand for Chinese exports has begun to cause inflation in the Chinese economy.

EXAM TIP

You must be able to use the *AD/AS* model and the circular flow of income to analyse how changes in exports and/or imports affect macroeconomic performance: that is, growth, employment, inflation and international competitiveness.

A fall in export demand and/or an increase in domestic demand for imports triggers an opposite effect to the one described above. There is a net leakage of demand from the circular flow of income, the *AD* curve shifts to the left, and both real output and the price level fall (or more realistically in the latter case, the rate of inflation slows down). Overall, the effect is *deflationary*.

CASE STUDY 22.3

Export-led growth

The pre-2008 UK boom resulted in large part from too much consumption and too little saving. For recovery from recession to lead into long-term growth, export-led growth is crucial.

But achieving export-led growth is much easier said than done, requiring UK goods and services to be quality competitive. Improved quality competitiveness, which involves good design and well-made products, may only be achievable in the long run if helped by appropriate supply-side policies implemented by the government, together with supply-side reforms undertaken by the private sector.

The need to export to BRIC countries

The continued crisis in the eurozone underlines just how important it is for the UK to diversify its export efforts to countries such as Brazil, Russia, India and China. But it is said we export more to Ireland than to the BRIC countries combined. The new middle classes in emerging economies have significant spending power and growing demands for some of the high-end goods which we can provide.

British products, talent and culture continue to command global appeal. If anything, the desirability of the 'Made in Britain' stamp is increasing — apparently in Japan it is more prestigious to own a Nissan car made in Sunderland than one made locally.

For a country that is home to just 1% of the world's population, the UK has remarkable dominance across several areas of global business. The City of London ranks alongside New York as the leading centre of global finance. Despite its often maligned reputation, the UK manufacturing sector is in the top ten in the world and responsible for 70% of UK research and development.

According to the CBI, industries with high export growth potential, which include construction, communication and financial services as well as electrical, optical and high-tech goods, could significantly increase our GDP.

Follow-up questions

1 Explain how supply-side policies and supply-side reforms may lead to export-led growth.
2 The extract is generally optimistic about the possibility of export-led growth. Explain **three** reasons for being more cautious.

Does a current account deficit pose problems?

While a *short-run* deficit or surplus on current account does not pose a problem, a persistent or *long-run* imbalance indicates fundamental disequilibrium. However, the nature of any resulting problem depends on the *size* and *cause* of the deficit: the larger the deficit, the greater the problem is likely to be. The problem is also likely to be serious if the deficit is caused by the uncompetitiveness of the country's industries. Although in the short run a deficit allows a country's residents to enjoy living standards boosted by imports, and thus higher than would be possible from the consumption of the country's output alone, in the long run, the decline of the country's industries in the face of international competition lowers living standards.

In a poor country, a current account deficit can be justified because of the country's need to import capital goods on a large scale to modernise the country's infrastructure and to promote economic development. However, there is always a danger, as the experience of countries such as Nigeria has shown, that the deficit soon becomes the means for financing the 'champagne lifestyle' enjoyed by the country's ruling elite.

Does a current account surplus pose problems?

While many people agree that a persistent current account deficit can pose serious problems, few realise that a balance of payments surplus on current account can also lead to problems. Because a surplus is often seen as a sign of national economic virility and success, a popular view is that the bigger the surplus, the better must be the country's performance.

Insofar as the surplus measures the competitiveness of the country's exporting industries, this is obviously true. There are, nevertheless, reasons why a large payments surplus is undesirable, though a small surplus may be a justifiable objective of government policy.

Two arguments against a persistently large surplus

One country's surplus is another country's deficit

Because the balance of payments must balance for the world as a whole, it is impossible for all countries to run surpluses simultaneously. Unless countries with persistently large surpluses agree to take action to reduce their surpluses, deficit countries cannot reduce their deficits. Deficit countries may then be forced to impose import controls from which all countries, including surplus countries, eventually suffer. In an extreme scenario, a world recession could be triggered by the resulting collapse of world trade.

At various times since the 1970s, the current account surpluses of the oil-producing countries have led to this problem, as has Japan's and more recently China's payments surpluses, which have been the counterpart to the US trade deficit. On several occasions, the US government has faced pressure from US manufacturing and labour interests to introduce import controls and other forms of protectionism. When introduced, US protectionism undoubtedly harms world trade.

Non-oil-exporting developing countries, almost without exception, also suffer chronic deficits, although these are very different from the US trade deficit. The imbalance of trade between more developed and less developed countries cannot be reduced without the industrialised countries of the 'North' taking action to reduce surpluses which have been gained at the expense of the developing economies of the 'South'.

A balance of payments surplus can be inflationary

A balance of payments surplus can be an important cause of domestic inflation, because it is an injection of aggregate demand into the circular flow of income, which increases the equilibrium level of nominal or money national income. If there are substantial unemployed resources in the economy, this has the beneficial effect of reflating real output and jobs. However, if the economy is initially close to full capacity, demand-pull inflation results.

SUMMARY

- The balance of payments measures the currency flows into and out of an economy.
- The two main parts of the balance of payments are the current account and capital flows.
- The main items in the current account are exports and imports.
- Balance of payments equilibrium occurs when exports more or less equal imports.
- A current account deficit usually occurs when imports are greater than exports. With a surplus, exports generally exceed imports.
- The balance of payments always 'balances', even when there is a deficit or surplus.
- Changes in exports or imports shift the *AD* curve rightward or leftward.
- An increase in exports or a fall in imports may be reflationary or inflationary, depending on circumstances.
- A decrease in exports or an increase in imports is deflationary.
- Current account deficits and surpluses both pose problems, though both may also have some advantages.

Exam-style questions

1 Explain how an improvement in the competitiveness of British industries may affect the UK current account of the balance of payments. (12 marks)

2 Explain how a large increase in investment in new productive capacity in the UK by overseas firms may affect the UK current account. (12 marks)

3 The UK has had a large current account deficit for several decades. Do you agree that a large payments deficit is bad for the UK economy? (25 marks)

4 Assess the effects of the growth of the UK's financial services industry on the country's macroeconomic performance. (25 marks)

Managing the economy: monetary policy

Chapter 23

This is the first of three chapters that cover the three main elements of macroeconomic policy. This chapter explains monetary policy, while Chapters 24 and 25 examine fiscal policy and supply-side policies. Monetary policy is an example of demand-side policy, which means it is used to manage aggregate demand. Along with fiscal and supply-side policies, it is also used to create a stable macroeconomic environment in the economy.

By contrast, fiscal policy is generally used these days as a supply-side policy. Supply-side policies aim at improving the economy's supply-side performance, rather than being used to manage aggregate demand.

LEARNING OUTCOMES

This chapter will:
- explain the meaning of monetary policy
- describe the Bank of England's role in implementing monetary policy
- distinguish between the objectives and instruments of monetary policy
- explain the meaning of the money supply
- discuss the extent to which UK monetary policy is 'monetarist' or 'Keynesian'
- use *AD/AS* analysis to distinguish between contractionary and expansionary monetary policy
- explain how changes in interest rates affect exports and imports via the exchange rate
- investigate how changes in the Bank of England's interest rate affect the economy

The meaning of monetary policy

Monetary policy is the part of economic policy that attempts to achieve the government's macroeconomic objectives by using monetary instruments, such as **controls over bank lending** and the **rate of interest**. Before 1997, monetary policy was implemented jointly by the Treasury (which is part of central government) and the Bank of England, which were known as the 'monetary authorities'. The Treasury abandoned its hands-on role in implementing monetary policy in 1997 when the government made the Bank of England operationally independent. Unless it is leaned on by the Treasury, there is now only one monetary authority, the Bank of England.

The Bank of England and monetary policy

Most banks, such as Barclays and HSBC, are **commercial banks**, whose main aim is to make a profit for their owners. The most significant exception is the **Bank of England**, which is the UK's **central bank**. For most of the period since its foundation in 1694, the

KEY TERMS

central bank: the central bank implements monetary policy on behalf of the government.

commercial bank: a commercial bank, such as Barclays, aims to make a profit from commercial banking business.

monetary policy: involves the use of interest rates to achieve the government's policy objectives.

Bank of England was a private enterprise company. Its principal function (besides printing banknotes) is to implement monetary policy on behalf of the government. Although profit is not its main objective, the Bank is highly profitable. However, as it is a nationalised industry, the profit goes to the state.

The objectives and instruments of monetary policy

To understand monetary policy, it is useful to distinguish between its objectives and instruments. A **monetary policy objective** is the target or goal that the Bank of England aims to hit. A **monetary policy instrument** is the tool or technique of control used to achieve the objective. Controlling inflation is the main monetary policy objective of the Bank of England, and the rate of interest has been the principal monetary policy instrument.

EXTENSION MATERIAL

What is money?

For most people, money is so desirable and so central to everyday life that what actually constitutes it hardly merits a second thought. For people living in England and Wales, money comprises coins and Bank of England notes, and any funds on deposit in banks such as HSBC and Barclays. Residents of Scotland and Northern Ireland would also include notes issued by local Scottish and Northern Irish banks. Building society deposits are now also regarded as money, although this was not the case until recently.

Where do we draw the line as to what is money? Is a credit card money? Is a foreign currency such as the US dollar or the Indian rupee, given the fact that we may not be able to spend a foreign banknote or coin in the UK? Do we include financial assets such as National Saving Securities, which possess some, but not all, of the characteristics of money?

Consider also the social relationship that takes place whenever modern banknotes are spent on goods or services. Why, for example, are shopkeepers prepared to hand over new and valuable goods to strangers, in exchange for grubby and unhygienic pieces of paper with no apparent intrinsic value of their own? The answer lies in a single word: 'confidence'. In a modern economy, people are prepared to accept such tokens in settlement of a contract or debt, because they are confident that these notes and coins will also be accepted when they decide to spend them.

The functions of money

Economists cut through these issues by defining money in terms of the functions it performs in an economy:

- **The medium of exchange function.** Whenever money is used to pay for goods or services, or for the purpose of settling transactions and the payment of debts, it functions as a medium of exchange or means of payment.
- **The store of value (or store of wealth) function.** Instead of being spent, money may be stored as a wealth asset in preference to other forms of wealth: for example, property or financial assets such as stocks and shares.
- **The unit of account function.** Money is the unit in which the prices of goods are quoted. The unit of account function of money allows people to compare the relative values of goods even when they have no intention of spending money and buying goods: for example, when we window-shop.
- **A standard of deferred payment.** This function allows people to delay paying for goods or settling a debt. Goods may be provided immediately, but payment occurs at a later date, at a price (in money units) agreed today.

Is a credit card money?

The main monetary policy objective: controlling inflation

For the last 30 years, control of inflation has been the main objective of UK monetary policy. However, at a deeper level, control of inflation should be viewed not as an *end* in itself, but as the *means* of creating the 'sound money' deemed necessary for competitive markets to deliver improved economic welfare.

KEY TERM

policy objective: a target or goal that policy-makers aim to 'hit'.

Since the 1990s, central government has set the inflation target for the Bank of England. In recent years, the target set by the Treasury has been a 2% rate of inflation (measured by the rate of change of the consumer prices index (CPI)). From 1997 onwards, the Bank of England's Monetary Policy Committee (MPC) has implemented monetary policy to try to achieve the inflation rate target set by the government.

Are there any other monetary policy objectives?

Prior to May 1997, monetary policy was concerned only with getting the inflation rate at or *below* the target set by the government. Critics argued that the policy had a built-in deflationary bias (i.e. reducing inflation was favoured at the expense of achieving other possible macroeconomic objectives).

This is no longer the case. The MPC is also now required to reduce interest rates to stimulate output and employment if the committee believes that, on unchanged policies, an inflation rate below 2% will be accompanied by an undesirable fall in output and employment. In the government's words: 'The primary objective of monetary policy is price stability. But subject to that, the Bank of England must also support the government's economic policy objectives, including those for growth and employment.'

UK monetary policy has thus become symmetrical, in the sense that the MPC is just as prepared to use monetary policy to increase aggregate demand as it is to deflate the economy. Indeed, if the inflation rate falls below 1%, the Bank of England has to explain to the government why the inflation rate target has not been met, in the same way that the Bank's governor must write a letter of explanation when the inflation rate rises above 3%.

EXAM TIP

When you take your exam, UK monetary policy might have become even more focused on increasing aggregate demand to stimulate the economy.

CASE STUDY 23.1

Regime change at the Bank of England

The government appoints Bank of England governors for terms of 5 years, subject to a maximum of two appointments. Mervyn King, the most recent governor, was first appointed in 2003, so his second term ended in 2013. King has been replaced by a surprise choice as new governor, a Canadian called Mark Carney, who was previously in charge of the Bank of Canada. At the time of his appointment, it was mooted that Carney will change significantly the central thrust of UK monetary policy: namely, pursuit of the 2% CPI inflation rate target, with control of inflation by far the main monetary policy objective. (Later in this chapter, it will be explained how the adoption of a new monetary policy instrument, quantitative easing, has already been changing monetary policy, from 2009 onwards).

Follow-up questions

1 To what extent, if any, has UK monetary policy changed under Mark Carney?

2 In implementing monetary policy, the governor is assisted by eight members of the Monetary Policy Committee (MPC). Find out how the MPC members have changed in recent years.

Monetary policy instruments

As explained in Chapter 16, policy instruments are the tools used to achieve policy objectives. In this chapter, it has already been briefly mentioned that the Bank of England's interest rate is the main monetary policy instrument.

Each month, the MPC either raises or lowers **Bank Rate** (usually by a quarter of 1%), or, more often, leaves the interest rate unchanged, to try to keep the inflation rate

KEY TERMS

Bank Rate: the rate of interest the Bank of England charges when lending money to commercial banks to increase their liquidity.

policy instrument: a tool or set of tools used to try to achieve a policy objective.

within a target range between 1% above and 1% below the 2% CPI target (i.e. between 3% and 1%).

It is important to realise that interest rate policy acts on the *demand* for credit and loans. When interest rates are raised, people generally decide to borrow less, because the cost of loans becomes too high. Conversely, falling interest rates encourage people to borrow more.

How changes in the Bank of England's rate of interest affect lending and credit in the economy

In order to understand how a change in the Bank of England's rate of interest affects credit or loans provided by commercial banks and other financial institutions, it is necessary to understand how a commercial bank makes a profit. A bank such as Barclays or Lloyds TSB is profitable because it 'borrows short and lends long'.

A bank 'borrows short', for example, by accepting deposits of money from people who have opened **current accounts** in the bank. The bank then lends this money to other people who wish to borrow from the bank. Many of the bank loans given to customers are long-term loans: for example, 25-year **mortgage** loans, or 5- or 10-year term loans. This type of banking business is profitable because the rate of interest that a bank pays when borrowing 'short' is less than the rate of interest it charges when lending 'long'.

However, there is an element of risk in this. If customers who have lent 'short' to a bank suddenly decide to withdraw most or all of their funds, it might be difficult for the bank to repay them. If other customers then fear that the bank cannot honour its liabilities, they may also decide to withdraw their funds. In a worst-case scenario, there is a run on the bank; the bank then crashes and goes out of business. In 2007 customers rushed to remove their money from the Northern Rock bank, which had to be rescued by the government before being sold to Virgin Money in 2011.

To maintain confidence in the commercial banking system, the Bank of England promises to lend to major banks in the event of large unexpected cash withdrawals, in order to preserve the **liquidity** in the banking system and to prevent runs on banks. The guarantee is part of the Bank of England's **lender of last resort function**. Even in 'normal' times, when there is no fear of a run on a bank, the Bank deliberately keeps the commercial banks slightly short of cash. It does this in order to engineer a situation in which, as a matter of routine, commercial banks have to borrow from the Bank of England. Bank Rate, the rate of interest the Bank of England charges when lending to commercial banks, is usually just above the rates of interest that commercial banks charge when lending money to each other (the LIBOR rate).

KEY TERMS

current account: a bank account that allows its owner to withdraw cash immediately by using a cheque or a plastic debit card.

lender of last resort function: the Bank of England's willingness to lend cash to commercial banks to increase their liquidity and to maintain confidence in the banking system.

liquidity: measures the ease with which assets can be turned into cash quickly and at a pre-known rate or price. Cash is the most liquid of all assets.

money supply or **stock of money:** takes the form of cash and bank deposits.

mortgage: a long-term loan to a house owner that is secured by the property.

At the next stage in the process, an increase in Bank Rate generally causes the commercial banks to increase the interest rates they charge their customers, because it now costs more for the banks to borrow from the Bank of England the funds they wish to lend on to their customers. With bank loans becoming more expensive, their customers reduce their demand for credit and repay existing loans wherever possible. This reduces the **money supply**, or stock of money in the economy.

Conversely, when the Bank of England cuts Bank Rate, commercial banks generally follow by reducing their own interest rates. If a commercial bank did not reduce its own interest rate, it would lose business and make less profit.

CASE STUDY 23.2

Bank Rate and the LIBOR

As well as paying interest to their customers who deposit money in savings accounts, commercial banks charge interest on money they lend to each other. The rate a bank pays when borrowing money from another bank is called the LIBOR rate (the London interbank offered rate).

In 'normal' times, the LIBOR rate hovers just above Bank Rate, but in 2007, during the 'credit crunch' which ushered in the current financial crisis, the gap between the two rates widened. One of the factors affecting interest

rates is the risk attached to a loan. In the financial crisis, the increased possibility of a bank collapsing made inter-bank loans much riskier. As Figure 23.1 shows, this caused the LIBOR rate to drift away from Bank Rate. With Bank Rate being cut to 0.5% in 2009, the fact that the interest rates that banks charge their customers are linked to LIBOR and not to Bank Rate undermined the effectiveness of the 0.5% Bank Rate in stimulating aggregate demand.

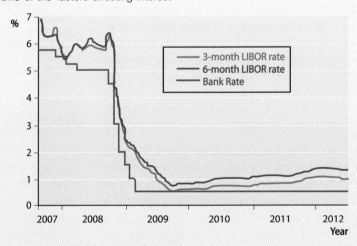

Figure 23.1 LIBOR and Bank Rate, 2007–12

Follow-up questions
1 Explain why the 6-month LIBOR is higher than the 3-month LIBOR in Figure 23.1.
2 In 2012 and 2013 a financial scandal erupted when UK banks such as Barclays admitted they been rigging the LIBOR. Find out about the scandal and discuss how LIBOR rigging affected the cost of loans to households and firms.

EXTENSION MATERIAL

Pre-emptive monetary policy

In the UK, monetary policy is meant to be pre-emptive: that is, based on foreseeing undesirable events likely to take place in the economy, and taking action *now* to prevent these events happening in the *future*.

In theory, the Bank of England's MPC estimates what the inflation rate is likely to be 18 months to 2 years ahead (the medium term), if policy (i.e. Bank Rate) remains unchanged. If the forecast rate of inflation is too far away from the target rate set by the government, the Bank may decide to change Bank Rate immediately to prevent the undesirable outcome becoming a reality.

The MPC is also prepared to raise or lower Bank Rate to head off any likely adverse effects of the inflation rate or an outside shock affecting the economy. A good example occurred in 2007 when the 'credit crunch' caused by the US sub-prime mortgage crisis destroyed confidence in the UK banking system. After a period of dithering, the Bank of England cut Bank Rate — even though the inflation rate was rising — to try to restore confidence in UK banks. Arguably, however, when monetary policy is determined in this way, it is *reactive* (responding to events that have already occurred in the economy), rather than *pre-emptive* (anticipating future events).

Monetarism and the money supply

When people react to higher interest rates by reducing the amount of money they borrow from banks, the stock of money in the economy shrinks. The stock of money in the economy is the money supply.

When macroeconomic policy in the UK was monetarist (from the late 1970s until about 1985), monetary policy attempted to control the rate of growth of the money supply. However, as was explained in some detail in Chapter 15, monetarist monetary policies did not last long, largely because they never worked properly.

Nevertheless, although the money supply these days is neither a policy objective nor a policy instrument, it does function as a **policy indicator**. Despite the money supply having been dropped as a monetary policy target, when setting Bank Rate, the MPC still takes account of changes in the money supply. This is because changes in the money supply provide information about the 'tightness' or 'looseness' of monetary policy. Also, changes in the money supply indicate whether monetary policy is 'on course' to achieve the inflation rate target.

> **KEY TERM**
>
> **policy indicator:** provides information about what is happening in the economy.

Is UK monetary policy now Keynesian?

Since the dropping of *monetarist* monetary policy in the 1980s, some commentators have argued that monetary policy is once again being used in a Keynesian way to manage aggregate demand.

However, current policy differs in significant ways from the Keynesian demand management policies practised for many years before the advent of monetarism:

> **EXAM TIP**
>
> Make sure you don't confuse monetarism with monetary policy.

- Only monetary policy, and not fiscal policy, is used in a discretionary way to manage aggregate demand.

- Control of inflation, rather than full employment, remains the principal (but not the only) policy objective.
- Control of inflation is regarded as a pre-condition for the success of the government's supply-side policies.

CASE STUDY 23.3

Hawks and doves at the MPC

The Bank of England's Monetary Policy Committee has nine members. Four are Bank of England officials, and four are 'independent' members appointed by the government. The governor of the Bank of England is the ninth member of the MPC, and has the casting vote.

It has become fashionable to divide the members of the MPC into 'hawks', who tend to resist interest rate cuts, and 'doves', who are much more prone to cutting interest rates and to resisting interest rate increases. The commentary below was accurate at the time it was written in December 2011, but it will be out of date by the time you read this book. Not only will some or all of the independent members have changed (each is elected for a term of 3 years), but the governor himself will have changed. In July 2013, the Canadian Mark Carney replaced Mervyn King, and at the time of writing (in June 2013) it was uncertain whether Carney would turn out to be a 'hawk' or a 'dove'.

Mervyn King, Governor of the Bank of England, 2003–13	
Having been 'hawkish', now 'dovish'.	
Bank of England employees	**'Independent' members (government appointees)**
Charles Bean, Deputy Governor, 2008–13 swing voter — more dove than hawk	David Miles, MPC member, 2009–12 dove
Paul Tucker, Deputy Governor, Financial Stability, 2009–14 swing voter — more hawk than dove	Ian McCafferty, MPC member, 2012–15 claims to be neither a hawk nor a dove
Spencer Dale, Executive Director, Markets, 2008–13 hawk	Martin Weale, MPC member, 2010–13 hawk
Paul Fisher, Executive Director, 2009–14 dove	Ben Broadbent, MPC member, 2011–14 neither hawk nor dove — sits in the middle
And Mark Carney...?	
'It is hard to place Carney as a dove or hawk relative to the views of others. Carney is generally seen as pragmatic and astute economist, rather than one with a predilection for one particular school of economic ideas' (Malcom Barr of JP Morgan). Time will tell whether Malcolm Barr is right.	

Follow-up questions

1 Is the Bank of England really independent when it implements monetary policy in the UK?
2 Research how the composition of the MPC has changed since 2011 and the 'hawish' or 'dovish' views of the current MPC members.

Using AD/AS diagrams to show how monetary policy affects the price level and real output

Monetary policy, rather than fiscal policy, is now used to manage the level of aggregate demand in the economy. To understand how monetary policy is used in this way, it is worth restating the aggregate demand equation:

$$AD = C + I + G + (X - M)$$

Whereas fiscal policy can affect aggregate demand by changing the level of government spending (G), monetary policy affects the other components of aggregate demand, C, I and $(X - M)$. An increase in interest rates causes the AD curve illustrated in Figure 23.2 to shift to the left, from AD_1 to AD_2.

There are three main ways in which an increase in interest rates decreases aggregate demand. Two of these are:

- **Higher interest rates reduce household consumption (C).** First, higher interest rates encourage people to save, and higher saving means that less income is therefore available for consumption. Second, the cost of household borrowing increases, which increases the cost of servicing a mortgage and credit card debt. Borrowers have less money to spend on consumption because more of their income is being used for interest payments. Third, higher interest rates may cause asset prices to fall (e.g. the prices of houses and shares). These falling prices reduce personal wealth, which reduces consumption. Fourth, falling house and share prices reduce consumer confidence, which further deflates consumption.

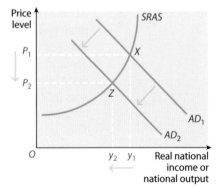

Figure 23.2 How an increase in interest rate causes the AD curve to shift to the left

- **Higher interest rates reduce business investment (I).** Investment is the purchase of capital goods such as machines by firms. Businesses postpone or cancel investment projects because they believe that higher borrowing costs make the purchase of capital goods unprofitable. This is likely to be exacerbated by a collapse of business confidence and increased business pessimism.

How changes in interest rates affect exports and imports via the exchange rate

The third way in which an increase in interest rates leads to a decrease in aggregate demand works through the effect of higher interest rates on net export demand $(X - M)$. As explained in Chapter 22, in the context of the balance of payments, higher interest increases the demand for pounds by attracting capital flows into the currency. The increased demand for sterling causes the pound's exchange rate to rise, which makes UK exports less price competitive in world markets and imports more competitive in UK markets. The UK's balance of payments on current account worsens, which shifts the *AD* curve leftward.

EXAM TIP

'Sterling' is a word often used when describing the role of the pound in the international economy. For example, economists write about the demand for sterling.

By contrast, a fall in interest rates triggers a capital outflow in the balance of payments. The exchange rate then also falls. Exports become more price competitive, and the current account of the balance of payments improves. Aggregate demand increases and the *AD* curve shifts rightward.

Contractionary monetary policy

Contractionary monetary policy involves raising interest rates in order to shift the *AD* curve to the left. However, the extent to which the price level then falls (or, more realistically, the rate of inflation falls), and/or real output falls, depends on the shape of the economy's *SRAS* curve. In Figure 23.2, the shift to the left of aggregate demand from AD_1 to AD_2 causes real output as well as the price level to fall. The price level falls from P_1 to P_2, and real output falls from y_1 to y_2. This illustrates the possibility that a contractionary monetary policy, which aims to control the rate of inflation in the economy, might also cause the economy to sink into a recession. This is especially likely if the contractionary monetary policy triggers a large multiplier which shifts the *AD* curve even further to the left. (See pages 285–87 for an explanation of the multiplier.)

Expansionary monetary policy

An expansionary monetary policy operates in the opposite way to that described above. A Bank Rate cut discourages saving, while stimulating consumption and investment spending. Exports also increase. Lower interest rates cause the exchange rate to fall, making exports more price competitive and imports less competitive. The *AD* curve shifts to the right, with the size of the shift depending on the size of the multiplier. Finally, the extent to which real output increases or the price level rises depends on the shape and slope of the economy's *SRAS* curve.

Neutral monetary policy

Before the 2008 recession, the Bank of England generally implemented a neutral monetary policy, rather than one that was overtly contractionary or expansionary. In a neutral monetary policy, interest rates neither boost nor hold back aggregate demand. It is broadly consistent with the economy growing at its sustainable trend rate over the medium term: that is, without positive or negative output gaps.

Evaluating the success of recent UK monetary policy

In May 1997, Gordon Brown, the incoming Labour chancellor of the exchequer, transferred to the newly independent Bank of England the task of using monetary policy to hit the government's inflation rate target, the 2% CPI rate.

Figure 23.3 shows that, for most of the time between 2000 and the end of the first quarter in 2008, the UK inflation rate was within its target range of 1% above and below the central target rate of 2%. Indeed, until early 2005, the inflation rate was always below 2%.

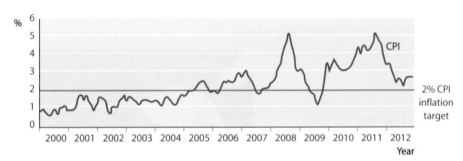

Figure 23.3 UK consumer prices index and the 2% CPI target, 2000–12

At the time, the Bank of England claimed that 'the proof of the pudding is in the eating'. Monetary policy had aimed to control inflation — inflation was low, therefore monetary policy was successful. The Bank's critics argued that, although monetary policy had been *partly* responsible for bringing down the rate of inflation, other factors also contributed in significant ways. First, there was the success of the supply-side reforms introduced by Thatcher's Conservative governments in the 1980s. When introduced, under the dictum 'first the pain and then the gain', supply-side policies contributed to high unemployment and a widening of income differentials. This was the 'pain'. From the mid-1990s onwards, the 'gain' arrived in the form of more competitive and efficient markets, which resulted in lower inflation rates.

Second, the policy-makers were 'lucky' in the last decade of the twentieth century and in the first few years of the twenty-first century. These were benign times, in which commodity, raw material and energy prices were generally falling, and when the ICT revolution increased productivity in manufacturing, communications and retailing.

But from 2008 onwards, times were much less benign. Rising oil and commodity prices, agri-inflation (the rising prices of crops such as wheat and corn) and the beginnings of inflation in Chinese manufacturing industries triggered a severe bout of cost-push inflation, which UK monetary policy cannot control. Government policies other than manipulating interest rates may be needed if the rate of inflation is to be brought down to 2%.

Monetary policy and inflationary expectations

UK monetary policy was successful in the 1990s and early 2000s partly because the Bank of England managed to control inflationary expectations. As long as monetary policy is credible, so the argument goes, people believe that the Bank of England can continue to control inflation. Policy credibility reduces expectations of future inflation and causes people to behave in ways consistent with the policy's future success. However, as the post-2008 experience shows, once credibility dissipates, the 'genie escapes from the bottle'. By 2013, people no longer had faith in the Bank's ability to control inflation.

EXTENSION MATERIAL

'One-club golf' and macroeconomic policy

In recent years, UK governments have been accused of relying on the 'one-club golfer' approach to macroeconomic policy. The accusation is based on the following analogy.

Rory McIlroy is one of the best golfers in the world today. Imagine, however, Rory playing in the Masters Golf Tournament in the USA with only one club in his golf bag. However great his talents as a golfer, Rory can't hope to win a major tournament playing under these conditions. Different golf clubs are needed for different shots: a driver for teeing off, a wedge iron for playing out of a bunker, and a putter for finishing off a hole on the putting green. So that Rory can show off his skills as a top-rate golf player, at the start of an 18-hole round, his caddy places ten or more different clubs in the golf bag to be carried round the greens. Part of Rory's skill then lies in selecting and using a particular club for a particular shot.

In the same way that Rory McIlroy selects different golf clubs for different shots, so the government needs different types of economic policy and policy instruments for achieving different policy objectives. Good government policy shouldn't rely just on interest rate policy or monetary policy. However sensible it is to raise interest rates in order to tackle demand-pull inflation, interest rates do not provide a panacea for *all* the macroeconomic problems that a government faces, particularly when policy conflicts and trade-offs are involved.

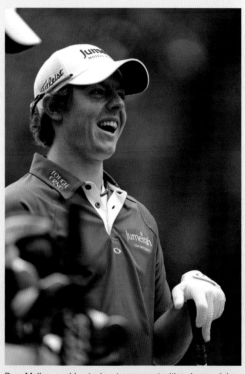

Rory McIlroy could not win a tournament with only one club

EXTENSION MATERIAL

Quantitative easing (QE)

In 2009, a new policy of quantitative easing (QE) was introduced to allow the Bank of England to escape from the 'one-club golfer' trap of solely using Bank Rate to implement monetary policy. QE is supposed to have the same effect as printing new money for people to spend. Of course, it is more complicated than this. The Bank does indeed create new money, but it is 'electronic' money with which the Bank purchases government bonds and other assets. These are sold to the Bank of England by commercial banks and other financial institutions. In theory, the general public then borrows and spends the newly created money, which increases aggregate demand. QE also raises asset prices, which causes long-term interest rates also fall. Both of these factors — asset owners feeling wealthier and falling long-term interest rates — also increase aggregate demand.

By 2013, QE had been used three times: QE1 in 2009, QE2 in 2011 and QE3 in 2012. Two important points to note are:
- The introduction and further use of QE marked the switching of monetary policy away from the control of inflation towards the deliberate boosting of aggregate demand. QE, combined with almost zero Bank Rate, is all about 'spending the economy out of recession', or out of very slow growth.
- QE's critics, who include many monetarists, claim that QE is leading to a massive erosion of the value of people's pensions and that it will eventually lead to inflation spinning out of control. Try and find out why this may be so.

As of 2013, QE has not been in the AS specification. QE will not therefore be mentioned in AS exam questions. This may change, however, and in any case a good answer to a question on how monetary policy operates, or on the success or otherwise of monetary policy, could show some knowledge of quantitative easing and the danger of relying solely on interest rate policy. QE is meant to support, but not to replace, Bank Rate policy.

SUMMARY

- Along with fiscal policy and supply-side policy, monetary policy provides a way of managing the national economy.
- In the UK, monetary policy is implemented by the country's central bank, the Bank of England.
- Control of inflation is the main monetary policy objective, but there are other objectives.
- Central government sets the inflation rate target of 2%, measured by the CPI.
- The Bank of England's Monetary Policy Committee (MPC) implements monetary policy to try to hit the 2% inflation rate target.
- Bank Rate is the main monetary policy instrument, but other instruments such as quantitative easing (QE) are now also used.
- Monetary policy is used to manage the level of aggregate demand.
- Changes in interest rates affect consumption, investment and net export demand, and shift the position of the *AD* curve.
- Monetary policy can be effective in controlling demand-pull inflation, but it is ineffective at controlling cost-push inflation.
- Monetary policy was successful in controlling inflation in the UK in the 1990s and early 2000s, but has been unsuccessful since 2008.

Exam-style questions

1 Explain the difference between the objectives and the instruments of monetary policy.   (12 marks)

2 Explain how changes in Bank Rate affect aggregate demand.   (12 marks)

3 Discuss the view that monetary policy is inappropriate for controlling cost-push inflation.   (25 marks)

4 Evaluate the Bank of England's success since 2008 in controlling the rate of inflation.   (25 marks)

Chapter 24

Managing the economy: fiscal policy

This chapter follows on from the coverage of monetary policy in Chapter 23. Unlike monetary policy, which is now used to manage the level of aggregate demand in the economy, these days fiscal policy is much more of a supply-side policy used for influencing personal incentives, particularly those to work, save, invest and to be entrepreneurial. Examination questions are set on demand-side and supply-side fiscal policy, so this chapter covers both forms of fiscal policy. However, the explanation of supply-side fiscal policy here is short, largely because the topic is dealt with in greater detail in Chapter 25.

LEARNING OUTCOMES

This chapter will:
- explain the meaning of fiscal policy
- describe the Treasury's role in implementing fiscal policy
- explain Keynesian or demand-side fiscal policy in the context of the short-lived fiscal stimulus from 2008 to 2010
- use *AD/AS* analysis to explain how fiscal policy has been used to manage aggregate demand
- discuss the significance of the government spending multiplier
- examine the nature of supply-side fiscal policy and its effect on the *LRAS* curve
- explain how government spending and taxation affect the pattern of economic activity

The meaning of fiscal policy

Fiscal policy is the part of a government's overall economic policy that aims to achieve the government's economic objectives through the use of the fiscal instruments of **taxation**, **public spending** and the **government's budgetary position**. As an economic term, fiscal policy is often associated with Keynesian economic theory and policy. Between the 1950s and 1970s, Keynesian governments used fiscal policy to manage the level of aggregate demand.

> **KEY TERM**
>
> **fiscal policy:** involves the use of taxation, public spending and the government's budgetary position to achieve the government's policy objectives.

> **EXAM TIP**
>
> Students often assume wrongly that fiscal policy is always used to manage aggregate demand.

However, it is misleading to associate fiscal policy exclusively with Keynesianism. After 1979, with the exception of the two years from 2008 to 2010, demand-side fiscal policy gave way to supply-side fiscal policy. But before comparing **demand-side** and **supply-side fiscal policy**, I will examine the government's budgetary position.

The government's budgetary position

Using the symbols G for government spending and T for taxation and other sources of revenue, the three possible budgetary positions of the government are:

$G = T$: **balanced budget**

$G > T$: budget deficit

$G < T$: budget surplus

A **budget deficit** occurs when public sector spending exceeds revenue. It is important not to confuse *financing* a budget deficit with *eliminating* a budget deficit. A budget deficit can be eliminated by cutting public spending or by raising taxation, both of which can balance the budget or move it into surplus. Assuming a budget deficit persists, the extent to which spending exceeds revenue must be financed by public sector borrowing.

EXAM TIP

Make sure you don't confuse the budget deficit with the balance of payments deficit.

The budget deficit and public sector borrowing

Various official terms are used by the Treasury for **public sector borrowing**, including the 'public sector's net cash requirement' and 'net public sector borrowing'. However, because the Treasury sometimes changes its terminology, the most important thing to learn is that public sector borrowing is 'the other side of the coin' to the budget deficit. Whenever there is a budget deficit, there is a *positive* borrowing requirement. Conversely, a **budget surplus** means the government can use the tax revenues it isn't spending to repay previous borrowing. In this case, the borrowing requirement is *negative*.

KEY TERMS

balanced budget: this is achieved when government spending equals government revenue ($G = T$).

budget deficit: occurs when government spending exceeds government revenue ($G > T$).

budget surplus: occurs when government spending is less than government revenue ($G < T$).

Keynesian fiscal policy and the budget deficit

During the Keynesian era, fiscal policy was used primarily to manage the level of aggregate demand in the economy. Keynesian fiscal policy centred on the use of **deficit financing** to inject demand into the economy. Deficit financing describes a situation in which the government runs a budget deficit, usually for several years, deliberately setting public sector spending at a higher level than tax revenues and other sources of government revenue. For each of the years in which the government runs a budget deficit, the shortfall of tax revenue has to be financed through a *positive* borrowing requirement.

KEY TERM

deficit financing: deliberately running a budget deficit and borrowing to finance the deficit.

Before the Keynesian revolution in the 1930s, UK governments believed they had a moral duty to balance their budgets. This has been called sound finance or fiscal orthodoxy.

The orthodox view was that a budget surplus placed the government in the moral position of a thief, stealing from taxpayers. If the government ran a budget deficit, it would be in the moral position of a bankrupt, perceived as not being able to manage its finances. Since both these budgetary positions were regarded as wrong or undesirable, the government's fiscal *duty* was to aim for a balanced budget.

However, in the 1930s, John Maynard Keynes established a new orthodoxy that legitimised deficit financing and overturned the view that a government should always aim to balance its budget. The new Keynesian orthodoxy lasted until the late 1970s, when, during the period in which monetarism held sway, there was a return to a belief in balanced budgets.

As was explained in Chapter 15, in the 1930s Keynes argued that mass unemployment in the Great Depression was caused by deficient aggregate demand. He believed that, in the economy as a whole, too little spending was taking place because households and firms in the private sector were saving too much and spending too little.

In the 1950s and 1960s, Keynes's followers, the *Keynesians*, argued that, in this situation, if the government deliberately runs a budget deficit, the deficit can be financed by the government, first borrowing, and then, in its public spending programme, spending the private sector's excess savings. This injects spending into the economy and (in Keynesian theory, at least) gets rid of demand-deficient unemployment.

Using *AD/AS* diagrams to illustrate Keynesian or demand-side fiscal policy

Before applying *AD/AS* analysis to Keynesian fiscal policy and its effects on the economy, it is worth reminding ourselves of the aggregate demand equation or identity introduced in Chapter 18:

$$AD = C + I + G + (X - M)$$

KEY TERM

demand-side fiscal policy: changes in the budget deficit are used to increase or decrease the level of aggregate demand (and to shift the *AD* curve to the right or to the left).

CASE STUDY 24.1

Budget day

The government's financial year runs for the 12 months beginning 5 April. A few weeks before, in March, the chancellor of the exchequer presents his budget to the House of Commons. Part of the budget speech, which is published in the 'Red Book' (formally called the Financial Statement and Budget Report (FSBR), but commonly named after the traditional colour of its cover), contains the chancellor's analysis of the state of the UK economy. This is the part of the budget which most interests economists.

By contrast, the general public is most interested in the announcement of tax changes, some of which come into effect within hours of the budget speech. Modern chancellors often use the trick of announcing tax increases a few months earlier, in the previous year's Autumn

Statement (or Pre-Budget Report as it used to be known). The chancellor hopes that taxpayers will not notice the announcement of stealth taxes (as the tax changes have come to be called), because the higher tax rates will not be paid until a few months later. The extract below has been taken from the Treasury website:

History of the budget

The word 'budget' derives from the term 'bougette' — a wallet in which either documents or money could be kept. The longest budget speech is believed to have been by William Gladstone on 18 April 1853, lasting 4 hours and 45 minutes. The budget box or 'Gladstone box' was used to carry the chancellor's speech from Number 11 to the House for over 100 consecutive years. The wooden box was hand-crafted for Gladstone, lined in black satin and covered in scarlet leather.

Before going to Parliament to deliver the statement, the chancellor holds up the red box outside No. 11 to waiting photographers. Chancellors are allowed to refresh themselves with alcoholic drinks during their budget speech — no other Member of Parliament can do this! Traditionally, the leader of the opposition — rather than the shadow chancellor — replies to the budget speech. This is usually followed by 4 days of debate on the Budget Resolutions (the basic parts of the budget that renew taxes), covering different policy areas such as health, education and defence.

Chancellor of the Exchequer George Osborne with his Treasury team on budget day 2013

Follow-up questions

1 What is the purpose of budget day?
2 What is a 'stealth tax'? Why are stealth taxes unpopular?

Government spending (G) is one of the components of aggregate demand. An increase in government spending and/or a cut in taxation increases the size of the budget deficit (or reduces the size of the budget surplus). Either way, an injection into the circular flow of income occurs and the effect on aggregate demand is expansionary.

EXAM TIP

Make sure you don't confuse demand-side and supply-side fiscal policy.

Figure 24.1 illustrates the effect of such an **expansionary** or reflationary **fiscal policy**. Initially, with the aggregate demand curve in position AD_1, macroeconomic equilibrium occurs at point X. Real income or output is y_1, and the price level is P_1.

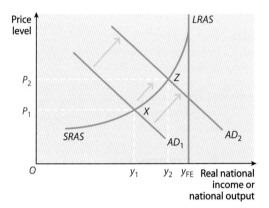

Figure 24.1 Keynesian or demand-side fiscal policy

To eliminate demand-deficient (cyclical or Keynesian) unemployment, the government increases the budget deficit by raising the level of government spending and/or by cutting taxes. The expansionary fiscal policy shifts the AD curve right from AD_1 to AD_2, and the economy moves to a new macroeconomic equilibrium at point Z.

However, the extent to which expansionary fiscal policy *reflates* real output (in this case, from y_1 to y_2), or creates excess demand that leads to demand-pull inflation (in this case, an increase in the price level from P_1 to P_2), depends on the shape of the $SRAS$ curve, which depends on how close, initially, the economy was to full employment. The nearer the economy gets to full employment, the greater the inflationary effect of expansionary fiscal policy and the smaller the reflationary effect. Once the full-employment level of real income is reached on the long-run aggregate supply curve at y_{FE}, a further increase in government spending or a tax cut solely inflates the price level. In this situation, real output cannot grow (except possibly temporarily), because there is no spare capacity. The economy is producing on its production possibility frontier.

Figure 24.1 can be adapted to illustrate the effect of a **contractionary** or deflationary **fiscal policy**. In this case, a cut in government spending and/or an increase in taxation shifts the AD curve to the left. The extent to which the demand deflation results in the price level or real income falling again depends on the shape and slope of the $SRAS$ curve.

KEY TERMS

contractionary fiscal policy: uses fiscal policy to decrease aggregate demand and to shift the AD curve to the left.

expansionary fiscal policy: uses fiscal policy to increase aggregate demand and to shift the AD curve to the right.

The national income multiplier

The **national income multiplier** measures the relationship between an initial change in a component of aggregate demand, such as government spending or private-sector investment, and the resulting larger change in the level of national income.

Suppose, for example, that government spending increases by £8 billion, but tax revenue remains unchanged. The resulting budget deficit initially injects £8 billion of new spending into the circular flow of income. This spending increases people's incomes. If we assume that everybody in the economy saves a small fraction of any income increase and spends the rest, the £8 billion generates multiple and successively smaller further increases in income, until the next stage is so small that it can be ignored. Adding up the successive stages of income generation, the total increase in income is a multiple of the initial spending increase of £8 billion — hence the name **multiplier theory**. If the size of the multiplier is 5, an increase in consumption spending of £8 billion causes national income to increase by £40 billion.

To capture the flavour of the multiplier process, think of ripples spreading over a pond after a stone is thrown into the water. Each of the ripples resembles a stage in the multiplier process. However, the ripples in a pond last only a few seconds, whereas the ripples spreading through the economy following a change in aggregate demand can last for months and even years.

There are in fact a number of different national income multipliers, each relating to the component of national income that initially changes. Besides the **government spending multiplier**, there is an **investment multiplier**, a **tax multiplier**, an **export multiplier** and an import **multiplier**. Taken together, the government spending and tax multipliers are known as **fiscal policy multipliers**. Likewise the export and import multipliers are **foreign trade multipliers**. An increase in consumption spending can also trigger a multiplier process.

In some circumstances, the multiplier process can reduce rather than increase national income. This happens when government spending, consumption, investment or exports fall. It also happens when taxation or imports *increase*. This is because taxation and imports are leakages from the circular flow of income, rather than injections. The tax and import multipliers are always negative.

The multiplier and Keynesian fiscal policy

During the Keynesian era from the 1950s to the 1970s, governments in many industrialised mixed economies, including the UK, based macroeconomic policy on the use of fiscal policy to manage the level of aggregate demand. This became known as **discretionary fiscal policy**. To achieve full employment, governments deliberately ran

KEY TERMS

government spending multiplier: the relationship between a change in government spending and the resulting change in national income.

investment multiplier: the relationship between a change in investment and the resulting change in national income.

national income multiplier: the relationship between a change in aggregate demand and the resulting change in national income.

tax multiplier: the relationship between a change in taxation and the resulting change in national income.

EXAM TIP

You will not be expected to calculate the value of the multiplier in AQA AS exams.

KEY TERM

discretionary fiscal policy: involves making discrete changes to G, T and the budget deficit to manage and 'fine-tune' the level of aggregate demand.

budget deficits (setting $G > T$). This expanded aggregate demand, but sometimes too much demand 'overheated' the economy. Excess demand pulled up the price level in a demand-pull inflation, or pulled imports into the country and caused a balance of payments crisis. In these circumstances, governments were forced to reverse the thrust of fiscal policy, cutting public spending or raising taxes to reduce the level of demand in the economy. The Keynesians used demand-side fiscal policy in a discrete way (supplemented at times by monetary policy), to 'fine-tune' the level of aggregate demand in the economy. Government spending and/or taxes were changed in order to stabilise fluctuations in the economic cycle, and to try to achieve the macroeconomic objectives of full employment and economic growth, without excessive inflation or an unsustainable deterioration in the balance of payments.

The larger the government spending multiplier, the smaller the increase in public spending needed to bring about a desired increase in national income. Similarly, the larger the tax multiplier, the smaller the required tax cut. It follows that if the government spending and tax multipliers are large (for example, equal to 5 as in my numerical example on page 285), and if the multipliers affect *real* output more than the *price level*, fiscal policy used as a demand management instrument can be an effective way of controlling the economy.

The multiplier in the UK economy

In reality, particularly in the case of the UK economy, neither assumption may hold. Free-market economists believe an increase in government spending stimulates *prices* rather than *real output*, and that government spending merely displaces or **crowds out** private sector investment.

> **KEY TERM**
>
> **crowding out:** a situation in which an increase in government or public sector spending displaces private sector spending, with little or no increase in aggregate demand.

Even without accepting this free-market argument, the size of the multiplier is likely to be small. The UK economy is open to imports, with relatively high income tax rates when national insurance contributions are included in the tax rate. A significant fraction of the income received from an increase in government spending leaks into taxation and imports, as well as into saving. This means that the main effect of an expansionary fiscal policy may be to pull imports into the economy — even when there is substantial unemployment — with relatively little increase in domestic output and employment.

EXTENSION MATERIAL

A closer look at the government spending multiplier

The multiplier process is essentially dynamic, taking place over time. To explain the government spending multiplier, it will be assumed that there is demand-deficient unemployment in the economy, and that the levels of taxation and imports do not change when aggregate demand increases. To reduce demand-deficient unemployment, the government decides to spend an extra £10 billion on road building.

In the first stage of the multiplier process, £10 billion is received as income by building workers who, like everybody in the economy, are assumed to spend 90p of every pound of income on consumption.

At the second stage of the multiplier process, £9 billion of the £10 billion income is spent on consumer goods and services, with the remaining £1 billion leaking into unspent savings. At the third stage, consumer goods sector employees spend £8.1 billion, or 0.9 of the £9 billion received at the second stage of income generation. Further stages of income generation occur, with each successive stage being 0.9 of the previous stage. Each stage is smaller than the preceding stage, to the extent that part of income leaks into savings (there being no taxes or imports that vary with the level of national income in this economy).

Assuming that nothing else changes in the time taken for the process to work through the economy, the eventual increase in income ΔY resulting from the initial injection of government spending is the sum of all the stages of income generation. ΔY is larger than ΔG, which triggered the initial growth in national income.

The multiplier process is illustrated in Figure 24.2, which captures the ripple-like nature of the process. In this example, the size of the multiplier is 10.

Figure 24.2 The government spending multiplier

The 'fiscal stimulus', the 'sovereign debt' problem and 'fiscal austerity'

In 2008 when recession began, Keynesian fiscal policy suddenly, but temporarily, came back into fashion. Barack Obama in the USA and the then Labour government in the UK justified the use of an expansionary demand-side fiscal policy, which became known as the **fiscal stimulus**. For a time, both monetary policy and fiscal policy were used in conjunction in the demand-side management of aggregate demand. The Labour government implemented tax cuts (the rate of VAT was cut temporarily to 15%), public spending increases and a burgeoning budget deficit to 'spend the economy out of recession'.

For a few months, the rebirth of Keynesian fiscal policy seemed to work, preventing the economy from slumping into a deep recession and triggering a weak recovery.

However, as in other EU countries such as Greece and Ireland, the massive increase in government borrowing that resulted from the fiscal stimulus led to a new problem: the **sovereign debt problem**. Put simply, the rest of the world was not prepared to lend to the UK government to help finance its budget deficit, except at ever-higher interest rates which the country could not afford. As in other deficit countries, Britain's 'Triple A' credit rating was threatened.

In May 2010, however, the newly elected coalition government, dominated by the Conservatives, was ideologically opposed to Keynesian economic policies. Under Chancellor George Osborne, the Conservatives immediately abandoned the fiscal stimulus and introduced a new fiscal policy based on swingeing public spending cuts and higher taxes (VAT was increased to 20% on 4 January 2011). The Labour government's Keynesian-inspired fiscal stimulus was replaced by a policy of **fiscal austerity** (known also as **fiscal consolidation** or **fiscal restraint**).

EXAM TIP

The AS specification mentions neither the national debt nor the sovereign debt, so you are not expected to know about them. However, answers to questions on fiscal policy can often be improved by applying knowledge of both concepts. The *national debt* is the stock of all past government borrowing that has not been paid back. The country's *sovereign debt* is a currently fashionable term for the same stock of debt. (The national debt or sovereign debt is an economic *stock*, whereas the budget deficit and the government's borrowing requirement are economic *flows*.)

Supply-side fiscal policy

Although the short-lived fiscal stimulus came to an end in 2010, fiscal policy continues to be an important part of government economic policy, but is now used once again primarily as a supply-side policy. Before the fiscal stimulus, on several occasions UK governments cut income tax rates, not to stimulate aggregate demand (though this has been an unintended consequence of the tax cuts), but to create supply-side incentives in the economy.

KEY TERM

supply-side fiscal policy: used to increase the economy's ability to produce and supply goods, through creating incentives to work, save, invest and to be entrepreneurial.

Along with other supply-side policies, **supply-side fiscal policy** is used to try and shift the economy's long-run aggregate supply curve (*LRAS*) curve to the right, thereby increasing the economy's *potential* level of output. The effect of successful supply-side fiscal policy on the *LRAS* curve is shown in Figure 24.3. (Note that an outward movement of the economy's production possibility frontier can also illustrate the intended effect of supply-side policies.)

Figure 24.3 The intended effect of supply-side fiscal policy

To find out more about supply-side fiscal policy, read Chapter 25 on supply-side economics and policies.

The Office for Budget Responsibility

The Office for Budget Responsibility (OBR) was created in 2010 to provide independent analysis of the UK's public sector finances. The OBR produces forecasts for the economy and public finances. The Treasury still produces the bulk of the forecasting. But, instead of the chancellor making judgements based on these data, the OBR rules on whether the government's policy has a better than 50% chance of meeting fiscal targets.

The OBR's spring forecast is published at the same time as the budget and incorporates the impact of any tax and spending policy measures announced in the budget.

The OBR also judges progress made towards achieving the two fiscal targets that the government aims to 'hit' in the medium term: that is, up to about 5 years ahead. The first target is to balance the cyclically adjusted current budget over a 5-year period. Budget deficits tend to rise during recessions and fall during the recovery and boom phases of the economic cycle. The cyclically adjusted budget balance is an estimate of what the budget balance would be if actual GDP were equal to potential (full-employment) GDP. Given that there has been a budget deficit in all recent years, the aim stated in 2010 of eliminating the deficit over the period extending to 2015/16 never seemed likely to be achieved.

The second target, announced when the OBR was set up in 2010, was to see the national debt falling by 2015/16. Again it is almost certain this will not be achieved. The budget deficit, which is a *flow*, may indeed fall — if the economy recovers rather than enters recession again. However, providing a budget deficit exists, the *stock* of accumulated borrowing (i.e. the national debt) must continue to rise.

Follow-up questions
1 Compare the OBR's role in UK fiscal policy to the MPC's role in UK monetary policy.
2 Why do budget deficits rise in recessions and fall in periods of recovery and boom? Discuss whether this is a good thing.

How government spending and taxation affect the pattern of economic activity

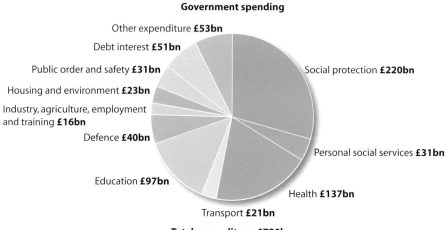

Government spending

Other expenditure **£53bn**

Debt interest **£51bn**

Public order and safety **£31bn**

Housing and environment **£23bn**

Industry, agriculture, employment and training **£16bn**

Defence **£40bn**

Education **£97bn**

Transport **£21bn**

Social protection **£220bn**

Personal social services **£31bn**

Health **£137bn**

Total expenditure: £720bn

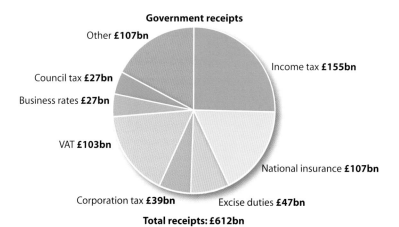

Government receipts

Other **£107bn**

Council tax **£27bn**

Business rates **£27bn**

VAT **£103bn**

Corporation tax **£39bn**

Income tax **£155bn**

National insurance **£107bn**

Excise duties **£47bn**

Total receipts: £612bn

Figure 24.4 Estimates of government spending and revenue, 2013–14

Source: March 2013 Budget Report, HM Treasury

As Figure 24.4 shows, at the time of the March 2013 Report, total UK government expenditure and revenue (mostly tax receipts) were expected to be £720 billion and £612 billion respectively during the financial year 2013–14. This means that the budget deficit for 2013–14 was expected to be £108 billion.

Perhaps more significant than the absolute totals of public expenditure is the ratio of public expenditure to national income or GDP, which indicates the share of the nation's resources taken by the government. Apart from the periods 1914–18 and 1939–45, which saw rapid, but temporary, increases in government spending to pay for the First and Second World Wars, the twentieth century witnessed a steady but relatively slow increase in government expenditure from around 10% to over 40% of GDP, reaching 46.75% in 1982–83. The ratio continued to rise in the early 1980s and fell in the late 1980s, before rising and falling again in the 1990s. By 2009–10, as Figure 24.5 shows, the ratio had increased again to nearly 48% in the depths of the recession. At the same time, tax revenues had fallen to about 36.5% of GDP. The spending figure fell to about 43.5% of GDP at the end of the 2011–12 financial year and tax revenues rose to about 37.6% of GDP. The forecast data up to the year 2015–16 seem very optimistic. When you read this chapter, check whether this optimism was justified.

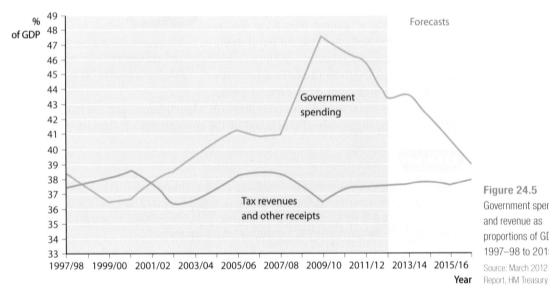

Figure 24.5
Government spending and revenue as proportions of GDP, 1997–98 to 2015–16
Source: March 2012 Budget Report, HM Treasury

A main explanation for the changes in the ratios of government spending and taxation as ratios of GDP lies in changes taking place in employment and unemployment, which in turn relate to the economic cycle. As Figure 24.4 shows, spending on social security (under the heading 'social protection'), which includes unemployment-related benefits, is by far the largest single category of public spending. When the economy booms, unemployment falls, so spending on social security also falls. The reverse is true in a recession.

Transfers and interest payments made by the government

A large part of government expenditure takes the form of **transfers**: for example, the state pension and unemployment-related benefits. As the name indicates, transfers are a redistribution of spending power from taxpayers in general to those receiving welfare benefits. By contrast, government spending on new hospitals or schools directly increases national output.

KEY TERM

transfers: the part of government spending in which tax revenues are paid to people such as pensioners, without any output being produced in return.

In Figure 24.4, transfers are the major part of the item 'social protection', which at £207 billion in 2012–13 dwarfed all other types of public spending, including health and education. When transfers are excluded, government spending falls from around 43.5% of GDP in 2012 to about 33%. This figure is a more accurate measure of the share of national output directly commanded by the state (and thus unavailable for use in the private sector) to produce the hospitals, roads and other goods and services which government collectively provides and finances, for the most part, out of taxation.

Figure 24.4 also shows the interest paid by the government to people who have lent to the state (i.e. to holders of the **national debt**). In 2012–13, interest payments on the national debt were expected to be £46 billion, or nearly 7% of public spending. This item of public spending rises when interest rates rise and falls when interest rates are cut. However, *total* interest payments are also affected by the government's budgetary position.

EXAM TIP

Don't confuse the national debt with the budget deficit. The national debt is a stock, but the budget deficit is a flow. Politicians sometimes confuse the two! Note that the borrowing which finances a budget deficit adds to the stock of the national debt, whereas a budget surplus allows the government to redeem part of the national debt.

A budget deficit generally increases interest payments because it increases the total *stock* of government debt. Conversely, a budget surplus allows the government to reduce the national debt by paying back past borrowing.

Microeconomic ways in which government spending affects the pattern of economic activity

Taxes and subsidies are used to alter the relative prices of goods and services in order to change consumption patterns. Demerit goods such as alcohol and tobacco are taxed in order to discourage consumption, while merit goods such as healthcare and education are subsidised and often publicly provided. Taxes are also used to finance the provision of public goods such as defence, police and roads. Under the 'polluter must pay' principle, taxes are also used to discourage and reduce the production and consumption of negative externalities such as pollution and congestion.

EXAM TIP

At AS, knowledge of public goods, merit and demerit goods, and externalities is tested in the Unit 1 exam and not in the Unit 2 exam.

How taxation and government spending affect people's spending power

The price mechanism is 'value neutral' with regard to the equity or social fairness of the distributions of income and wealth resulting from the action of market forces in the economy. If the government decides that the distributions of income and wealth produced by free-market forces are undesirable, taxation and transfers in its public spending programme can be used to modify these distributions and to try to reduce this market failure resulting from 'inequity'.

Before 1979, British governments of all political complexions used **progressive taxation** and a policy of transfers of income to the less well-off, in a deliberate attempt — albeit with limited success — to reduce inequalities in the distribution of income. A tax is progressive when the proportion of income paid in tax *rises* as income increases. Progressive taxation, combined with transfers to lower-income groups, reduces the spending power of the rich, while increasing that of the poor. However, some taxes, particularly those designed to reduce consumption of the demerit goods alcohol and tobacco, are regressive and fall more heavily on the poor. A tax is regressive when the proportion of income paid in tax *falls* as income increases.

> **KEY TERM**
>
> **progressive tax:** a tax where the proportion of income paid in tax rises as income increases.

Regional and EU considerations

Government spending and taxation also contribute to a redistribution of income between different regions and member countries of the UK. On average, people living in London and southeast England receive higher pre-tax incomes than those living in Northern Ireland, Scotland and Wales and in western and northern England. However, part of the tax revenue collected from households and businesses in the southeast is transferred and spent by the government in the poorer regions of the UK.

The UK is also a net contributor to the European Union's budget. Although the poorer parts of the UK benefit from EU spending on regional regeneration projects, taken as a whole, the UK pays more into the EU budget than it gets out. The UK's net contribution was less than 1% of UK public spending in 2011.

The influence of supply-side theory on government spending, taxation and the pattern of economic activity

Between 1979 and 1997, and under the influence of supply-side theory, Conservative governments changed the structure of both taxation and public spending to *widen* rather than *reduce* inequalities in the distributions of income and wealth. The Conservatives believed that greater incentives for work and enterprise were necessary in order to increase the UK's growth rate. For the Conservatives, progressive taxation and transfers to the poor meant that people had less incentive to work harder and to engage in entrepreneurial risk. The ease with which the poor could claim welfare benefits and the level at which they were available created a situation in which the poor rationally chose unemployment and state benefits in preference to wages and work. In this dependency culture, the unwaged were effectively married to the state. Many of the poor, obviously not enjoying this marriage, drifted into antisocial behaviour, attacking bus shelters and other public property, as well as privately owned property.

From 1997 until losing office in 2010, Labour governments tried to use fiscal policy both to improve the economy's supply-side performance and to make the distribution of income once again more equal. The policy had only limited success. Although the real incomes of most of the poor increased in these years, income inequalities continued to grow, largely because high incomes grew at a much faster rate than low incomes. Since the 2008 recession, however, average incomes have fallen by near-record amounts, and, according to the Institute of Fiscal Studies, inequality has fallen back to levels last seen in the mid-1990s.

SUMMARY

- Fiscal policy uses government spending, taxation and the budgetary position to try to achieve the government's economic policy objectives.
- Keynesian fiscal policy (or demand-side fiscal policy) manages the level of aggregate demand.
- Changes in the government's budget deficit or surplus are important in Keynesian fiscal policy.
- The size of the government spending multiplier affects the power of Keynesian fiscal policy.
- Government spending is a component of aggregate demand.
- Changes in government spending and/or taxation shift the *AD* curve.
- The effect on real output and employment depends on the shape and slope of the *SRAS* curve.
- Supply-side fiscal policy affects the position of the *LRAS* curve.
- In supply-side fiscal policy, tax changes are used to try to change incentives in the economy.
- A significant proportion of government spending takes the forms of transfers and debt interest payments.
- Progressive taxation and transfers have redistributed income from higher-income groups to lower-income groups, but income inequalities have widened since the 2008 recession.

Exam-style questions

1 Explain how Keynesian fiscal policy differs from supply-side fiscal policy. (12 marks)

2 Explain the relationship between a budget deficit and the government's borrowing requirement. (12 marks)

3 Do you agree that the fiscal stimulus should have been continued after 2010 in order to 'spend the UK economy out of recession'? Justify your answer. (25 marks)

4 Evaluate the view that cuts in the higher rates of income tax are necessary in order to create the incentives necessary for stimulating economic growth. (25 marks)

Managing the economy: supply-side economics and supply-side policies

Chapter 25

This is the last of three chapters which explain the different forms of economic policy used to manage the national economy. Supply-side policy has already been mentioned in Chapters 23 and 24, and the meaning of supply-side economics was introduced in Chapter 15. In Chapter 23, it was mentioned that monetary policy, which is now used to manage aggregate demand, has little to do with supply-side economics, except in the sense that supply-side economists deem 'sound money' and control of inflation as essential prerequisites for successful supply-side policy. As Chapter 24 explained, things are different with fiscal policy.

This chapter explains how, when supply-side economics first came into existence, it was based on a rejection of Keynesian fiscal policy and on the need to use taxation to create incentives rather than to manage aggregate demand. Most economists now agree that the economy's supply side is important, although many argue that the central premise of supply-side economics, that lower taxes pay for themselves through the extra tax revenue they generate, is not proven.

LEARNING OUTCOMES

This chapter will:
- explain the meaning of supply-side economics
- relate supply-side economics to the free-market revival
- distinguish between the original meaning of supply-side policy and its later, broader meaning
- use *AD/AS* analysis to contrast supply-side and Keynesian views on the macroeconomy
- examine the role of fiscal policy in supply-side economics
- describe a number of supply-side policies that are used, or have been used, in the UK

The meaning of supply-side economics

> Supply-side economics provides a framework of analysis which relies on personal and private incentives. When incentives change, people's behaviour changes in response. People are attracted towards positive incentives and repelled by the negative. The role of government in such a framework is carried out by the ability of government to alter incentives and thereby affect society's behaviour.

Professor Arthur Laffer, University of Southern California, 1983

The term **supply-side economics** was first used in 1976 by Jude Wanniski, a journalist at the *Wall Street Journal*, and by Herbert Stein, a professor at the University of Virginia. A few years later, in 1980, supply-side economics became an important part of the economic policy programme promised by Ronald Reagan in his successful campaign for the US presidency. These policies became known as **Reaganomics**.

KEY TERM

supply-side economics: a branch of free-market economics arguing that government policy should be used to improve the competitiveness and efficiency of markets.

The ideology and policies of other free-market orientated governments were also strongly influenced by supply-side theories in the 1980s, in particular the Conservative administrations of Margaret Thatcher in the UK from 1979 to 1990. During the 1980s, Thatcherism became the UK equivalent of Reaganomics in the USA.

CASE STUDY 25.1

Supply-side economics and American politics

The term 'supply-side economics' was coined in 1976 by Jude Wanniski, then an economics journalist for the *Wall Street Journal*. Wanniski got his ideas from two right-wing economists, Herbert Stein and Art Laffer, who themselves went on to become prominent supply-side economists. Wanniski's crude but popularist arguments in favour of tax cuts, especially cuts from which the rich would benefit most, were adopted by US President Ronald Reagan in the 1980s (becoming perhaps the most important part of 'Reaganomics'). More recently, Wanniski's arguments in favour of tax cuts formed an important part of the neo-conservative (neo-con) political agenda in the USA, an agenda implemented by the Republican president George W. Bush from 2001 to 2009.

Democratic President Barack Obama does not of course accept supply-side arguments, but Mitt Romney, Obama's unsuccessful opponent in the 2012 presidential race, did promise that, if elected, he would reintroduce supply-side policies. As Michael Tomasky stated immediately after the 2012 election: 'Economics played a strong and even pivotal role in this election, and "extreme" supply-side economics came out a huge loser, while the Democrats have started to wrap their arms around a simple, winning alternative: the idea that government must invest in the middle class and not the rich.'

Follow-up questions
1 What is meant by 'supply-side economics'?
2 Contrast the views of Keynesian and supply-side economists on the role of tax cuts in fiscal policy.

Margaret Thatcher in 1986

Supply-side economics and the free market revival

As explained in Chapter 15, supply-side economics grew in significance in the 1980s as a part of the free-market revival. The growing fashion for the term 'supply-side economics' was partly a response to the decline of monetarism, which for a number of years in the late 1970s and early 1980s had been the label most often associated with the free-market revival. Free-market economics, monetarism and supply-side economics, which overlap each other, all accompanied and contributed to the decline of Keynesianism.

Although there is some disagreement over points of emphasis and detail, free-market economists believe in the virtues of capitalism and competitive markets — a belief which is matched by a distrust and dislike of 'big government' and state intervention in the economy.

> **EXAM TIP**
>
> Even if an exam question on UK macroeconomic performance does not mention supply-side economics or policies, it may be appropriate to bring supply-side analysis into your answer.

The original meaning of supply-side economic policy

When supply-side economics first came to prominence around 1980, it focused narrowly on the effects of fiscal policy on the economy. During the Keynesian era, most economists regarded fiscal policy — and especially taxation — as a demand management tool. In Keynesian economics, the government's budget deficit lay at the centre of fiscal policy. The Keynesians largely ignored the impact of public spending and tax changes on the supply side of the economy, focusing instead on how changes in government spending and taxation affect aggregate demand.

By contrast, supply-side economics initially grew out of the concern expressed by free-market economists in the 1970s about the microeconomic effects of demand-side Keynesian fiscal policy. Indeed, in many respects, supply-side economics is a revival of the old pro-free market theory that largely disappeared from view during the Keynesian era. The central idea of supply-side economics is that a tax cut should be used, *not* to stimulate aggregate demand Keynesian-style, but to create incentives by altering relative prices, particularly those of labour and leisure, in favour of work, saving and investment, and entrepreneurship, and against the voluntary choice of unemployment.

> **EXAM TIP**
>
> It is important to understand that supply-side economics is part of the free-market revival.

The wider meaning of supply-side economic policy

Supply-side economic policy now encompasses more than just fiscal policy; it is the set of government policies which aim to change the underlying structure of the economy and improve the economic performance of markets and industries, and of individual firms and workers within markets. For the most part, supply-side policies are also *microeconomic* rather than simply *macroeconomic*, since, by acting on the motivation and efficiency of individual consumers, workers and entrepreneurs within the economy, the policies aim to enhance general economic performance and the economy's underlying production potential by improving microeconomic incentives.

> **KEY TERM**
>
> **supply-side policies:** interpreted narrowly, supply-side policies focus on the role of tax cuts in increasing personal incentives. Interpreted broadly, they aim to improve the economy's ability to produce and supply more output.

Supply-side economists, and free-market economists in general, believe that the economy is usually close to its equilibrium, or 'natural', levels of output and employment. However, due to distortions and inefficiencies resulting from Keynesian neglect of the supply side, towards the end of the Keynesian era these equilibrium levels became unnecessarily low. To increase levels of output and employment (and to reduce unemployment), supply-side economists recommend the use of appropriate microeconomic policies to remove distortions, improve incentives and generally make markets more competitive.

> **EXAM TIP**
>
> You should appreciate that many supply-side policies are microeconomic rather than macroeconomic.

During the Keynesian era in the 1960s and 1970s, government microeconomic policy in the UK was generally interventionist, extending the roles of the state and of the planning mechanism. Interventionist policies, such as regional policy, competition policy and industrial relations policy (which were known collectively as industrial policy), generally increased the role of the state and limited the role of markets.

By contrast, supply-side microeconomic policy is anti-interventionist, attempting to roll back government interference in the activities of markets and of private economic agents, and to change the economic function of government from *provider* to *enabler*. Along with tax cuts to create incentives to work, save and invest, and cuts in welfare benefits to reduce the incentive to choose unemployment rather than a low-paid work alternative, supply-side economic policy includes policies of **privatisation**, **marketisation** (commercialisation) and **deregulation**.

In essence, the supply-siders, together with the other free-market economists, wish to create an *enterprise culture*. In this broad interpretation, supply-side policies aim to promote entrepreneurship and popular capitalism and to replace the *dependency culture* and statism that had been part of the Keynesian mixed economy.

EXTENSION MATERIAL

The Laffer curve

Supply-side economists believe that high rates of income tax and the overall tax burden create disincentives, which, by reducing national income as taxation increases, also reduce the government's total tax revenue. This effect is illustrated by a Laffer curve, such as the one in Figure 25.1.

The Laffer curve, named after the leading supply-side economist Arthur Laffer, quoted at the beginning of this chapter, shows how the government's total tax revenue changes as the average tax rate increases from 0% to 100%. Tax revenue must be zero when the average tax rate is 0%, but Figure 25.1 also shows that total tax revenue is also assumed to be zero when the tax rate is 100%. With the average tax rate set at 100%, all income must be paid as tax to the government. In this situation, there is no incentive to produce output other than for subsistence, so with no output produced, the government ends up collecting no tax revenue.

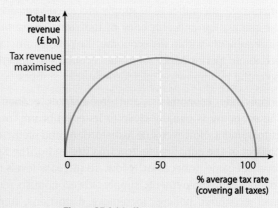

Figure 25.1 A Laffer curve

Between the limiting tax rates of 0% and 100%, the Laffer curve shows tax revenue first rising and then falling as the average rate of taxation increases. Tax revenue is maximised at the highest point on the Laffer curve, which in Figure 25.1

occurs at an average tax rate (for all taxes) of 50%. Beyond this point, any further increase in the average tax rate becomes counterproductive, causing total tax revenue to fall.

Supply-side economists argue that the increase in the tax burden in the Keynesian era, needed to finance the growth of the government and the public sector, raised the average tax rate towards or beyond the critical point on the Laffer curve at which tax revenue is maximised. In this situation, any further tax increase has the perverse effect of reducing the government's total tax revenue. Indeed, according to supply-side theory, if the government wishes to increase total tax revenue, it must cut tax rates rather than increase them.

A reduction in tax rates creates the incentives needed to stimulate economic growth. Faster growth means that total tax revenue increases despite the fact that tax rates are lower. Arguably, the effect is reinforced by a decline in tax evasion and avoidance, as the incentive to engage in these activities reduces at lower marginal tax rates.

CASE STUDY 25.2

How supply-side economics came into being

Before the advent of supply-side economics in the 1970s, it was thought that tax reductions had to be financed by either cutting government spending or increasing government borrowing. Supply-siders took a different view. Economist Arthur Laffer and politician Dick Cheney (who later became Secretary of State in George W. Bush's Republican administration) argued that taxes could be cut, public spending could be increased, and government borrowing and inflation could be held down, all at the same time. This view of the world, from which 'extreme' supply-side economics grew, stemmed from the proposition that if taxes are cut, the rate of economic growth substantially increases, and fast growth then boosts government tax revenues in a way that more than makes up for the earlier cuts in tax rates.

At a lunch-time meeting attended by fellow true believers in southern California, Laffer drew a parabola-shaped curve on a napkin. The curve showed that if the tax rate is set at zero, the government receives no revenue. But if the tax rate is set at 100%, it will also receive zero tax revenue, since all income would be taxed away. Between these two, Laffer drew an arc, which suggested that at higher levels of taxation, reducing the tax rate would produce more revenue for the government. In this way, the Laffer curve was born.

According to journalist Johann Hari, the Laffer curve became the supply-siders' 'Sermon on the Mount'. For Cheney, it was 'a revelation, for it presented in a simple,

easily digestible form the messianic power of tax cuts'. Economic performance hinges almost entirely on how much incentive investors and entrepreneurs have to attain more wealth, and this incentive hinges almost entirely on their tax rate. The Laffer curve was an economic recipe for tax cuts for the rich. Others, such as Paul Krugman, saw the idea as preposterous. However, a string of right-wing economists supported Laffer's idea, and many were then employed by Republican politicians on the make, such as Ronald Reagan and later George W. Bush.

The term 'voodoo economics' was coined to describe extreme supply-side theory. However, promises of tax cuts are always popular with voters, despite the lack of economic evidence to justify them. For this reason, every Republican presidential candidate in the USA promises to cut taxes (and some Democratic presidential candidates too), using the supply-side argument to support their case. Fairly recently, neo-conservative politicians in the administration of President George W. Bush (the Republican predecessor of Democrat Barack Obama) used the supply-side argument to justify greatly increased government spending on arms, combined with large tax cuts, especially for high income earners. The neo-conservatives believe that higher tax revenues, allegedly resulting from the tax cuts, pay for military spending, without the government's budget deficit growing. However, as was the case in the 1980s, the evidence does not support this extreme supply-side argument.

Follow-up questions

1 Contrast supply-side and Keynesian views on the role of tax cuts in the economy.
2 Explain why supply-side economists believe that tax cuts stimulate economic growth.

Supply-side policy: using a production possibility frontier to show the possible effect of a cut in government spending

A production possibility graph is one of the most fruitful diagrams for you to use in AS (and A2) economics. It is useful in both macroeconomic and microeconomic analysis. A macroeconomic production possibility graph usually shows capital good and consumer good production on the two axes of the diagram. However, Figure 25.2 is different. The vertical axis of the diagram shows public sector output and spending (i.e. government output and spending), while the horizontal axis shows private sector output and spending.

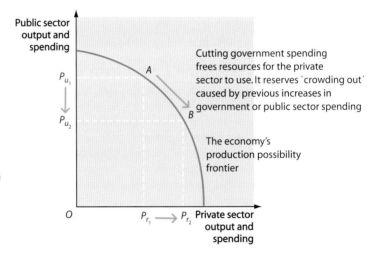

Figure 25.2 A possible 'crowding-in' effect resulting from a cut in public sector output and spending

Suppose that, initially, the economy is on its production possibility frontier, producing at point A. As a result of previous increases in public sector spending undertaken by a Keynesian-inspired government, public sector output is Pu_1, and private sector output is Pr_1. Supply-side (and other free-market) economists generally take the view that a cut in public sector output and spending frees resources for the private sector to use. Thus a cut in public sector spending from Pu_1 to Pu_2 creates sufficient 'slack' (i.e. unemployed resources) for the private sector to mop up and employ. The optimistic view that private sector output would grow was one of the justifications used by chancellor George Osborne for swingeing tax cuts when the coalition government took office in 2010.

CASE STUDY 25.3

Have UK politicians been influenced by supply-side theory?

On 18 December 2012, Chancellor George Osborne spoke to a gathering of American supply-side economists at the Manhattan Institute for Policy Research in New York City. In answer to a question about the division between American Republicans and British Conservatives on the power of tax rate cuts to generate tax revenue, George Osborne replied:

Well I'm a fiscal Conservative, and I don't want to take risks with my public finances on an assumption that we are at some point on the Laffer curve. What I would say is, let's see the proof in the pudding: in other words, I'm a low-tax Conservative, I want to reduce taxes, but I basically think you have to do the hard work of reducing government spending to pay for those lower taxes. If you want to cut taxes, cut welfare and cut spending, and that's what I'm doing.

Osborne seemed to be rejecting the 'extreme' supply-side argument, based on the Laffer curve, that tax cuts can be self-financing and that they are all that is needed for growth generation. Osborne, along with other Conservative members of the UK government (in 2013), is best regarded as a 'moderate' rather than an 'extreme' supply-sider.

Many Labour and Lib Dem politicians now also accept *moderate* supply-side arguments, though they continue to reject extreme supply-side calls for swingeing tax cuts and greater income inequality in order to incentivise the population. Especially since the emergence of the sovereign debt problem, few politicians now call for continuous large budget deficits as the way to achieve growth and

full employment, and there is general agreement that the tax structure should be used in a supply-side way to create incentives for work, entrepreneurship, saving and investment.

George Osborne

Follow-up questions
1 Describe the difference between 'extreme' and 'moderate' supply-side views on the role of tax cuts.
2 How has the emergence of the sovereign debt problem affected fiscal policy?

The 'trickle-down' effect

These days, few supply-side economists (at least in the UK) support the 'extreme' supply-side argument that tax cuts can be self-financing. However, all supply-siders, moderate and extreme, reject the view that fiscal policy should be used to manage aggregate demand. Along with other free-market economists, they believe that expansionary fiscal policy simply leads to inflation, with no long-run increase in real output.

Some supply-side economists believe that, although the rich benefit most from supply-side tax cuts, the poor would also benefit through a **trickle-down effect**. The rich, whose disposable income increases the most as a result of tax cuts, respond by employing more servants, nannies and gardeners, and in this way the poor benefit.

> **KEY TERM**
>
> **trickle-down effect:** income paid by rich people to the poorer people they employ.

Many economists, especially Keynesians, question the strength and even the existence of trickle-down effects. J. K. Galbraith, for example, caustically quipped the less than elegant metaphor that if one feeds the horse enough oats, some will pass through to the road for the sparrows. Galbraith went on to argue that 'we can safely abandon the doctrine that the rich are not working because they have too little money and the poor because they have too much'. And even if a 'trickle-down' effect operates, it stems from increasing significantly income inequalities that most regard as far too inequitable or unfair.

EXTENSION MATERIAL

Microeconomic theory and the effect of supply-side fiscal policy

The supply-side theory of the effects of taxation on labour market incentives, which lies at the heart of free-market supply-side economics, depends significantly on the shape of the supply curve of labour.

Supply-side economists usually assume a conventional upward-sloping supply curve of labour. Such a curve, which is illustrated in Figure 25.3(a), shows that workers respond to higher wage rates by supplying more labour.

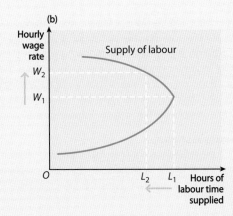

Figure 25.3 Labour supply curves

Since a cut in the rate at which income tax rates are levied is equivalent to an increase in the wage rate, the upward-sloping supply curve implies that workers respond to cuts in the marginal rate of income tax by working harder. (The marginal rate of income tax is the percentage of the last pound of income paid in tax.) If this is the case, a reduction in income tax rates creates the incentive for workers to supply more labour (and for entrepreneurs to become more enterprising), while an increase in income tax rates has a disincentive effect on effort and the supply of labour.

However, as the extension material in Chapter 4 noted (see page 33), the supply curve of labour need not necessarily slope upward throughout its length. The backward-bending labour supply curve drawn in Figure 25.3(b) is another possibility. It shows that, above the hourly wage rate W_1, any further wage rate increase (or income tax decrease) causes workers to supply *less* rather than *more* labour. In this situation, workers prefer to enjoy extra leisure time rather than to work. Following an increase in the hourly wage rate from W_1 to W_2, the hours of labour time supplied fall from L_1 to L_2.

It is important to note that, if supply curves of labour bend backward, the supply-side argument, that tax reductions increase national output and efficiency through their effect on labour market incentives, becomes much weaker. Far from encouraging people to work harder, a wage rise or income tax cut might have the opposite effect, causing people to work fewer hours and to enjoy more leisure time instead.

Examples of supply-side economic policies

This final chapter will conclude with some examples of supply-side policies other than those that relate to the effect of fiscal policy on personal incentives.

All the policies listed below have been implemented in the UK over approximately the last 30 years. However, some policies, such as creating internal markets in the provision of state healthcare and education, have been partially implemented and then largely withdrawn.

Industrial policy measures

- **Privatisation.** The sale or transfer of assets such as nationalised industries from the public sector to the private sector.
- **Marketisation (or commercialisation).** Shifting economic activity from non-market provision (financed by taxation) to commercial or market provision for which the customer pays.
- **Deregulation.** The removal of previously imposed regulations in order to promote competition. Deregulation removes barriers to market entry to make markets contestable, and gets rid of unnecessary 'red tape' or bureaucracy, which had increased firms' costs of production.
- **Internal markets.** In the National Health Service and education, where the state continues to be a major producer and provider of services, internal markets can be introduced to provide a form of commercial discipline and to improve efficiency. In an internal market, which is a substitute for privatisation, the taxpayer continues to finance hospitals and schools, but hospitals and schools 'earn' the money according to how many patients and pupils they attract.
- **Encouraging the private sector to introduce its own supply-side reforms**.

Labour market measures

- **Lower rates of income tax.** Reducing marginal rates of income tax to create labour market incentives, and raising tax thresholds or personal tax allowances to remove the low-paid from the tax net.
- **Reducing state welfare benefits relative to average earnings.** Lower benefit levels create incentives to choose low-paid employment in preference to claiming unemployment-related benefits. In addition, welfare benefits can be made more difficult to claim, and available only to claimants genuinely looking for work. Making benefits less attractive may also reduce the unemployment trap.
- **Changing employment law to reduce the power of trade unions.** Removing trade unions' legal protection, restricting their rights, and extending the freedom for workers not to belong to unions, and for employers not to recognise and negotiate with unions. Replacing collective bargaining with individual wage negotiation and employer determination of pay. Restricting the right to strike and to undertake industrial action.
- **Introducing short-term contracts.** Replacing 'jobs for life' with short-term labour contracts, and introducing profit-related and performance-related pay. Critics of these policies believe they lead to even greater poverty and inequality for ordinary workers in an increasingly casualised and exploited part-time labour force.

- **Repealing legislation which limits employers' freedom to employ.** This makes it easier for employers to 'hire and fire' workers.
- **More flexible pension arrangements.** Encouraging workers to 'opt out' of state pensions and to arrange private pension plans so as to reduce the burden on taxpayers. Allowing workers to transfer private sector pensions between employers when changing jobs.
- **Improving the training of labour.** Establishing training agencies and academies to develop vocational technical education. However, UK governments have rejected the proposal to impose a 'training tax' on all employers to prevent free-riding by firms with no training schemes, which poach trained workers from firms that do train their workers.

Financial and capital market measures

- **Deregulating financial markets.** Creating greater competition among banks and building societies, and opening up the UK financial markets to overseas banks and financial institutions. These reforms increase the supply of funds and reduce the cost of borrowing for UK firms. Financial deregulation and the removal of foreign exchange controls also encourage 'inward' investment by overseas firms such as Samsung and Nissan.
- **Encouraging saving.** Governments have created special tax privileges for saving. They also encouraged saving by giving individual shareholders first preference in the market for shares issued when former nationalised industries such as British Gas were privatised. However, most individual shareholders quickly sold their shares to institutional shareholders, which negated one of the main reasons for privatisation. It is also worth noting that in recent years, very low interest rates, brought about by the government's monetary policy, have discouraged saving.
- **Promoting entrepreneurship.** Governments have encouraged the growth of popular capitalism and an enterprise culture. Company taxation has been reduced and markets have been deregulated to encourage risk taking.
- **Reducing public spending and public sector borrowing.** This has been done to free resources for private sector use and avoid crowding out.

SUMMARY

- Supply-side economics argues that government policy should be used to improve incentives and the competitiveness and efficiency of markets.
- In its early years, supply-side economics focused on how, via increased incentives, tax cuts promote economic growth and are self-financing.
- The growth of supply-side economics was part of the free-market revival.
- Supply-side economists are anti-interventionist and wish to reduce the economic role of the state.
- There is little or no evidence to support the 'extreme' supply-side argument that tax cuts are self-financing.
- Nevertheless, most economists now accept the moderate or mainstream supply-side argument that the supply side of the economy is just as important as the demand side.
- Many supply-side policies are microeconomic rather than macroeconomic.

Exam-style questions

1 With the help of *AD/AS* diagrams, explain the difference between supply-side and Keynesian views on the effect of an increase in aggregate demand on the economy. (12 marks)

2 Explain the role of fiscal policy in supply-side economic policy. (12 marks)

3 To what extent do you agree that supply-side reforms are needed if UK macroeconomic performance is to improve? Justify your answer. (25 marks)

4 Assess the view that a cut in income tax rates inevitably leads to an increase in total tax revenue. (25 marks)

accelerator: a change in the level of investment in new capital goods induced by a change in national income or output. The size of the accelerator depends on the economy's capital–output ratio.

aggregate demand: the total planned spending on real output produced within the economy.

aggregate supply: the level of real national output that producers are prepared to supply at different average price levels.

balance of trade in goods: the part of the current account measuring payments for exports and imports of goods. It is sometimes called the 'balance of visible trade'.

balance of trade in services: the part of the current account measuring payments for exports and imports of services. It is sometimes called the 'balance of invisible trade', though the two terms are not strictly identical.

balanced budget: this is achieved when government spending equals government revenue $(G = T)$.

Bank Rate: the rate of interest the Bank of England charges when lending money to commercial banks to increase their liquidity.

budget deficit: occurs when government spending exceeds government revenue $(G > T)$.

budget surplus: occurs when government spending is less than government revenue $(G < T)$.

capital–output ratio: the ratio between the output that firms are currently producing and their existing stock of fixed capital assets.

central bank: the central bank implements monetary policy on behalf of the government.

ceteris paribus: holding all other factors in the economy constant when examining one part of the economy. It is an important assumption in microeconomics, but not generally in macroeconomics.

claimant count: the method of measuring unemployment according to those people who are claiming unemployment-related benefits.

closed economy: an economy with no international trade.

commercial bank: a commercial bank, such as Barclays, aims to make a profit from commercial banking business.

consumption: total planned spending by households on real output produced within the economy.

contractionary fiscal policy: uses fiscal policy to decrease aggregate demand and to shift the *AD* curve to the left.

cost-push theory of inflation: a rising price level is caused by an increase in the costs of production, shown by a shift of the *SRAS* curve to the left.

crowding out: a situation in which an increase in government or public sector spending displaces private sector spending, with little or no increase in aggregate demand.

current account: (1) the part of the balance of payments measuring payments for exports and imports, investment income and transfers; (2) a bank account that allows its owner to withdraw cash immediately by using a cheque or a plastic debit card.

current account deficit: occurs when currency outflows in the current account exceed currency inflows. It is often shortened to 'exports less than imports ($X < M$)'.

current account surplus: occurs when currency inflows in the current account exceed currency outflows. It is often shortened to 'exports exceeding imports ($X > M$)'.

cyclical unemployment: also known as Keynesian and demand-deficient unemployment. As this name suggests, it is unemployment caused by a lack of aggregate demand in the economy.

deficit financing: deliberately running a budget deficit and borrowing to finance the deficit.

deflation: a persistent or continuing fall in the average price level.

demand-pull inflation: a rising price level caused by an increase in aggregate demand, shown by a shift of the *AD* curve to the right.

demand-side fiscal policy: changes in the budget deficit are used to increase or decrease the level of aggregate demand (and to shift the *AD* curve to the right or to the left).

depression: this term has no generally agreed definition. It is best to think of it as a long and deep recession. In the UK, a recession is defined as a period of negative economic growth lasting at least 6 months.

deregulation: involves removing previously imposed regulations.

discretionary fiscal policy: involves making discrete changes to *G*, *T* and the budget deficit to manage and 'fine-tune' the level of aggregate demand.

economic cycle: the fluctuation of real output above and below the trend output line.

economic growth: an increase in the economy's potential level of real output, and an outward movement of the economy's production possibility frontier.

equilibrium national income: the level of income at which withdrawals from the circular flow of income equal injections into the flow. In a two-sector model of the economy, national income is in equilibrium when $S = I$.

expansionary fiscal policy: uses fiscal policy to increase aggregate demand and to shift the *AD* curve to the right.

export: a domestically produced good or service sold to residents of other countries.

fiscal policy: involves the use of taxation, public spending and the government's budgetary position to achieve the government's policy objectives.

free-market economists: these are also known as neoclassical economists.

frictional unemployment: voluntary unemployment, occurring when a worker switches between jobs.

full employment: according to Beveridge's definition, full employment means 3% or less of the labour force unemployed. According to the free-market definition, it is the level of employment occurring at the market-clearing real wage rate, where the number of workers whom employers wish to hire equals the number of workers wanting to work.

government spending multiplier: the relationship between a change in government spending and the resulting change in national income.

import: a good or service produced in another country and sold to residents of this country.

inflation: a persistent or continuing rise in the average price level.

interest rate: the reward for lending savings to somebody else (e.g. a bank) and the cost of borrowing.

investment: total planned spending by firms on real output produced within the economy.

investment income: profit and interest income flowing into a country that is generated from assets that residents of the country own abroad.

investment multiplier: the relationship between a change in investment and the resulting change in national income.

Keynesian economists: followers of the economist John Maynard Keynes.

Labour Force Survey: a quarterly sample survey of households in the UK. Its purpose is to provide information on the UK labour market. The survey seeks information on respondents' personal circumstances and their labour market status during a period of 1–4 weeks.

lender of last resort function: the Bank of England's willingness to lend cash to commercial banks to increase their liquidity and to maintain confidence in the banking system.

liquidity: measures the ease with which assets can be turned into cash quickly and at a pre-known rate or price. Cash is the most liquid of all assets.

macroeconomic equilibrium: the level of real national output at which $AD = AS$ or at which planned injections into the circular flow of income equal planned withdrawals from the flow.

macroeconomics: involves the study of the whole economy at the aggregate level.

marketisation: involves shifting provision of goods or services from the non-market sector to the market sector.

monetarism: the belief that, as inflation is assumed to be caused by excessive growth of the money supply, monetary policy should be used to control its growth.

monetary policy: involves the use of interest rates to achieve the government's policy objectives.

money supply or **stock of money:** takes the form of cash and bank deposits.

mortgage: a long-term loan to a house owner that is secured by the property.

national debt: the stock of all past government borrowing that has not been paid back.

national income or **national output:** the *flow* of new output produced by the economy in a particular period (e.g. a year).

national income multiplier: the relationship between a change in aggregate demand and the resulting change in national income.

open economy: an economy with exports and imports.

output gap: the difference between actual output and the trend output line.

policy conflict: occurs when two policy objectives cannot both be achieved at the same time: the better the performance in achieving one objective, the worse the performance in achieving the other.

policy indicator: provides information about what is happening in the economy.

policy instrument: a tool or set of tools used to try to achieve a policy objective.

policy objective: a target or goal that policy-makers aim to 'hit'.

privatisation: involves shifting ownership of state-owned assets to the private sector.

progressive tax: a tax where the proportion of income paid in tax rises as income increases.

recession: a fall in real output for 6 months or more.

reflation: an increase in the level of real output following an increase in aggregate demand.

saving: income which is not spent.

seasonal unemployment: unemployment caused by factors such as the weather and the end of the Christmas shopping period.

structural unemployment: unemployment caused by structural change in the economy: for example, when industries decline without being replaced by new industries.

supply-side economics: a branch of free-market economics arguing that government policy should be used to improve the competitiveness and efficiency of markets.

supply-side fiscal policy: used to increase the economy's ability to produce and supply goods, through creating incentives to work, save, invest and to be entrepreneurial.

supply-side policies: interpreted narrowly, supply-side policies focus on the role of tax cuts in increasing personal incentives. Interpreted broadly, they aim to improve the economy's ability to produce and supply more output.

tax multiplier: the relationship between a change in taxation and the resulting change in national income.

technical progress: improvements in methods of production resulting from invention, innovation and research and development. It often leads to the production of new types of goods and better-quality goods.

trade off between policy objectives: governments often do this because it may be impossible to achieve two or more objectives simultaneously. They aim for a satisfactory combination.

transfers: (1) the part of government spending in which tax revenues are paid to people such as pensioners, without any output being produced in return; (2) payments flowing between countries in forms such as foreign aid, grants and gifts.

trickle-down effect: income paid by rich people to the poorer people they employ.

wealth: the stock of assets, or things that have value, which people own.

Index

Page numbers in **bold** refer to **key term definitions**.

Index